## OTHER BOOKS BY DAVID L. HAYWARD

*The Economic Value of Water Utility Services: A Survey of Theory, Methods, and Applications*
(Infinity Publishing Company)

*Valuing an Electric Utility: Theory and Application*
Co-authored with Dr. Michael R. Schmidt,
(Public Utility Reports, Inc.)

*Valuing a Water Utility*
2nd ed.
(National Association of Water Companies)

*EWRA Cost of Service Training Self-Study Course, Vol. 1–4,*
(Hayward Consulting Group)

*Valuing a Utility Company: What You Absolutely Need to Know*
(National Association of Certified Valuation Analysts, Hayward Consulting Group)

# WATER UTILITY COSTS, VALUES, RATES, AND SUBSIDIES

## A STRATEGY FOR REGULATORY REFORM

DAVID L. HAYWARD

INFINITY PUBLISHING

Library of Congress Control Number: 2011940356

ISBN 978-0-7414-6941-0

Printed in the United States of America

Published June 2013

INFINITY PUBLISHING
1094 New DeHaven Street, Suite 100
West Conshohocken, PA 19428-2713
Toll-free (877) BUY BOOK
Local Phone (610) 941-9999
Fax (610) 941-9959
Info@buybooksontheweb.com
www.buybooksontheweb.com

# CONTENTS

# AUTHOR'S NOTE

The target audience of this book is key decisionmakers involved in the U.S. water utility industry and technical staff with an interest in applying economic concepts to problems in the sector. The audience may include state utility commissioners, city council members, state legislators, other individuals involved in the water utility regulatory process, and analysts with economics, finance, or accounting backgrounds. The audience may also include governmental officials involved in public or government-owned utilities (GOU).

The framework of the book generally uses three steps: (a) explaining concepts, (b) describing methods used in the analyses, and (c) providing case studies and numerical examples to illustrate the concepts and methods.

The problems facing the U.S. water utility industry are vast and include numerous stakeholders. However, this book addresses only water utility costs, prices, values, and subsidies, and does not include related topics such as integrated resource planning (IRP), [1] water quality, [2] reform of social institutions, and other issues. Various utility regulatory commissions such as the California Public Utilities Commission (CPUC) through their *2010 Water Action Plan* have attempted to address water issues in an integrated, comprehensive manner.

The book is the second in a series of three books related to reforming the U.S. water utility industry. The first book was *The Economic Value of Water Utility Services: A Survey of Theory, Methods, and Applications.* In *Water Utility Costs, Values, Rates, and Subsidies*, the relationships among a water utility's costs, values, rates, and subsidies are explored. It also provides recommendations for utility regulators for ratemaking and regulatory reform. The last book in the series addresses performance-based regulation (PBR) for the industry.

A comprehensive bibliography is provided for the advanced reader (e.g., technical staff economists at a utility regulatory commission). References to other books are provided for additional explanations of various terms and concepts.

The quantitative analysis of the cost–benefit case study in chapter seven could appeal to an individual with an advanced understanding of economics. Finally, implementing the ideas in this book is generally for large investor-owned utilities (IOU) or GOUs.

---

1 A related (and, in many respects, more comprehensive) practice is integrated water resource management. See Appendix F for the definition.

2 The U.S. EPA establishes maximum containment levels (mcl) for drinking water contaminants. The current levels can be found at www.epa.gov/drink/contaminants/index.cfm.

# EXECUTIVE SUMMARY

## Overview

Nearly fifty years ago, economist Jerome Milliman evaluated costing and pricing (rate) mechanisms in the water utility industry and found them deficient. He predicted that in the near future, water utilities would undergo significant changes with reform occurring in both costing methods and rate design. [3] Clearly he was wrong. The water utility industry has been historically slow to adopt water pricing and costing changes. One possible reason for this is that, unlike the natural gas and electric utility industries, water is both a private and public good. Water utility managers have a unique responsibility for stewardship over this resource, which includes protecting the environment, maintaining or increasing the value of the utility's asset base, [4] ensuring that water resources are not depleted and thus available for future generations, and making decisions that maximize the public's economic welfare. [5] For example, in California, under the Public Trust Doctrine, water is owned by the people and the State serves as trustee of the navigable waters and underlying beds within the State. As an extension of the State, the public utilities commission and other decisionmakers (e.g., city councils) have the affirmative duty to take the public trust into account in planning and allocating water resources. A common method of allocating water resources is through rates established by the regulators.

Economic regulation in the water utility industry often focuses on two groups—the utility and its customers. Clearly, based on a broader public interest obligation, policymakers should add a third stakeholder in its decisionmaking. For instance, excluding societal benefits (e.g., recreation) can affect the cost effectiveness of conservation programs and ultimately the availability of water for all stakeholders. The application of more rigorous economic analysis (e.g., cost-benefit analysis, and consumer surplus) can help decisionmakers in formulating policy decisions that maximize net benefits to society. For instance, chapter seven provides an example of the use of consumer surplus and net present value (NPV) in analyzing the welfare impact of a change in ownership from a publicly-owned utility to an investor-owned utility.

The book contains 24 case studies or examples of lessons learned in the water utility industry from around the world. These studies are related to: (a) costing methodologies including value of service and marginal costs; (b) subsidies; (c) the use of economic analysis including cost–benefit analysis; and (d) various pricing policies and rate design options. Based, in part, from these experiences, a strategy is presented for regulatory reform. *This book argues that water utility regulators should adopt the policy of full-cost pricing and set rates based on marginal costs.*

3 Patrick C. Mann, "Water Utility Regulation: Rates and Cost Recovery" (Los Angeles: Reason Institute, March 1993), 3.

4 Under government accounting—Government Accounting Standards Board (GASB)—governments must show how they will maintain the value of their assets.

5 Welfare economics is a branch of economics that deals with the principles and criteria of evaluating alternative economic states and policies from the viewpoint of efficiency or social well-being. It involves an assessment of the condition of society as a whole and not individuals or groups—e.g., residential and commercial customers, and utility. Welfare economics should not be confused with the layperson's concept of welfare which relates to government programs such as Aid to Families with Dependent Children.

The book first highlights some of the serious problems facing the water utility industry. Next, the following topics are addressed: costs and pricing; subsidies; the value of water; economic analysis applied in the industry; and economic regulatory policy.

**The Problems.** For decades most economists in the field of utility ratemaking have agreed that water is priced at ridiculously cheap rates and used inefficiently. From an economic perspective, inefficient use of a resource leads to waste and lost economic welfare. This book provides examples of where low water rates are associated with numerous industry problems, including:

1) A decaying utility infrastructure (with a grade of "D–" given by the American Society of Civil Engineers), and ultimately lost economic activity for a region;

2) Irrational pricing and use; and

3) Water utilities' insufficient cash flow from operations necessary for growth and replacing a utility's infrastructure; and a low return on invested capital (ROIC).

In addition, water utilities often have poorly defined (and in many cases ignored) sustainability metrics. Needless to say, the above-mentioned problems are interrelated. Moreover, the current methods of water utility regulation are unlikely to result in significant improvements. Thus, the need exists for regulatory reform.

With thousands water utilities in the United States one should not make a blanket statement regarding the causes of the problems. Some of the possible explanations include: (a) insufficient revenues to maintain utility assets, (b) wasteful spending on the part of the utility, and (c) an insufficient number of regulatory staff members available to properly regulate the water utilities. (Usually water utilities have a lower priority of regulatory oversight at state public service commissions as compared to electric and natural gas utilities.) Whatever the reasons, the industry must get its arms around the problem of the deteriorating water utility infrastructure. Because of the mounting deficit problems currently at the federal level, funding for upgrading the infrastructure will likely be even more challenging.

**Costs and Pricing.** Often a utility's costs form the basis for its rates (prices). In the U.S., the most common practice in rate regulation is to use a utility's historical *supply costs* (e.g., O&M expenses, taxes, interest expense, depreciation, and return on capital) to determine its revenue requirements. Unfortunately, these components do not necessarily capture all of the utility's costs. In some cases, externalities and opportunity costs should be included to reflect the utility's *full costs*. Dr. James C. Bonbright, a well-respected utility economist and whose ratemaking criteria are often cited in rate decisions, states that rates should reflect:

> *"All of the present and future private and social costs and benefits occasioned by a service provider (i.e., all internalities and externalities)."* (emphasis added)

This book argues that a water utility's full costs (not just supply costs) equal the full value of water service. In effect, full costs and full value are two sides of the same coin. Denmark is an example of a country that recognizes full-cost pricing. A case study in the United States of underpricing (i.e., not setting rates based on full costs) revealed that prices were approximately one-half the price based on full costs. The primary area of underpricing was related to infrastructure recapitalization and maintenance. Similar to the United States, economic utility regulators in developing countries dismiss certain costs as legitimate expenses.

In contrast with supply costs, marginal costs as the basis for pricing are common in the United Kingdom, Canada, and Australia. A deviation of marginal costs—average incremental costs (AIC)—is often used for practical reasons. The World Bank endorses AIC-pricing and it is used in Bank-funded projects. Chapter two on utility costs examines various types of marginal cost analyses and provides several case studies. Price theory based on microeconomic principles is used to support the recommendation of using marginal-cost pricing. Limitations of both embedded-cost pricing and marginal-cost pricing are discussed.

Finally, a case study related to Sydney Water Company (Australia) found that tariffs that produced the maximum efficiency gains were non-uniform two-part tariffs based on short-run marginal costs. The least effective tariffs (from an efficiency perspective) were uniform rates based on average costs. Setting rates based on a utility's average costs is common in the United States.

**Subsidies.** Inefficient pricing can also lead to various subsidies that should be identified, justified, quantified, and may not be intended or even recognized by utility regulators. Once a subsidy is in place, it tends to remain indefinitely. Current pricing practices incorporate up to eighteen subsidies, depending on the characteristics and ownership of a water utility. In many cases, subsidies do not reach the targeted groups (e.g., low-income water utility customers). A case study of water utility reform in Scotland illustrates how the government is committed to unwinding subsidies. One option U.S. utility regulators might consider is having the government directly fund and distribute subsidies as is the case in Chile.

**Value.** The full value of water includes: intrinsic value, value to society, value to end users (the most common), and externalities (positive or negative). Various methods of estimating nonmarket values such as externalities are presented. Many participants in the water utility industry claim that water is underpriced; therefore it is a great value. A commonly used phrase in the industry is: "Water costs less than a penny a gallon." However, one problem for the water utility industry is defending the truthfulness of the above statement without the supporting evidence. Furthermore, such a statement is meaningless in the context of determining the effectiveness of utility regulation and pricing utility services. Without the evidence, normally utility regulators are legally constrained in changing customers' water rates.

Experts in the field of natural resource economics have long known the methods of valuing water, but other analysts in the field of public utility economics have generally failed to incorporate this knowledge in the context of pricing water utility [6] services (i.e., the water as a resource—commodity—and the infrastructure [7] [8] to provide safe, reliable water delivery when customers demand it). In both cases—natural resource economics and utility economic regulation [9] [10]—

6 For purposes of this book, government-owned water utilities (GOU) and investor-owned water utilities (IOU) are used interchangeably.

7 David Monsma, Executive Director, The Aspen Institute claims that "the traditional definition of water infrastructure must evolve to embrace a broader, more holistic definition of sustainable water infrastructure that includes both traditional man-made water and wastewater infrastructure and natural watershed systems." See "A Report of the Aspen Institute's Dialog on Sustainable Water Infrastructure in the U.S." Presentation at NARUC Winter Meeting (February 16, 2010), 4.

8 Mr. Eric Thornburg, President and CEO of Connecticut Water Company claims: "[The] Traditional definition of infrastructure must evolve to include not just pipe and plant but the natural system as well." See "Sustainable Water Systems: Redefining the Nation's Infrastructure Challenge." Presentation at Aspen Institute's Dialogue on Sustainable Water Infrastructure, NARUC Winter Meeting (February 16, 2010), 5.

9 In this book, the terms *economic regulation* and *regulation* are used interchangeably.

10 As defined by the World Bank, utility economic regulation involves the rules and organizations that set, enforce, and change the allowed tariffs and service standards for service providers. Currently, five state public service commissions (North Dakota, South Dakota, Michigan, Minnesota and Georgia) do not oversee price regulation.

prices are estimated because true markets do not exist. Natural resource economists performing nonmarket valuations assign monetary values of individuals' preferences for outcomes of policy proposals or events. However, for regulated utilities, the rates (prices) authorized by economic regulators generally reflect accounting (book) costs but not necessarily customers' value. In contrast to book costs, many economists and institutions including the European Union (EU) and the World Bank prefer to base utility rates on full economic costs (FEC) and not accounting costs.

A working definition of value of service is assigning monetary measures of individuals' preferences for outcomes of policy proposals or events (e.g., water delivered with a specified reliability). When the value of water or water services is being estimated, what is being measured is the welfare change associated with some policy-induced change in the attributes of the commodity or service (e.g., reliability). To estimate the value of water utility service to customers, a willingness-to-pay (WTP) study is often conducted. These studies are rare in the United States; however, they are common in developing (third-world) countries. Various WTP studies have found that some water utility customers were willing to pay three to five percent of disposable income to receive reliable water service.

While many factors play into setting water utility rates, the differences between the cost of service (the most common ratemaking approach) and value of service approaches are rarely known even by large water utilities. Thus, the cost of being wrong—lost economic welfare—can be in the billions of dollars and affect generations of customers. Stated differently, the "cost" of low water rates for current customers may be lost future economic activity and a reduction in society's welfare. As an example of value of service, one study concluded that residential customers value water reliability ranging from $109 to $421 (2003 U.S. dollars) per year. [11]

**Economic Analysis.** To properly set water utility rates that reflect full value and full costs, the proper economic analytical tools should be used. In particular, this includes marginal cost and cost–benefit analysis (CBA), and leads to the fulfillment of one of Dr. Bonbright's criteria of a sound rate structure. Other types of economic analysis include net present value (NPV), cost-effectiveness, internal rate of return (IRR), and consumer's surplus (CS). The use of consumer's and producer's surplus is broadly accepted as appropriate for welfare analysis in public utility economics. An examination of consumer's surplus was used to evaluate a water supply project in New York City. One estimate of the project showed the City spending $2.9 billion (reflected in 1960 U.S. dollars) more than alternatives providing similar benefits. (The book also contains commonly used formulas and numerical examples used in economic analyses.)

**Economic Regulation Policy.** Currently, regulatory policies and decisions are often defended by using vague phrases such as "just and reasonable rates," and "balancing the interests of a utility and its customers." Instead, utility regulators should defend their policies on the basis of more concrete measures such as maximizing the value of the market (i.e., making producer and consumer surplus as large as possible). As an example, the following table illustrates how a policy change can be evaluated. If the total change is positive the new policy should be implemented. (The letters—a, b, and c—represent hypothetical values.) Assume that prior to a policy change (e.g., a change in water rates) consumer and producer surplus is equal. At the result of the rate increase consumers lose by the amount "b" (however they gain as a result of a more reliable water system) and producers gain by the same amount. Society also gains an amount "c" as the result of changes in water acquisition policies (e.g., water from groundwater—thus avoiding damage to an aquifer—is replaced by purchased water). The net gain is the amount "c".

---

11 Robert S. Raucher et al., *The Value of Water: Concepts, Estimates, and Applications for Water Managers* (Denver, CO: Awwa Research Foundation, 2005), 95.

Thus, decisionmakers should approve the changed policy which affects all stakeholders—utility, customers, and society.

**Analysis of Policy**
**Rate Increase**

| | **Consumer surplus** | **Producer surplus** | **Society** | **Total change** |
|---|---|---|---|---|
| Pre-policy | a | a | | |
| Post-policy | a – b | a + b | c | |
| Change | - b | + b | c | c |

The necessary regulatory steps to implement water utility costing and pricing reform is presented. As mentioned above, this book argues that water utility regulators should adopt the policy of full-cost pricing based on marginal costs and when appropriate incorporate rates based on value of service. This recommendation is reflected in a *proposed* National Association of Regulatory Utility Commissioners (NARUC) resolution for consideration by its members. In addition, and as a matter of public policy, utility economic regulators should give capital attraction and consumer rationing the highest priorities among the various criteria used in setting rates. If regulators choose to adopt the above-mentioned pricing policy, various alternatives are identified to address any excess operating revenue generated by the utility. However, excessive utility profits may not necessarily result from pricing based on full costs. Pricing and policy approaches used by the thirty countries as members of the Organization for Economic Co-operation and Development (OECD) are also examined.

# LIST OF FIGURES

**Figure No.** **Page No.**

# LIST OF TABLES

# LIST OF TABLES (CONT.)

# LIST OF CASE STUDIES AND APPLICATIONS

# LIST OF NUMERICAL EXAMPLES

# ACKNOWLEDGMENTS

I would like to thank Infinity Publishing Company for their help in editing and designing the front and back covers of the book.

# CHAPTER ONE

# Introduction

## 1.1 Overview

Economic regulation of water utilities has historically focused on analyzing water utilities' costs—particularly embedded costs. However, at least three other issues are interrelated with costs. These are:

1) The value of water and delivery services to a utility's customers;
2) Rates and charges customers pay through their tariffs; and
3) Subsidies either known or unknown to policymakers, consumers, and/or utilities.

These are interrelated issues that could affect the public for years or decades. For example, underpricing water (e.g., setting rates that do not reflect a utility's true costs) could ultimately result in infrastructure decay and lost regional economic activity. An example of this is the City of Escondido, California, presented later in the chapter.

It is fair to say (almost with certainty) that rates are the primary focus of decisionmakers. For instance, in one regulatory jurisdiction (which remains confidential) regulators were almost exclusively concerned with rates and not the long-term economic and environmental consequences of their decisions. In particular, they were interested in the combination of fixed charges and rates that would be politically acceptable to the public. Needless to say, almost an infinite number of combinations could be tested so as to accomplish this objective. Moreover, a computer instead of humans employing economic principles, facts, logic, and reasoning would be a much more effective tool in accomplishing the task.

### 1.1.1 Value

Experts in the fields of natural resource and environmental economics have long known the methods [12] of valuing water supply, but other analysts in the field of public utility economics have generally failed to incorporate this knowledge in the context of pricing water utility services. Value of service is a concept in utility ratemaking whereby the usefulness or necessity of the service to a customer (e.g., residential) replaces the cost of service as a major (not necessarily exclusive) influence on the rates charged. Price discrimination (the result of value-of-service pricing) results when a firm sells the same service at rates that are not proportional to costs. The mechanics of implementing a system of prices based on value of service is called "differential pricing." In traditional cost-of-service pricing, rates (prices) are primarily based on accounting (embedded) costs [13] and not value of service. [14]

One of the conclusions of a study [15] by the American Water Works Association Research Foundation (AwwaRF) was that very little is known about how much value customers place on water and delivery services. [16] The American Water Works Association (AWWA) understands the importance of valuing water. Its Strategic Plan states that it will engage the public, elected officials, and key decisionmakers about the value of water and AWWA's role in maintaining that value. [17] Other organizations such as the National Association of Water Companies (NAWC) and California Public Utilities Commission (CPUC) have similar goals. [18]

In assessing value, one should be clear regarding the definitions of utility "goods" and "services." In the context of water utilities, *goods* represent the end products (e.g., tap water for the utility's customers that is safe, aesthetic, and affordable). *Services* are the reliable delivery (i.e., service on demand) to a customer's tap of ample quantities of water. For analytical, value of service, and potentially rate unbundling purposes, water utility goods and services can be broken down into two components:

1) Water supply as a commodity; and

2) Water treatment and delivery services (e.g., treating, transporting, storing, and delivering water).

An example of valuing water *supply* is the California Water Bank where farmers have been paid to release supplies primarily for urban customers. In effect, urban customers value the water supply more than farmers and are willing to pay for it. An example of valuing water *delivery*

---

12 The general methods of valuing a natural resource such as water are summarized in Appendix B.

13 Costs usually include reasonable and prudent: O&M expenses, taxes, book depreciation, interest expense, and a return on equity.

14 For a more detailed discussion of a utility's cost of service, see *Public Utilities Reports Guide: Principles of Public Utilities Operations and Management*, vol. 4, Rates and Ratemaking (Vienna, VA: Public Utilities Reports, Inc., 2004).

15 Bob Raucher, "The Value of Water: What It Means, Why It's Important, and How Water Utility Managers Can Use It," AWWA Journal (April 2005), 93.

16 Other services a water utility or its subsidiary may provide include, but are not limited to: water and sewer line maintenance, well rehabilitation and repair, community irrigation, utility billing and collections, water system contract operations, wastewater system contract operations, water system surveys and leak detection, control system services, meter services, cross connection services, collection services, public information services, mapping/drafting, and engineering services.

17 Neil S. Grigg, *Total Water Management Practices For a Sustainable Future* (Denver, CO: American Water Works Association, 2008), 138.

18 For example, see Walton Hill's (United Water) presentation at the July 2010 NARUC summer meeting; and the CPUC's *2010 Water Action Plan*, 1.

*service* is: In California, residential customers were willing to pay an additional $1 billion per year to ensure reliable water service. Willingness-to-pay [19] is discussed in more detail in chapter four. Several studies have concluded that households value water reliability ranging from $135 to $421 (2003 U.S. dollars) per year. [20] However, in the United States, a major problem with pricing water based on value of service is that utilities rarely determine how much reliability its customers want and are willing to pay. In contrast to the United States, in the United Kingdom a water utility's commercial customers are allowed to self-select into two rate classes depending on the service reliability they desire.

### 1.1.2 Subsidies

Subsidies are often hidden. They represent the difference between actual costs underlying calculations of the water price and full economic costs. Decisionmakers approving water utility rates usually have not identified, quantified, or justified subsidies included in a water utility's rates and charges. Often the results of these subsidies transfer wealth from some customers to other customers without any economic justification. In addition, in the case of investor-owned utilities regulated by a state public service commission (PSC), some experts question if the goal of transferring wealth is within the agency's charter.

### 1.1.3 Analytical Framework

Figure 1.1, Water Costing and Pricing Framework, shows how conceptually the issues of cost, rates, values, and subsidies are interrelated. For a sophisticated water utility, the rate process is as follows. First, a demand forecast for each customer class and for the company as a whole is prepared. This forecast feeds into the utility's integrated resource plan (IRP). Second, using cost–benefit analysis, demand-side and supply-side resources are evaluated on a comparable basis. The IRP must also consider constraints. Examples of constraints include: (a) maximum containment levels of contaminants required by the EPA; (b) reliability goals; (c) financial; (d) environmental, such as withdrawals from aquifers; (e) asset maintenance; and (f) operational. Third, all of the resource costs necessary to produce reliable service are calculated. In addition to the full supply costs included in traditional ratemaking, externalities (environmental and economic) should be estimated. This is also true of opportunity costs. Together these cost components make up full costs. At this point, the utility must make a critical decision. That being: Is financial sustainability likely? In other words, is the utility likely to be a going concern? Fourth, once total revenues are estimated, a water utility's management needs to address its pricing policy. Key issues in this step are the relative importance of economic efficiency [21], social issues such as affordability, and subsidies. Value of service for customer classes can also be an important component to a utility's pricing policy. To estimate a customer's value of service, willingness-to-pay studies are often completed.

Fifth, the utility should evaluate various rate structures. For example, if a water utility has significantly higher demand in the summer months, perhaps seasonal rates are appropriate. Finally, the new rates (tariffs) due to price elasticity of demand may change the utility's demand

---

19 Willingness to pay is based on the area under a customer's demand curve. For a general overview of willingness to pay, see David L. Hayward, *The Economic Value of Water Utility Services: A Survey of Theory, Methods, and Applications* (West Conshohocken, PA: Infinity Publishing Co., 2009), 55.

20 Raucher et al., 69.

21 From an efficiency perspective, business attempt to maximize profits, and consumers maximize utility.

forecast. If this is the case, the process iterates back to the IRP. Usually one iteration of the price elasticity impact on demand is sufficient. All of these components are discussed throughout the book.

**Figure 1.1**
**Water Costing and Pricing Framework**

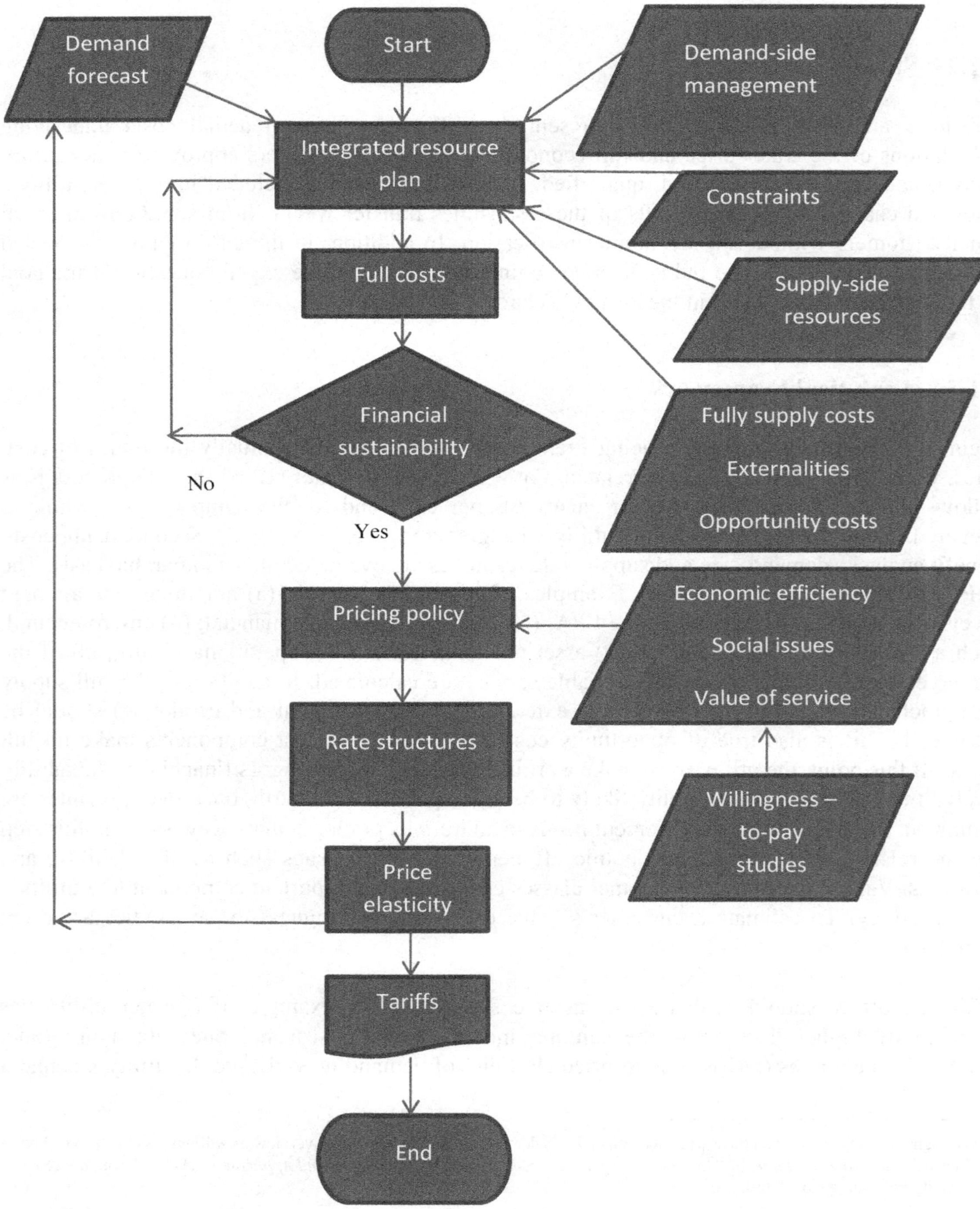


Source: Author's construct.

## 1.2 A Central Problem: Underpricing Water Utility Services

For more than fifty years, some water utility economists [22] have argued that water is underpriced and used inefficiently. Many economists agree that the price of water has historically been too low from a social perspective. [23] One study estimates that water rates are underpriced by approximately 50 percent in some cities. [24] Case studies presented in chapter six document an even higher level of underpricing. Finally, it should be noted that Europeans pay 50–350 percent *more* than Americans for their water service. [25] But, is underpricing water (i.e., not including full costs in prices) in the best long-term interests of society? Most economists agree that underpricing goods and/or services generally results in overconsumption and misuse of a resource. Appendix A builds a case that the U.S. water utility industry is in serious trouble as a result, in part, of underpricing water and delivery services. [26]

Utility managers and regulators have a unique responsibility of stewardship of a resource such as water, and providing for the greater good of the community. [27] Components of stewardship are: (a) maintaining and rehabilitating capital assets; (b) creating comprehensive asset management systems; [28] and (c) providing environmental sustainability. Stewardship of a resource can also be described as "affected with a public interest"—a phrase used by the U.S. Supreme Court [29] that will be discussed in chapter eight. Given this stewardship responsibility, underpricing water utility services may not be in a society's long-term best interest.

For most water utilities, historical average costs (AC) for both the commodity (water) and the capacity are much lower as compared to the marginal costs (MC) of new water supplies and additional capacity. (Marginal cost is the cost of producing or providing one more unit of output.) Hence, the likelihood is high that water and water utility services (e.g., delivery) will be underpriced.

Related to underpricing water, key questions for utility regulators are:

1) Does underpricing water contribute to the deteriorating infrastructure discussed in Appendix A?

---

22 Jack Hirshleifer, James C. DeHaven, and Jerome W. Milliman, *Water Supply Economics, Technology, and Policy* (Chicago: The University of Chicago Press, 1960), 107. Also, see Mann, 4.

23 W. Douglass, Shaw, *Water Resource Economics and Policy* (Northampton, MA: Edward Elgar, 2005), 101. Also, see Mann, 4.

24 Ibid, 114.

25 Shaw, 13.

26 Care must be used in applying this general industry trend to individual utilities. In fact, many water utilities are viable from a financial, managerial, and operational perspective.

27 In California, the State Constitution requires all claimants' use of water be reasonable and beneficial. "Beneficial" uses include: (a) irrigation; (b) municipal; (c) domestic; (d) industrial; (e) recreational use; (f) protection of fish, wildlife, and their habitat; and aesthetic enjoyment. Reasonable use is not precisely defined. See *Layperson's Guide to Water Marketing* (Sacramento, CA: Water Education Foundation, 2005), 6.

28 One definition of asset management is a combination of management, financial, economic, engineering, and other practices applied to physical assets with the objective of maximizing the value derived from an asset stock over the whole life cycle, within the context of delivering appropriate levels of service to customers, communities, and the environment at an acceptable level of risk. See David R. Marlow and Stewart Burn, "Effective Use of Condition Assessment within Asset Management," *Journal AWWA* 100:1 (Jan. 2008): 54.

29 *Munn v. Illinois*, 94 U.S. 113, 74 L.Ed. 77 (1877).

2) Is underpricing water (i.e., not including full costs in prices) in the best long-term interests of society?

### 1.2.1 Graphical and Numerical Illustration of the Problem

Figure 1.2 provides a graphical and numerical illustration of the potential range between the "social tariff" (a subsidized rate for low-income residential customers) and full economic costs based on long-run average incremental costs (LRAIC). (Costs are in Egyptian pounds per cubic meter.) Figure 1.2 is based on a tariff study for Alexandria Water Company (Alexandria, Egypt). 30 Some of the details of the study are presented in Appendix D. In this example, the Company's LRAIC is approximately twelve times higher than the social tariff and three times higher than average costs. Time did not permit an examination of externalities. (Externalities are unintended side-effects of the actions of an individual, company, or community on others or the environment, and these effects are not taken into account in the decision making of the parties causing them.) Externalities can be either positive or negative values. In all likelihood including externalities would have increase total costs. Clearly, pricing water at the social tariff rate illustrates underpricing as compared to the utility's LRAIC. The social tariff, LRAIC, and other forms of costs will be described in more detail throughout the book.

With respect to the incremental or marginal costs of new water *supplies* as a component of LRAIC in Figure 1.2 (i.e., the commodity), policymakers might want to consider the lessons from the natural gas industry. In that industry, the prices of various categories of gas (e.g., "old gas" and "new gas") were averaged to generate a "rolled-in" average price. This pricing practice quite logically resulted in a decline in natural gas exploration, and natural gas shortages resulted in various markets (e.g., Eastern United States). When the United States government eventually lifted price controls, the so-called natural gas "shortages" disappeared. In comparison to the natural gas industry, in the water utility industry the cost of "old water" and "new water" supplies can be even more dramatic. This is because, in many cases, for the initial source of water supply a utility does not pay for the water but rather the cost of pumping and transporting it. In summary, the practice of average-cost pricing in the water utility industry does not result in maximizing efficiency and society's welfare. In economics, efficiency is where price equals marginal cost. These concepts will be discussed in more detail throughout the book.

As will be illustrated in an example regarding the City of Escondido, California, the outcome of underpricing water does not necessarily result in the greater long-term good of the community. In fact, underpricing water can result in low economic growth. Furthermore, some people even expect that an entity (e.g., government or private business) should provide water for free since it falls from the sky. In fact, water is a scarce resource and a method of allocating, transporting, treating, and storing it is needed. In the context of the water utility industry, the pipes, plumbing, and engineering are very expensive—especially the costs of replacing this infrastructure. In short, not properly valuing and pricing water and water utility services (i.e., price does not equal marginal cost) has contributed to the challenges in the water industry.

In various areas of the world, people do not believe that some expenses and investments are true costs. This is particularly true in Africa. In the case of Egypt, many people believe that water should be free or, at the maximum, customers should pay for only operating and maintenance (O&M) expenses. Many Egyptians believe that the capital is free since it comes from the

30 Water Policy Regulatory Reform (WPRR) project in Egypt and funded by the United States Agency for International Development (USAID). Task Order No. EPP-I-00-04-00020-00, January 2011.

government. Even in the United States, many people believe that externalities are not true costs and therefore should be excluded in utility rates. However, in the United States, the case law and economic regulatory theory related to externalities from the natural gas and electric utility industries is clear—externalities are legitimate costs and can be included in rates.

**Figure 1.2**
**Social Tariff and Economic Costs (LE/m³)**
**Alexandria Water Company (Egypt)**

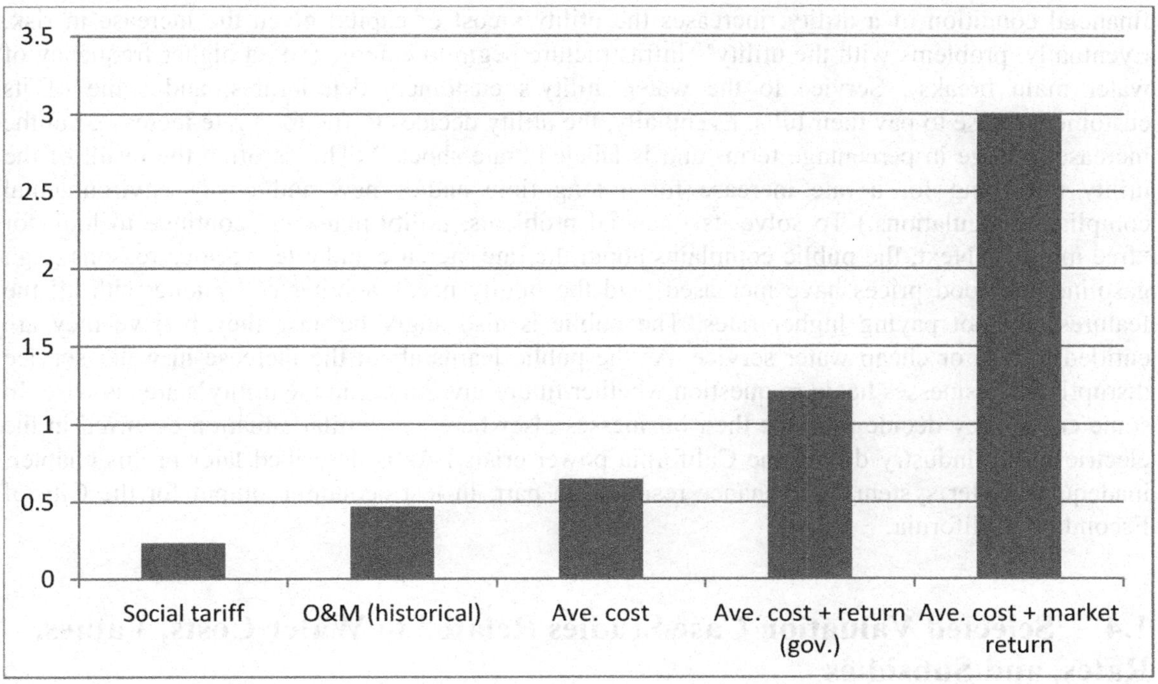


Source: Author's construct.

## 1.3 The Cycle of Decaying Utility Infrastructure

As mentioned in Appendix A, the American Society of Civil Engineers (ASCE) has given the U.S. water utility industry an overall grade of D– with respect to its infrastructure. ASCE assigns letter grades to 15 categories of public works. These grades are determined on the basis of condition and performance, capacity versus need, and funding versus need. [31]

The decaying water utility infrastructure in the United States, however, is not an isolated case. Ever since the end of the old Soviet Union and the fall of communism in Eastern Europe, numerous multilateral institutions such as the World Bank, United States Agency for International Development (USAID), the European Union (EU), have provided developing countries with assistance rebuilding their utilities (e.g., natural gas, electric, and water) and regulatory institutions. Thus, utility policymakers have more than 20 years of case studies that

31 Marlow and Burn, 55.

illustrate how to avoid costly mistakes related to a decaying utility infrastructure. Over this twenty-year period, a clear cycle has emerged.

In a very simplistic manner, the cycle of decaying utility infrastructure observed throughout the world is as follows. First, underpricing water utility services can lead to deferred system maintenance. The utility has insufficient cash flow from operations (a key measure of financial health). Realizing this insufficient cash flow from operations, utility managers invest time finding and securing cheap money (e.g., government grants and low-interest loans) to maintain the utility as a going concern. In the case of government-owned systems, often funds from other government sources are diverted to the utilities. The investment community, realizing the real financial condition of a utility, increases the utility's cost of capital given the increase in risk. Eventually, problems with the utility's infrastructure begin to emerge (i.e., a higher frequency of water main breaks). Service to the water utility's customers deteriorates, and some of its customers refuse to pay their bills. Eventually, the utility decides to file for a rate increase, but the increase is large in percentage terms and is labeled "rate shock." (This is often the result of the utility not filing for a rate increase for a long time and/or new and costly environmental compliance regulations.) To solve its financial problems, utility managers continue to look for "free money." Next, the public complains about the rate increase and cites various reasons (e.g., gasoline and food prices have increased, and the family needs another cell phone with all the features) for not paying higher rates. The public is also angry because they believe they are entitled to free or cheap water service. As the public learns about the increase in water service disruptions, businesses begin to question whether future investment in the utility's area is wise. In some cases, they decide to move their businesses elsewhere. (A similar situation occurred in the electric utility industry during the California power crisis.) As is described later in this chapter, inadequate water system maintenance resulted, in part, in lost economic output for the City of Escondido, California.

## 1.4 Selected Valuation Case Studies Related to Water Costs, Values, Rates, and Subsidies

Table 1.1 identifies various case studies related to utility costs, values, rates, and subsidies from throughout the world. These case studies will be discussed in more detail throughout the book.

**Table 1.1**
**Case Studies Related to Costs, Values, Rates, and Subsidies**

| No. | Study Description | Topic |
|---|---|---|
| 1 | Willingness to pay for water service in Manaus, Amazonas, Brazil | Value |
| 2 | Willingness to pay for water supply service in the Gaza Strip | Value |
| 3 | Consumer surplus of water in New York City | Value |
| 4 | Consumer surplus (shortage costs) water shortages Atlanta Metro area | Value |
| 5 | Metropolitan Water District of Southern California reliable water supply | Value |
| 6 | A comparison of life-cycle cost analyses for a typical college dormitory using subsidized versus full-cost water pricing (U.S.) | Costs/subsidies |
| 7 | Full cost water pricing strategy for South Carolina rural water utilities | Costs |
| 8 | Long-run average incremental costs (LRAIC), Alexandria Water Utility (Egypt) | Costs |
| 9 | Ipswich River (Massachusetts) exploitation (negative externality) | Costs |
| 10 | The cost of water utility infrastructure failure (U.S.) | Cost/value |
| 11 | Bristol Waterworks Company (U.K.) marginal cost study | Costs |
| 12 | Australia's water scarcity pricing approach | Rates |
| 13 | Sydney Water (Australia) tariff efficiency study | Rates |
| 14 | Cost-benefit analysis of water efficiency programs in commercial buildings (U.S.) | Cost-benefit analysis |
| 15 | Estimating the benefits of water use efficiency programs for Denver Water | Cost-benefit analysis |
| 16 | Cost-benefit analysis of the concession of a water utility | Cost-benefit analysis |
| 17 | Water recycling | Cost-benefit analysis |
| 18 | Reform of water tariffs in Chongqing, China | Rates/subsidies |
| 19 | Cross subsidies in the Scottish water industry | Subsidies |
| 20 | Subsidies in Chilean public utilities (water and electricity) | Subsidies |
| 21 | World Bank's Analysis of Water Utility Subsidies (Africa, Latin America, and Asia) | Subsidies |
| 22 | Cost recovery, equity, and efficiency in water tariffs: Evidence from African utilities | Cost/rates |
| 23 | Marginal cost-based rates for U.K. water utilities | Costs/rates |
| 24 | Massachusetts-American Water Company marginal cost study | Costs/rates |

Source: Author's construct.

## 1.5 The Cost to Society Resulting from Underpricing Water Utility Services

If the above discussion of underpricing water utility services seems abstract the following real-world example may clarify the concept. In March 2011, the *North County Times* (a newspaper distributed primarily in North San Diego County) printed an article entitled: "Antiquated pipes stall city's dream." The article described how the City of Escondido's plan for economic development was delayed if not abandoned as the result of outdated water and sewer pipes. The article described the developer essentially abandoning plans for building condominiums and retail shops. The developer planned to spend approximately $2 million remodeling the area. Assuming that the city agreed to proceed with updating its water and wastewater master plan (requiring another study), the time frame for implementing the project was at least two years. In conclusion the article stated:

> *"It's hard enough for Escondido to attract investment required to transform its downtown into a sort of "Gaslamp North, [referring to the famous Gaslamp district in San Diego] and that investors might be discouraged by needing to wait for water and sewer upgrades.*" 32

From the developer's perspective, the city should have been steadily upgrading the water pipes over the years and that city officials were *irresponsible* to let the system become so antiquated. In short, one could argue that the city officials were not good stewards of the water and wastewater assets under their control. Unfortunately, the above example is not an isolated case. Newspaper articles from throughout the United States describe how an outdated water and wastewater infrastructure has resulted in supply interruptions, lost productivity, and ultimately lower economic growth. To economists, lost productivity generally results in lower economic output (usually measured by a region's gross domestic product—GDP) and ultimately a lower standard of living for the people in the region.

While the above story would be considered an economic disaster (i.e., foregone GDP) by most economists, many water utility analysts using traditional utility ratemaking methods might believe that nothing is wrong. To them, if O&M costs and capital charges (i.e., full supply costs—FSC) reflected in Figure 1.3 (and the water rates derived from the revenue requirements) could be observed, verified, and justified, then a problem does not exist. On the other hand, economists would also consider opportunity costs and externalities as "full costs." The magnitude of the difference between full costs and full supply costs depends on the utility. Said another way, the "cost" of low rates in the historical and current period could result in forgone economic growth in the future. Thus, regarding pricing policies, the following are key questions for utility regulators:

1) Is average-cost pricing good public policy?

2) If not, what are the alternative pricing approaches?

32 David Garrick, *North County Times*, 1, col. 4; and 4 col. 1–6 (March 6, 2011).

**Figure 1.3**
**Components of the Full Cost of Water (Not Drawn to Scale)**

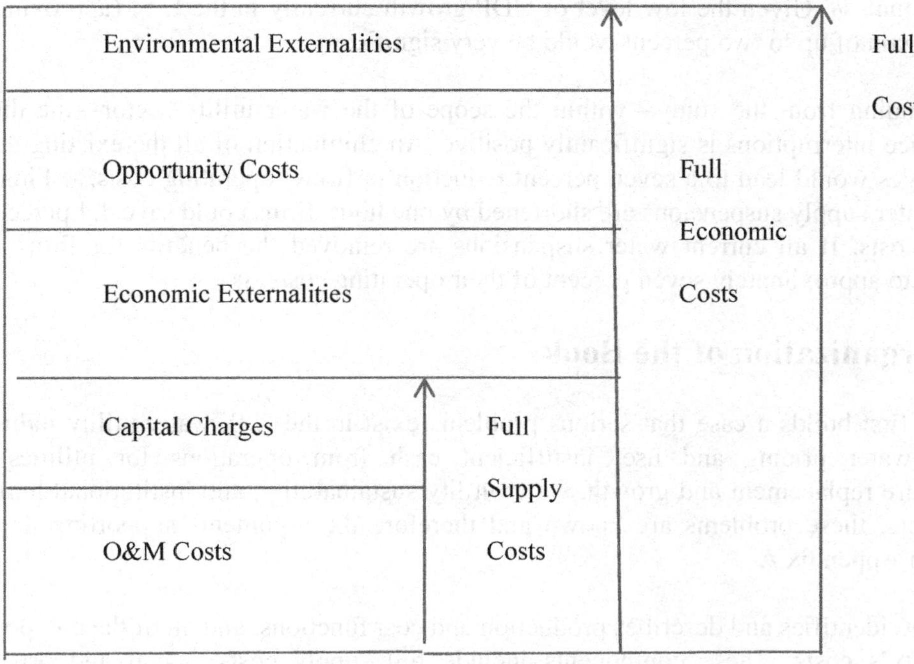


Source: Adopted from R. D. Raucher et al., *The Value of Water: Concepts, Estimates, and Applications for Water Managers* (Denver, CO: American Water Works Research Foundation, 2005), 42.

---

## 1.6 The Correlation Between Infrastructure and Economic Growth

Every major economy on Earth needs to have essential public services supplied in order to accomplish day-to-day business commerce. In fact, there is a strong correlation between economic development in terms of GDP and access to water. 33 Several World Bank studies from different time periods and areas of the world have reached this conclusion. 34 For those individuals skeptical of the above statement just go to a developing country that does not have basic utility services such as reliable water and electricity.

In a significant public policy paper for the World Bank, Atsuhi Iimi studied the marginal impacts on firm costs of infrastructure quality using firm-level data for 4,300 businesses in 26 countries in Europe and Central Asia. 35 The study included water, electric, and telecommunication utilities. For each sector, two dimensions were used to measure the level of service quality perceived by individual firms: (a) annual frequency, and (b) daily duration of service suspensions. The results suggested that the reliability or continuity of services is important for business performance. In

---

33 Fredrik Segerfeldt, Water For Sale, How Business and the Market Can Resolve the World's Water Crisis, (Washington, DC: Cato Institute, 2005), p. 49.

34 Atsushi Iimi, "Effects of Improving Infrastructure Quality on Business costs: Evidence from Firm-Level Data," Policy Research Working Paper No. 4581, (Washington, DC: The World Bank, 2008), p.2.

35 Ibid.

the water sector, increased hours of water supply suspensions reduce firms' competitiveness. If all water suspensions were removed, the economy could receive a *gain* of approximately one-half of one percent to three percent of gross domestic product (GDP). Residential welfare gains are also additional. 36 Given the low level of GDP growth currently in the U.S. (approximately one percent) a gain of up to two percent would be very significant.

Another finding from the study—within the scope of the water utility sector—the duration of water service interruptions is significantly positive. An elimination of all the existing duration of water outages would lead to a seven percent reduction in firms' operating costs. 37 Finally, if the existing water supply suspensions are shortened by one hour, firms could save 4.4 percent of their operating costs. If all current water suspensions are removed the benefits for firms would be equivalent to approximately seven percent of their operating costs. 38

## 1.7 Organization of the Book

This book first builds a case that serious problems exist in the U.S. water utility industry (e.g., irrational water pricing and use, insufficient cash from operations for utilities to fund infrastructure replacement and growth, water utility sustainability, and institutional hurdles). For most readers, these problems are known and therefore the arguments supporting the case are included in Appendix A.

Chapter two identifies and describes production and cost functions, and all of the components of a water utility's costs. These components include full supply costs, social and private costs, opportunity costs, and externalities. Second, the costs associated with externalities are illustrated. Third, various methods of abating externalities are discussed. Fourth, various issues related to marginal costs are discussed, including the methods used and a short-run marginal cost case study. Fifth, Massachusetts-American Water Company and United Kingdom marginal cost case studies are summarized. Finally, United States and international marginal-cost pricing practices are described.

Chapter three summarizes price theory as it pertains to regulated water utilities. First, the assumptions related to two market structures—perfect competition and monopoly—are discussed. Second, the relationship between a water utility's average and marginal costs is highlighted; and the reasons that average-cost pricing provides an outcome where society's overall economic welfare is reduced. Third, the concepts of consumer's and producer's surplus are discussed and illustrated. Fourth, the regulator's pricing challenges are presented. Finally, two case studies related to consumer's surplus are provided.

Chapter four defines and illustrates customers' willingness to pay (including price elasticity of demand) and the methods of estimating demand. The results of two willingness-to-pay studies are summarized. All of the components of total economic value are discussed. One key component of value in the water utility industry—reliability of service—is highlighted. Finally, the result of one study quantifying the value of water by sector of the U.S. economy is presented.

36 Ibid, p. 19.

37 Ibid, p. 16.

38 Ibid, p. 21.

Chapter five discusses an issue at the heart of utility economic regulation: water rates. The chapter starts by identifying economic regulation policy goals and factors influencing tariffs. Next, various pricing (rate) options are presented, and common rate structures are identified. Third, the perspectives and concerns of the three common stakeholders in utility regulation—consumer, utility, and society—are listed. Fourth, the criteria of a sound rate structure developed by a prominent utility economist (Dr. James Bonbright) are presented.

Chapter six discusses subsidies in the water industry. The chapter begins by identifying sources of revenues for water utilities. Next, subsidies and social policy goals are identified and discussed.

Economic analysis is the topic of chapter seven. Cost–benefit analysis and cost-effectiveness analysis is compared and contrasted. Six case studies using the concepts and methods of economic analysis are summarized.

Since utility economic regulation is significantly influenced by state and federal laws, chapter eight outlines the legal framework in ratemaking as well as identifies key U.S. Supreme Court decisions regarding utility pricing. The chapter also discusses the legal precedents and limitations related to value-of-service pricing.

Chapter nine summarizes the key points made in the book.

Chapter ten concludes by analyzing the status of various rate and cost recovery mechanisms presented years ago by a prominent water utility expert, Dr. Patrick Mann. Next, various policy recommendations for utility regulators are presented. Finally, the chapter concludes by identifying the necessary steps for utility regulators to implement costing and pricing reform. The option of implementing full-cost pricing is recommended. This recommendation is reflected in a proposed National Association of Regulatory Utility Commissioners (NARUC) resolution for consideration by its members. In addition to this resolution and as a matter of public policy, utility economic regulators should give capital attraction and consumer rationing the highest priorities among the various criteria used in setting rates. If regulators choose to pursue implementing full-cost pricing, various alternatives are identified to address any excess operating revenue generated by the utility. However, this method of pricing may not necessarily result in excessive utility profits.

# *CHAPTER TWO*

# WATER UTILITY COSTS

## 2.1 Overview

A natural place to begin analyzing a water utility's rates (discussed in chapter five) is its costs. This is a good starting place because of the long-standing proposition that utility rates should be primarily linked to its costs; 39 and that the customers who cause a utility to incur costs should pay for them. A water utility incurs costs in the production or provision of its services. These are called direct costs. Also, a water utility could have indirect costs that may include the impact on nonusers of a good or service such as externalities. Also, opportunity costs—the monetary value or foregone value of a good or service in its next best alternative use—may exist. Externalities and opportunity costs along with examples are provided in this chapter. Finally, marginal costs—the costs of producing or providing an additional unit (e.g., cubic meter of water)—are defined and discussed, including their limitations and application issues. Also in this chapter, various case studies of marginal-cost pricing are presented.

Various terms and phrases related to water utility economics need to be defined and explained, since they cannot be used interchangeably. Examples related to costs include: (a) embedded (full supply), (b) full, (c) opportunity, (d) externalities, (e) fixed or sunk, (f) variable, (g) social, (h) private, (i) depreciation, (j) implicit, (k) explicit, (l) long-run, (m) short-run, and (n) marginal (incremental). In chapter three, these cost concepts will be used in the context of utility price theory. These cost concepts are discussed below.

---

39 Not all economic regulators recognize this relationship for setting water utilities' rates. For example, in Chile a water utility's rates are derived from a cost model of a "proxy company."

## 2.2 Production and Cost Functions

A production function is a physical relationship between a firm's inputs and its output. In the case of a water utility, the output is an amount of water (usually of a minimum quality) delivered to a customer when he wants it (i.e., service on demand). An example of a production function is equation 2.1.Production of a good or service is a process through which resources (i.e., factor inputs such as land, labor, capital, and entrepreneurial ability) and/or other products are transformed into different products either for final use or use in another production process. Included in production are services.

$$Q = f(L, N, K, E) \tag{2.1}$$

Where:

Q = quantity,

L = land,

N = labor,

K = capital, and

E = entrepreneurial ability.

A utility's production possibility is the maximum output from inputs with a given level of technology and within a specified time frame. Two types of efficiency exist—technical and economic. Technical efficiency is the production process (given the current state of technology) that requires the least amount of inputs in order to produce a particular level of output. Economic efficiency is the least-cost production. For a specific level of output, economic efficiency is the production process that utilizes the lowest per unit cost for that output. As discussed in chapter five, economic efficiency is one of the most important criteria of a sound rate structure and is closely tied to technical efficiency.

A cost function expresses costs as a function of quantity and is represented as equation 2.2.

$$C = f(Q) \tag{2.2}$$

Where:

C = costs, and

Q = quantity.

An empirical question is what mathematical form this function takes. Economists often assume that cost functions are cubic in quantity. Frequently, the following assumptions are included in cost functions: (a) with the exception of purchased water, raw water is generally not included in costs; (b) at every level of quantity, the most cost-effective techniques are used; (c) in the long run, all costs are considered variable; (d) as the amount of delivered water increases, total costs strictly increase; (e) marginal costs decline as usage increases up to a point; after this point they begin increasing; and (f) at the bottom of the marginal cost function total costs increase at an increasing rate.

## 2.3 Embedded (Full Supply) Costs

In traditional cost-of-service ratemaking, embedded costs generally refer to accounting costs that can be verified from a utility's books and records, and reflect all the activities associated with providing water services to end users. Usually, if these embedded (i.e., accounting) costs are determined by the economic regulator to be "prudent," they are included in the utility's revenue requirements. (The terms "cost of service" and "revenue requirements" are synonymous.) The traditional revenue requirements formula in equation 2.3 is as follows:

$$RR = O\&M + D + Tax + RoR(RB) \quad (2.3)$$

Where:

| | | |
|---|---|---|
| RR | = | Revenue requirements, |
| O&M | = | Operating and maintenance expenses, |
| D | = | Depreciation, |
| Tax | = | Taxes, |
| RoR | = | Rate of return authorized by utility regulators, and |
| RB | = | Rate base |

The definitions of these terms are included in Appendix F. Full supply costs include the expenses and investment related to producing/securing, treating, storing, and delivering water. These costs are frequently broken down into operation and maintenance (O&M) costs, depreciation and amortization, taxes, and capital charges. (For an economist, depreciation expense is based on a decrease in value of a capital asset due to wear or obsolescence; however, in utility ratemaking, the accounting concept is traditionally used.) In Figure 1.3, embedded costs used in traditional ratemaking are reflected as capital charges and O&M costs. [40] Together, they constitute "full supply costs." In the United States, these are the costs typically included in a utility's revenue requirements that are used in setting rates. [41]

For 2007, the full supply cost structure of the average large investor-owned water utility (IOU) in the United States is as follows: (a) return on equity (ROE), 12 percent; (b) interest on debt, 8 percent; (c) depreciation and amortization, 13 percent; (d) taxes, 15 percent; and (e) O&M costs, 52 percent. [42] Thus, on average, approximately 50 percent of an IOU's cost structure (constituting its revenue requirements) is fixed costs. Figure 2.1 reflects this cost structure.

40 In Figure 2.1, O&M costs include depreciation and taxes.

41 A numerical example of revenue requirements and rate design can be found in Hayward, Appendix B.

42 *2007 Financial Summary for Investor-Owned Water Utilities, Economic Research Program* (Washington, DC: National Association of Water Companies, 2008), 10.

**Figure 2.1**
**Revenue Requirements Components**

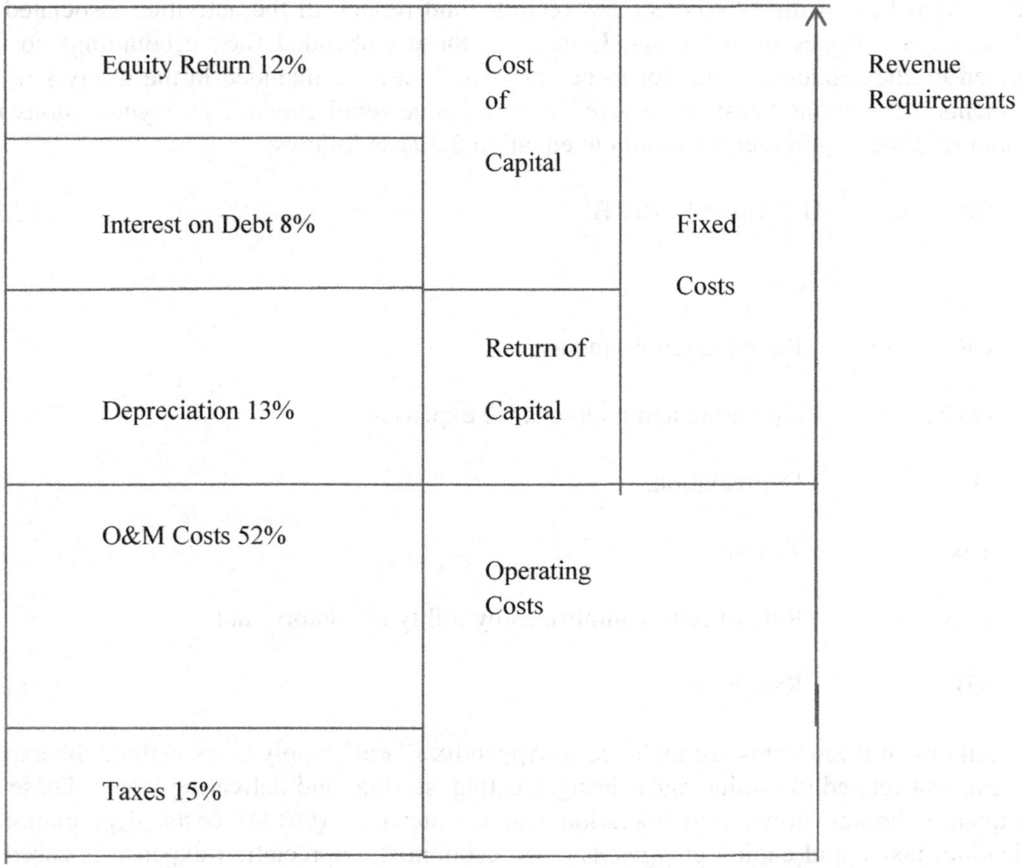


Source: Author's construct.

## 2.3.1 Rate Base and Revenue Requirements Numerical Example

Full supply costs using traditional cost-of-service ratemaking is illustrated through the following numerical example in Tables 2.1 and 2.2.

**Table 2.1**
**Rate Base and Rate of Return**

| Line No. | Item | Amount ($) |
|---|---|---|
| 1 | Plant in Service (without CWIP) | 320 |
| 2 | Construction work in progress (CWIP) (+) | 35 |
| 3 | Plant acquisition adjustment (+) | 10 |
| 4 | Plant held for future use (+) | 0 |
| 5 | Materials and supplies (+) | 15 |
| 6 | Cash working capital (+) | 20 |
| 7 | Accumulated depreciation (-) | 30 |
| 8 | Customer advances & contributions in aid of construction (CIAC) (net) (-) | 20 |
| 9 | Deferred income taxes (-) | 50 |
| **10** | **Rate base** | **300** |
| | | |
| 11 | Operating revenues (+) | 80 |
| 12 | Income and other taxes (-) | 8 |
| 13 | Depreciation expense (-) | 10 |
| 14 | Operating and maintenance expenses (O&M) (-) | 32 |
| 15 | Net operating income (11-12-13-14) | 30 |
| 16 | Rate of return (15/10) | .10 |

**Table 2.2**
**Revenue Requirements**

| Line No. | Item | Amount ($) | Percent |
|---|---|---|---|
| 1 | Rate base | 300 | |
| 2 | Cost of equity (Line 1 * .50 * .12 | 18 | 23 |
| 3 | Income tax (Line 2 * .43) | 8 | 10 |
| 4 | Subtotal (Line 2 + Line 3) | 26 | 32 |
| 5 | Interest expense ($300 * .5 * .08) | 12 | 15 |
| 6 | Depreciation expense ($300 * .0333) | 10 | 12 |
| 7 | Operation and maintenance expense | 32 | 40 |
| 8 | Total (Lines 4 through 7) | 80 | 100 |

Assumptions:

1/ The utility's capital structure is composed of 50% equity at a cost of 12% (weighted cost of 6%) and 50% debt at a cost of 8% (weighted cost of 4%). Total weighted average cost of capital is 10%.

2/ The income tax rate is 43%.

3/ The value of depreciable assets is $300 and the composite depreciation rate is 3.33% using a 30-year straight-line method of depreciation.

Source: Author's construct

### 2.3.2 Full Supply Costs from an Economic Perspective

In contrast to embedded full supply costs, an economist views the components of a water utility's cost of service from a resource or opportunity cost perspective. Table 2.3 identifies a utility's cost of service from accounting and economic perspectives. Accounting costs are historical in nature, while opportunity costs are forward-looking. For instance, employees' historical salaries can be observed, yet at the same time most employees have alternative employment opportunities. It is generally assumed that resources (e.g., labor) will flow to the opportunities with the highest monetary compensation.

**Table 2.3**
**Primary Methods of Analyzing Full-Supply Costs**

| Line No. | Cost Description | Accounting/Regulatory Books | Economic/Resource Cost |
|---|---|---|---|
| | O&M | | |
| 1 | Salaries | Observed/historical | Current/expected market rate |
| 2 | Electricity | Observed/historical | Current/expected |
| 3 | Raw materials | Observed/historical | Expected (futures) |
| 4 | Depreciation | Book life of asset | Usefulness of asset |
| 5 | Amortization | Determined by regulator | None |
| 6 | Other taxes | Observed/historical | Expected tax rate applied to base |
| 7 | Income taxes | Actual (consolidated or stand alone) | Marginal (based on law) |
| 8 | Assets (rate base) | Usually book (historical) | Replacement or reproduction |
| 9 | Operating income | Calculated from above | Calculated from above |
| 10 | Interest expense | Historical | Current/expected |
| 11 | Net income (profit) | Historical (if any) | Expected (implied) |

Source: Author's construct.

## 2.4 Full Costs, Social Costs, and Private Costs

In contrast with full supply costs, to an economist, "full costs" (also called full economic costs) reflected in Figure 1.3 include: (a) full supply costs; (b) externalities (i.e., economic and environmental); and (c) opportunity costs. From Figure 1.3, note how different the traditional ratemaking definition of cost of service (i.e., full supply costs) is relative to full costs (FC) from an economic perspective. Some economists argue that administrative and governance costs needed to sustain services should be added to full costs. [43] Another possible set of costs that one could reasonably argue should be added to full costs are those associated with water resource management activities needed for the stewardship of the water resource base, and therefore for the long-term sustainability of service. [44]

Full-cost pricing is an attempt to represent the true market value of the water to decisionmakers. By representing the true market cost of the water, the impacts and tradeoffs of policy decisions can be evaluated more thoroughly. For example, within a multi-attribute decision model

43 OECD, *Pricing Water Resources and Water and Sanitation Services* (London: IWA Publishing, 2010), 20.

44 Ibid.

incorporating both economic and noneconomic factors, it is important for decisionmakers to have a thorough understanding of the comparative systems under analysis. If the difference between economic value scores is exaggerated by failure to include all costs, the decision calculus could be biased to the detriment of noneconomic (i.e., environmental) criteria.

In discussing average and marginal costs, implicit in the discussion is that all of the costs are private; in other words, firms or individuals themselves directly incur the costs. On the other hand, social costs are different. They are imposed by individuals or firms on others. An example of a social cost is traffic congestion. At certain times of the day, such as late at night, few cars are on the road. At rush hour, more traffic is on the road, and drivers begin to slow each other down. For example, Driver A imposes a cost (in the form of greater travel time) on all other drivers; however, Driver A does not bear the full cost of his actions. Economists call this action an external cost or "externality." Externalities are explained in more detail later in this chapter.

Historically, utility regulators have considered only private costs in ratemaking. It was not until the late 1980s that utility regulators became interested in environmental costs, particularly related to electric generation. Then they began considering ways to "internalize" external environmental costs into rates (i.e., include the costs associated with externalities in prices). Often utility regulators were skeptical of externalities because they are difficult to quantify. In the water utility industry, pollution is an example. If a water utility does not treat the water, the public may become ill and cause people to incur medical expenses to get well. To counteract this social cost, regulators require utilities to incur costs related to water treatment; thus, water utilities will internalize this externality and include the costs of water treatment in rates.

Ideally, these externalities are included in full costs. Price signals based on full-cost rates encourage efficient production and use. In the absence of full-cost pricing, subsidies (discussed in chapter six) may exist and a utility's long-run sustainability is questionable. In the United States, many water utility experts claim that full-cost water pricing is essential for a utility's sustainability (e.g., financial, operational, and managerial), as well as economic efficiency. [45] Other areas of the world have recognized the need to use water more efficiently. For example, the Water Framework Directive of the European Union (EU) requires countries to ensure that water pricing policies (discussed in chapter five) provide incentives to use water efficiently, and for sectors to contribute to full cost recovery (FCR) *including* environmental costs. [46] Denmark is an example of a country that has adopted a policy of FCR. [47] In the EU, all of the *potential* costs included in FCR include:

1) Operation and maintenance (O&M);

2) Capital costs;

3) Opportunity costs;

4) Resource costs;

5) Social costs;

---

45 Janice A. Beecher, "Full-Cost Pricing," presentation at the 2007 National Drinking Water Symposium, La Jolla, California, October 1–2, 2007, 1.

46 Eva Roth, "Water Pricing in the EU: A Review" (Brussels, Belgium: The European Environmental Bureau, 2001), 2.

47 OECD, 22.

6) Environmental damage (i.e., externalities); and

7) Long-run marginal costs (LRMC). 48

An alternative to FCR is sustainable cost recovery (SCR), which includes the following components:

1) An appropriate mix of tariffs, taxes, and transfers to finance recurrent and capital costs, and to leverage other forms of financing;

2) Predictability of public subsidies to facilitate investment (planning); and

3) Tariff policies that are affordable to all, including the poorest, while ensuring the financial sustainability of service providers. 49

Sustainable cost recovery requires more involvement from government as compared to FCR.

Figure 1.2 and Appendix D shows estimates of long-run average and marginal costs for Alexandria Water Company, Alexandria, Egypt, under different costing methods. The Company's long-run average incremental costs—LRAIC (used as a proxy for long-run marginal costs) is approximately three times higher than its "average cost plus return to the Government of Egypt." Thus, basing rates on full costs (FC) can be substantially different than rates based on full supply costs. In Figure 1.2, in the long-run, setting average rates at the social tariff level and below full costs (i.e., LRAIC) will not allow a utility to remain sustainable.

### 2.4.1 Opportunity Costs

In contrast to embedded costs, full costs include opportunity costs. Opportunity costs are the monetary value or foregone value of a good or service in its next best alternative use; or, the maximum amount it could receive elsewhere for use as a production input for final consumption. 50 An extreme example of opportunity cost in the water utility industry are the costs incurred by a residential customer buying and hauling treated water from a water truck to the point of use (e.g., his bath). This situation actually occurs in many developing countries. Other alternatives to delivering treated drinking water from a utility include:

1) Under-sink reverse osmosis system for nitrate removal ($194–279 per household, per year); and

2) Whole-house reverse osmosis system or other point of effect system ($643–786) per household, per year). 51

---

48 Ibid.

49 OECD, 22–24.

50 In the context of the natural gas industry, the value of natural gas for electric generation (i.e., transportation costs and commodity costs) is generally not higher than No. 6 residual fuel oil.

51 Shaw, 238.

Typically in water-abundant regions where the volume of water is large relative to overall demand, the opportunity cost for the water *resource* is low. When water is abundant and therefore cheap, a water utility's primary costs are O&M expenses (including pumping and chemical costs), taxes, and capital costs associated with their treatment plants, distribution networks, and other fixed, utility-related assets.

In contrast to water-abundant regions, in arid regions or where water is in relatively short supply, every acre-foot (AF) of water used by water utility customers is an AF of water taken away from alternative uses. Potential alternative uses of water could be for recreation or ecological preservation, or for activities such as farming. Thus, where water is relatively scarce, the opportunity cost of water allocated to one type use (e.g., agriculture) can be high. The opportunity cost of extracting large volumes of water for municipal and industrial uses can include significant sums of money foregone in the agriculture sector. Another example of opportunity costs is water extraction for municipal water supply purposes, which can reflect values in competing uses by other residential and commercial utility customers in different locations and at different time periods.

Another way to view opportunity costs is reflected in Figure 2.2. As illustrated previously (and assuming that externalities do not exist) the economic cost of water consists of use cost (i.e., full supply costs) and opportunity costs. The combination of use costs and opportunity costs equals full economic costs. In chapter four an argument is made that full economic costs equals full economic value. Therefore, the optimum outcome is the amount of full economic costs reflected as the point in the upper right-hand corner of Figure 2.2. If we analyze one input—water—the larger the number of alternative uses the higher its value. Another example of an input would be labor. If an individual can sell his skills to hundreds or thousands of employers his value would be much higher than if he could sell his services to only one employer.

Three reasons exist for few utilities operating at level IV (the economic optimum) in Figure 2.2. First, in areas where water supplies are abundant, the marginal cost of water supply may not be significantly different from average costs. Second, setting tariffs to cover average costs is a simple, transparent process, which mimics that of commonplace financial transactions. Third, opportunity costs may not be visable to utilities.

**Figure 2.2**
**Full Economic Costs**
**One Input (Water)**

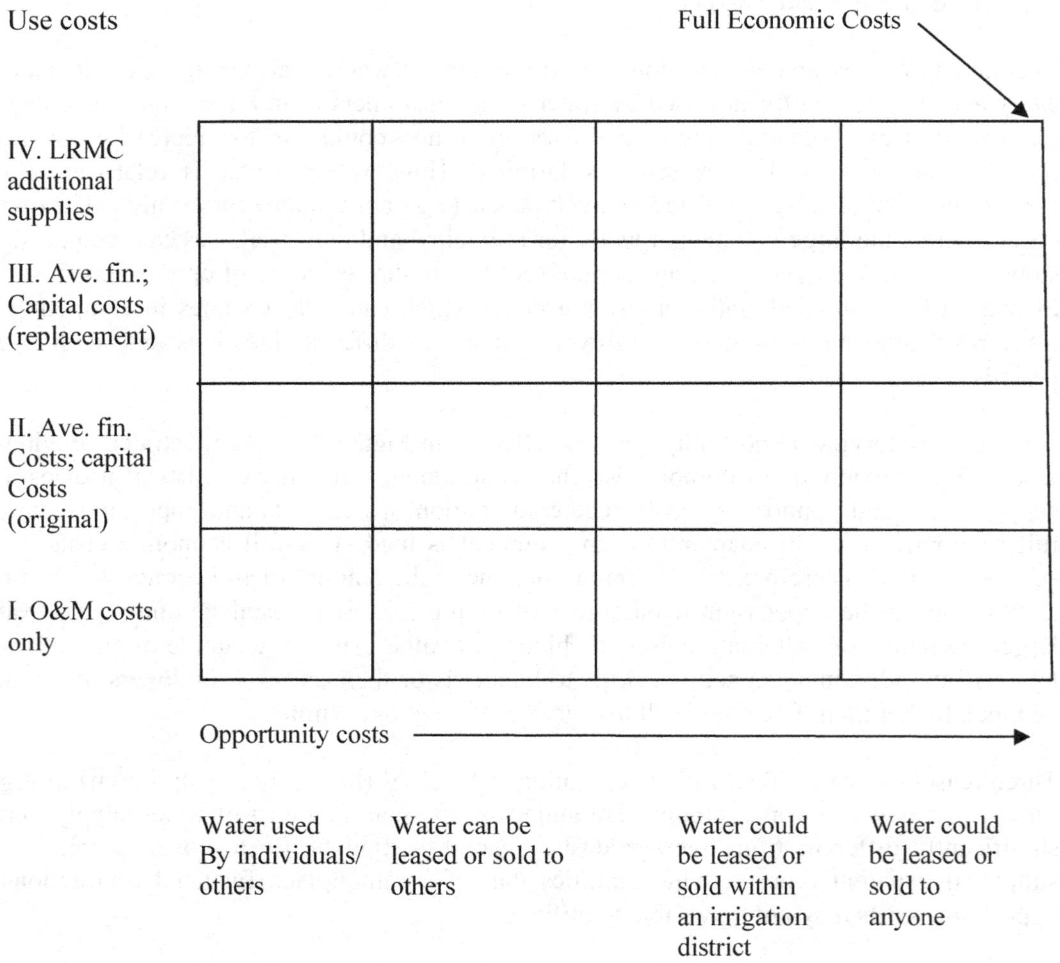


Source: Adopted from Roy Brouwer and David Pearce, Cost-Benefit Analysis and Water Resources Management, (Northampton, MA: Edward Elgar Publishing Limited, 2005), p. 56.

---

## 2.4.2 Externalities

The final element of full costs is externalities. An externality (either negative or positive) is an impact on a third-party associated with the use of a good or service. An example of a negative externality in the water industry is a water utility over-pumping an aquifer, which may reduce the amount of water for future generations. A second example is the impact of removing water from a stream, which causes an adverse impact to the agricultural sector and a loss in the market value of its output. In a similar manner, diverting water could adversely impact downstream anglers.

From an economist's perspective, these externalities are overlooked costs and should be reflected in the costs borne by entities as they make their decisions. As discussed in chapter five, the criteria for a sound rate structure developed by Dr. Bonbright, a renowned utility economist, involves including externalities in the utility's costs and rates. Specifically, criteria No. 5 states:

> *"Reflection of all the present and future private and social costs and benefits occasioned by a service's provision (i.e., all internalities and externalities)."*[52]

When externalities exist, the supply and/or demand curves [53] no longer represent the marginal costs and marginal benefits to society. Other examples of economic externalities include:

1) Inconvenience to customers;

2) Disruption of business activity;

3) Human injury; and

4) Diminished fire-fighting capability.

As described in chapter eight, economists and the courts have determined that externalities are legitimate costs. Therefore, they should be included in utility rates. In France, water tariffs include a 15 percent tax that represents environmental externalities. [54] This is not a trivial amount. The impact of these costs on prices is discussed in chapter three.

In the water utility industry, the repair-replace-refurbish (RRR) decision-making process usually does not reflect the entire array of social costs (i.e., an externality) that result from infrastructure failures. [55] When considering RRR decisions, water utilities typically consider the cost of a hypothetical failure as one criterion in prioritizing projects. The cost of a main break is often estimated using actual cost data from previous breaks in similar mains within the utility's system. However, utilities usually do not quantitatively estimate nor include less tangible social costs that result from a failure (e.g., property loss, water damage, service outage, traffic delays). The AwwaRF claims that quantifying and including these costs will provide a more accurate and effective tool for prioritizing main rehabilitation and replacement choices than exists with current practices. [56]

In contrast with economic externalities, environmental externalities are effects on the environment, outside of the common decision-making process. These externalities include the effects of surface water extraction on downstream ecological health. These downstream effects can impose real costs on society (e.g., the costs associated with remediation). Externalities might also include the loss of important fish species and ecological consequences. For example, in California the courts have held that in order to protect the Delta Smelt (a very small fish in the Sacramento delta in northern California), almost one-third of southern California's water supplies have been withheld. Therefore, when taking full account of water use, externalities should be

---

52 James C. Bonbright, Albert L. Danielsen, and David R. Kamerschen, *Principles of Public Utility Rates*, 2nd ed. (Arlington, VA: Public Utilities Reports, Inc., 1988), 383.

53 A supply curve is a graphical representation of the relationship between price and quantity supplied. A demand curve is a graphical representation of the relationship between price and quantity demanded.

54 "Water pricing in some EU countries," www.emwis.org/topics/waterpricing/water-pricing-some-eu-countries, 2.

55 Scott Rubin, "A Call for Water Utility Reliability Standards: Regulating Water Utilities Infrastructure Programs to Achieve a Balance of Safety, Risk, and Cost" (Silver Spring, MD: NRRI, 2010), 1.

56 Ibid., 3.

included in the overall calculations of costs and benefits. The real cost of withholding this water is the monetary value of replacing a similar amount of water with a comparable quality.

Chapter seven provides a discussion of cost–benefit analysis (CBA). In a rigorous cost–benefit analysis, all externalities are included. As noted previously, Dr. Bonbright developed criteria of a sound rate structure that includes reflecting the present and future private and social costs and benefits (i.e., all internalities and externalities) incurred by a water utility. These criteria will be discussed in more detail in chapter five.

**Cargo shipping.** A hypothetical example of externalities in the water utility industry relates to the falling level of the Great Lakes of North America.[57] Assume that as the result of excessive pumping by water utilities, water levels in Lake Superior and Lake Michigan have declined over the past two decades. As a result, the cost of transporting merchandise and raw materials on giant cargo ships has been affected. Also assume that for every one-inch reduction in the level of either lake means that these ships must reduce their loads by 100 tons. Next, assume that a round trip for a cargo ship between Windsor, Ontario, and Chicago, Illinois, would cost a shipping company $100,000 for any size load excluding fixed costs. Third, assume that the ship could hold up to 10,000 tons in cargo absent any constraints imposed by lower lake levels. Lines $TC_0$ and $AC_0$ in panels A and B of Figure 2.3 show that the resulting total and average cost curves of total monthly tonnage carried between Windsor and Chicago. Both panels are drawn under the assumption that the shipping company fills all but the last ship required to service demand over the month. Observe that total costs climb in steps and average cost projects a saw-tooth shape. This is because variable costs increase only by the trip and because average variable costs would be minimized at $10 per ton only if the shipping company could always operate full ships. That is, if the last ship of the month were full just like the others. The extra cost of the last load's being partially empty does, however, become smaller, on average, as the company arranges to complete more round trips during the month.

Finally, assume that the levels of Lakes Michigan and Superior fall by 50 inches. As the result of this decline, each ship could accommodate only 5,000 tons of cargo. Lines $TC_{50}$ and $AC_{50}$ in panels A and B of Figure 2.3 show the resulting cost curves. Notice that the steps are steeper for total costs and that the saw-tooth pattern for average variable costs are higher after the lake level falls for every monthly total in excess of one shipload, ore 5,000 tons.

In this example the additional shipping costs (i.e., the externality) were caused by utilities' pumping excessive water from the lakes. Thus, water rates should increase to compensate the shipping company for its additional costs.

---

57 This example is from Edwin Mansfield and Gary Yohe, Microeconomics Theory/Applications, 11th ed., (New York: W.W. Norton & Company, 2004), pp. 256-258.

**Figure 2.3**
**Cost Curves for Lake Transport with**
**Different Levels of Bottom Clearance**

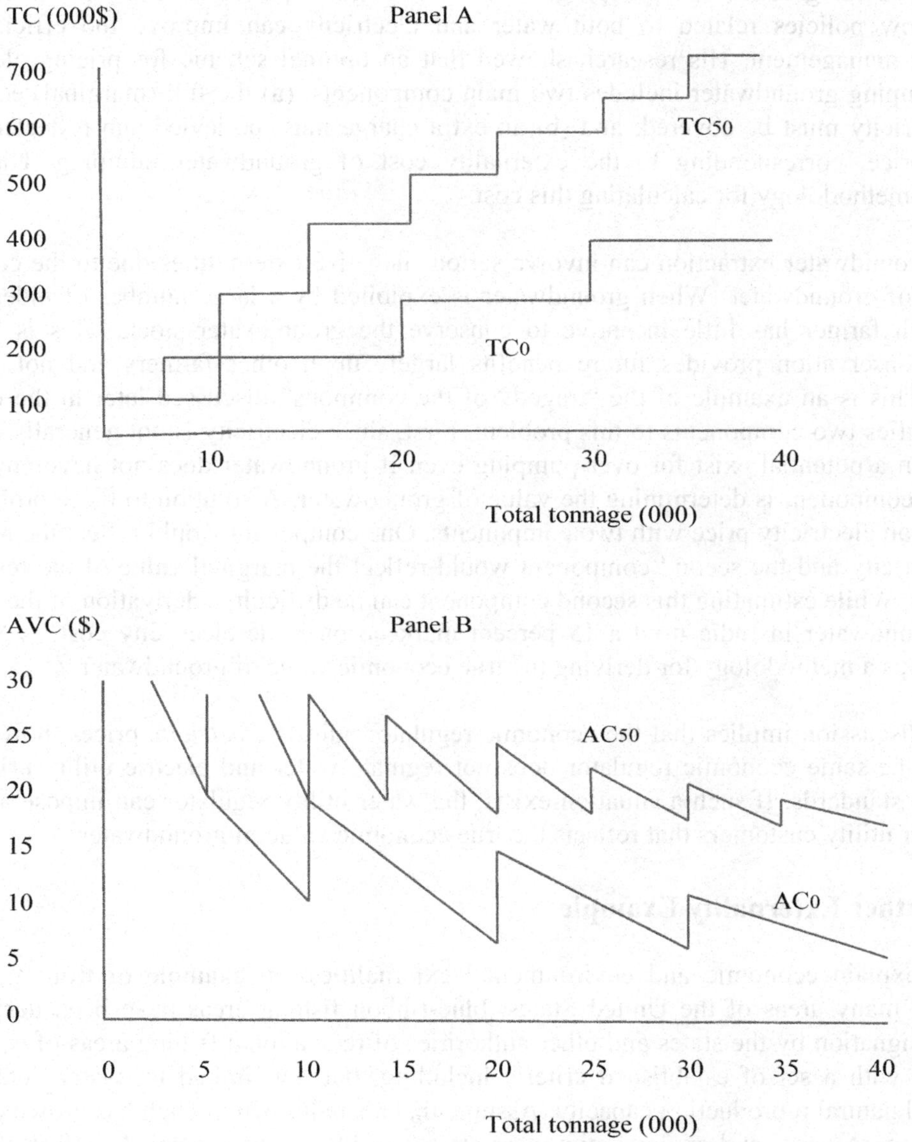


Notes: AVC = Average variable costs, TC = total costs

Source: Modified from Edwin Mansfield and Gary Yohe, Microeconomics, (New York, NY: W.W. Norton & Company, 2004), p. 257.

**Groundwater extraction**. Many economists and research organizations (e.g., NRRI) have been studying the nexus between water and electricity. When a groundwater basin has been exploited by a large number of farmers, acting independently, each farmer has little incentive to practice conservation that would primarily benefit other farmers. A situation like this can lead to excessive groundwater extraction. This problem in enhanced when farmers pay less than the full cost of electricity used for groundwater pumping. In a World Bank paper [58] on this topic, Jon Strand examined how policies related to both water and electricity can improve the efficiency of groundwater management. His research showed that an optimal scheme for pricing electricity used for pumping groundwater includes two main components: (a) the full (marginal) economic cost of electricity must be covered; and (b) an extra charge must be levied and reflected in the electricity price, corresponding to the externality cost of groundwater pumping. His paper includes the methodology for calculating this cost.

Excessive groundwater extraction can involve serious negative externalities due to the common-pool nature of groundwater. When groundwater is exploited by a large number of independent farmers, each farmer has little incentive to conserve the groundwater stock. This is because individual conservation provides future benefits largely upon other farmers and not just the individual. This is an example of the "tragedy of the commons" discussed later in the chapter. Strand identifies two components to this problem. First, since electricity is not generally charged at the margin a potential exist for over-pumping even if groundwater does not have any value. The second component is determining the value of groundwater. A solution to these problems is establishing an electricity price with two components. One component would reflect the marginal cost of electricity and the second component would reflect the marginal value of the remaining groundwater. While estimating this second component can be difficult, a derivation of the shadow price of groundwater in India used a 15 percent mark-up on basic electricity cost. [59] Strand's paper develops a methodology for deriving the true economic value of groundwater. [60]

The above discussion implies that the economic regulator adjusts *electricity* prices; however, in some cases the same economic regulator does not regulate water and electric utility prices and performance standards. If such a situation exists, the water utility regulator can impose a "pump tax" on water utility customers that reflects the true economic value of groundwater.

### 2.4.3 Another Externality Example

To further explain economic and environmental externalities, an example of trout fishing is provided. In many areas of the United States, blue-ribbon fishing areas have been designated. This is a designation by the states and other authorities of recreational fishing areas of extremely high quality with a set of established criteria including, but not limited to, water quality and quantity, and natural reproduction capacity. Assume that a small town in Utah has grown over the years to support tourists and anglers enjoying a stretch of blue-ribbon water. In effect, the town has one industry—fishing. Other businesses are in a supporting role to the fishing industry. Now assume that in order to support the town's growth, water is extracted from the river, causing it to lose its blue-ribbon designation. As a result, business declines to the point that it becomes a ghost town. The economic externality would include the net present value of lost income for the town.

---

58 Jon Strand, "The Full Economic Cost of Groundwater Extraction," Policy Research Working Paper 5494, (Washington, DC: The World Bank, 2010).

59 Ibid, p. 2.

60 Ibid, pp. 2-6.

The environmental externality would include the cost of remediation (i.e., restoring the stream to its original condition).

### 2.4.4 Methods of Abating Externalities

The different methods of dealing with externalities include: (a) direct regulation, (b) incentive policies (tax and market), and (c) voluntary measures. These methods are discussed below.

An example of direct regulation is the Environmental Protection Agency (EPA) establishing maximum containment levels (MCL) of various substances in a utility's water (e.g., arsenic). A second example is where the government (such as the state engineer's office) regulates pumping water from an aquifer to prevent its permanent damage.

A second method of abating externalities is incentive policies (tax and market). The traditional economic method of modifying externalities is referred to as the Pigouvian tax-subsidy approach. In 1962, A. C. Pigou wrote his famous book *The Economics of Welfare,* in which he argued that taxes and subsidies could be used to encourage economic agents to internalize externalities (i.e., include the costs associated with externalities in prices). Pigou's solution was that the producer (polluter) must compensate parties who are affected by negative externalities or be taxed to the extent that the marginal private cost (MPC), including the tax, is equal to the marginal social costs (MSC) including the negative externality. The amount of the tax should be equal to the difference between the MSC and the MPC. Figure 2.4 illustrates this relationship. This cost of compensation (i.e., included in full costs) serves as the price signal that becomes part of the basis of how the entity producing the pollution will consider its future actions. For instance, if an upstream polluter is forced to pay a fine, a tax, or compensate downstream parties adversely affected by their pollution, then under the "polluter pays" approach, hopefully the polluter will be motivated to reduce his future pollution. The "polluter pays" concept is firmly established in UK water regulations. This tax either induces the party who imposes the externality to:

1) Eliminate or reduce the externality to limits set by the government; or

2) Compensate the parties adversely affected through proceeds from the tax.

**Figure 2.4**
**Marginal Private Costs and Marginal Social Costs**

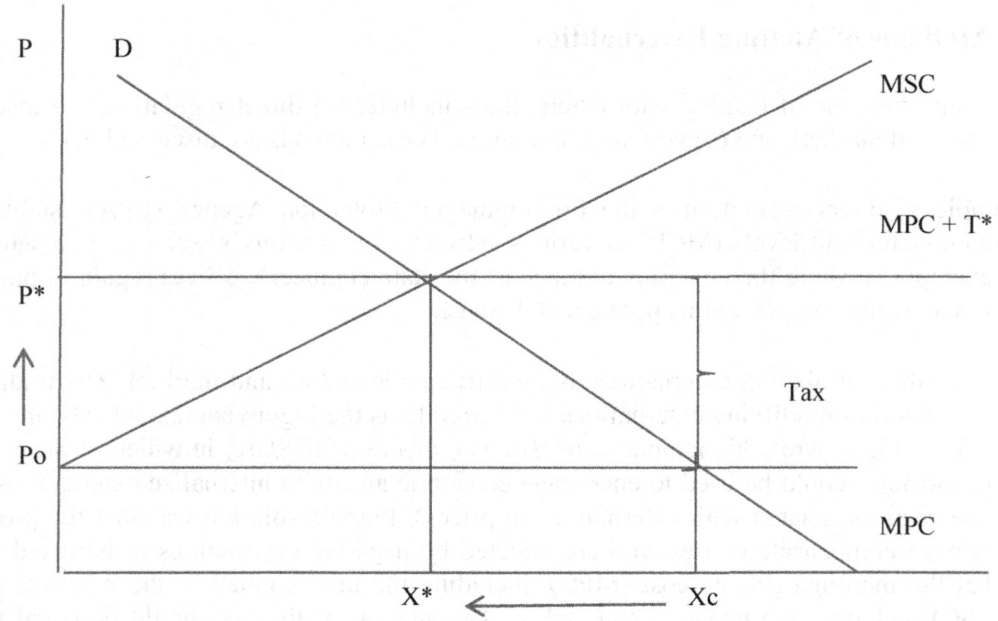


Source: Adapted from Jonathan A. Lesser and Leonardo R. Giacchino, *Fundamentals of Energy Regulation* (Vienna, VA: Public Utilities Reports, 2007), 253.

---

An alternative to the Pigouvian tax-subsidy approach is the Coasian property rights approach. This approach is named after Ronald Coase, a Nobel Laureate in Economics, who in 1960 authored the famous paper, "The Problem of Social Cost." The paper examined how the assignment of property rights can be used to overcome the problems of pollution and proposed "the Coase Theorem." The theory postulates that the assignment of a property right can be used to internalize an externality and it does not matter, in terms of economic efficiency, which party—the polluter or the persons suffering from the pollution—is assigned the right. Said differently, the Coase Theorem states that if: (a) property rights are well defined, and (b) transaction costs do not exist, then externalities will not exist. The Coase Theorem addresses one of the most common mistakes concerning how environmental policies are implemented: the assumption that *any* amount of pollution, regardless of the magnitude, represents an environmental externality that not only must be eliminated, but also must be paid for by the polluter. This assumption is false. It is only economically efficient to reduce pollution to a level where the marginal costs of further pollution reduction equals the marginal benefits of a cleaner environment.

### 2.4.5 Examples of Taxes and Surcharges on Utilities

Surcharges to reflect the costs of externalities have been addressed by various state public utility commissions (PUC). For example, the Massachusetts Department of Public Utilities (DPU) *requires* an "externality adder" to the avoided cost of electric resource planning. The DPU urges its utilities to determine the externality estimate to reflect the various emissions characteristics of different equipment and end-users and the costs of controlling such emissions. 61

In another example, the Wisconsin Public Service Commission (PSC) has approved the inclusion of the costs to reduce greenhouse emissions as part of any planned electric system. They have even specified dollar amounts for carbon dioxide, methane, and nitrous oxide. 62 Thus, logic would suggest that if utility regulators allow the costs associated with externalities for electric utilities, they should also recognized the costs (or benefits) of externalities related to water utilities.

### 2.4.6 Market Incentive Policies

Another way to correct for externalities is a market incentive policy. This is a policy that requires market participants to certify that they have reduced total consumption—not necessarily their own individual consumption—by a specific amount. If a participant chooses to reduce consumption by more than the required amount, he is given a certificate that could be sold to someone who has chosen to reduce consumption by less than the required amount. In the water utility industry, pumping water from an aquifer is an example. An example of this policy in the electric utility industry is emissions certificates and is often referred to as "cap and trade."

Another example of market incentive policies is through marketable permits. In the water utility industry, a marketable permit program was instituted in California to deal with droughts. In this case, the only way a construction firm is allowed to build a new house is if it reduces existing water usage by a specific amount. To accomplish this, the firm approaches existing home owners offering to install free water-saving devices. In some areas, more than 60 percent of the existing homes have introduced these devices that were paid for by the construction companies and indirectly by the new home owners. 63

### 2.4.7 Voluntary Measures

In the water industry (especially in times of drought), utilities have asked the public to voluntarily conserve water. This has been the most common approach. For example during droughts in California, local governments identify various water-use restrictions. Scarcity pricing in Australia was proposed as an alternative to water restrictions that involve complex rules that govern the use of outdoor water by urban households. 64 This form of pricing is discussed in more detail in chapter five. The scarcity pricing study found that water restrictions are a relatively inefficient method of demand management, as they impose inconvenience costs, generate allocative efficiency losses, and require substantial enforcement effort and cost. 65

---

61 Leonard Saul Goodman, *The Process of Ratemaking*, vol. II (Vienna, VA: Public Utilities Reports, Inc., 1998), 982–84.

62 Ibid.

63 David Colander, *Microeconomics* (New York: McGraw-Hill Irwin, 2001), 333.

64 As of May 2011, it is unclear if the scarcity pricing proposal was implemented.

65 Neal Hughes, Ahmed Hafi, Tim Goesch, and Nathan Brownlowe, "Urban Water Management: Optimal Price and Investment Policy under Climate Variability" (Canberra, Australia: Australian Bureau of Agricultural and Resource Economics, 2008), 29.

### 2.4.8 Total or Full Costs

Previously, the revenue requirement formula (equation 2.3) was presented as:

$$RR = O\&M + D + Tax + RoR(RB) \qquad (2.3)$$

These are the utility's direct or supply costs. To the extent that other costs (e.g., externalities and opportunity) exist, they must be added to RR. Thus, equation 2.3 can be restated as equation 2.4.

$$FC = [O\&M + D + Tax + RoR(RB)] + [OC + Ext] \qquad (2.4)$$

Where:

FC = full costs,

OC = opportunity costs, and

Ext = externalities (environmental and economic).

### 2.4.9 Difficulties Estimating Full Costs

In the EU, disagreements exist regarding how to estimate full costs of water and sanitation services. For example, difficulties exist with computing the resource cost of water, due to its nature as a renewable flow and non-appropriated stock. A clear difficulty derives from the distinction between "blue water" (i.e., outflows that can be abstracted and used), and "green water" (the stock of water that is stored in the land and represents the substance of living beings). Ecosystems mostly rely on both blue and green water, and humans mainly use blue water; thus, it is not appropriate to simply sum their requirements. This complicates the calculation of water balances, and therefore the calculation of the scarcity of water. The correct determination of resource cost would require an understanding of the relationship that green and blue water have in a given territorial context. This relationship is, for the most part, site-specific and depends on external circumstances such as climate variability. Hence, it is very difficult to compute proper resource and environmental costs that can be simply added to other economic costs. [66]

## 2.5 Marginal Costs

According to microeconomic theory, a water utility customer will purchase a good or service up to the point where the marginal benefits he receives (reflected by his demand curve) equals the marginal costs of production (reflected by the water utility's supply curve). Marginal costs are the costs of producing or providing an additional unit and can be either short-run or long-run, and refer to commodity or capacity costs. As such, it does not make economic sense for the consumer to purchase more than that quantity since the cost of consuming each additional unit will exceed the benefit he or she receives. The price of the product or service should be set equal to the marginal cost because the costs represent the value water consumers and water suppliers place on the resources used up, or the goods sacrificed elsewhere, in producing one more unit of output. *As*

66 OECD, 21.

*is shown in chapter three, the profit-maximizing price level for a firm is where price equals marginal costs.*

Also in chapter three, it will be shown that what is good about equilibrium prices in competitive markets is that it makes the combination of consumer's and producer's surplus as large as possible and *increases* society's welfare. At the policy level, with respect to water utility rates, two major questions are frequently debated by stakeholders. These are:

1) Do water rates contribute to economic efficiency?

2) Are the resulting water rates "equitable"?

Chapter five addresses these questions.

The problem of maximizing society's welfare is one of combining economic efficiency with distributional equity such that the well-being of the individuals in a community is maximized. Using the Pareto-optimum criteria 67, economic efficiency (also known as neutral economic efficiency) is achieved when resources are allocated such that it is impossible to increase the welfare of one individual without decreasing the well-being of another. Another term—"aggregate efficiency"—treats the values experienced by different people as commensurate and then maximizes total value summed over all water users. This second definition permeates the customary conduct of water resource economics so completely such that the "aggregate" adjective is dropped. 68

As noted above, efficiency is achieved when price equals marginal cost. However, rate structures that satisfy economic efficiency criteria may not be considered "equitable." In a similar fashion, rate structures that are considered equitable may not be efficient. The basic problem of welfare economics applied in the water utility industry is one of defining an optimal plant size and rate structure without impeding society's desired income distribution.

### 2.5.1 Marginal-Cost Pricing Is a Forward-Looking Concept

Ratemaking decisions can be backward-looking, forward-looking, or a mixture of the two. Backward-looking ratemaking is based on historical (primarily accounting) costs and assumes that the utility's future operations will be identical to its past. An example is sunk costs that were incurred in the past. Aside from income tax effects, they are irrelevant for current decisions. In making efficiency decisions, only those costs and benefits that are incremental (i.e., forward-looking) to the analysis are to be taken into account as relevant.

In the United States, it is standard ratemaking practice in the water utility industry to base prices on an allocation of historical joint costs to user classes. Many economists regard standard allocating procedures as wholly erroneous. In economic analysis, marginal costs are the only relevant costs. Dr. Alfred Kahn, the former Chairman of the New York Public Service Commission, was a strong supporter of marginal-cost based rates and emphasized the forward-looking concept. He stated:

---

67 A Pareto-optimal condition exists when a policy benefits some people and hurts no one.

68 Ronald C. Griffin, *Water Resource Economics* (Cambridge, MA: The MIT Press, 2006), 13.

> *"Marginal costs look to the future, not to the past: it is only future costs for which additional production can be casually responsible; it is only future costs that can be saved if that production is not undertaken...If capital costs are to be included in price, the capital costs in question are those that will have to be covered over time in the future if service is to continue to be rendered. These would be the depreciation and return (including taxes) of the future investments that will have to be made...These incremental capital costs per unit of output will be the same as average capital costs of existing plant only in a completely static world, and under conditions of long-run constant cost. As for the former and by far the most important qualification, in a dynamic economy, with changing technology as well as changing factor prices, there is every reason to believe that future capital costs per unit of output will not be the same as the capital costs historically incurred installing present capacity"* 69 (emphasis added).

This forward-looking view implies the existence of a water utility's long-term capital plan (or IRP). In chapter three, an example of a long-term plan is provided. It is related to the analysis of a water project in New York City.

### 2.5.2 Short-Run versus Long-Run Marginal Costs

Marginal costs can be either a long-run (LRMC) or short-run (SRMC). The primary difference between the two is the time frame under consideration and the water utility's ability to adjust its production process to minimize costs. During water or capacity shortages, SRMC can rise dramatically primarily because production capacity is operating at the limits of its design capability. Before additional investment or the acquisition of water supplies is made, marginal costs are somewhat flat until the next capital expansion phase. Figure 2.5 illustrates this situation.

69 Jacob Marsden Associate, "Estimation of Long-Run Marginal Cost (LRMC) A Report Prepared by Marsden Jacob Associates for the Queensland Competition Authority" (Camberwell, Victoria: Jacob Marsden Associates, 2004), 7.

**Figure 2.5**
**A Water Utility's Capital Expansion Plan**

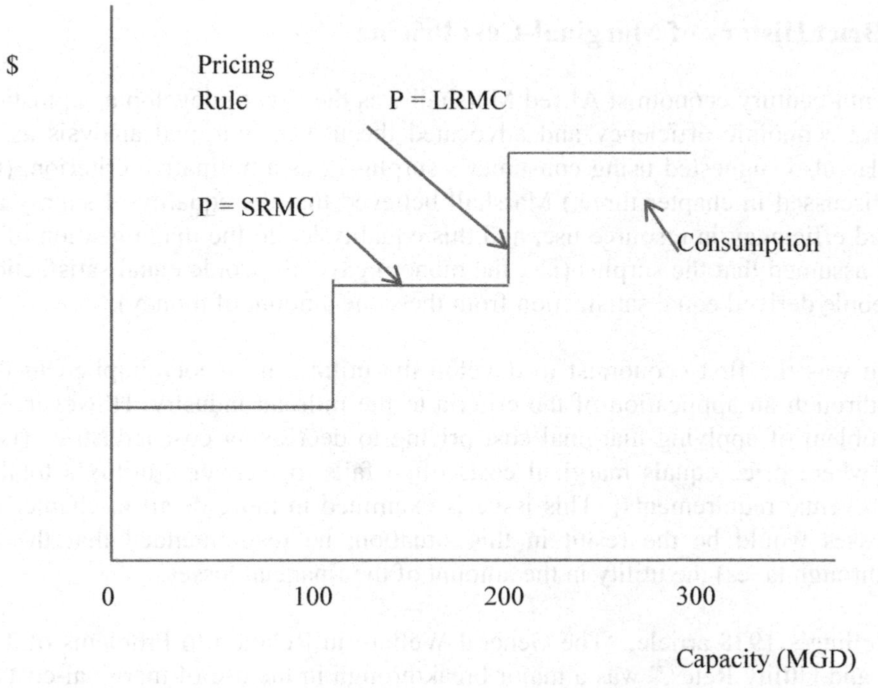


Source: Modified from Janice A. Beecher, Patrick C. Mann, and James R. Landers, "Cost Allocation and Rate Design for Water Utilities" (Columbus, OH, The National Regulatory Research Institute, 1990), 76.

---

In an extreme case, additional supplies or capacity can only be secured if supplies or capacity are reduced by an existing customer (i.e., another customer releases his claim to water and/or capacity such as through interruptible service). In that case, SRMC rises to the value of water to the customer who is not being served, rather than being defined by production costs. In contrast, when both excess capacity and water supply exist, SRMC are normally very low—primarily limited to energy and chemical costs. However, several economists (e.g., Turvey and Mann) believe that LRMC are preferable to SRMC as the appropriate basis for cost-reflective pricing. Their conclusions are based primarily on the recognition of the socially unacceptable instability in SRMC over time. 70 In chapter five, one of the criteria of a sound rate structure is rate stability. All the criteria of a sound rate structure are included in chapter five.

In practice, the long-run has been interpreted based on:

1) The water utility's planning horizon;

2) The average life of utility assets; or

---

70 Marsden, 9.

3) The time period until the next capacity expansion project is needed to meet growth in demand. [71]

### 2.5.3 A Brief History of Marginal-Cost Pricing

The nineteenth-century economist Alfred Marshall was the first to develop a sophisticated model for analyzing economic efficiency and advocated the use of marginal analysis as a means to achieve it. He also suggested using consumer's surplus [72] as a normative criterion. (Consumer's surplus is discussed in chapter three.) Marshall believed that the equality of supply and demand characterized efficiency in resource use, and this equality led to the maximization of consumer's surplus. He assumed that the surplus (i.e., the money) gave all people equal satisfaction (i.e., rich and poor people derived equal satisfaction from the same amount of money).

A. C. Pigou was the first economist to develop the utility rate theory implied in the marginal conditions through an application of the criteria to the railroad industry. However, he struggled with the problem of applying marginal cost pricing to decreasing cost industries (i.e., a natural monopoly) where price equals marginal costs often fails to recover a utility's total production costs (i.e., revenue requirements). This issue is examined in more detail in chapter three. Since financial losses would be the result in this situation, he recommended that the government subsidize (through taxes) the utility in the amount of the financial losses.

Harold Hotelling's 1938 article, "The General Welfare in Relation to Problems of Taxation and of Railway and Utility Rates," was a major breakthrough in the use of marginal-cost pricing as a policy prescription for public utilities. Specifically, he defended the proposition that *marginal-cost pricing is the proper policy in establishing utility rates*. Hotelling is noted for his example of a toll bridge. He argued that in the case of a bridge where the marginal cost (the extra cost involved in allowing an additional vehicle to cross) is zero, the socially optimal price for crossing the bridge is also zero. In addition, its costs should be supported by general taxation. If a toll is charged, the conditions of optimal resource allocation are violated. With respect to the problem that a utility's decreasing costs would result in financial losses, he recommended the government subsidize the losses through the income tax rather than a tax on commodities.

More than fifty years ago, in 1960, Jack Hirshleifer, James C. DeHaven, and Jerome W. Milliman (hereinafter referred to as Hirshleifer et al.) presented a plan for water utilities to charge marginal costs for water that takes into account the differences in providing services to different customers. They stated:

> *"The price...should be equal to all users (since otherwise employments with higher marginal values in use are being foregone in favor of employments with lower values. Suppose that at a certain moment of time this price is $30 per unit. Then, if the community as a whole can acquire and transport another unit of water for, say, $20 [the marginal cost is $20 per unit], it would clearly be desirable to do so: in fact, any of the individual customers to whom the unit of water is worth $30 would be happy to pay the $20 cost, and none of the other members of the community is made worse off thereby [referring to a Pareto optimal condition]. We may say that, of efficiency grounds, additional units*

71 Marsden, 8–9.

72 An alternative measure of consumer surplus is the Hicks compensation criterion. This book focuses on Marshall's consumer's surplus since it is the most widely used measure in applied welfare economics.

> *should be made available so long as any members of the community are willing to pay the additional or marginal costs incurred. To meet the criterion of equal-marginal value in use however, the price should be made equal for all customers. So the combined rule is to make the price equal to the marginal cost and equal for all customers.*" [73] (emphasis added)

In order to allocate water efficiently and fairly, they developed a simple rule for determining how much to charge water customers. Their rule stated that customers served under identical cost conditions should be charged equal prices. This is still a commonly accepted principle even among rate analysts using embedded (accounting) costs. In addition, the commodity (e.g., water) should be supplied and priced in such a way that the price for each customer class should equal the marginal cost of serving that class. Where marginal costs differ, prices should also differ. [74]

The exception to the rule exists where the marginal costs of serving different customers is not the same. The challenge for utilities and regulators is to group customers into classes that can be served under identical conditions (or as close to identical as possible). However, between customer classes, prices should differ, and the difference should be precisely the difference in marginal costs in serving the classes. [75]

### 2.5.4 Marginal Cost Methods

Four marginal cost methods used in utility costing include:

1) Simple marginal costs (SMC);

2) Traditional (textbook) marginal costs (TMC);

3) Turvey marginal costs (TVMC); and

4) Average marginal costs (AMC).[76]

The primary differences among the methods relate to:

1) Short-run versus long-run (i.e., not a time dimension but the capacity of the firm to adjust production);

2) O&M costs (i.e., marginal operating costs) as compared to capacity costs; and

3) Consumption in different time periods (e.g., peak versus off-peak).

---

73 Leonard S. Hyman et al., *The Water Business: Understanding the Water Supply and Wastewater Industry* (Vienna, VA: Public Utilities Reports, Inc., 1998), 228–29.

74 Ibid., 229.

75 Ibid.

76 The formulas for these four methods came from: Janice A. Beecher, Patrick C. Mann, and James R. Landers, "Cost Allocation and Rate Design for Water Utilities" (Columbus, OH: The National Regulatory Research Institute, 1990), 82–85.

### 2.5.4.1 Simple Marginal Costs

The simple marginal cost method focuses primarily on short-run O&M cost. Thus, it has a relatively short planning horizon. The formula for calculating simple marginal costs is reflected in equation 2.5

$$SMC_t = ((O\&M_t - O\&M_{t-1}) + K_t) \div (Q_t - Q_{t-1}) \tag{2.5}$$

Where:

SMC = simple marginal costs;

Q = water output at a point in time;

K = capital investment becoming operational;

O&M = O&M expenditures; and

t = the year for which the calculation is being made.

### 2.5.4.2 Traditional Marginal Costs

The formula for traditional or textbook marginal costs (TMC) consists of two components: (a) short-run marginal costs (SRMC), and (b) marginal capacity costs (MCC). This method also has a relatively short planning horizon. The formula is expressed in equations 2.6 and 2.7.

$$TMC_t = SRMC_t + MCC_t \tag{2.6}$$

$$= ((O\&M_t - O\&M_{t-1}) + rK_t) \div (Q_t - Q_{t-1}) \tag{2.7}$$

TMC uses the same formula as SMC, however, $K_t$ is replaced by $rK_t$. The coefficient "r" represents the capital recovery factor or the annual payment that would repay the unit loan over the economic life, "n" years, of the capital expenditure with compound interest of "i" on the unpaid balance. The equation for the capital recovery factor is shown in equation 2.8.

$$r = (i(1 + i)^n) \div ((1 + i)^{n-1}) \tag{2.8}$$

### 2.5.4.3 Turvey Marginal Costs (TVMC)

In 1968, Ralph Turvey devised the TVMC method and first applied it to pricing electricity. It takes a long-term view of marginal cost pricing. It is forward-looking and is based on a utility's future investment and planning decisions. His concept has been applied by the World Bank. This method calculates the present value of the cost increment resulting from the same permanent increment in demand starting at the beginning of year t-1 *minus* the present value (PV) of the cost increment resulting from the same permanent increment in demand at the beginning of year t. Another way of saying this is that the TVMC method reflects the difference in the PV of the future cost streams (capital and operating) by shifting back a *specified* capacity increment by one year. The focus of this method is on the change in costs of postponing or accelerating an increment of capacity. In the time between capacity increments, Turvey marginal cost is zero. The formula for TVMC is shown in equation 2.9.

$$TVMC = ((MCC_t - MCC_{t-1}) + (SMC_t - SMC_{t-1})) \div \Delta Q \qquad (2.9)$$

Turvey marginal costs differentiate a water utility's distribution network (which expands through many small investments) and the utility's central system (which expands through a small number of large additions to capacity sometimes separated by lengthy time intervals). For example, in England the Metropolitan Water Board produced a plan for new reservoirs and associated works to be commissioned in 1916, 1924, 1931, and 1934. For the central system, while the timing of the expansion may change, usually there is no doubt that it will occur. The marginal cost is associated only with changes in quantity not quality. For example, an investment in a water-softening plant changes the quality of water, not the quantity of water; thus, it is excluded from marginal costs.

Some activities are related to system expansion and other activities should be excluded in the calculation. Take for instance the replacement of an old, inefficient pumping station with one that is more efficient. It would be incorrect to divide the cost of the new station between replacement and expansion. It is the impact on the system costs of any such change in timing that is relevant to marginal costs.

#### 2.5.4.3.1 Numerical Example of Turvey Marginal Costs—Bristol Waterworks Company (UK) [77]

Ralph Turvey, before becoming Economic Adviser to the International Labour Office, applied the methods in his book—*Economic Analysis and Public Enterprises*—in a case study of Bristol Waterworks Company. For the period 1962–1974 the Company planned to provide a safe daily yield from all sources that was never less than the projected average daily demand during the peak week. The Company has three distinct service areas with differing marginal costs. These areas are: North Kent, Kent, and South Kent.

To create a numerical example, Turvey assumed that a new capital program was to be commissioned at the beginning of 1979. The relevant facts are as follows:

1) Total expenditure of £1.2 million of which plant and equipment was £0.9 million (1979 present value);
2) Demand was forecasted to grow by 10 million cubic meters per year from 1978 to 1979;
3) The change in demand of 10 million cubic meters would not change the reliability of water supply;
4) A thirty-year life for the plant and equipment was assumed and an infinite life for the civil works; and
5) Capital recovery factors were 0.1 for the civil works and 0.106 for the plant and equipment;

77 Ralph Turvey, "Analyzing the Marginal Cost of Water Supply," *Land Economics*, 1976, 160–61.

The impact of a one-year change in timing was £215,400 (£1.2 * 0.1) + (£0.9 * 0.106) divided by 10 million cubic meters is 2.154 pence per cubic meter. This number represented the marginal *capacity* costs (MCC) per cubic meter for the central system. This marginal capacity cost is different from textbook marginal costs in that it arises only in those years when demand is at or near the reliable yield of existing capacity. This situation was illustrated in Figure 2.5.

Marginal operating costs were added to marginal capacity costs to yield total marginal costs. This was done by assuming that the marginal operating costs were 0.75 pence per cubic meter. By adding the two costs (capital and operating), the long-run marginal costs (LRMC) for the central system were as follows:

1) 2.904 pence upward in 1978;

2) 0.75 pence downward in 1978;

3) 2.904 pence upward in 1979;

4) 0.75 pence upward in 1979; and

5) 0.75 pence in succeeding years.

The above central system marginal costs related to water supply to the distribution network. Distribution losses were assumed to be one-sixth of total supply at the source. The above-mentioned marginal costs were multiplied by five-sixth and added to the marginal distribution costs to derive the cost of water per cubic meter to consumers.

To estimate demand, twice the average predicted weather-corrected hourly supply was assumed. This amount was assumed because it is common for water utilities to include a reserve margin in capacity planning. Data was collected from the three service areas for thirteen years (March 31, 1961 to March 31, 1973). For each service area, the length of main and each diameter of pipe at March 31 were regressed against the average daily supply thus calculated for the preceding twelve months. Several main sizes were omitted from the calculations for various reasons (e.g., negligible total length). Finally, ten sizes of water mains were used ranging from four inches to thirty-six inches. Ultimately, extra yards of water main per extra thousand gallons of daily water supply were calculated.

After the incremental water main requirements (in yards) were calculated, they were adjusted for water losses and multiplied by the 1997 cost per yard of installation. Finally, an additional cost for storage was added. The amount of additional storage was assumed to be in proportion to the additional gallons of daily water demand. This was assumed to be £35 and added to the costs of main pipe. The result of these calculations is presented in Table 2.4.

**Table 2.4**
**Marginal Distribution Costs (Bristol Waterworks Company)**

| | North | Kent | South |
|---|---|---|---|
| Marginal distribution capital costs | | | |
| Per 1,000 gallons/day consumed | | | |
| At 1973 prices (£) | 413 | 640 | 713 |
| | | | |
| Per 1,000 gallons consumed | 1.13 | 1.75 | 1.95 |
| | | | |
| Annuitized over eighty years at 10 percent (pence) | 11.3 | 17.5 | 19.5 |
| | | | |
| Marginal annuitized distribution | | | |
| Capital cost per cubic meter consumed (pence) | 2.5 | 3.9 | 4.3 |

Source: Ralph Turvey, "Analyzing the Marginal Cost of Water Supply," *Land Economics* (May 1976): 167.

---

Marginal costs were analyzed as the impact on total system costs of an extra connection or cubic meter supplied in a particular year. Marginal costs relate to decisions for more than one year. They relate to a series of years. For example, for a ten-year period, prices could change each year, or a uniform amount could be calculated for the entire period. For ratemaking purposes, this single amount could be desirable. The only adjustment for the uniform amount would be for inflation.

### 2.5.4.4 Average Marginal Costs (AMC)

This method is also called long-run average incremental costs (LRAIC). It is a compromise between pure short-run and pure long-run marginal costs. It includes all future capital and O&M expenditures for a specified planning period (e.g., thirty years). The terms "marginal" and "incremental" are interchangeable. Thus, it is referred to as average incremental costs (AIC), or long-run average incremental costs (LRAIC). The formula for this method is listed in equation 2.10.

$$AMC = PV(K) \div PV(Q) \qquad (2.10)$$

An example of this method is the long-run average incremental costs for Alexandria Water Company found in Appendix D. AMC can be used for each functional account (e.g., transmission, storage) based on the National Association of Regulatory Utility Commissioners (NARUC) Uniform System of Accounts. Note that functional categories are also used in embedded cost-based ratemaking. The average marginal cost method is probably the most widely used method of estimating marginal costs in the water utility industry.

Table 2.5 provides a summary of marginal cost methods that involve various time horizons and cost types (i.e., operating and capacity).

**Table 2.5**
**Summary of Marginal Cost Methods**

| Method | Cost Type | Time Horizon |
|---|---|---|
| | | |
| Simple | Operating | Short-run |
| Traditional | Operating and capacity | Short-run |
| Turvey | Operating and capacity | Long-run |
| Average (LRAIC) | Operating and capacity | Average of short-run and long-run |

Source: Author's construct.

In summary, the key steps in a marginal cost analysis are as follows:

1) Identify all potential supply options;

2) Choose the most viable supply option;

3) Develop cost allocation assumptions and methodologies;

4) Perform the cost estimation for the most viable supply option; and

5) Use the marginal cost estimate in rate design.

## 2.5.5 Short-Run Marginal Cost Case Study (South Carolina)

In 1988 as part of his doctoral work at Clemson University, Gordon L. Carriker undertook a study [78] with the specific objective of deriving a general short-run marginal cost function and to use it to obtain economically efficient and financially sufficient water prices for a sample of rural water systems in South Carolina. (A rural system is defined as one with less than ten thousand total customers including residential and nonresidential accounts.) The data for the study came from a financial survey of 307 South Carolina water systems conducted in 1984 and 1985, and the 1983 Inventory of Regulated Systems maintained by the Water Supply Division of the South Carolina Department of Health and Environmental Control.

An underlying objective of the study was to develop a model that was practical to use. Therefore, a single-equation model was developed. The first step in the study involved derivation of a general short-run marginal cost function for water delivery was to estimate a general short-run average cost function. The short-run average cost estimate is the minimum per-unit average total revenue a water system must collect to cover the basic costs of operation (i.e., O&M expenses). [79] Initially, two single-equation average cost functions were specified for South Carolina rural water utilities by applying ordinary least squares (OLS) regression to the sample data. The general marginal cost function was obtained from the short-run average cost function. Together, the

78 Gordon L. Carriker and Buddy L. Dillman, "A Full-Cost Water Pricing Strategy for South Carolina Rural Water Utilities" (Clemson, SC: The Strom Thurmond Institute, 1988), 5.

79 This study did not account for any externalities or opportunity costs, therefore they were assumed to be zero. Full costs in this context refer to supply costs.

average cost and marginal cost schedules provide the foundation for a pricing rule that is economically efficient and financially sound when combined with the estimated demand schedules faced by the sample systems.

The general average cost function estimate used in the remaining empirical analysis was chosen on the basis of the expected coefficient signs, best statistical fit as measured by the $R^2$ statistic, and the absence of violations of the Gauss-Markov assumptions for ordinary least squares analysis. 80 To obtain a system-specific average cost function, one need only to substitute the appropriate values in for the number of meters and treatment capacity. Equation 2.11 was chosen because it met the criteria listed above. The equation is provided below:

$$ANTC = b_0 + b_1 (QS - CAP)^2 + b_2CAP + b_3RM + b_4NRM \quad (2.11)$$

Where:

ANTC = average total cost net of depreciation, interest, and principal expenses divided by the quantity of water sold in million gallons per year (MGY);

QS = quantity of water sold, in MGY;

CAP = treatment capacity (size), in MGY;

RM = total number of residential meters; and

NRM = total number of non-residential meters.

A transformation of equation 2.11 (i.e., taking its derivative) facilitates the derivation of a general marginal cost function. By multiplying the average cost function by quantity, the corresponding general total cost function is obtained. Next, taking the derivative of the general total cost function with respect to quantity provides the general marginal cost function. A system-specific marginal cost function was arrived at by following the same procedure of substituting the appropriate values for the number of meters and treatment capacity as that described for the general average cost function.

In order to compare the derived marginal cost pricing rule to the unit-pricing policies of a water system, it is necessary to approximate the system-specific demand function. An estimate of a demand function can be derived by combining the quantity and average revenue information for a particular system with an accepted estimate of price elasticity of demand for water service. The study assumed a constant price elasticity of demand. For reasons of computational simplicity, a price elasticity of demand of -0.50 was assumed. (This estimate is within the range of many water demand studies.) A demand function with constant price elasticity and zero income elasticity may be specified in the Cobb-Douglas functional form as in equation 2.12.

$$Q = \phi P^{\varepsilon} \quad (2.12)$$

Where:

Q = quantity demanded at price P;

---

80 See a basic econometrics textbook for a description of these terms.

$\phi$ = a constant;

P = the demand price (average revenue); and

$\varepsilon$ = the price elasticity of demand.

Given the price elasticity data and substituting the system-specific values for Q and P into this equation and solving for $\phi$ provides a system-specific demand equation. By equating the approximation of the system-specific demand function with that of the system-specific short-run marginal cost function, the equilibrium quantity resulting from pricing according to marginal cost may be determined. Substituting this quantity into either the marginal cost function or the demand function provides the marginal cost price estimate. If this price is below average cost, a deficit results. Therefore, a fixed charge must be calculated that covers the deficit and which is apportioned based on customer classes' capacity requirements. The fixed charge refers to the percentage of capacity that is required by each customer group.

A direct comparison of the actual prices and quantities to the marginal cost prices and equilibrium quantities for six of the eight systems suggests that the average per-unit prices charged by rural water systems was higher than the price based on marginal costs. This results in customer water use levels being less than optimal. An additional finding of the study was that the water utilities in the study do not price according to either marginal or average cost. More likely, they priced their services according to custom and public pressure. [81]

### 2.5.6 U.S. and International Marginal-Cost Pricing Practices

In terms of application in the United States, Wisconsin was one of the first states to implement utility rates based on estimated marginal costs. In 1974, in a Madison Gas and Electric case, the Wisconsin Public Service Commission put forth four basic propositions, which included the:

1) Desirability of long-run incremental pricing;

2) Significance of flattening rates in circumstances of diminishing economies of scale;

3) Possibility of reflecting externalities in rate design; and

4) Usefulness of peak-load pricing as the ultimate outcome of cost-based pricing principles. [82]

In 1977, the World Bank researched alternative concepts of marginal costs for application in the water supply sector. Regarding marginal-cost pricing in the water sector, the World Bank staff concluded:

1) It is not possible to establish a set of precise marginal cost estimation rules that can be followed in all circumstances; and

---

81 Carriker and Dillman, 33.

82 Bonbright, Danielsen, and Kamerschen, 415–16.

2) Compromises are required that depend on the degree of capital indivisibility, the elasticity of demand, and prices which currently prevail. The [average incremental cost] AIC method, however, is now well recognized within the World Bank and frequently used in water supply projects." [83]

In 1978, the U.S. Congress passed the Public Utility Regulatory Policies Act (PURPA). This legislation required the state utility commissions to consider the applicability of a number of marginal cost-pricing principles in the electric utility industry.

In 1993, the Canadian Water Waste Water Authority (CWWWA) published a rate manual that set out the Canadian approach to rate setting. The CWWWA recognizes a two-part rate structure featuring a constant volumetric charge plus a meter charge that varies by meter size. (Rate structures are discussed in more detail in chapter five.) The volumetric charge is based on LRMC and is calculated using the AIC method. [84]

Two states—New York and Massachusetts [85]—have encouraged marginal-cost pricing in setting water utility rates. Many state regulatory commissions leave the door open with respect to using marginal-cost pricing. [86] In the United States, the number of government-owned water utilities (GOU) employing marginal cost pricing is not known.

### 2.5.6.1 Massachusetts-American Water Marginal Cost Study

Table 2.6 shows the results of a 1990 Massachusetts-American Water Company marginal cost study. Details on the supporting schedules are included in Appendix G. This study is an example of the LRAIC method. The general approach used in the study for each functional category (e.g., supply) is as follows:

1) For capital investment, identify the capital cost, life cycle, present value, and equal periodic payment;

2) For unit variable costs, identity each cost category (e.g., purchased power and maintenance) and divide it by total system sales during the year; and

3) The unit marginal costs are then allocated to customer classes based on sales.

The estimated total unit marginal cost was $7.96 per 1,000 gallons or $.00796 per gallon—less than a penny.

---

83 Marsden, 23.

84 Marsden, 22.

85 Massachusetts-American Water Company case before the Massachusetts Department of Public Utilities, June 1990.

86 *Utility Regulatory Policy in the United States and Canada, Compilation 1995–1996* (Washington, DC: NARUC, 1996), 644.

**Table 2.6**
**Summary: Marginal Cost Analysis for Massachusetts-American Water Company**

| Line No. | Customer Class | Cost Component | Annual Marginal Cost ($) | Effective Sales (TGs) | Unit Marginal Cost ($/TG) |
|---|---|---|---|---|---|
| | Residential | | | | |
| 1 | | Supply | 106,129 | 118,443 | 0.90 |
| 2 | | Pumping | 50,134 | 118,443 | 0.42 |
| 3 | | Treatment | 22,143 | 118,443 | 0.19 |
| 4 | | Storage | 48,079 | 84,607 | 0.57 |
| 5 | | **Total** | **226,486** | | **2.08** |
| | Commercial | | | | |
| 6 | | Supply | 106,129 | 148,081 | 0.72 |
| 7 | | Pumping | 50,134 | 148,081 | 0.34 |
| 8 | | Treatment | 22,143 | 148,081 | 0.15 |
| 9 | | Storage | 48,079 | 84,607 | 0.45 |
| 10 | | **Total** | **226,486** | | **1.66** |
| | Other Industrial | | | | |
| 11 | | Supply | 106,129 | 169,214 | 0.63 |
| 12 | | Pumping | 50,134 | 169,214 | 0.30 |
| 13 | | Treatment | 22,143 | 169,214 | 0.13 |
| 14 | | Storage | 48,079 | 131,619 | 0.37 |
| 15 | | **Total** | **226,486** | | **1.43** |
| | Large Industrial | | | | |
| 16 | | Supply | 106,129 | 211,518 | 0.50 |
| 17 | | Pumping | 50,134 | 211,518 | 0.24 |
| 18 | | Treatment | 22,143 | 211,518 | 0.10 |
| 19 | | Storage | 48,079 | 164,506 | 0.29 |
| 20 | | **Total** | **226,486** | | **1.13** |
| | Public Authorities | | | | |
| 21 | | Supply | 106,129 | 148,081 | 0.72 |
| 22 | | Pumping | 50,134 | 148,081 | 0.34 |
| 23 | | Treatment | 22,143 | 148,081 | 0.15 |
| 24 | | Storage | 48,079 | 105,777 | 0.45 |
| 25 | | **Total** | **226,486** | | **1.66** |
| 26 | **Total** | | | | **7.96** |

Source: Janice A. Beecher, Patrick C. Mann, and James R. Landers, "Cost Allocation and Rate Design for Water Utilities" (Columbus, OH: The National Regulatory Research Institute, 1990), 164.

### 2.5.6.2 Long-Run Marginal Costs in the United Kingdom

Long-run marginal cost pricing for water utilities has been implemented in the United Kingdom. In 2001, the utility economic regulator in England and Wales—Ofwat—produced a report called: "The Role of Long Run Marginal Cost in the Provision and Regulation of Water Services." The goal of the report was to explain Ofwat's views on the relevance of LRMC pricing in the water utility industry. In 2003, Ofwat published a report "Tariff Structure and Charges 2002-03" that included estimates of marginal costs for water and wastewater utilities under its jurisdiction. Ofwat periodically updates the Tariff Structure and Charges Report.

Ofwat does not strongly recommend a specific approach in calculating LRMC but requires that companies should identify the methodology used. Most regulated water utilities in the United Kingdom have adopted the AIC approach. 87 In the United Kingdom, water utilities are required by Ofwat to break down LRMC into the following four functional categories:

1) Resources;

2) Treatment;

3) Bulk transportation; and

4) Local distribution.

Table 2.7 shows the marginal costs of these four categories for seven water utilities in the United Kingdom. Note that the marginal cost components—resources, treatment, bulk transport, and local distribution—are additive to yield total long-run marginal costs. Also note that these cost components are different from those used by Massachusetts-American Water Company.

**Table 2.7**
**Estimates of Water Utility Marginal Costs in the United Kingdom**

| Company | Resources | Treatment | Bulk Transport | Local Distribution | Total LRMC |
|---|---|---|---|---|---|
| | p/cubic meter | p/cubic meter | p/cubic meter | p/cubic meter | p/cubic meter |
| Bristol | 14 | 2 | 0 | 0 | 16 |
| Cambridge | 40 | 4 | 0 | 9 | 54 |
| Deer Valley | 10 | 19 | 0 | 25 | 54 |
| South East (Northern) | 16 | 9 | 11 | 23 | 60 |
| South East (Southern) | 24 | 45 | 30 | 23 | 123 |
| Portsmouth | 3 | 0 | 1 | 5 | 9 |

Notes: P = Pence.

Source: Ofwat, "Tariff Structure and Charges, 2002-03," (Birmingham, England: Ofwat), 210.

87 Marsden, 19–21.

Observations regarding the above marginal cost estimates include:

1) A huge range of LRMC exists (i.e., 9 p/cubic meter to 123 p/cubic meter);

2) Some utilities such as Bristol appear to have excess capacity of bulk transport and local distribution (i.e., the unit marginal costs are zero); and

3) Regional LRMC variation exists (e.g., South East Northern and Southern).

### 2.5.7 Marginal-Cost Pricing Limitations and Application Issues

Marginal-cost pricing maximizes economic welfare in the absence of complexities. These complexities include:

1) Relevant externalities (e.g., public health and sanitation);

2) Income distribution problems;

3) A utility's joint costs (e.g., to meet peak and off-peak water use);

4) Interdependent peak and off-peak demands;

5) Indivisibilities (i.e., size of the plant); and

6) Decreasing costs.

These complexities will now be discussed.

**Externalities** were discussed previously and to the extent possible that they should be included in a utility's cost of service. Marginal-cost pricing has also been attacked on the grounds that it fails to come to grips with potential income distribution problems. As discussed previously, advocates of marginal-cost pricing frequently avoid the income distribution issues by assuming that the net welfare gains are distributed in a manner that either adequately compensates the losers or does not lead to an inferior income distribution. Furthermore, governments can often better address income distribution issues through tax policies (or direct payments such as a "water stamp" program) as compared to distorting water utility rates. Potential problems related to externalities and income distribution also exist with average cost pricing.

**Joint costs.** With respect to a water utility's joint costs, if one commodity or service is supplied together with another commodity or service (e.g., peak and off-peak water service), the use of marginal-cost pricing is complicated by the inability to identify the marginal costs of the separate products or services. However, this is also true for average-cost pricing.

**Indivisibility.** Another criticism or limitation to marginal-cost pricing relates to input-indivisibility, which could lead to profits or losses rather than a breakeven solution. With respect to demand, this would result in a utility's capacity being underbuilt or overbuilt. A water utility's plant investment tends to be "lumpy." That is, periodically relatively large increments of plant are added to a water utility's existing plant in somewhat of a "step-wise" manner. Figure 2.5 illustrates this process. A water utility's system that is underbuilt will usually yield profits under marginal cost pricing. After the new plant is added, the water utility will usually have excess capacity (and may incur financial losses) until load growth catches up to the excess capacity.

**Decreasing costs.** A final criticism of marginal-cost pricing relates to a water utility with decreasing average costs. The argument that long-run marginal-cost pricing will not recover a utility's total cost is more theoretical than practical and does not have much empirical justification in today's market when:

1) Sources of new water are scarce and very expensive to develop; and

2) The cost of new plant is much more expensive than existing plant.

Table 2.8 summarizes the general and specific marginal cost application issues.

**Table 2.8**
**Marginal Cost Application Issues**

| **General Issues** | **Specific Issues** |
|---|---|
| | |
| Allocative (demand) efficiency | Income distribution impact |
| | Barriers to economic efficiency |
| | Competing policy goals 1/ |
| | |
| Cost and rate stability | Needle and shifting peaks 2/ |
| | Possible large rate changes |
| | |
| Financial viability | Insufficient revenues (P < MC) |
| | Excessive revenues (P > MC) |
| | Customer bypass 3/ |
| | |
| Administrative feasibility | Data requirements and availability |
| | Predictive accuracy |
| | Time lags |
| | Public opposition |

Notes:

1/ Examples include providing: (a) customers with proper price signals, and (b) service to low-income water utility customers.

2/ In general, if a water utility's pricing policies cause a shift in the time of the system peak the utility's costs do not change.

3/ Customer bypass is a situation where a customer no longer utilizes utility services and provides its own services.

Source: Adopted, in part, from Janice A. Beecher, Patrick C. Mann, and James R. Landers, "Cost Allocation and Rate Design for Water Utilities" (Columbus, OH, The National Regulatory Research Institute, 1990), 73.

# CHAPTER THREE

# PRICE THEORY

## 3.1 Overview

Historically, the focus of economic regulation has been on a utility's costs. Chapter two contains a discussion of various costs for a water utility including: (a) supply costs, (b) full costs, (c) externalities, (d) opportunity costs, (e) private and social costs, and (f) marginal costs. The analytical framework used in economic analysis is the standard supply-demand model used in microeconomics. In particular, producer's surplus, consumer's surplus, and welfare economic principles are used. These concepts are explained in this chapter. As was mentioned previously, the use of consumer's and producer's surplus is now broadly accepted as appropriate for welfare analysis in public utility economics. This chapter contains two real-world applications of consumer's surplus. A third example is included in chapter seven. This chapter also compares and contrasts two market structures—perfect competition and monopoly. Finally, this chapter discusses the regulator's challenges under different marginal- and average-cost relationships. Chapter five discusses how price theory can be applied to setting water utility rates.

## 3.2 Perfect Competition Market Structure

Economic concepts including price theory are often best explained through the use of illustrations and diagrams. A common place to start a discussion of price theory is with the perfectly competitive market structure. Figure 3.1 shows an individual firm and industry equilibrium under a perfectly competitive market structure. [88] The market supply and market demand for water is from a hypothetical water utility.

88 Two other market structures—oligopoly and monopolistic competition—are not discussed in this book.

**Figure 3.1**
**Individual Firm and Industry Equilibrium—Perfect Competition**

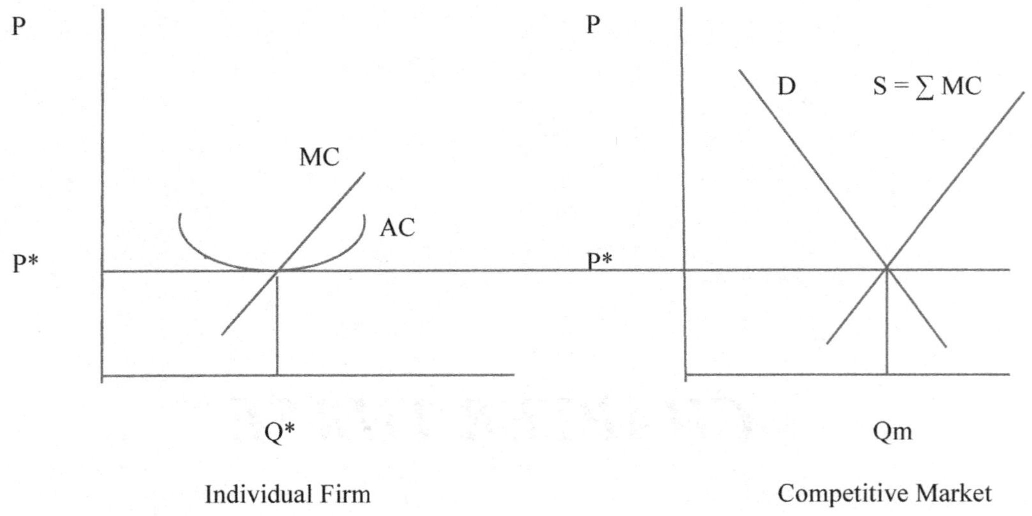


Source: Adapted from Jonathan A. Lesser and Leonardo R. Giacchino, *Fundamentals of Energy Regulation* (Vienna, VA: Public Utilities Reports, 2007), 18.

---

The key assumptions underlying the perfectly competitive market structure include:

1) All quantities (Q) of water are identical in quality (i.e., homogeneity of product);

2) A large number of independent buyers and sellers exist;

3) Firms are price-takers, and individual sellers cannot influence price;

4) Free entry and exit of firms into the industry; that is, there are no barriers to getting into or out of the market;

5) Buyers and sellers have perfect information of market conditions;

6) Constraints on the market do not exist; and buyers and sellers act in their own self-interest, thus the movement of prices is not constrained;

7) For the firm, demand (D) is perfectly elastic (horizontal) and equals price (P), and marginal revenue (MR)—not shown;

8) The analysis is for a specific point in time;

9) Technology is constant; and

10) For the market. the demand curve is linear and slopes downward from left to right and represents a normal good. In the long-run, average costs (AC) and marginal costs (MC)

are increasing. The supply curve (S) represents the utility's long-run marginal cost (LRMC) curve, and it too is assumed to be linear.

The left-hand side of Figure 3.1 shows the costs and market equilibrium production decsion for an individual firm in an industry. This firm is characterized by its average cost (AC) and marginal cost (MC) curves. Average cost equals the firm's total costs (TC)—fixed plus variable—divided by the total qualtity of output produced (Q). For the individual firm marginal revenue (MR) equals average revenue (AR) (not shown in Figure 3.1).

As explained in chapter two, marginal cost reflects the change in total cost associated with each incremental change in the firm's output. Once a water company is operating, producing one more unit may be less expensive than the average cost of all the output produced. For a typical water utility, marginal operating costs include small increases primarily in power and chemical costs. However, if the water utility is operating at full capacity, the marginal costs may be very high (or infinite—perfectly vertical) because additional output would require the utility to build additional capacity. This concept was illustrated in Figure 2.5.

### 3.2.1 Numerical Examples of Cost Curves

The cost curves such as those illustrated in Figure 3.1 are derived from data from a hypothetical utility. Tables 3.1 and 3.2 show the relationships among average fixed costs (assuming a value of 1,000), average variable costs, average total costs, and marginal costs. Note that in Table 3.2 the average costs begin increasing after the 11th unit; and marginal costs begin increasing after the 2nd unit.

**Table 3.1**
**Hypothetical Output and Costs**

| Units of | Total Fixed Costs | Variable Costs | Total Costs |
|---|---|---|---|
| 0 | 1,000 | 0 | 1,000 |
| 1 | 1,000 | 50 | 1,050 |
| 2 | 1,000 | 90 | 1,090 |
| 3 | 1,000 | 140 | 1,140 |
| 4 | 1,000 | 196 | 1,196 |
| 5 | 1,000 | 255 | 1,255 |
| 6 | 1,000 | 325 | 1,325 |
| 7 | 1,000 | 400 | 1,400 |
| 8 | 1,000 | 480 | 1,480 |
| 9 | 1,000 | 570 | 1,570 |
| 10 | 1,000 | 670 | 1,670 |
| 11 | 1,000 | 780 | 1,780 |
| 12 | 1,000 | 1,080 | 2,080 |

Source: Edwin Mansfield, *Microeconomics: Theory and Application* (New York: W.W. Norton Co., Inc., 1970), 160.

**Table 3.2**
**Hypothetical Output, Average and Marginal Costs**

| Units of Output | Ave. fixed Costs | Ave. variable Costs | Ave. total costs | Marginal Costs |
|---|---|---|---|---|
| 1 | 1,000 | 50.00 | 1,050 | 50 |
| **2** | **500** | **45.00** | **545** | **40** |
| 3 | 333 | 46.67 | 380 | 50 |
| 4 | 250 | 49.00 | 299 | 56 |
| 5 | 200 | 51.00 | 251 | 59 |
| 6 | 168 | 54.17 | 221 | 70 |
| 7 | 143 | 57.14 | 200 | 75 |
| 8 | 125 | 60.00 | 185 | 80 |
| 9 | 111 | 63.33 | 174 | 90 |
| 10 | 100 | 67.00 | 167 | 100 |
| **11** | **91** | **70.91** | **162** | **110** |
| 12 | 83 | 90.00 | 173 | 300 |

Source: Edwin Mansfield, *Microeconomics: Theory and Application* (New York: W.W. Norton Co., Inc., 1970), 164.

### 3.2.2 Supply Curve

An individual water utility's supply curve is its marginal cost curve. The reason for this is that the firm will be willing to supply more units of output up to the point where the market price just equals the marginal cost of production. For example, if the market price for a gallon of water is $0.005, the firm will be willing to sell output as long as it costs not more than $0.005 per gallon to supply the water. Since we assume that all the individual firms are the same size and have identical cost structures, each firm will produce the same quantity of output (Q).

The right-hand side of Figure 3.1 illustrates the aggregate result of all of the firms' individual production decisions. In Figure 3.1, price (P*) and quantity ($Q_m$) represent market equilibrium levels. This is the price and quantity relationships that economic utility regulators attempt to replicate.

An individual water utility is assumed to use the least-cost resources in providing service. For instance, resources from the least cost to the most expensive could be: (a) local groundwater, (b) treated local surface water, (c) conservation, (d) reclaimed water, (e) treated imported surface water and (f) desalination. Supply enhancements could include: (a) building or enlarging dams, (b) drilling or improving water wells, (c) building interbasin water transfer facilities, (d) repairing leaky infrastructure, (e) building desalinization plants, and (f) reprograming reservoir operations (e.g., more storage with less flood protection).

There are six points to remember when considering a supply curve. These are: (a) a supply curve follows the law of supply—when prices increase, the quantity supplied increases and vice versa; (b) the quantities are all the same quality; (c) quantity as represented on the horizontal axis has a time dimension; (d) price, as reflected on the vertical axis, assumes all other prices remain constant; (e) the supply curve assumes everything else is held constant; and (f) the effect of price changes are shown by movements along the supply curve, and the effects of non-price determinants shift the entire curve.

### 3.2.3 Demand Curve

An overall market demand curve, D, equals the sum of all individual consumers' demand curves. The reason that a demand curve does not exist on the left-hand side of Figure 3.1 is that individual firms are assumed to be price-takers, and their individual production decisions are assumed not to have an impact on the market price. This is an important assumption because the main thrust of economic regulation is to address cases where an individual firm's production decisions (i.e., their costs) *can* affect market price, and in the limiting case, the individual firm is a monopolist (i.e., the sole provider of the good or service in question in the relevant market).

The right-hand side in Figure 3.1 also shows the market supply curve (S), which is the horizontal sum of all the individual firms' marginal cost curves. The intersection of the market supply and market demand curves determines the market equilibrium price, P*, and total market demand, $Q_m$. In the perfectly competitive market structure, a single firm cannot affect the market price by its production decisions. In this market structure, the level of output produced by each individual firm will correspond to the point where each firm's average costs are at the minimum. In addition, the minimum of the firm's average cost curve coincides with its marginal cost curve. This is why: assume that demand increases (shifting the demand curve up and to the right). This increased demand leads to a higher market price. The higher market price results in the firms already in the market earning additional profits. The higher prices attract other firms to enter the market in search of higher profits. As new firms enter the market, supplies increase, and the price falls until *excess* profits can no longer be generated.

The *market* demand curve is the primary interest to a water utility. For the market, the law of demand is based on two phenomena: (a) at lower prices, new demanders enter the market, and (b) at lower prices, existing demanders buy more. When considering a demand curve there are six points to remember. These are: (a) the law of demand—for a normal good, when prices rise quantity demanded falls and vice versa; (b) the horizontal axis, quantity, has a time dimension; (c) the quantities are the same quality; (d) the vertical axis—price—assumes all other prices remain the same; (e) the demand curve assumes everything else is held constant; and (f) effects of price changes are shown by movements along the demand curve and the effects of anything else are shown by shifts of the entire demand curve.

Demanding a good or service is different from wanting it. Demand for a good or service reflects both the willingness and capacity to pay. For a normal good, prices are the tool by which the market coordinates individual desires. A demand schedule (often expressed as a straight line) shows the relationship between quantities of a commodity that would be purchased at various prices, and *demand* is the quantity of a good or service demanded at a particular price, at a particular time, and at a particular place. The law of demand for normal goods and services states that the quantity demanded falls as price rises, *ceteris paribus* (other things constant). In the context of water, those "other things" may include, and not limited to: (a) individuals' tastes and preferences, (b) prices of other goods, and (c) the weather. Thus, the curve is normally downward sloping from left to right. The demand curve is a graphic representation of the law of demand.

Movements along a demand curve reflect the effects of a change in price on the quantity demanded. A shift in the demand curve refers to the effect of anything other than the price on demand. Important shift factors include: (a) society's income, (b) the prices of other goods, (c) tastes, and (d) expectations. An inward shift may be the result of a water utility's non-price related conservation programs.

Demand enhancements may include: (a) increasing water rates, (b) educating water users about conservation options, (c) buying/leasing/selling water rights, (d) establishing drought contingency plans, (e) establishing water-conserving plumbing codes requiring certain fixture types (e.g., low-flow toilets and showerheads, and (f) rationing water or constrain water use (e.g., alternative-day watering schedules).

## 3.3 Consumer's and Producer's Surplus

### 3.3.1 Overview

The equlibrium point where supply equals demand is the ideal outcome because at this point the overall value of the market is maximized. This is the only point where consumer's willingness-to-pay as reflected by the demand curve and the producer's willingness to sell (i.e., the supply curve) exactly equals the market price. This outcome is reflected in Figure 3.2. The competitive market outcome of Figure 3.1 is reproduced in Figure 3.2.

**Figure 3.2**
**Consumer's and Producer's Surplus**

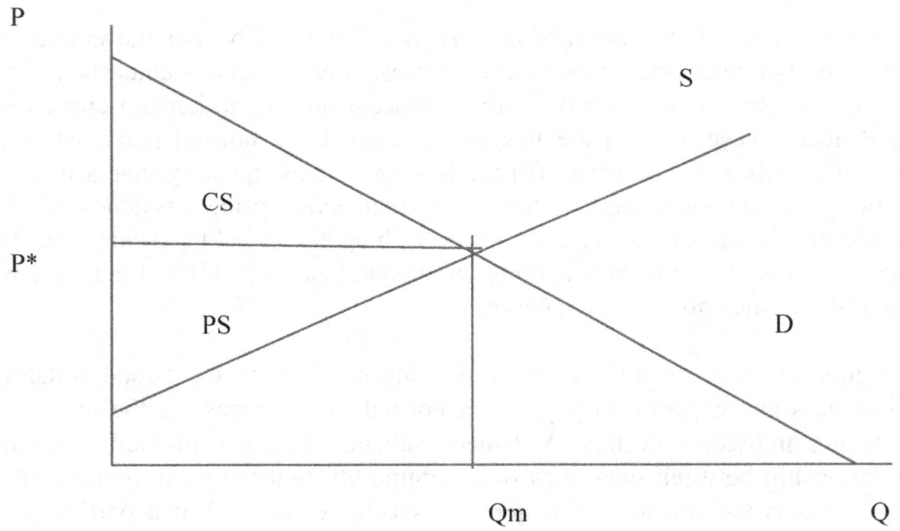


Source: Adapted from Jonathan A. Lesser and Leonardo R. Giacchino, *Fundamentals of Energy Regulation* (Vienna, VA: Public Utilities Reports, 2007), 20.

---

The top triangle labeled "CS" represents consumer's surplus. This is the area below the demand curve and above the competitive price, P*. Said another way, this is the aggragate difference between consumer's willingness-to-pay (WTP) for the good or service and the price (P*) they actually pay. Consumer's surplus is either increased or decreased by a change in quality of the good, or its price. The mathematical formula for consumer's surplus is shown in equaton 3.1.[89]

$$CS = \int D(Q) - P_0Q_0 \quad (3.1)$$

Where:

CS = consumer's surplus; D(Q) = demand with respect to quantity;

$P_0$ = equilibrium price, and

$Q_0$ = equilibrium quantity.

Similarly, the bottom triangle "PS" is the producer's surplus. The producer's surplus is the difference between the market price and the price at which producers are willing to sell. The formula for producer's surplus is shown in equation 3.2.[90]

$$PS = P_0Q_0 - \int S(Q) \quad (3.2)$$

Where:

PS = producer's surplus,

S(Q) = supply with respect to quantity.

The total value of the market (V) is the sum of PS and CS. At the competitive equilibrium price and quantity, the sum of PS and CS will be a maximum. For this reason, economists refer to perfect competition as the optimum market structure.

### 3.3.2 Consumer and Producer Surplus Numerical Examples

A numerical example of consumer and producer surplus is as follows. Assume that the demand function is $P = 30 - Q_d$ and the supply function is $P = 15 + 2Q$. Also assume that a purely competitive market structure exists. First, one must fine the equilibrium price which is derived by setting supply and demand and solving for Q.

$$30 - Q = 15 + 2Q$$
$$30 - 15 = 2Q + Q$$
$$15 = 3Q$$
$$5 = Q$$

Using Q = 5, and filling it into either the supply or the demand function we find P = 25. Therefore $Q_m = 5$ and P* = 25.

Therefore, the consumer surplus for the area 0 to 5 is:

89 The integral of the quantity from 0 to $Q_0$

90 The integral of the quantity from 0 to $Q_0$

$$\int (30 - Q)dq - (5)(25)$$
$$\left[30Q - (Q^2 \div 2\right] - 125$$
$$\left[30(5) - (25 \div 2)\right] - 125 = (25 \div 2) = 12.5$$

The producer's surplus for the area 0 to 5 is:

$$5(25) - \int (15 + 2Q)\,dq$$
$$125 - \left[15Q + Q^2\right]$$
$$125 - \left[15(5) + (5)^2\right]$$
$$125 - \left[75 + 25\right] = 25$$

A second numerical example of consumer surplus is as follows. Assume a market equilibrium price of $2,000, the maximum willingness to pay of $3,600, and equilibrium quantity of 40. The area of the rectangle is $64,000 (($3,600 – $2,000) * (40 – 0). One-half of this amount is $32,000. Thus, the value of the consumer surplus is $32,000.

### 3.3.2.1 Consumer and Producer Surplus--Rate Increase [91]

Assume the following facts: (a) a water utility is considering a 5 percent rate increase; (b) the utility delivers 180 million gallons of water per year; (c) the utility's annual revenues are $740,000 of which $520,000 is related to volumetric charges (and the difference, $220,000, is derived from fixed charges); (d) a price elasticity of demand of -.3; (e) a linear demand function; (f) the analysis is for only one year; and (g) the average customer pays $2,889 per million gallons of water.

A 5 percent increase in fixed charges will produce an additional $11,000 for the utility. This increase would result in an $11,000 "injury" to consumers. The above information provides a point estimate of (180, $2,889). (The point estimate method used for deriving a demand schedule is discussed in chapter 4.)

The point estimation method yields the demand function, Q = 234 – 0.0187(P). Increasing the price to $3,033 will yield a quantity demanded of 177.3 million gallons.

The change in net benefits resulting from the change in policy (e.g., the rate increase) is as follows:

$$\Delta NB_{consumers} = \int (234 - 0.0187P)dp = -\$25{,}805$$

$$\Delta NB_{utility} = (3{,}033 - 2{,}889) \times 177.3 - 2{,}889 \times (180 - 177.3) = \$17{,}731.$$

The water utility gains $28,731 ($11,000 in fixed charges plus $17,731 in volumetric revenue) in benefits; and the consumers lose $36,805 (i.e., $740,000 x .05). The net result is a total loss of $8,074 (-$36,805 + $28,731 = -$8,074) in net benefits. On the basis of this calculation, the

---

91 Griffin, 153.

proposal should be rejected since the change in net benefits is negative. (The proposed rate increase would result in a reduction of 2.7 million gallons which would lower the utility's O&M costs. However, this cost savings is not accounted for in the above analysis.)

### 3.3.3 A Brief History of Consumer's Surplus

The concept of consumer's surplus was originated by J. Dupuit in 1944, who used it in the the evaluation of public works projects. (A similar application was made for a water supply project discussed later in this chapter.) In looking for criteria to evaluate public works projects, he argued that the total satisfacton derived from the construction of a bridge or rail works should not be measured in terms of profit derived from the project but from how much consumers were willing to pay for it. Thus, consumer's surplus is defined as the maximum a consumer would be willing to pay for a good or service rather than to do without it. In 1890 the famous economist, Alfred Marshall, popularized the tool as a classical measure of welfare change. In 1938 Harold Hotelling applied the concept to public utility pricing.

Despite consumer's surplus being the most widely used measure in applied welfare economics, it is surrounded by conroversy. The Marshallian consumer's surplus measure is critized because it includes the effect of an income change (a complicated set of price changes that can sometimes affect nominal, though not real income). An alternative to Marshallian consumer's surplus is the Hicks compensation criteria designed by J. R. Hicks. Compensating variation is defined as the minimum amount the consumer would need to be paid after a price change to make his final well-being the same as before the price change. However, despite the controversy surrounding consumer's surplus, it is considered a rigorous measure of welfare if there are no income effects, or in the case of constant marginal utility of income, which is only possible in certain exceptional circumstances. 92

Estimating consumer's surplus is usuful in evaluating public policy proposals. Chapter seven provides a case study of a water utility concession where the consumer's surplus is quantified. From the perspective of pure economic efficiency, total value of the market (V) does not depend on who gets what. If a monopolist can perfectly price discriminate (i.e., charge customers different prices based on their willingness to pay), it will capture all of the CS. That is, under perfect price discrimination, CS is zero. Chapter five discusses three forms of price discriminaiton. The following are results from three examples of consumer's surplus studies applied to the water utility industry.

### 3.3.4 Consumer's Surplus for Residential Water Utility Customers

In Diana C. Gibbons' book, *The Economic Value of Water*, she estimates the household WTP, or consumer's surplus, for a 10 percent reduction from a baseline of average prices from three cities. 93 Table 3.3 is a reproduction of various portions of her analysis and shows that the marginal values are higher in the winter as compared to the summer. For example, in Raleigh, North Carolina, the marginal values are approximately five times higher as compared to the summer.

---

92 Nadira Barkatullah, *Pricing, Demand Analysis and Simulation: An Application to a Water Utility* (Sydney, Australia: University of Sydney, 1997), 67.

93 Diana C. Gibbons, *The Economic Value of Water* (Washington, DC: Resources for the Future), 18.

**Table 3.3**
**Marginal Values for Residential Water Demand Reduction**

| Locality | Date | Season | Price | Elasticity | Ave. Use | $ (10% Reduction) |
|---|---|---|---|---|---|---|
| Tucson, AZ | 1979 | Winter | 0.72 | -0.23 | 9.44 | 82 |
| | | Summer | 0.83 | -0.70 | 16.43 | 28 |
| | | | | | | |
| Raleigh, NC | 1973 | Winter | 1.27 | -0.305 | 7.82 | 105 |
| | | Summer | 1.23 | -1.390 | 8.81 | 21 |
| | | | | | | |
| Toronto, Ontario | 1967 | Winter | 0.79 | -0.75 | 5.30 | 25 |
| | | Summer | 0.79 | -1.07 | 6.55 | 17 |

Notes: 1/ Prices in 1980 dollars.

2/ Usage in ccf/household/month.

Source: Diana C. Gibbons, *The Economic Value of Water* (Washington, DC: Resources for the Future, 1986), 18.

---

The above results assume that price elasticity is constant over some interval. The estimates of marginal value range from $17 to $105; however, they are not very meaningful because they do not identify the quantity of water related to the changes in consumer's surplus. By making a few assumptions, W. Douglass Shaw—professor at Texas A&M University—performed some calculations to identify what the consumer's surplus numbers represent with standardized usage units. 94 He claims that a 10 percent reduction from this baseline level translates into about 0.045 acre foot. The marginal value for this amount of water is about $28. Thus, the average consumer in the above cities would be willing to pay $28 rather than face a reduction of about 0.045 acre feet per year, or season.

## 3.3.5 Lost Consumer's Surplus for Water in New York City

The period 1949–1950 was the beginning of a five-year drought in the New York City area. In 1955, this drought caused City officials to examine new water supply options. These options included:

1) Building a new dam and reservoir on the Delaware River (the Cannonville project);

2) Tapping water supplies from a nearer connection on the Hudson River; or

3) Using water meters and fixing water leaks.

An obvious fourth option—increasing water rates—was not politically acceptable. In 1955, only about 25 percent of the water used was metered. Those customers where usage was metered were primarily the large industrial and commercial customers. The customers that used the remaining

94 Shaw, 53.

75 percent of water paid a flat fee and thus had no incentive to economize using water, to fix leaks, or even to turn off the faucets. Thus, the average water rate resulted in excess consumption that was not sustainable. As a result of this overconsumption, the City considered the above-mentioned options.

Three economists involved in the study, Jack Hirshleifer, J. W. Milliman, and James C. DeHaven determined that water from the Hudson River would have been more attractive than the Cannonville project. At the time of their analysis (1960) other supplies then on-stream were more than adequate to meet water demand for the foreseeable future. For the years 1960–1965, a reserve margin of approximately 25 percent was forecasted *before* the 310 million gallons per day (mgd) output from the Cannonville project. In *addition* to this reserve margin, storage capacity of 500 billion gallons (over a year's supply) was available, resulting from tapping excess runoff water in wetter years. In comparison to the Cannonville project, competent studies showed that just fixing serious leaks in the City mains and extending metering could provide an increment of supply equal to the Cannonville project at a small fraction of its cost. [95]

An additional factor in the analysis was New York City's claim to Delaware River water—the operative Supreme Court decree having granted New York not a legal right to the water but only permission to use the water subject to reconsideration at any time. In June 1965, New York City unilaterally stopped releasing Delaware River water downstream.

In 1960—the last year of normal rainfall—City officials delayed the Cannonville project to 1996–1997. Ultimately, the City decided to build the dam and reservoir. At a later date, two of the economists who conducted the original analysis—Jack Hirshleifer and Jerome W. Milliman—studied the case to determine if the correct decision had been made. [96] According to various estimates, the cost of providing water with the new dam would be about $1,000 per million gallons per day. According to the City's Committee on Management Survey, the cost of metering would be about $50 per million gallons per day. This cost did not include the lost consumer's surplus arising from the fact that the public would consume less water. In order to make a fair comparison of the cost of metering with the cost of a new dam, those losses should be included in the analysis. The question for City officials was how to measure the monetary value of the losses. The economists attempted to answer this question using an economic welfare model. They hypothesized that suppose a consumer is obligated to consume Q gallons of water per day rather than $Q + \Delta$ gallons of water per day. (The symbol "$\Delta$" represents change.) To measure the monetary value of the loss of $\Delta$ gallons of water per day, the economists used the maximum amount that the consumer would be willing to pay for the $\Delta$ gallons per day (i.e., the marginal value of water). Thus, if a water customer was willing to pay up to ten cents a day to avoid losing a hundred gallons of water per day, this would be the monetary value to him of the loss of this amount of water. The monetary value to the consumer of the $\Delta$ gallons of water—that is, the maximum amount that he would pay for the $\Delta$ gallons of water—may be considerably more than the consumer actually pays for the $\Delta$ gallons.

A technique exists to tell from a consumer's demand curve how much, at most, he is willing to pay to avoid the loss of $\Delta$ gallons of water per day. [97] That is, to calculate the minimum amount a water utility consumer is willing to pay to avoid having to consume Q gallons of water per day

95 James C. DeHaven, "Water Supply, Economics, Technology and Policy" (Santa Monica, CA: RAND Corporation, 1963), 5–6.

96 Jack Hirshleifer and J. W. Milliman, "Urban Water Supply, A Second Look" (American Economic Association, 1967), 169–73.

97 For more details on the analysis, particularly consumer indifference curves, see Edwin Mansfield, *Microeconomics* (New York: W.W. Norton & Co., 1970), 69–71.

rather than Q + Δ gallons of water per day, one simply computes the area under his demand curve for water between Q and Q + Δ.

The economists also assumed that a consumer's demand curve was approximately linear. Under this assumption, the area under the demand curve for each consumer would be about 7.5 cents per hundred cubic feet times the number of cubic feet that was saved and amounts to about $100 per million gallons per day. Thus, the total cost of saving water through metering was estimated to be about $150 per million gallons per day. This result was lower than the cost of providing water from the new dam ($1,000 per million gallons per day). Therefore, the study suggested that metering might have been less expensive than building the dam.

At a later date, one of the authors of the original study, Dr. James C. DeHaven, concluded that:

> *"It is strongly suggested that the correct application of economic principles to the distribution of out present water supplies, especially pricing in proper relation to cost, will so extend these present supplies through the reduction of waste that many of the grandiose schemes for increasing our supplies can be put off for the future."* (emphasis added) 98

In summary, deferring large investments can provide huge financial savings for a utility and its customers. He went on to comment that:

> *"Perhaps the most important conclusion of our initial survey was that the economic understanding of water supply is indeed a primitive state."* 99

Finally, as an alternative to large and expensive projects such as Cannonville, the three economists were more optimestic about the future costs and returns of some of the possibilities for water conservation techniques. This statement was made in 1963, almost fifty years ago. Conservation techniques in the water utility industry are now part of a wide spectrum of demand-side management (DSM) techniques that have been implemented by some water utilities in roughly the past 10 to 15 years.

### 3.3.6 Economic Beneftis of Municipal and Industrial (M&I) Water Supply Reliability for Metropolitan Atlanta

Lake Lanier is a large reservoir located in the upper Chattahoochee River Basin in Northern Georgia and is the principal source of drinking water for the Metropolitan Atlanta area. The Apalachicola-Chattahoochee-Flint Basin Water Control Plan gives priority to hydropower and navigation objectives in deciding to release water from the resevoir for other uses (e.g., urban water). Alternative sources of drinking water do not exist to meet Atlanta's growing water demands. In addition to the water shortage issue, the problem was magnified by federal and state jurisdictions, the interests of various states (e.g., Alabama, Florida and Georgia), and other stakeholders (e.g., recreation, electric generation, and water basin jurisdiction).

The state of Georgia sought to reallocate a portion of Lake Lanier's conservation storage from hydropower and navigation to water supply as its best alternative to assure reliable water supplies

---

98 DeHaven, v.

99 Ibid., 1.

for the Atlanta Metro area. In 2001, a study [100] was prepared for the Atlanta Regional Commission to address various issues related to water supply for the area. The primary issue in the study was: What would be the reduction in National Economic Development (NED) benefits if water supplies to Metro Atlanta were capped for the year 2000 at water withdrawal levels and no new supply alternatives existed? In other words, what are the direct measures of NED benefits foregone by failing to reallocate Lake Lanier water to the Atlanta Metro area?

The economic analysis of NED benefits broadly hinged on:

1) The cost of water (i.e., the cost of alternative water supplies or programs that may reduce the need for alternative water supplies); and

2) The cost of shortages (i.e., drought management program costs, lost profits, and reduced consumer surplus).

Since alternative water supplies did not exist the cost of this option was not evaluated (i.e., ignored) and the analysis focused on estimating shortage costs which included:

1) The costs of shortage management including conservation and reclamation;

2) Water agency revenue lost from reduced water sales;

3) Lost consumer surplus due to shortages; and

4) Economic losses to the region as a result of water shortages or water supply capacity limitations. (This issues was not addressed in the analysis; however, for a region the size of Atlanta's Metro area the economic losses could be enormous.)

Typically in federal water project analysis, NED benefits are capped at the cost of the next best alternative. In the case of Metro Atlanta, with no supply alternatives other than reallocating water stored in Lake Lanier, consumer surplus was estimated as a component of NED benefit values. The cost of the water plus the consumer surplus was the total value of the water to the consumer.

Four potential approaches to estimating benefit values have been used in various studies. These approaches include:

1) Alternative costs;

2) Contingent values;

3) Marginal loss function; and

4) Consumer surplus (willingness to pay) based on observed water prices, demand elasticity, and water use levels.

The alternative cost, contingent valuation, and marginal loss function methods of estimating NED benefits were rejected for various reasons. Thus, estimating consumer surplus was the focus of the study. Estimates of consumer surplus requires a demand curve. Baseline water price and

100 George F. Mahon, William W. Wade, and Brian Roach, "Lake Lanier National Economic Development Update: Evaluation of Water Supply, Hydropower and Recreation Benefits," Draft Report, November 2001.

quantities were combined with information on water demand elasticity to estimate demand curves. The approach to M&I water valuation used in the analysis relied on verifiable water price and quantity combinations and secondary studies regarding price elasticity of demand. A constant price elasticity estimate of -.16 was used for all demand functions in the study.

The arc convention was used to measure the price elasticity of demand and is discussed in chapter four. The formula for arc elasticity is presented in equation 3.3.

$$\varepsilon = [(Q_1 - Q_0) \div ((Q_1 + Q_0) \div 2)] \div [(P_1 - P_0) \div ((P_1 + P_0) \div 2)] \quad (3.3)$$

Where:

$\varepsilon$ = Price elasticity of demand;

$Q_0$ = Forecast quantity of demand before the shortage;

$Q_1$ = Water withdrawals limited by shortage;

$P_0$ = Retail price before the shortage; and

$P_1$ = Retail price after the shortage.

Since the starting prices and forecast quantities of water usage were known, one can estimate the change in consumer surplus under the linear demand curve in such a way as to yield that component of legitimate NED benefits. The other component is the amount actually paid for the reduced quantity of water (i.e., $P_0 * (Q_0 - Q_1)$.

The welfare loss is often calculated assuming a market equilibrium solution implicit in a competitive market. Assuming a market equilibrium solution, Figure 3.3 shows the area (a and b) under the linear demand curve between the before and after price and quantity changes as the loss in consumer surplus as a porton of the NED benefits (The area is exactly equivalent to the NED measure that could be measured as lost revenue plus lost consumer surplus. That is, the rectangle $(P_1 - P_0) * Q_1$ exactly (area a) equals the rectangle $(Q_0 - Q_1) * P_0$ (area c), everything else held constant.)

Normally, to reach a market equilibrium a rate regulated water utility will not increase prices during a supply shortage. Thus, price ceilings will result in excess demand during a shortage. Therefore, regulators will not allow prices to increase to $P_1$ during a shortage as implied in Figure 3.3.

**Figure 3.3**
**Linear Demand Function – Market-Clearing Solution**

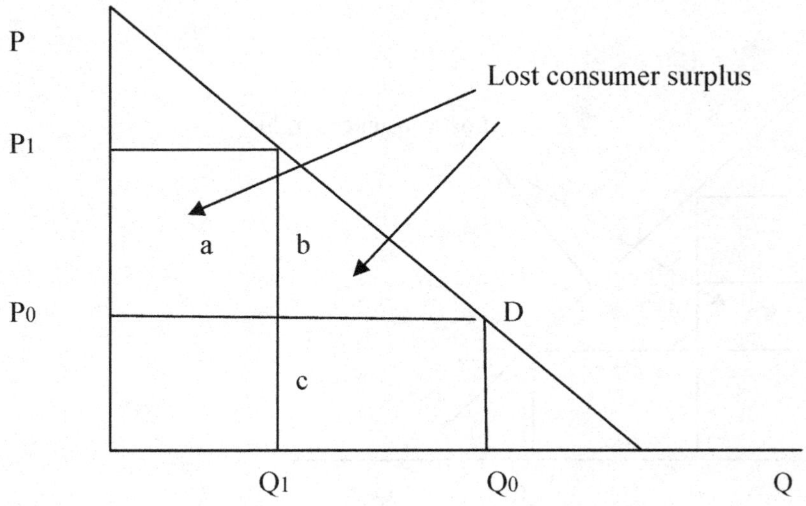


Source: Author's construct.

---

In Figure 3.4, the market clearing price is $P_c$. The regulated price will increase only to $P_1$. The lost consumer surplus (i.e., the area c and d in Figure 3.4) is noticeably smaller than the area (a and b) in Figure 3.4. In the study, the area c and d was the conceptual value that was measured as NED benefits.

The market clearing price (Pc) must be computed to estimate the amount of lost welfare. The formula for calculating the market clearing price is presented in equation 3.4.

$$P_c = P_0 + (((Q_0 - Q_1) \div (Q_0 - (Q_0 * (0.01 * \varepsilon) + 1))) * 0.01 * P_0 \qquad (3.4)$$

**Figure 3.4**
**Linear Demand Function – Regulated Monopoly Solution**

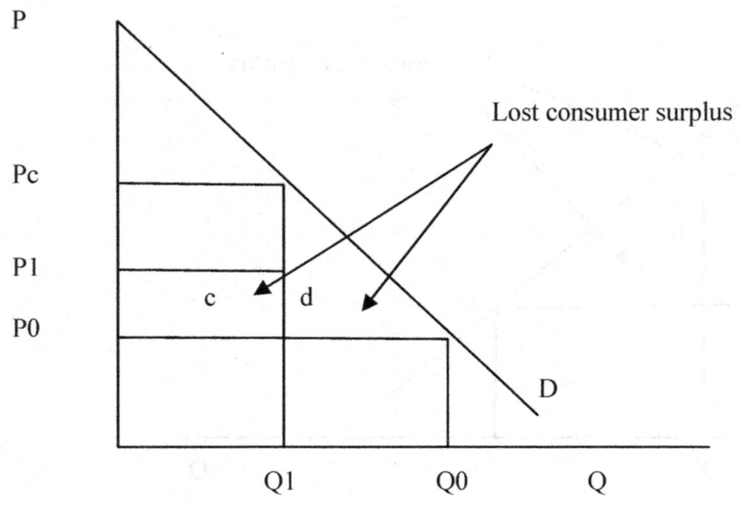


Source: Author's construct.

Ignoring the arc elasticity convention, the corrected equation to estimate the monopoly linear consumer surplus (CS) is shown in equation 3.5.

$$CS = ((P_1 - P_0)) * Q_1 + ((P_c - P_o) * (Q_o - Q_1) * .5) \quad (3.5)$$

The price to maintain regulated revenues is estimated with equation 3.6.

$$RR = P_1Q_1 = [Q_0P_0 - (Q_0 - Q_1)(T + D + R) + C_c(Q_0 - Q_1)] \quad (3.6)$$

Where:

RR = Revenue requirements;

T, D, R = Treatment, distribution, and other costs per 1,000 gallons water saved because of the shortage;

$Q_0$-$Q_1$ = Shortage before purchases of other make-up supplies (which are assumed to be zero); and

Cc = Cost of conservation programs and devices to achieve user reductions equal to the shortage (not induced by price changes).

These prices vary with the starting price (based on a survey in the Atlanta Metro area), shortage and conservation costs, assuming that T, D, and R costs are constant over time. The estimated prices are shown on Table 3.4. These are prices that satisfy a utility's revenue requirements. However, these prices are lower than the market clearing levels. That is, the water districts are price regulated to prevent excessive prices.

**Table 3.4**
**Revenues Satisfying Price ($P_1$)**

| Year | $P_0$ (low end) ($/1,000 gallons) | $P_0$ (high end) ($/1,000 gallons) |
|---|---|---|
| | | |
| 2000 | 2.00 | 3.50 |
| | | |
| 2010 | 2.36 | 4.16 |
| 2020 | 2.97 | 5.10 |
| 2030 | 3.52 | 5.83 |
| 2040 | 4.37 | 6.94 |
| 2050 | 5.84 | 8.68 |

Source: George F. Mahon, William W. Wade, and Brian Roach, "Lake Lanier National Economic Development Update: Evaluation of Water Supply, Hydropower and Recreation Benefits," Draft Report, November 2001, p. 14.

---

Table 3.5 provides estimated welfare losses derived from the linear demand model. The losses are estimated and shown at ten-year intervals. These annual estimates increase with the increasing shortage of water through time and vary positively with the starting water prices. The authors of the study claim that the estimates were consistent with economic theory.

**Table 3.5**
**Lost NED Benefits**
**($ Millions)**

| Year | $P_0$ = $2.00 ε = -.16 | $P_0$ = $3.50 ε = -.16 |
|---|---|---|
| | | |
| 2010 | 91.1 | 164.0 |
| 2020 | 280.1 | 474.6 |
| 2030 | 434.0 | 706.7 |
| 2040 | 678.5 | 1,074.6 |
| 2050 | 1,038.4 | 1,569.3 |

Source: George F. Mahon, William W. Wade, and Brian Roach, "Lake Lanier National Economic Development Update: Evaluation of Water Supply, Hydropower and Recreation Benefits," Draft Report, November 2001, p. 14.

---

In conclusion, the study estimated that water utility customers in the Atlanta Metro area would be willing to pay higher prices to avoid a water shortage. The economic solution would imply that urban water utility consumers would be willing to pay hydropower and navigation interests to reallocate water from Lake Lanier.

## 3.4 Factors that Preclude a Competitive Outcome

The ideal outcome of utility economic regulation from an efficiency perspective is to replicate the long-run price and output conditions of a firm in a perfectly competitive market. This outcome is illustrated in Figure 3.5. Note that at a level of output greater than Q* the long-run average cost curve begins increasing, which means that economies of scale have been exhausted. Average cost is total cost divided by total quantity. A firm can have multiple short-run average cost curves but only one long-run average cost curve.

**Figure 3.5**
**Price and Output Under Long-Run Perfect Competition**

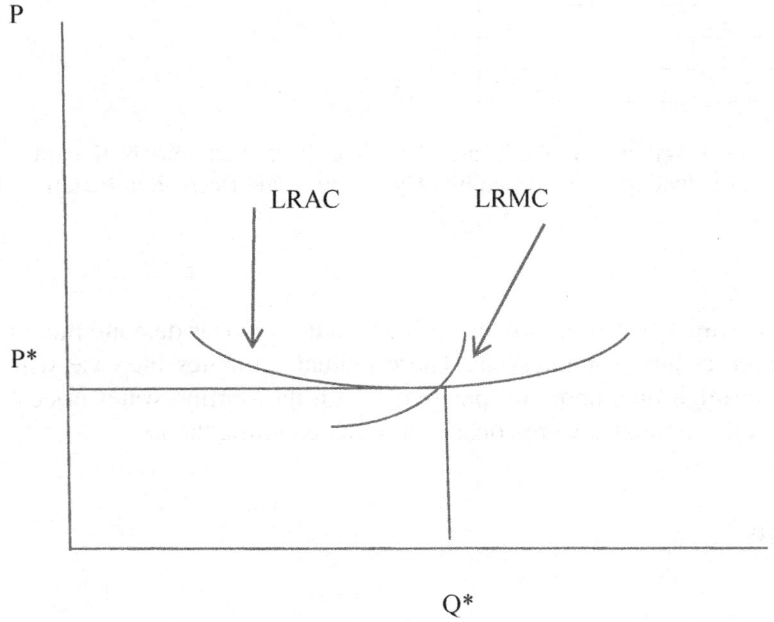


Source: Author's abstract.

If water utility markets were perfectly competitive, a need would not exist to regulate prices charged to consumers. However, water utility markets are not perfectly competitive and have characteristics that preclude purely competitive outcomes. This situation is called market failure. Market failure exists in situations where the market does not lead to desired results. Types of market failure include: (a) imperfect information to guide purchasing or production decisions; (b) limits to competition, including barriers to market entry; (c) externalities, (d) failure to protect or preserve the commons, including natural resources; (e) failure to produce public goods and services, such as environmental protection; (f) adverse social or economic impacts, undesirable distributional consequences, or threats to basic rights or core values (including universal access to services); and (g) the tendency toward monopoly formation and the potential abuse of monopoly power. [101]As the result of the above conditions, the prices charged by water utilities to

101 Janice A. Beecher, "Economic Regulation of Water Utilities: A Primer," (Washington, DC: National Association of Water Companies, September 2001), 3-4

consumers in those market segments should be regulated if society is to obtain various social objectives. (Social objectives are discussed in chapter five.) Two specific characteristics—natural monopoly and high barriers to entry—are discussed below.

### 3.4.1 Natural Monopoly and Barriers to Entry

The natural monopoly characteristic has traditionally served as the basis for regulating utilities. A natural monopoly is a firm characterized by average costs that decrease as the amount the firm produces increases (i.e., the firm has declining average costs). The result is that it is less costly for one firm to produce all of the goods or services demanded than for two or more firms combined to produce the same amount. The primary reason for this is economies of scale. Economies of scale mean that the more units of a good produced, the lower the per-unit production cost. In addition, economies of scope may exist. Economies of scope exist when the average cost of combined services (e.g., water for consumption and fire protection services) is less than the cost of providing the services separately and when the unit cost of providing multiple services is less than if they were provided by separate utilities. For a water uility, water treatmet usually has economies of scale. After approximately eight miles from water treatment plants that provide about 0.018 million gallons per capita per year, water distribution has diseconomies of scale. 102

Figure 3.6 illustrates the cost structure of a natural monopoly. In this figure, the market demand for the good or service is characterized by the demand curve, D. Assume that the firm has high fixed costs and constant marginal costs. As the firm's output increases, its average costs decrease, since its fixed costs are spread over more units of output. A distinguishing characteristic of a natural monopoly is that the individual firm exhibits economics of scale through the relevant range of the market demand. Although the firm's average costs will evenutally increase, the level of market demand necessary for that to occur will be far greater than the observed market demand. Therefore, at the idealized competitive market price equal to marginal cost, total demand would equal $Q_m$. At that level of demand, AC is still decreasing as a result of economices of scale and/or economies of scope.

102 Shaw, 104.

**Figure 3.6**
**Natural Monopoly**

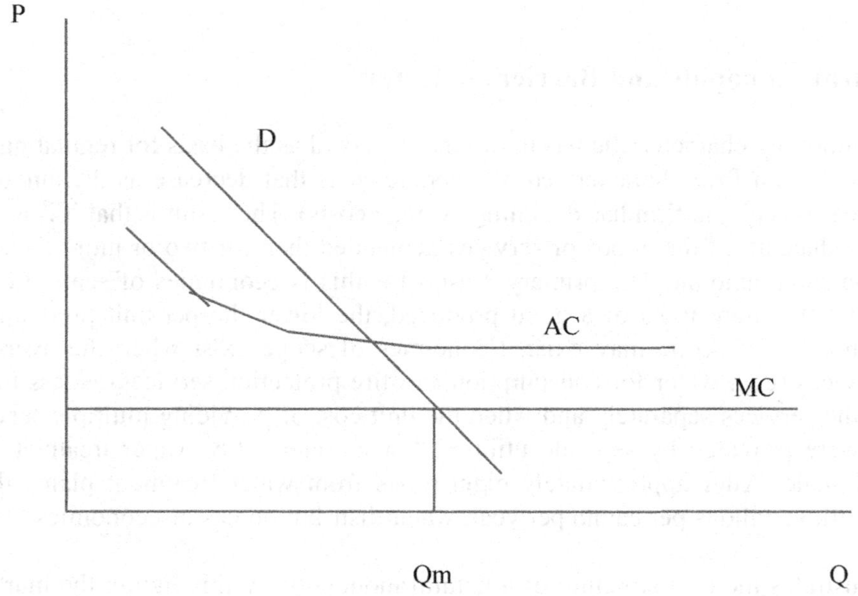


Source: Adapted from Jonathan A. Lesser and Leonardo R. Giacchino, *Fundamentals of Energy Regulation* (Vienna, VA: Public Utilities Reports, 2007), 24.

---

In addition to economies of scale, historically, a second reason for utility economic regulation has been the presence of barriers to entry. Barriers to entry are defined as any costs that must be borne by firms seeking to enter (or exit) an industry that are not borne by incumbent firms. In the context of utilities, many economists consider economies of scale and large initial capital expenditures to be barriers to entry. This is particularly true in the water utility business because of high capital costs and immobile assets. The water utility industry is one of the most capital-intensive industries, with a ratio of approximately $3.2 in fixed assets (e.g., plant) for each $1 in revenue. As a consequence of these characteristics, the losses associated with firms' unsuccessful market entry can be quite large. Barrers to entry and exit make it easier for incumbent firms to charge prices above the competitive ideal. Because the threat of entry is low, without regulation, firms could get away with price gouging.

Numerical examples of total price, output, profits, average price, and marginal costs are provided in Appendix H.

## 3.5 Monopoly Market Structure

In a perfectly competitive market, all resources are optimally allocated; therefore, the maximum social benefit is equal to the maximum producer benefit. Monopolies arise due to conditions of imperfect competition in the market in which a firm has control over prices. When a perfectly competitive market structure cannot be achieved, it is useful to see how an unconstrained monopolist would behave and the resulting economic impact of that behavior. Figure 3.7 illustrates the price and output under a monopoly market structure. Unlike firms in a competitive market, a monopolist is a price setter and not a price taker; and a monopolist's level of output affects the market price. That is, to sell another unit, the monopolist must lower its price on all units sold. As a result, the monopolist will set the *quantity* of output and the price at the point where MR equals MC—the same as a firm in a perfectly competitive market. The MR curve lies below the industry demand curve, D, since each additional unit the monopolist produces and sells results in a lower market price for all units sold.

For illustration purposes, assume that the marginal cost (MC) of producing each unit of water is constant. (This is likely to occur when a firm has excess capacity, and the marginal costs only represent variable operating costs such as electricity and chemicals.) The competitive outcome would be to produce Q* with a resulting market price P*. In Figure 3.7, this is represented as point "a". The monopolist will restrict output to $Q_m$ where the firm's marginal revenue equals its marginal cost. This will result where output falls to $Q_m$ and price increases to $P_m$. This decision by the monopolist results in point "b". One of the results of this production decision is a decrease in the overall value of the market. Specifically, consumer's surplus (CS) is reduced because consumers are forced to pay a higher price for fewer units of output. As a result, the monopolist transfers some of the CS profits to itself. Because the monopolist also restricts output below the competitive ideal, a welfare loss exists and is represented as the triangle (abc) in Figure 3.7. The reason this area is called "welfare loss" is that consumers are willing to pay more for an additional level of output (Q* - $Q_m$) units than it costs the monopolist to produce those units, which is in a perfectly competitive market would be produced.

**Figure 3.7**
**A Monopolist's Price and Output**

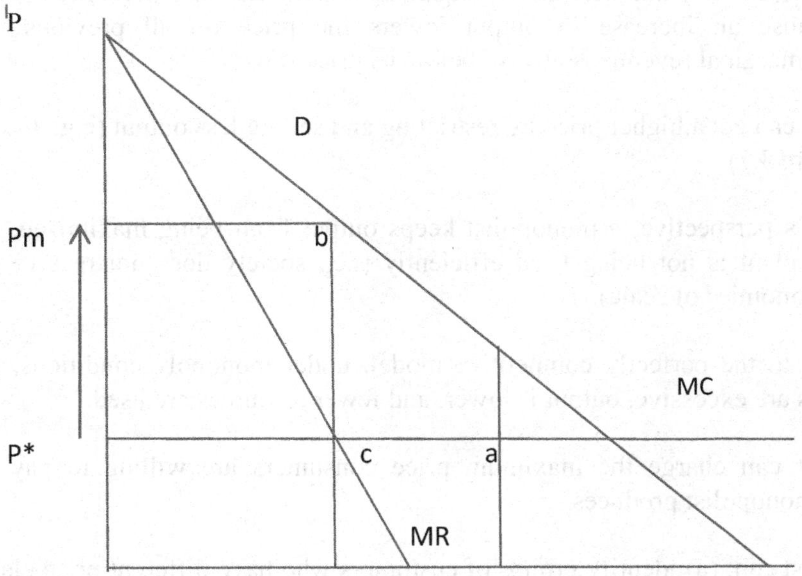


Source: Adapted from Jonathan A. Lesser and Leonardo R. Giacchino, *Fundamentals of Energy Regulation* (Vienna, VA: Public Utilities Reports, 2007), 27.

### 3.5.1 Monopoly Market Structure Summary

Pure monopoly is the opposite of perfect competition. Characteristics of the monopoly model include:

1) A single seller of a product exists.

2) The extent of the monopolist's power is the availability of close substitutes (e.g., bottled water, water supplied from a standpost).

3) In the long run, just like the firm operating in a perfectly competitive market, the monopolist's goal is to maximize profits. This exists when marginal costs equal marginal revenues.

4) The demand curve (D) for a monopolist is the industry's demand curve as compared to the horizontal demand curve faced by a firm in a perfectly competitive market.

5) A supply curve for a monopolist does not exist because: (a) the output produced by a monopolist depends on the position and slope of the demand curve, and (b) any single monopoly price can result in a variety of rates and quantities produced.

6) In the short run, there is no reason to believe that a monopolist always makes a profit; however, in the long run the monopolist must at least make a *normal* profit; the monopolist will at least attempt to minimize its losses.

7) Marginal revenue (MR) and price are not equal, as was the case in a perfectly competitive market. Because an increase in output lowers the price on all previous units, a monopolist's marginal revenue is always below its price. [103]

8) A monopolist can get a higher price by restricting and selling less output (e.g., $Q_m$ instead of $Q^*$ in Figure 3.7).

9) From society's perspective, a monopolist keeps output from being maximized, and the monopolist's plant is not being used efficiently (i.e., society does not receive the full benefits of economies of scale).

10) As compared to the perfectly competitive model, under monopoly conditions, price is higher, profits are excessive, output is lower, and fewer resources are used.

11) A monopolist can charge the maximum price consumers are willing to pay for the quantity the monopolist produces.

12) If a monopolist can: (a) identify groups of customers who have different price elasticities of demand, (b) separate them in some way, and (c) limit their ability to resell its product between groups, it can price discriminate.

103 The marginal revenue curve will intersect the x axis halfway between the origin and where the demand curve intersects the axis.

13) A price-discriminating monopolist earns more profit than a normal monopolist because it can charge a higher price to those with less elastic demands and a lower price to those with more elastic demands.

14) Because monopolists reduce output and charge a price higher than marginal cost, monopolies create a welfare loss to society.

15) Natural monopolies exist in industries with strong economies of scale. Because their average total costs are always falling, it is more efficient for one firm to produce all of the output.

## 3.6 The Regulator's Pricing Challenge

### 3.6.1 Setting Prices When Average Costs Are Declining

In industries characterized as natural monopolies, utility regulators face a challenge of setting an appropriate price. (Chapter five addresses utility rates. For now, the appropriate price is assumed to be based exclusively on economic efficiency criteria.) As previously stated, a natural monopoly has a declining average cost curve in the relevant range. In this range, marginal costs are lower than average costs. This situation is illustrated in Figure 3.8. When this cost structure occurs, a pricing dilemma exists for the utility regulator. If a utility's short-run marginal costs are constant and below its average costs (AC), setting the price based on short-run marginal costs results in total revenues lower than total costs.

If this situation continues, the monopolist (i.e., the water utility) will go out of business. A primary challenge presented to utility economic regulators is to obtain the results (i.e., price and quantity) that would result in a competitive market. In other words, in Figure 3.8, the regulator would prefer the output equal to Q* and the price equal to P* at the same time as the monopolist earns enough revenues to recover all of its costs, including earning a normal profit.

A frequently used solution for the above-mentioned problem is for regulators to set price equal to the firm's average cost. This situation is shown in Figure 3.9. If the utility regulator sets the price at Pac, the total quantity demanded will decrease relative to the optimum quantity, Q*. At this level of price and output, the monopolist will recover its costs, but society will still experience a welfare loss—but less than in the case of Figure 3.7. This welfare loss is shown by the triangle abc in Figure 3.9. This loss results because the total value of the market is less than it would have been in a purely competitive market. The solution to this problem will be discussed in chapter five.

Another pricing alternative that does meet the discussed welfare criteria employs the marginal cost price as a per-unit charge to customers. The difference (if any) between the revenues generated through a per-unit charge and the utility's costs is collected through fixed fees. Ideally, these fixed fees are based on the customer-specific requirements for surplus capacity. Most water utilities maintain surplus capacity and water in order to meet unexpected, higher-than-average loads on the system caused by drought, fires, or other unusual circumstances.

**Figure 3.8**
**Marginal Costs Less Than Average Costs**

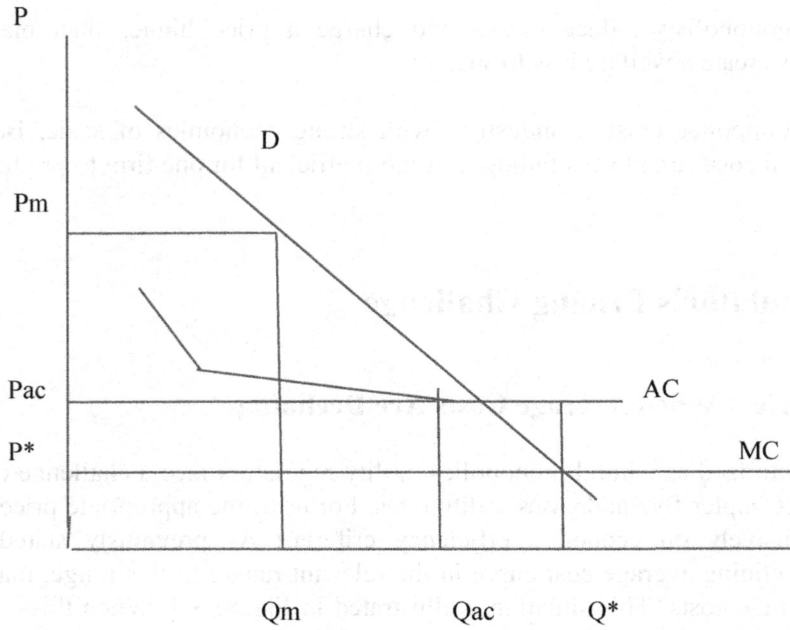


**Figure 3.9**
**Average-Cost Pricing**

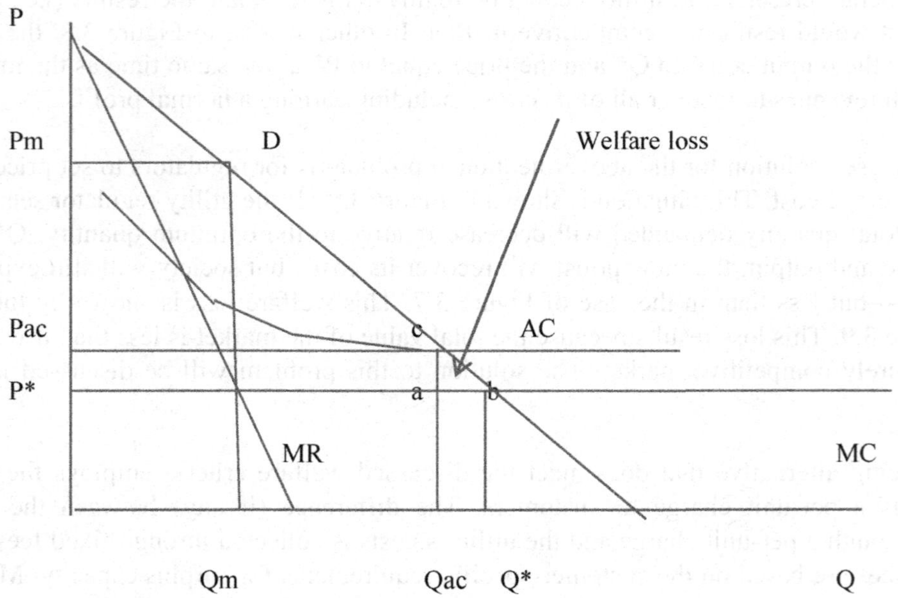


Source: Adapted from Jonathan A. Lesser and Leonardo R. Giacchino, *Fundamentals of Energy Regulation* (Vienna, VA: Public Utilities Reports, 2007), 30.

The previous pricing discussion was in the context of a water utility's declining average costs. Currently, in the water utility industry, many economists argue that average costs are not declining; rather, they are increasing. Some causes of increasing average costs are:

1) The result of meeting more stringent water quality standards;

2) Replacing infrastructure due to growth and/or assets that are no longer useful (e.g., they are past their expected life); and

3) More expensive water supplies.

Unlike the situation of marginal costs lower than average costs producing a revenue shortfall, marginal-cost pricing when a utility's marginal costs are higher than average costs results in excessive revenues. Figure 3.10 shows various prices and quantities when average costs are increasing in the relevant range (i.e., in excess of Q*. If the regulator sets the price at P*, the monopolist will earn excessive profits equal to the rectangle, P*ACqab. If the regulator sets the price equal to the monopolist's average cost (Pac), the monopolist will produce too much output (Qac), resulting in a welfare loss to society equal to the area in the triangle.

**Figure 3.10**
**Pricing When Average Costs Are Increasing**

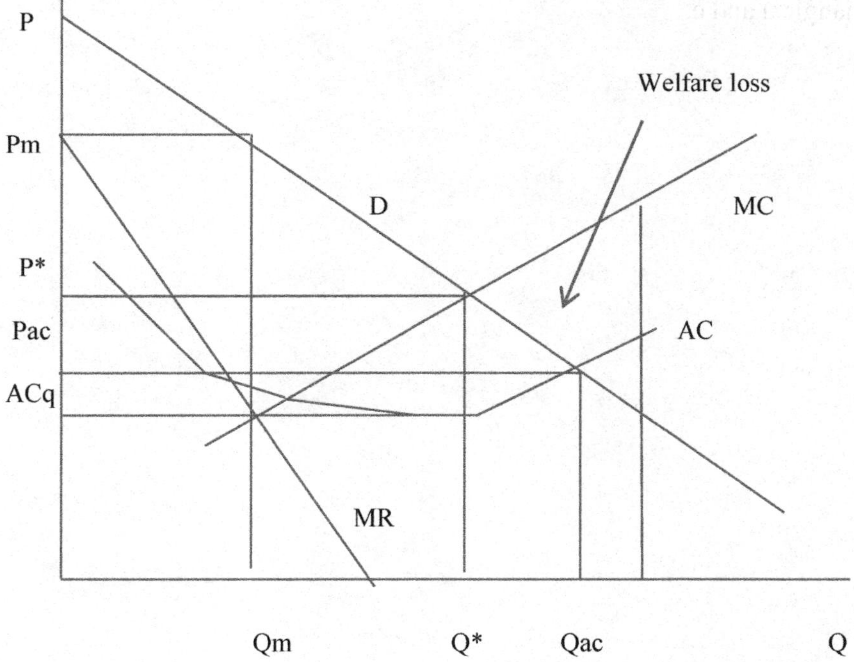


Source: Adapted from Jonathan A. Lesser and Leonardo R. Giacchino, *Fundamentals of Energy Regulation* (Vienna, VA: Public Utilities Reports, 2007), 32.

## 3.7 Price Ceilings and Price Floors

In almost all cases, regulators have imperfect information regarding a utility's costs. Despite this lack of information, they should attempt to set prices that would have resulted in a competitive market. Often, utility regulators miss the mark (either intentionally or unintentionally) and set prices (rates) that result in a price ceiling or a price floor. A price ceiling is a government-set price below market equilibrium price. In effect, it is an explicit tax on producers and an implicit subsidy to consumers. The impact of a price ceiling is reflected in Figure 3.11 (upper figure). If the price were at the market equilibrium level, the total surplus would be the combination of areas a through f. But with an effective price ceiling at Pc, the quantity supplied falls to Qc from Q*. The combined producer's and consumer's surplus is reduced by the triangles c and e. The loss of surplus represents those consumers who would like to make trades—the consumption represented by the demand and supply curves between Q* and Qc—but cannot do so because of the price ceiling. This loss of consumer's and producer's surplus is identical to the welfare loss from taxation. The price ceiling is a combination implicit tax on suppliers, shown by area d, and an implicit subsidy to consumers of that same area. The result is as if the government places a tax on suppliers (i.e., the utility) when they buy the good, and then gives that tax revenue to consumers when they consume the good (e.g., water).

Price floors have the opposite effect on the distribution of consumer's and producer's surplus. Price floors—the government-set prices above the equilibrium price—transfer consumer's surplus to producers. Price floors can be viewed as a tax on consumers represented by area b and a subsidy to producers of the same amount. Price floors also impose a deadweight loss shown by the welfare triangle a and e.

**Figure 3.11**
**Effect of Price Controls on Consumer's and Producer's Surplus**

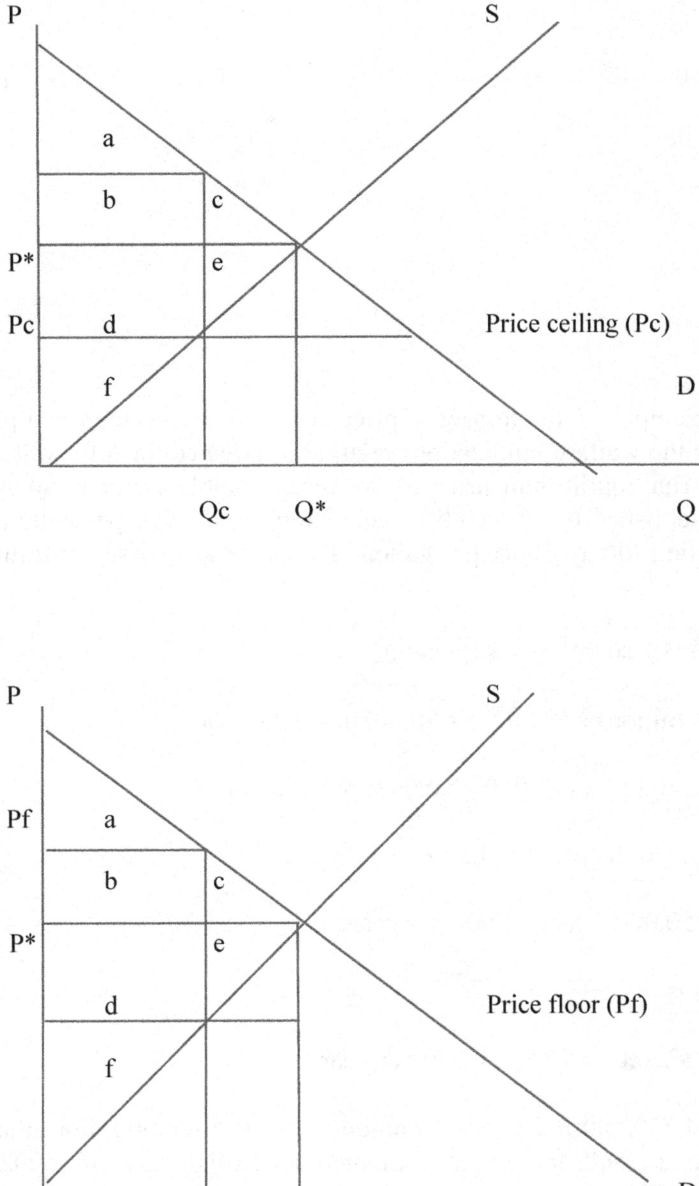


Source: Source: Adapted from David Colander, *Microeconomics* (Boston: McGraw-Hill Irwin, 2001), 165.

The general methodology of calculating deadweight loss is as follows. First draw the supply and demand curves. Second, calculate the price and quantity demanded at market efficiency. Third, keeping supply constant, calculate the new quantity demanded and price after the tax (if any) has been applied or the inefficiency has been introduced. Fourth, calculate the deadweight loss using the formula in equation 3.7. The value, 0.5, is referred to as the "rule of half" and will be described later in the book.

$$DL = (0.5) * (\Delta P * \Delta Q) \qquad (3.7)$$

Where:

DL = deadweight loss;

P = price; and

Q = quantity.

The following is a numerical example of the impact of price controls on consumer and producer surplus.[104] Figure 3.12 reflects the welfare implications relating to price ceilings for water utility service. Assume that the long-run equilibrium price of delivered potable water is $0.0075 per gallon and the ceiling price established by water utility regulators is $0.0050 per gallon. Water utility customers would be willing to pay $0.01 per gallon. The gains and losses resulting from price ceilings are as follows:

U = 1.8 billion x ($0.0075 - $0.0050) = $4,500,000

W = ½(2.0 billion – 1.8 billion) x ($0.0075 - $0.0050) = $250,000

V = ½(2.0 billion – 1.8 billion) x ($0.010 – $0.0075 = $250,000

The gain in consumer surplus due to the price ceiling is:

U – V = $4,500,00 - $250,000 = $4,250,000 per year;

and the loss in producer surplus is:

U + W = $4,500,000 + $250,000 = $4,750,000 per year.

In other words, utilities lose $4,750,000 per year—an amount that is $500,000 more than what water utility customers gain. As a result, there is an estimated deadweight loss of $500,000 per year. This is a measure of the efficiency cost of price ceilings—the reduction in the aggregate welfare of the utility and its customers.

104 This example was derived from Mansfield and Yohe, pp. 334-335.

**Figure 3.12**
**Gain in Consumer Surplus**
**Related to Price Ceiling**

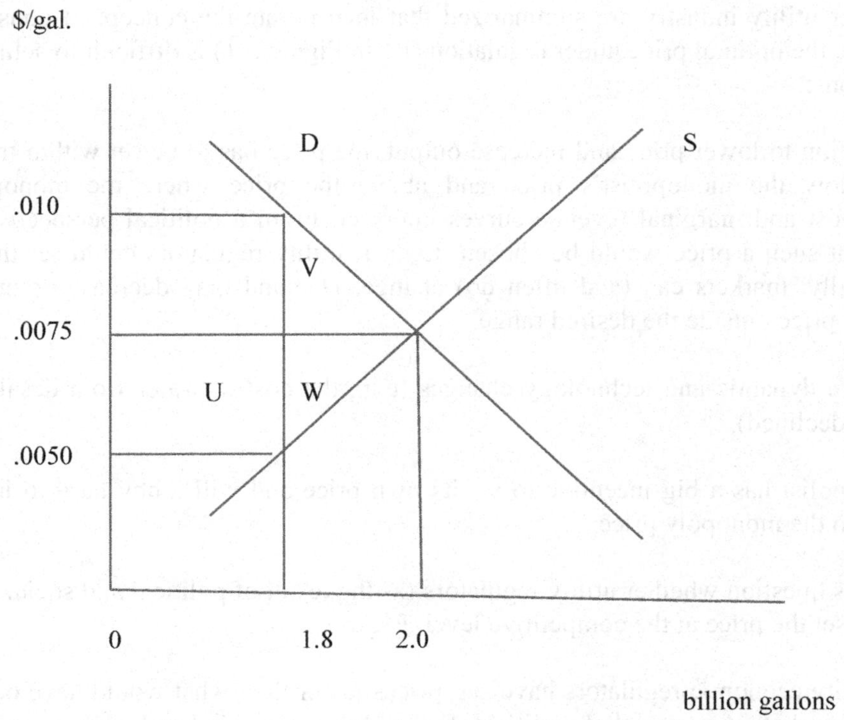


Source: Adopted from Mansfield and Yohe, p. 334.

## 3.8 Chapter Summary

As stated previously, economic regulation attempts to replicate the outcome of an efficient market in situations where, in the absence of regulatory intervention, it would not otherwise occur. This chapter identifies two market structures: perfect competition and monopoly.

If utility regulators set prices based on SRMC when average costs are declining, a revenue shortfall will occur. On the other hand, if regulators set prices based on marginal costs when average costs are increasing and marginal costs are higher than average costs, a revenue surplus will occur. When regulators set prices based on average costs, a welfare loss will result; however, the loss will be less than under conditions of monopoly pricing.

The welfare loss of monopoly is one reason economists oppose this market structure. This loss is summarized as follows: because monopolies charge a price higher than marginal cost, people's decisions do not reflect the true costs to society. Because of this, people's choices are distorted. That is, they choose to consume less output (e.g., water) and more of some other goods or services than they would if markets were competitive. That distinction means that the marginal cost of increasing output is lower than the marginal benefit of increasing output, so there is a welfare loss.

Optimal pricing will result in a maximum value (welfare) to society. The value represents the sum of producer's surplus and consumer's surplus. The use of consumer's and producer's surplus is now widely accepted as appropriate for welfare analysis in public utility economics. Two case studies in the water utility industry are summarized that incorporate the concept of consumer's surplus. In practice, the optimal price under regulation (P* in Figure 3.1) is difficult to achieve for the following reasons:

1) For regulation to lower price and increase output, the price has to be set within the right range—below the monopolist's price and above the price where the monopolist's marginal cost and marginal revenue curves intersect. From a political perspective, it is unclear that such a price would be chosen. Even if utility regulators could set the right price initially, markets can (and often do) change. Demand may decrease or increase, putting the price outside the desired range.

2) Markets are dynamic and technology changes (e.g., the cost of water from desalination plants has declined).

3) The monopolist has a big incentive to set its own price and will lobby hard to increase prices up to the monopoly price.

4) Economists question whether utility regulators (as the result of political and social forces) will try to set the price at the competitive level, P*.

In many cases, utility economic regulators have set prices lower than what would have occurred in a competitive market. Assume that political forces have overwhelmed economic forces, causing regulators to limit the regulated price. The result of this pricing decision is called "lost surplus" or "deadweight loss." In economic theory, lost surplus results in lower economic welfare for society. In this case, the lost surplus results in a gain in consumer's surplus and a loss in producer's surplus. This is akin to rent control, and the result is usually a deterioration of the owner's assets and property. That is, regulators have set prices based on full supply costs instead of full costs (see Figure 1.3). This price distortion is the exact opposite from that mentioned above. The result (cost) is summarized as follows: Because regulators set prices lower than long-run marginal cost, people's decisions do not reflect the true cost of resources to society. The long-run marginal costs exceed the price, and because of this, people's choices are distorted. That is, they choose to consume more output and less of some other goods or services than they would if prices were set in a perfectly competitive market.

# *CHAPTER FOUR*

# WATER VALUE

## 4.1 Overview [105]

In chapter one, the concept was introduced that for some goods and services price tags do not exist. In those cases, the demand for the goods or services is not revealed. However, that does not mean that people do not value them. Water, as we know, is essential for human life. For such nonmarket goods and services a consumer's willingness to pay (WTP) can be considered their price. Nonmarket valuation is the study of economic behavior—especially consumption, demand, production, and supply relationships—for the purpose of assigning economic values in contexts where market prices are absent or distorted.

This chapter defines WTP and provides two case studies summerizing how it was estimated. Also included in the chapter is a case study regarding how consumers value reliable water service. A key component of WTP is price elasticity of demand, which is defined and illustrated. Next, the components of value are described and discussed. The primary categories include use and nonuse values which are components of total economic value (TEV). The chapter concludes by identifying utility regulatory policy issues related to TEV and the value of water by sectors of the U.S. economy.

Utility economic regulation was created as a substitute for competition where true market prices do not exist. The WTP of an individual indicates part of his income that he or she is willing to give up in order to secure a good or service. Graphically, it is represented as the area below the demand curve. (A demand curve is a schedule that indicates the quantities of a good or service that individuals purchase at various prices.) WTP is often used to refer to the amount that a

105 This discussion regarding value is from a consumer's perspective. We are not discussing various approaches to valuing a utility's assets such as original cost, replacement cost, or reproduction cost.

consumer would pay for a hypothetical good (e.g., a liter of water), service, or change in the state of the environment. Figure 4.1 shows a customer's WTP for three units of a hypothetical good at a point in time, at a specific location, and assuming equal quality of all units.

**Figure 4.1**
**A Water Utility Customer's Willingness to Pay**

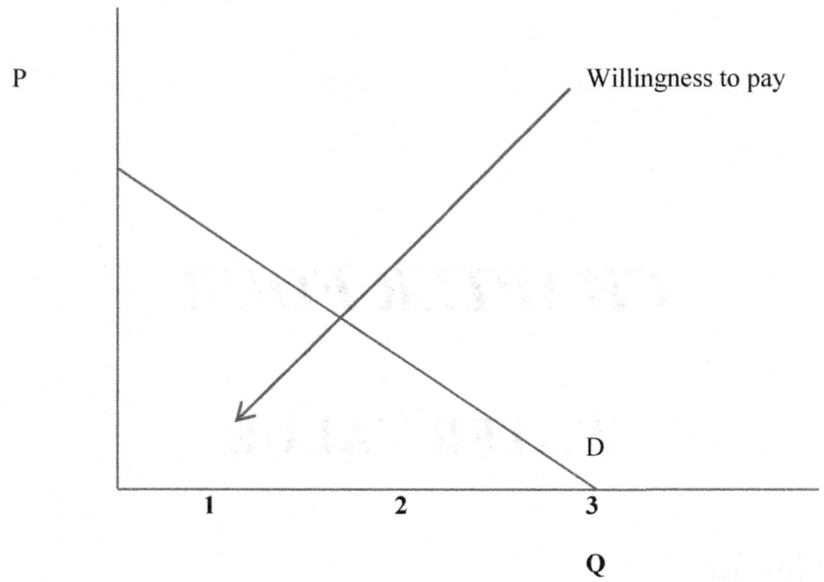


Source: Katar Singh and Anil Shishodia, *Environmental Economics: Theory and Application* (Los Angeles: Sage Publications, 2007), 76.

---

Another term—willingness to accept (WTA) compensation—is sometimes used as a surrogate for the price of a nonmarket good or service. WTA is the compensation that an individual is willing to accept for giving up the consumption of a good. It is presumed that the compensation is sufficient to return the individual to his original state of economic well-being. A water utility's customer that accepts a lower rate in exchange for the possibility of having his service interrupted (i.e., interruptible service) is an example of WTA. In many cases, WTA is considered to be inferior to the WTP as a measure of economic value. Empirical studies—mainly in applications of the contingent valuation method (CVM) and defined in Appendix B—have shown that fairly large differences exist between WTP and WPA. For example, studies have shown that WTA is typically two to six times larger than WTP for public goods that do not have substitutes. 106

If a commodity such as water is priced at zero, it is considered a free good; however, it most likely has value. Normally, this situation results in overconsumption of the good. Related to the overconsumption of a public good or a common pool resource (CPR), in 1968 a biologist, Garret Hardin, developed a hypothesis called "The Tragedy of the Commons." Hardin explained why CPRs, like a river or lake, are frequently overexploited, degraded, and/or depleted. He argued that the reason for these situations is purely economic. That is, the marginal private benefits (MPB) to

106 Raucher, 69.

an individual from the increased use of the resource exceed the marginal private costs (MPC) associated with the increased use. This leads to overexploitation of the resource. The CPR problem is basically the existence of an externality—a divergence between the private cost and the social cost of exploitation, which eventually leads to either depletion of a resource, overcrowding, or congestion. (Externalities were discussed in chapter two.) The CPR problem is a reflection of either the absence of exclusive private property rights or the breakdown of the structure of property rights.

### 4.1.1 Example: Ipswich River in Massachusetts

As an example of The Tragedy of the Commons, the AWWA Research Foundation cites a study of the Ipswich River in Massachusetts, where local groundwater and river water in the Ipswich Basin have been seen as free goods that are available to anyone with properties that provide land-based access. Not surprisingly, increasing groundwater withdrawals and direct river water extraction have resulted in situations where the river has experienced extremely low and zero-flow conditions (i.e., negative externalities) in summer months. The low water flow from the river had several adverse consequences in terms of losses in values for ecological, recreational, and aesthetic purposes that would otherwise be provided by retaining higher summertime in-stream flows. 107

Seven options were considered to solve the problem, including:

1) Encouraging water conservation;
2) Importing water from the Massachusetts Water Resources Agency (MWRA);
3) Providing more in-basin return flows from treated wastewater;
4) Improving storm-water management;
5) Increasing water storage;
6) Improving land-use planning; and
7) Desalination. 108

At the time of the case study, the costs and benefits of these various options were not fully estimated. Since water from the Ipswich River is seen as a free good, one alternative solution is to assess a fee to all users based on the volume of water extracted. That is, the water resource itself is paid by users. Hopefully the associated price signals would help regulate use levels.

## 4.2 Estimating Demand

To estimate a customer's demand for water such as in Figure 4.1, various demand forecasting methods exits. These methods include: (a) point expansion, (b) residual imputation, (c) math

107 Raucher et al., 141.

108 Ibid., 201–6.

programming (multiple-activity analysis; linear or nonlinear), (d) production function, (e) statistical regression (econometrics), (f) contingent valuation, (g) hedonic pricing, and (h) travel cost. These methods are summarized in Appendix B. 109 The choice of the method used can be based on a number of factors such as: (a) the availability and quality of the data, and (b) being conceptually compatible with particular water uses.

Table 4.1 provides a summary of the methods, data/input types, and customer classes or use.

**Table 4.1**
**Methods of Demand Estimation**

| No. | Technique | Data/input types | Customer classes or use |
|---|---|---|---|
| 1 | Point expansion | A known P, Q, and elasticity | Potentially useful for all sectors |
| 2 | Residential imputation | Output amount and price; and a cost-of-production budget | When water is a large input to production (especially irrigation) |
| 3 | Math programming | Multiple activities (i.e., output/prices and budgets for each) | When water is a large input to production (especially irrigation and possibly industry) |
| 4 | Production function | Experimental data or physical relationships | Irrigation, hydropower, individual manufacturing processes |
| 5 | Statistical regression | Behavior (agent level or aggregate) under administered prices; market transactions; or metadata | Residential, commercial, industrial |
| 6 | Contingent valuation | Survey data from consumers | Urban/residential, recreation |
| 7 | Hedonic pricing | Market transactions for land and/or water | Recreation, irrigation |
| 8 | Travel cost | Survey data for recreation participants | Recreation |
| 9 | End use | Number of fixtures and use per fixture | Primarily residential |

Source: Adopted in part from Ronald C. Griffin, *Water Resource Economics* (Cambridge, MA: The MIT Press, 2006), 278.

---

One method of estimating demand is point estimation or extrapolating historical data. This method is the simplest and least expensive. An example of the extrapolation method is using a compound growth rate. However, the factors influencing a water utility's growth are not specified explicitly. Extrapolation of historical data can produce reasonable results as long as the factors contributing to the growth are stable over long periods of time.

A second forecasting method is using econometric (regression) models. These models include equations that attempt to describe the causal relationships between water usage (the dependent variable) and various factors (independent variables). An econometric model was used in the pricing strategy for the South Carolina rural water utilities case study.

A third forecasting method is end-use forecasts. Usually this method is the most sophisticated and the most expensive to implement. This method disaggregates demand into end uses (e.g., lawn watering) for each customer class. These forecasts are based on:

---

109 For more details regarding these methods and case studies see: David L. Hayward, *The Economic Value of Water Utility Services.*

1) Estimates of water consumption for each end use;

2) Saturation levels (e.g., number of dishwashers per household); and

3) Usage patterns (e.g., the number of times toilets are flushed per day).

End-use forecasts generally produce the most precise forecasts and allow a water utility's management to incorporate changes in technology and the impact of water conservation.

### 4.2.1 Point Estimation and Numerical Example

Assume that historical data for residential consumers shows that, on average, monthly consumption is 7,000 gallons per month and the utility has 5,000 customers. Also, assume that the utility has a uniform rate structure (discussed in chapter five) and charges \$3.00 per 1,000 gallons of tap water. In this case, the data (35 million gallons, \$3.00) is an ordered pair on the city's demand curve for tap water. This relationship is reflected in Figure 4.2

**Figure 4.2**
**Demand Using Point Estimation**

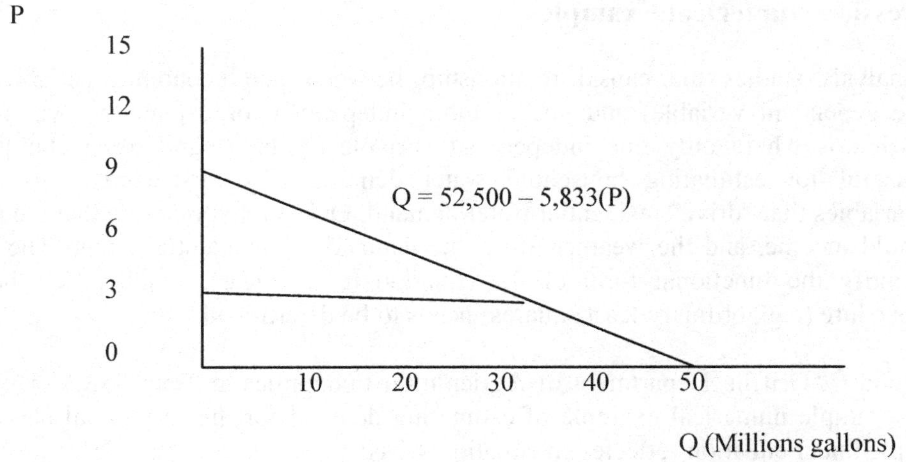


Source: Adopted from Ronald C. Griffin, *Water Resource Economics*, (Cambridge, MA: The MIT Press, 2006), pp. 32-33.

---

Next, assume that the price elasticity of demand (ε) is estimated at -.5. Even though these price elasticities are negative numbers, economists refer to them as absolute numbers. For instance, -0.7 is referred to as 0.7. Finally, assume that the demand function exhibits constant price elasticity through the relevant range of consumption. Assume that the demand function is a linear function of price in the form Q = a + b(p) where a is an intercept, and b is the slope

The first step is to determine the slope (b) of the demand curve. Using the price elasticity formula: $(dQ_w \div Q_w) \div (dP/P)$ and rearranging terms produces:

$$\varepsilon = (dw/dp) * (P/Q)$$

$$.5 = dw/dp * 3/35$$

$$b = -5{,}833.3$$

Using the ordered pair (35,000, 3), the slope (b), and the linear demand equation, the intercept term a can be derived as follows:

$$35{,}000 = a + -5{,}833.3(3)$$

$$a = 52{,}500$$

Therefore,

$$Q = 52{,}500 + -5{,}833.3(P)$$

$$35{,}000 = 52{,}500 - 5{,}833.3(3)$$

## 4.2.2 Regression Numerical Example

Regression analysis studies the causal relationship between one economic variable to be explained (the dependent variable) and one or more independent or explanatory variables. A simple regression is where only one independent variable exists. Regression techniques are particularly useful for estimating household water demand. The first step is to identify explanatory variables that "drive" residential water demand. One can hypothesize that the price of water, household income, and the weather affect the demand for residential water. The second step is to identify the functional form of the equation (e.g., linear). Finally, the choice of regression procedure (e.g., ordinary least squares) needs to be determined.

Professor Ronald C. Griffin, Department of Agricultural Economics at Texas A&M University has provided a simple numerical example of estimating demand for the residential class. 110 A relatively simple linear equation reflected in equation 4.1 is:

$$Q = D(AP, I, C) \qquad (4.1)$$

Where:

Q = production (i.e., water pumped into the supply system) for the entire community, minus all industrial water use, divided by the number of days in the month as well as by the community's entire population;

AP = average price (monthly water bill divided by Q) for an average household using Q gallons of water per person per day;

---

110 Griffin, 295.

I = annual personal income in thousands of dollars per capita for the community; and

C = a climate variable postulated to affect water use (defined as the month's average daily temperature times the number of days in the month not having significant rainfall).

The estimated demand equation is:

$$Q = 32.81 - 26.64AP + 9.590I + 0.07253C$$

The above coefficients have the expected sign (e.g., demand is inversely related to price). Finally, the coefficient of determination—$R^2$—(i.e., the portion of the total variation in the dependent variable explained by the regression of the dependent variables on the independent variable) is 0.46 (i.e., the independent variables in the equation can explain 46 percent of the variation in demand (the dependent variable)..

## 4.3 Willingness-to-Pay [111]

There are two basic approaches to quantifying customers' willingness-to-pay to avoid the consequences of a change in service such as a water supply shortage. These approaches are the survey and the demand curve analysis. Regarding the survey approach, individuals can be surveyed to directly elicit their willingness to pay for a good or service. Estimates of a water utility's customers' value of service (as measured by their WTP) can provide very useful information to policymakers regarding a water utility's service. For instance, willingness-to-pay is the method used for assessing the value of electric power for federal government projects. Appendix B provides a summary of methods used to estimate the value of nonmarket goods and services. The most common methods are:

1) Contingent valuation method (CVM);

2) Travel cost method; and

3) Hedonic property valuation approach or method; [112]

For example, using the CVM, a 1987 study for the Metropolitan Water District of Southern California (MWD) found that:

> *"Consumers were willing to make significant financial sacrifices to have a reliable water supply. Under one of four scenarios, in order to avoid a 30-35 percent reduction from baseline use in two out of five years, households were willing to pay approximately $2.3 billion per year."* [113]

The advantage of the survey approach is that it directly focuses on the question of interest and can measure willingness-to-pay caused by all different types of impacts. One disadvantage of this

---

111 Numerous willingness-to-pay studies exist in the water utility industry. A sample of studies from diverse countries include: Brazil, United Kingdom, Nigeria, China, Egypt, Kenya, Pakistan, Lesotho, Gaza Strip, Ethiopia, Mali, Rwanda, Kabwe, and Dares Salaan. See www.amazon.com/books/water willingness to pay.

112 Shaw, 254.

113 Raucher et al., 69.

approach is that respondents do not actually have to make the payments they report and thus may over- or understate their willingness to pay to avoid a consequence (e.g., becoming ill). A second disadvantage of the survey approach is that respondents may have little experience valuing these types of losses and may not give realistic answers.

The demand curve approach using econometric models estimates water demand relationships. For instance, the relationship among water price, household income, drought management strategies other variables, and household water use as the basis for analytically determining willingness-to-pay. Demand curve analysis offers the promise of measuring willingness to pay more quickly and more cheaply than the survey approach. However, this method has several drawbacks and limitations. First, the demand curve approach will be inexpensive if pre-existing demand relationships can be used in the analysis. However, these relationships may not accurately capture consumption responses to the various policies adopted during an event (such as a drought) because the range of variation in prices and other policies is much larger during the event (e.g., drought). Thus, time-consuming empirical work using data on water use during the event may be necessary.

### 4.3.1 Price Elasticity of Demand

As previously noted, a customer's willingness to pay is the area under his demand curve. The law of demand states that the quantity demanded of a product (e.g., water) falls as the price of a product (e.g., water) rises, other things being held constant. In economics, elasticity refers to responsiveness. Price elasticity of demand is defined as the percentage change in quantity demanded divided by the percentage change in price. In mathematical terms, the formula for price elasticity of demand is reflected in equation 4.2.

$$\varepsilon = (\%\Delta Q_W) \div (\%\Delta P_W) \quad (4.2)$$

Where:

$\%\Delta$ = percentage change;

$\varepsilon$ = elasticity;

$P_W$ = price of water; and

$Q_W$ = quantity of water.

A more formal definition is given in equation 4.3.

$$\varepsilon = ((dQ_W \div Q_W)) \div ((dP \div P)) \quad (4.3)$$

In economics, common elasticities include price elasticity of demand, cross-price elasticity of demand, price elasticity of supply, and income elasticity of demand. One example of cross-price elasticity of demand is the percentage change in the price of bottled water and the percentage change in the demand of water from the water utility. The focus in this chapter is on price elasticity of demand.

The general equation in 4.2 for estimating the point elasticity of a linear demand function can be used to solve for the point where the shortage quantity $Q_1$ crosses the demand curve at $P_1$. This can be used to calculate the lost consumer surplus under competitive market conditions. The formula for consumer surplus was provided in equation 3.1.

One problem with the point elasticity formula is that the elasticity depends on the starting point. For example assume two prices, $P_0$ and $P_1$. Therefore, more than one consumer surplus value may be found between two quantities. This problem becomes more serious the larger the magnitude of the price change. One way to avoid any ambiguity in measuring elasticities is to use the arc convention. This approach uses the average price and quantities as the denominators. The arc elasticity formula is presented in equation 4.4.

$$\varepsilon = [(Q_1 - Q_0) \div ((Q_1 + Q_0) \div 2)] \div [(P_1 - P_0) \div ((P_1 + P_0) \div 2)] \qquad (4.4)$$

A numerical example of arc elasticity of demand is as follows. Assume that the range in price is \$20 to \$26 and the quantity range is 10 to 14. Using the above formula the percentage change in price is 26 percent, and the percentage change in quantity is 33 percent. Therefore, the price elasticity using the arc convention is 33/26 or 1.27 or $\varepsilon = -.27$.

The arc convention yields the same elasticity whether a price increase or decrease is assumed. Figure 4.3 shows a hypothetical residential water customer's demand. (The units for quantity on the horizontal axis is cubic meters.) Figure 4.3 reflects changes to a hypothetical residential water customer's demand curve given various uses. The figure shows a relatively steep demand curve for basic necessities such as drinking and bathing (i.e., relatively inelastic demand). The demand curve becomes more elastic for indoor discretionary uses (e.g., cooking) and outdoor discretionary uses (e.g., landscape, pool, and irrigation). (Price elasticity of demand is explained in more detail later in the chapter.) The price elasticity of demand assumptions in the case study in chapter seven used a range between .20 and .70 with an expected value of .40.

**Figure 4.3**
**A Hypothetical Residential Water Customer's Demand**

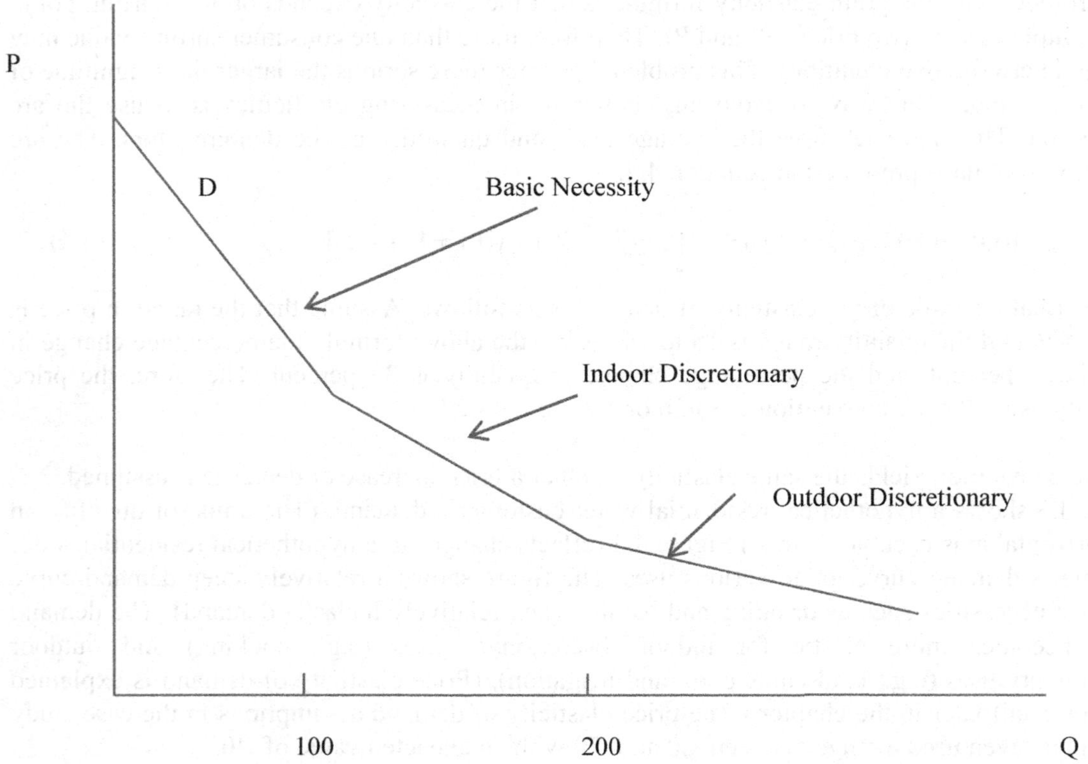


Source: Adopted from R. D. Raucher et al., *The Value of Water: Concepts, Estimates, and Applications for Water Managers* (Denver, CO: American Water Works Research Foundation, 2005), 35.

### 4.3.1.1 Characteristics of Price Elasticity

The more substitutes a good or service has, the greater the price elasticity. Factors affecting the number of substitutes are:

1) The time interval;

2) Whether the good is a luxury or necessity (e.g., minimal quantities of water are essential for humans to survive, and therefore they are a necessity);

3) How specifically the good is defined; and

4) The good's proportion of one's budget.

One of the most important factors affecting the number of substitutes a good or service has is time. As the time interval lengthens, in most cases, demand becomes more elastic. Five elasticity measurements are:

1) Elastic (i.e., elasticity greater than one);

2) Inelastic (i.e., elasticity less than one);

3) Unit elastic (i.e., elasticity equal to one);

4) Perfectly inelastic (i.e., elasticity equal to zero); and

5) Perfectly elastic (i.e., elasticity equal to infinity).

For products and services that have close substitutes, the demand is usually relatively elastic. When a supplier raises the price of a good or service, if demand is inelastic, total revenues increase; if demand is elastic, total revenues decrease; and if demand is unit elastic, total revenues are constant. Knowing the price elasticity of demand for a good or service allows economists to be more precise about the effects of changing prices on demand and revenues. A case study of a water concession reflected in chapter seven incorporates both price elasticity and income elasticity of demand.

Frequently, non–price regulated companies attempt to segregate a market into two categories: consumers with elastic demands and those with inelastic demands. This was done in the railroad industry. If companies make this separation and charge different prices, they practice what is called "price differentiation." An example of price differentiation is in the airline industry. Often, airlines price tickets with a Saturday-night stay-over lower than fares to the same destination but at different times. The motivation for this differential pricing is that businesspeople have relatively inelastic demands and do not like to stay over Saturday nights. In contrast, leisure travelers (if the price discount for the ticket is sufficient) would be willing to stay over Saturday nights. By requiring individuals to stay over Saturday night, airlines can separate out businesspeople from other passengers and charge them more for the service.

Table 4.2 provides key features of water price differentiation. As illustrated in the table, water prices can be differentiated by customer class, volume, connection charge and volume charge, time of day, season of year, and quality of water.

## Table 4.2
## Water Price Differentiation

| No. | Price differentiated by | Cities/Countries |
|---|---|---|
| 1 | Customer class (e.g., residential, commercial, industrial) | Most cities |
| 2 | Volume consumed based on metering; increasing, decreasing, uniform block | Many cities in the world |
| 3 | Connection charge and volume charge | Many cities in the world |
| 4 | Time of day | Antwerp, Le Havre |
| 5 | Season of the year | Many cities in France, United States, Netherlands |
| 6 | Quality of water (e.g., treated and raw) | Hong Kong, United States, Denmark, Japan, Germany, France, Australia, Italy |

Source: Michael Klein, "Economic Regulation of Water Companies," Policy Research Working Paper No. 1649 (Washington, DC: The World Bank, 1996), 13.

#### 4.3.1.2 Water Price Elasticity Studies

For residential water utility service price elasticity studies have focused on:

1) Region of the country;

2) Season (e.g., winter and summer); and

3) Time series or cross-sectional data.

The empirical evidence suggests that the price elasticity of demand for residential water is inelastic, in that 90 percent of the studies reported estimates of elasticity between 0 and 0.75 (i.e., less than one in absolute terms). [114] Studies of residential water demand indicate that in-house water use is consistently price inelastic (-0.23), while so-called sprinkling (outdoor) use is more elastic and differs significantly between the Eastern (-1.6) and the Western U.S. (-0.7). [115] The relative price inelasticity of basic necessity water use (for such purposes as drinking, bathing, and cooking) reflected in Figure 4.3 makes intuitive sense.

#### 4.3.1.3 Caveats Regarding Price Elasticity of Demand

Several caveats should be mentioned regarding price elasticity of demand. First is the assumption of constant price elasticity over the interval (i.e., the section of the demand curve). Generally, the smaller the interval the more valid is the elasticity estimate. Price elasticity of demand estimates are only valid for small (or marginal) changes in prices (i.e., up to a few percentage points). It cannot accurately predict the effect of a large (e.g., 25 percent) increase in price. Second, elasticities are relative to the total quantity of water currently being consumed and the prices paid. Thus, comparisons across households, let alone regions or sectors, should be made with caution.
Third, the price data used in the various demand studies are limited. For example, in the United States, the water bills of most consumers are a very small fraction of their incomes (approximately .75 percent). [116] Also, the range of observed prices is narrow. These points are even more significant when real prices and incomes (i.e., adjusted for inflation) are considered. This is true because per capita income appears to be the single most important statistical determinant of residential water demand. The apparent inelasticity of use at current levels may be a result of the low price relative to income. [117]

The final caveat concerns the purchase of water rights by water utilities. Frequently, a water utility incurs the transportation costs but not the acquisition costs of water. Occasionally, a municipal utility such as a city will buy water rights, in effect acting as a broker for the consumers in the aggregate. The methodology used to calculate marginal values relies on the assumptions that the water price accurately reflects the water utility's costs, and that the utility's costs do not include expenditures for raw, in-stream water. If raw water is purchased by the utility, the net willingness to pay (WTP), as measured by the consumer's surplus, would

---

114 Shaw, 122.

115 Gibbons, 9–10.

116 Sharon Gascon, Deputy Executive Director, National Association of Water Companies, presentation at the 27th Annual Western NARUC Utility Rate School, May 14–19, 2006, San Diego, California.

117 Gibbons, 19–20.

underestimate the value of water in municipal use. Where water is purchased, the prices paid by the utility can be used to calculate an average WTP for the quantity. 118

## 4.4 Willingness-to-Pay Studies

### 4.4.1 Manaus, Amazonas Brazil 119

The city of Manaus, Brazil, has approximately 1.5 million residents and forms the epicenter for economic activity and development in the Amazon Basin. Since the original water treatment facilities were built, the population has increased 15-fold. This large population increase has made access to safe drinking water a major health concern. The segments of the population who cannot purchase bottled water are susceptible to water-borne diseases and illnesses. The University of Amazonas Center for Environmental Sciences conducted a survey of more than 1,600 residents to determine their willingness to pay for universal access to water services delivered to their homes. The researchers used the CVM to estimate willingness-to-pay. (This method is summarized in Appendix B.) The results from the study indicated that residents were willing to pay more than USD6.12 per month (USD72 per year) for service. This amount is approximately 2.5 percent of household income and is consistent with previous studies in Brazil, India, and urban Nepal. 120

### 4.4.2 Water Supply Service in the Gaza Strip 121

In the Gaza strip, groundwater is the primary source of supply and it suffers from rapid decline in both quality and quantity. As such, in 1998 researchers from the consortium of consulting firms—Lyonnaise Des Eaux Khatib and Alami (LEKA)—studied the ability and willingness of the population to pay for improved water supply service. The study was in the context of helping design a water tariff for municipal water departments and a coastal water utility in the Gaza Strip. The study used a CVM approach with prefilled questionnaires and bidding games to determine consumers' own hypothetical estimates of their WTP. Since 1987, the CVM has been tested in several developing countries. The mean WTP is the key component of the cost–benefit analysis that compares the present value of investment benefits to the present value of costs.

The ability to pay criterion used a broad guideline that households should not be obligated to pay more than five percent of their income for water. The study showed that the average monthly per capita income was 225.7 New Israeli Shekel (NIS) where the exchange rate at the time of the study was NIS=USD 0.21. The mean amount for which the respondents were willing to pay was 3.06 NIS for each cubic meter of improved water. At the time of the study, the average price in the Gaza Strip was 1.08 NIS per cubic meter. Thus, on average, the public was willing and able to pay almost a 300-percent increase in water rates in spite of serious economic problems in the region.

---

118 Ibid., 20.

119 James F. Casey, James R. Kahn, and Alexandre Rivas, "Willingness to pay for improved water service in Manaus, Amazonas, Brazil," Ecological Economics, vol. 58, Issue 2, (June 2006): 365–72.

120 Ibid., 371–72.

121 Yusuf Al-Ghuraiz and Adnan Enshassi, "Ability and Willingness to Pay for Water Supply Service in the Gaza Strip," *Building and Environment*, vol. 40, Issue 8 (August 2005): 1093–1102.

## 4.5 Regulatory Use of Willingness-To-Pay Studies in the United States

So why do water utilities in the United States often fail to use information regarding customers' WTP in setting water rates? The answer to this question may involve the following elements:

1) Economic regulators are unaware of the various survey methods to estimate the price of nonmarket goods and services and therefore do not require utilities to prepare them. (See Appendix B for a description of various methods.)

2) The analysis and studies to estimate WTP have not been completed, in part, because they are perceived to be time-consuming and expensive;

3) The political implications—for instance, possible dramatic increases (also called "rate shock") in water utility rates—may be undesirable for regulators;

4) Charging customers their full WTP may seem inconsistent with the very goals of regulation (e.g., protecting the consumer from abuse by a monopolist);

5) Rates based on accounting prices may be easier for the public to understand; and

6) Historically, economic theory and economists' tools are rarely used in utility ratemaking. One exception is setting some water rates (e.g., the tail block in a multi-tiered rate structure) based on marginal costs. [122] This rate structure is discussed in more detail in chapter five. A second exception is the Federal Energy Regulatory Commission's (FERC) use of WTP to value benefits of power projects.

## 4.6 Reliability of Water Service

In the water utility business, an attribute of WTP is service reliability. The reliability of water service is often an overlooked or ignored concept in utility ratemaking, yet price and service go hand-in-hand. A regulated firm's tariff structure almost always includes prices and service terms; the overall regime usually includes other provisions such as: (a) policies related to disconnection for customers who do not pay their bills; (b) access to the utility's transmission and distribution network; and (c) rates derived from negotiations with customers related to economic development.

A recent paper by the National Regulatory Research Institute (NRRI) calls upon state public service commissions (PSC) to establish reliability standards for water utilities before billions of dollars are spent replacing aging infrastructure. [123] Regulators should consider that reliability standards can vary for different types of customers. For instance, an industrial plant with access to a private well as a backup water supply and delivery system for its manufacturing process might require a lower level of reliability from that needed or desired by a typical residential customer. On the other hand, a hospital or nursing home that must have water to maintain sanitation might require a higher level of reliability than typical residential customers. The NRRI paper also argues that lowering the reliability target by less than 12 percent could defer a multi-

122 However, this is rarely done. In the United States, only a few state PSCs recognize marginal costs for purposes of setting water utility rates. For the most part, rates are often based on a cost of service study using historical accounting costs.

123 Rubin, iii.

million-dollar construction program by as much as ten years. [124] Therefore, using the same logic, if water utility customers require a higher degree of reliability and have *both* the ability and willingness to pay for it, regulators should consider raising rates for these customers. The increase in rates is associated with the cost of providing a higher level of service. Thus, in this case, price discrimination does not exist. This pricing policy assumes that a number of regulatory safeguards are in place and are discussed in chapter five.

### 4.6.1 Metropolitan Water District of Southern California Water Reliability Study

To identify water reliability needs would suggest that a utility should identify what their customers want and supply it. This is a common goal among a whole spectrum of businesses, including water utilities. For example, the Metropolitan Water District of Southern California (MWD) incorporates reliability in its integrated resource planning (IRP) process. The starting point in the planning process is establishing a goal for service reliability. Next, various resource options such as: (a) conservation, (b) local resources, (c) imported supplies, and (d) storage facilities are identified and evaluated in terms of costs, reliability, risk, and flexibility. Finally, water utility planners should ask: Is the resource mix affordable and balanced in terms of IRP objectives? If the answer to this question is yes, the reliability analysis is complete.

Finally, Table 4.3 reflects households' annual willingness to pay for water reliability from three studies in the United States during the period 1987 through 2000. The annual WTP range is from $80 to $421.

124 Ibid., 9.

**Table 4.3**
**Annual WTP for Household Water Reliability (2003 USD)**

| Source | Shortfall % | Frequency (Years) | Probability % | WTP ($) |
|---|---|---|---|---|
| Carson 1/ | 10–15 | 1 in 5 | 20 | 135 |
| Carson 1/ | 10–15 | 2 in 5 | 10 | 248 |
| CUWA | 20 | 1 in 30 | 3.3 | 143 |
| Carson 1/ | 30–35 | 1 in 5 | 20 | 186 |
| Carson 1/ | 30–35 | 2 in 5 | 10 | 421 |
| CUWA | 50 | 1 in 10 | 5 | 253 |
| Griffin 2/ | N.A. | N.A. | N.A. | 109 |
| Griffin 2/ | N.A. | N.A. | N.A. | 125 |
| Howe 3/ | .16–9.2 5/ | N.A. | N.A. | 80 4/ |
| Howe 3/ | .23–12.2 5/ | N.A. | N.A. | 92 6/ |

N.A. = not applicable.

Notes: 1/ Carson and Mitchell (1987); 2/ Griffen and Mjelde (2000); 3/ Howe and Smith (1994).

4/ Value represent the average of the WTP range given in the study ($70 to $90 per year). If there are not any respondents for this increased probability range included in the data set (respondents' WTP = $0), the WTP range is from $16/year to $28/year per respondent.

5/ This percentage range does not represent the magnitude of the shortfall, as is the case in the other studies. Rather, this range represents increased probability over the base probabilities of the SASE. The actual percentage increase is dependent on the city. The associated dollar values are the annual WTP per respondent for an increase over their current reliability.

6/ Value represents the average WTP range given in the study ($64 to $119 per year). If there are not any respondents for this increased probability range included in the data set, the WTP range is from $15/year to $29/year per respondent.

Source: Adopted from R. D. Raucher, et al., *The Value of Water: Concepts, Estimates, and Applications for Water Managers* (Denver, CO: American Water Works Research Foundation, 2005), 75.

## 4.7 Types of Goods

### 4.7.1 Overview

Water and other natural resources can be both public and private goods. It is a public good in the sense that it is nonexclusive (anyone can use it) and non-rivalrous (the number of users does not affect the benefits from its consumption). A lake is an example of a public good. A private good or service, on the other hand, is where one person's consumption reduces the amount available to other consumers and from which nonpayers can be excluded.

Public goods range in geographical scope from local or regional to national or global. The oceans are examples of an international public good, since it is not possible to exclude other nations from benefiting from their use. Thus, in a free market, it is not reasonable to expect the good to be provided in sufficient quantities by an individual entity.

A public good is characterized by jointness in supply, in that to produce the good for one consumer, it is necessary to produce it for all consumers. In many cases, no individual can be excluded from the enjoyment of a public good or service. For example, an individual cannot be excluded from the benefits of public fire protection.

Since nobody can or should be excluded from the benefits of a public good or service, consumers would not voluntarily pay for it, and therefore businesses would not find it profitable to provide the good or service. This is because it would not be possible for the business to recover its costs of production through the market. Thus, the market mechanism would fail to supply a public good even though the good or service would likely contribute to society's wellbeing. As a result, a free market would tend to under-produce the good or service. This is an example of market failure discussed previously.

Because public goods belong to the entire community, individual rights of ownership do not exist. In summary, the three main characteristics of public goods are:

1) Non-excludability;

2) Non-rivalrous consumption; and

3) Indivisibility.

### 4.7.2 Public and Private Goods

Sometimes water is a mixture of public and private goods. A mixed collective good is one which, like a pure collective good, is used in common by a large number of individuals and from whose use free riders cannot easily be excluded. A free rider is an individual who benefits from the actions and efforts of others without contributing to the costs incurred in generating the benefits. An example of a free rider would be a visitor to the United States who enjoys public lakes and beaches yet does not pay to use them. Its use by one individual reduces its availability to other people.

As stated previously, many public goods and services do not have markets or price tags; and the role of utility regulators is to set a price (usually lower) and establish a quantity of service (usually higher) than a monopolist would charge. Usually, a producer of public goods will not provide the service unless the government (e.g., state public service commission) provides a regulatory framework such that the firm has an opportunity to earn a reasonable return on its investment.

Since individual consumers cannot adjust the amount of many environmental goods and services they consume, a market for those goods and services cannot exist. When a market does exist, it does not provide the goods in sufficient quantities. This situation provides a rationale for establishing government enterprises for the purpose of providing these goods. For the government to provide a public good, it is necessary to know each individual's marginal rate of substitution between the public and private goods, which would determine the optimum level of the public good and perhaps each individual's share of the costs. However, consumers may not reveal their true preferences for public goods and services. Thus, they are usually produced or contracted out by public agencies on the basis of collective decisions that are financed from general taxation. Thus, although consumers consume the same amount of the public good, they pay different prices whereas in the case of a private good (such as water from a utility), consumers pay the same price but consume different quantities.

Some goods are referred to as "publicly provided private goods" because of the large marginal cost associated with supplying additional individuals. The rationale for the public supply of such goods is their large set-up costs and the high transaction costs of running a market for these goods. When private goods are freely provided they are over-consumed. Since the consumer does not pay for the good, he demands and uses it up to the point where the marginal benefit he receives from the good is zero, although the marginal cost to society is positive and often substantial. The social loss from overconsumption is the difference between the individual's willingness to pay and the marginal cost. A good example of a publicly provided private good, or mixed collective good, is irrigation water. In this case, overconsumption can result in a double loss—a direct welfare loss from excessive consumption, and an indirect loss from water-logging (a form of externality) resulting from overconsumption.

To the extent that some environmental goods such as water are of a mixed collective type, the conventional theory of the firm could be used to determine the optimum level of their production, given a fixed quantity of inputs or factors available for their production. An alternative to this solution would be the least-cost combination of inputs used to produce a given quantity of the good.

A rationing system is needed to control consumption of publicly provided private goods. Three possible rationing devices are:

1) Uniform provision;

2) Queuing; and

3) User charges.

In a uniform provision system everyone gets the same amount of the good or service. The problem of a uniform provision is that everyone gets the same amount regardless of his or her needs or desires. The problem with queuing is that it requires payment in waiting time and rewards those whose opportunity cost of time is lowest. User charges are particularly well-suited to publicly provided goods because users could be charged the marginal cost of providing the good, which is often substantial, though not sufficient to cover the total cost of the public good. User charges result in both improved efficiency of use and partial cost recovery. This is particularly relevant to irrigation water pricing.

### 4.7.3 Reliability as a Public Good

Previously in this chapter, reliability of water service was discussed. One can ask: does a market exist for reliability as a public good? The answer is yes. Water reliability is not simply a tradable commodity like wheat; it is also a public good. The existence of a secure water supply and delivery system is essential in waste removal and putting out wild fires. A water utility that diligently repairs leaks produces benefits for all members of society (e.g., firefighting capability).

### 4.7.4 Social Benefits, Social Costs, and Economic Welfare

Groups or society as a whole are involved in making choices related to water and its use. As such, one must understand why and how groups of individuals behave and interact with the environment. Social benefits refer to the total increase in society's welfare from an economic action. It is the sum of two benefits:

1) The benefit to the agent performing the action (producer's surplus); and

2) The benefit accruing to society as a result of the action (consumer's surplus).

As an example, in the water utility industry a utility receives profits for supplying a good or service and residential customers receive benefits (e.g., drinking, bathing, and cooking) from the service.

Ideally, social costs should represent the total cost to society of an economic activity. It is the sum of two costs—private costs borne by the agent performing the action, and the cost to society or the value of externalities. For example, if a steel mill is polluting a river (and treating it as a free resource), then the mill is imposing a cost on society as a whole (i.e., external cost or externality). This cost is in addition to the internal (private) costs of producing the steel.

Similar to a production function, a social welfare function states the relationship between social utility and the factors that affect it. The utility of all individuals in society can be summed and the aggregate utility of all individuals can be derived. The advantage of such a function is that each individual's utility depends only upon his or her own consumption. Then standard economic efficiency rules apply and Pareto-efficient allocations and welfare maximization are intimately related.

Figure 2.4 shows the quantity of water consumed ($X_C$) when the price only reflects marginal private cost (MPC) and the effect of a tax (T*) to capture the effects of an externality such as over-pumping water from an aquifer. The sum of the MPC and T* yields the MSC. Therefore, if the market is to maximize social welfare, government intervention may be necessary to reduce production from $X_C$ to $X^*$ and raise prices from $P_o$ to $P^*$. In fact, a restriction regarding pumping water from an aquifer is an example of government intervention. Total revenues collected by imposing this tax on output represents a transfer of wealth from consumers to the government.

## 4.8 Components of Value

When the value of water or water services is being estimated what is being measured is the welfare change associated with some policy-induced change in the attributes of the commodity or service (e.g., reliability). Various attributes include: (a) long-run versus short-run values; (b) at-site versus at-source values; (c) per period versus capitalized values; and (d) use, nonuse, and total economic values. These values are discussed below.

### 4.8.1 Use, Nonuse, and Total Economic Value

As reflected in Figure 4.4, the total economic value (TEV) of an environmental asset such as water can be broken down into two general categories. The first category is use value and consists of direct use and indirect use. In the context of groundwater, use values would include waste disposal, recreation/fish and wildlife habitat, hydroelectric power, navigation, irrigation, domestic, thermoelectric power, and industrial processing. 125 For groundwater, TEV is the sum of the extractive and *in situ* (in place, within an aquifer) values. Use values relates to the preferences that people have for using the environmental asset in question such as drinking water, fishing in a river, bathing, or valuing the recreation at a beach site.

Non-use values arise when the asset is valued by people who do not currently or directly use the asset. Non-use values (often called passive use values) include existence value and option value. These values are often more controversial than use values when it comes to measuring and validating them. Non-use values are public goods in the usual sense of the term, meaning that they are non-rivalrous and non-excludable. They are now well-accepted in environmental theory and practice. TEV is another way to represent full value reflected in Figure 4.5. 126

**Figure 4.4**
**Components of Total Economic Value**

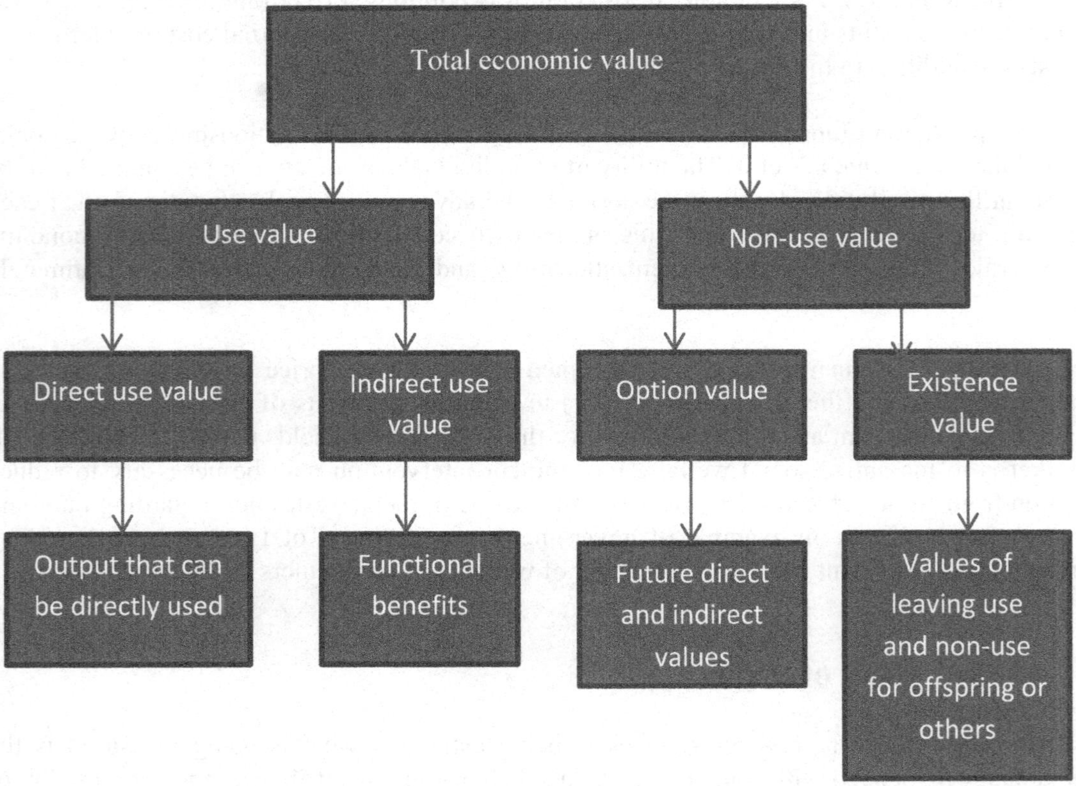


Source: Katar Singh and Anil Shishodia, *Environmental Economics: Theory and Application* (Los Angeles, Sage Publications, 2007), 126.

---

125 Kenneth D. Frederick, Tim VandenBerg, and Jean Hanson, "Economic Values of Freshwater in the United States" (Washington, DC: Resources for the Future, 1996), 9.

126 Another type of value is referred to as cultural value. These values include but are not limited to: (a) spiritual and ceremonial water, and (b) water fountains. An example of cultural value is the use of water to support and maintain the way of life of Native Americans. See Raucher et al., 95–96.

**Figure 4.5**
**Components of the Full Value of Water (not drawn to scale)**

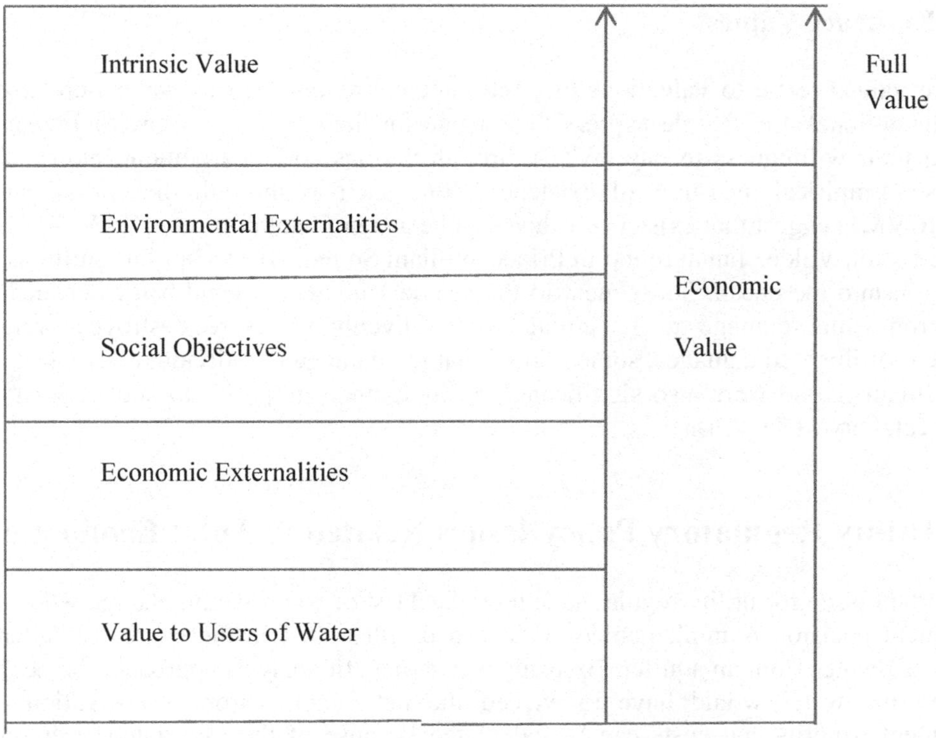


Source: Adopted from R. D. Raucher et al., *The Value of Water: Concepts, Estimates, and Applications for Water Managers* (Denver, CO: American Water Works Research Foundation, 2005), 43.

---

## 4.8.2 Option Values

Options values relate to the amount that individuals would be willing to pay to conserve a resource. That is, the resource is not used now but may be used in the future. One way to conceptualize option value is to view it like an insurance premium—to ensure the supply of something of which would otherwise be uncertain. While there can be no presumption that an option value is positive, it is likely to be if the resource is in demand and its supply is threatened. 127 Options can be quite valuable such as the case with natural gas and petroleum products.

In an environmental context, in 1964 the concept of option value was introduced. The context was an individual who was not sure if he would visit a recreational site. However, he would be willing to pay a sum in excess of his expected consumer's surplus to guarantee that the site would be available should he wish to visit it in the future. This extra sum was called the option value. The option value should be measured and added to the expected consumer's surplus. The resulting sum would represent the full value of providing an environmental service or amenity. Option values cannot be measured separately and can only be calculated if enough information

127 Ibid., 20.

exists about people's preferences to establish both the expected consumer's surplus and option price. 128

### 4.8.3 Existence Values

Existence values relate to valuations of environmental assets such as water unrelated to either current or optional use. People express their value for the existence of environmental assets by revealing their willingness to pay (WTP) through various charities without taking part in their direct use. Empirical measures of existence value such as through the contingent valuation method (CVM) suggest that existence values can be a significant portion of TEV. For instance, in 1989 the Exxon Valdez ran aground in Prince William Sound, Alaska spilling millions of gallons of crude oil into the ocean. Subsequent to the accident numerous legal battles ensued. Although the environmental damage to fisherman whose livelihoods were destroyed were a major component of litigated damages, some argued that the damage to individuals who had never seen Price William Sound were also significant. 129 Some analysts prefer to add bequest value as a separate category of TEV. 130

## 4.9 Utility Regulatory Policy Issues Related to Total Economic Value

An important issue for utility regulators is how the TEV of water would change when a policy or management decision is implemented. TEV can be illustrated in the context of alternatives of using groundwater from an aquifer. By using a cost–benefit analysis approach, the net benefits of extracting the water would have to exceed the net benefits from conservation. Typically, development benefits and costs can be calculated because of the associated cash flows. For a water utility's residential consumers, the use value could include, but are not limited to, water for drinking, bathing, cooking, and so on. For industrial use, the benefits may include water as part of a production process (e.g., making beer). Non-use values could be water as objects of intrinsic value such as a gift to others or as a responsibility (stewardship). An obvious non-use value would be future economic activity as a result of an aquifer being preserved.

## 4.10 Other Values

### 4.10.1 Long-Run versus Short-Run Values

For both producers and consumers, a distinction is necessary between the long-run and the short-run. In economic theory, in the long-run all of a firm's production costs are variable. The long-run is the most appropriate time frame for most of the important investment decisions in the water resources field. Failure to observe this distinction has caused analysts to ignore certain costs and to erroneously value water uses. In some cases, however, such as in drought planning, short-run values are appropriate. For example, during a drought some water utilities impose higher short-run commodity rates during the summer months. In contrast to the short run, in the analysis of a water utility concession summarized in chapter seven, a thirty-year period was assumed.

---

128 Singh and Shishodia, 140–41.

129 Lesser and Giacchino, 258.

130 Pearce, 21.

### 4.10.2 At-Site and At-Source Values and Quality

At-site and at-source water values represent different economic products. A water utility usually commits significant resources capturing, treating, storing, and delivering water for its customers. Therefore, a method is necessary to input the consumer's surplus from at-site domestic water demand to derive the measure of the at-source water value. A standard formula (i.e., point expansion) has been developed for the integral of a constant elasticity demand function to estimate an at-source value of residential water. To implement the analysis, a demand function is developed by assuming a functional form and inferring an empirical demand function from an observed price-quantity point on that function. Gross economic value of some assumed change in water availability is found by integrating (i.e., using calculus) under the inferred demand function for the assumed quantity change. Next, after subtracting for the cost of supply, consumer's surplus is isolated. Finally, an at-source water value is derived after adjusting for water losses incurred as the result of delivering the water. For simplicity, a constant-elasticity demand function is used. The application of this formula requires only four data items which include:

1) A price-quantity point—an observed price in effect during a specified period;

2) The water deliveries observed during the same period;

3) A hypothetical change in quantity that is to be valued; and

4) The price elasticity of demand that is assumed.

The procedure infers a second point on an empirical demand function from an initial point—the price-quantity observation. We have assumed the constant-elasticity form of the demand function. If residential water can be assumed to be priced to recover all the costs of supplying it, the average revenue can be subtracted from the total willingness to pay to derive the net consumer's surplus attributable to raw water. Finally, to reflect water losses resulting from meter error, leakage, and pilferage, an adjustment must be made. Multiplying the derived value per unit times the percentage available for customers—1.0 minus the percentage lost—yields the final estimated value of raw water to the utility's customers. The resulting net benefit is the value of raw water. 131

Marketed economic commodities such as water are priced according to quality, time, and space. For instance, crude oil is always priced in terms of grade, time of delivery, and location. With respect to location, because water has a low value at the margin, the energy and capital costs for: (a) treatment, (b) transportation, and (c) storage tend to be high relative to the economic value at the point of use. Thus, the economic value of water of similar quality at the point of use may differ widely from the value at its source. Water in its untreated form is a distinctly different commodity from treated water delivered under pressure by a public utility to its various customers. Another important variable affecting the value of water is the season of the year water delivery occurs. For instance, water may have little value for irrigation during the winter.

131 Raucher, 99.

### 4.10.3 Per Period versus Capitalized Values

Some values can be expressed for a single period while others represent the value of a capital asset. Water values are usually expressed as a single period such as a year. The alternative to expressing the value as a single period is to capitalize the present value of a stream of periodic values. In this case, the capitalized value is sometimes called a capital asset.

## 4.11 Value of Water by Sectors of the U.S. Economy

As a final illustration regarding the value of water, the AwwaRF has summarized the value of water in specific sectors in the U.S. economy. In addition to surveys regarding WTP, various other methods (discussed in Appendix B) were used to estimate these values. Table 4.4, Relative Value of Water by Sector (2003 USD), provides a low and high range in dollars per acre-foot.

**Table 4.4**
**Relative Value of Water by Sector (2003 USD)**

| Sector | Low ($/AF) | High $/AF |
|---|---:|---:|
| Agriculture | 21 | 1,447 |
| Residential | 1,400 | 4,000+ |
| Commercial/Industrial | 28 | 805 |
| Instream 1/ | 10 | 770+ |
| Cultural | Unknown | Unknown |

Notes: 1/ Recreation

Source: Adopted from R. D. Raucher et al., *The Value of Water: Concepts, Estimates, and Applications for Water Managers* (Denver, CO: American Water Works Research Foundation, 2005), 99.

---

The authors of the data in Table 4.4 qualify the information by stating:

> *"These ranges of values are not necessarily due to imprecise measurement of the value of water but in fact represent the true situation that the value of water is site, time, and use specific, such that one value does not fit all."* 132

Table 4.5 shows water values by use in the United States. Prices are in 1994 dollars.

---

132 Raucher, p. 99.

**Table 4.5**
**National Water Values by Use ($/AF)**

| Water Use | Classification | Ave. | Median | Min. | Max. | Number |
|---|---|---|---|---|---|---|
| **Major** | **Minor** | 2/ | | | | **Of Values** |
| **In-stream** | | | | | | |
| | Waste Disposal | 3 | 1 | 0 | 12 | 23 |
| | Recreation/F&W habitat 1/ | 48 | 5 | 0 | 2,642 | 211 |
| | Navigation | 146 | 10 | 0 | 483 | 7 |
| | Hydropower | 25 | 21 | 1 | 113 | 57 |
| **Withdrawal** | | | | | | |
| | Irrigation | 75 | 40 | 0 | 1,228 | 177 |
| | Industrial processing | 282 | 132 | 28 | 802 | 7 |
| | Thermoelectric power | 34 | 29 | 9 | 63 | 6 |
| | Domestic | 194 | 97 | 37 | 573 | 6 |
| **Total number of values** | | | | | | **494** |

Notes: 1/ F&W = fish and wildlife

2/ Each estimate is given equal weight in calculating the averages.

Source: Kenneth D. Frederick, Tim VandenBerg, and Jean Hanson, "Economic Values of Freshwater in the United States," (Washington, DC: Resources for the Future, 1996), 9.

---

Table 4.5 indicates that industrial and domestic uses are the highest values based on both the average and median figures. Note that the median values of the withdrawal uses are all higher than those of the in-stream uses. The primary valuation methods for valuing the water use in Table 4.5 are those listed in Appendix B.

# CHAPTER FIVE

# WATER RATES

## 5.1 Overview

To understand water tariffs [133] (and rates in particular), recall that one of the fundamental goals of utility economic regulation is to replicate the outcome of a competitive market. In a competitive market, for efficiency reasons, price should equal marginal cost and the amount of output produced should provide the greatest overall level of benefit to society. To the extent that regulated water utilities are natural monopolies, they have an incentive to charge higher prices than under competitive conditions; furthermore, they have an incentive to restrict output. These concepts were discussed in chapter three. Thus, utility regulators step in and set rates to prevent such undesirable social outcomes.

In the water utility context, rates (usually based on embedded costs) generally refer to the prices established by governing bodies (e.g., state PSCs or PUCs, city officials) and included in a utility's tariffs. However, in the case of certain goods (e.g., the *value* of a unpolluted stream to a fisherman) and services, price tags do not exist. In these cases, economists attempt to determine what are called "shadow prices." Shadow prices are the values used in economic analysis when market prices are unknown or judged not to be an appropriate measure of economic value. In an environmental context, economists have been estimating these for years. In the public utility context, economists have occasionally (but not often) attempted to assign monetary measures of individuals' preferences for outcomes of policy proposals or events (e.g., value-of-service pricing).

133 Tariffs are the authorized rates, charges, and terms and conditions under which utilities provide services.

This chapter begins by identifying economic regulation policy goals. Next, the factors influencing tariffs are identified and briefly discussed. Third, various pricing policies and approaches used in setting water rates are described. Fourth, utility, consumer, and society ratemaking perspectives are mentioned. Fifth, Dr. Bonbright's frequently cited criteria of a sound rate structure is presented and analyzed. Sixth, commonly used water utility rate structures are explained. Seventh, the lessons learned related to water utility ratemaking from African utilities are presented. Finally, the pros and cons of rates based on value of service are discussed.

## 5.2 Economic Regulation Policy Goals

From a purely economic efficiency perspective, rate design boils down to the following question: Is there a way to structure rate design to induce utilities to produce the proper level of output and sell it at the correct price? Pricing and economic efficiency, however, are not the exclusive goals of utility regulation. Table 5.1 lists common policy goals of utility regulation. [134] What is noticeably absent from Table 5.1 are environmental concerns.

**Table 5.1**
**Common Policy Goals of Utility Regulation**

| No. | Description |
|---|---|
| 1 | Ensure just and reasonable rates |
| 2 | Prevent excessive (monopoly) profits |
| 3 | Prevent unreasonable price discrimination among customers and places |
| 4 | Provide regulated firms with adequate earnings |
| 5 | Provide service to the largest number of customers |
| 6 | Promote economic development and employment |

Source: Author's construct.

---

Not all countries are in agreement as to the policy goals of utility economic regulation. In contrast to Dr. Phillip's policy objectives listed above, the Organization for Economic Co-operation and Development (OECD) [135] has organized their objectives around four sustainable dimensions which include:

1) Environmental sustainability;

2) Financial sustainability;

3) Economic efficiency; and

4) Social concerns.

134 Charles F. Phillips, Jr. *The Regulation of Public Utilities Theory and Practice*, 3rd ed. (Arlington, VA: Public Utilities Reports, Inc., 1993), 172–73.

135 Member countries include: Australia, Austria, Belgium, Canada, the Czech Republic, Denmark, Finland, France, Germany, Greece, Hungary, Iceland, Ireland, Italy, Japan, Korea, Luxembourg, Mexico, the Netherlands, New Zealand, Norway, Poland, Portugal, the Slovak Republic, Spain, Sweden, Switzerland, Turkey, the United Kingdom, and the United States.

These dimensions are examined in more detail below.

**Environmental sustainability** involves discouraging the depletion of critical natural resources by:

1) Guaranteeing the preservation of ecological functions related to water;

2) Minimizing the use of supply-side solutions to water scarcity;

3) Using water efficiently by encouraging water savings and discouraging wasteful water use; and

4) Minimizing the alteration of natural flow patterns.

**Financial sustainability** provides for the long-term reproduction of physical assets and continuity of service. Measures or metrics of this goal involve the following:

1) Cash flow should allow for the replacement of physical assets;

2) Cost recovery should be for prudently incurred investment and expenses;

3) *Full* payment for the resources (i.e., the factors of production identified in chapter two) that are used as inputs in water-related activities; and

4) Cost efficiency (i.e., minimizing the present value of the utility's future revenue requirements subject to any constraints related to providing service).

**Social concerns** involve adequate access to affordable water that are fair and under equitable conditions. Benchmarks for achieving these goals involve:

1) Structuring tariffs so that lower-income users can have access to and can afford water services;

2) Identifying customers' water needs and allocate water in a way that is not skewed by concentration of political power; and

3) Achieving an equitable way to share the cost of managing water resources.

**Economic efficiency** is defined by OECD such that water is allocated to the most beneficial uses and economic resources are not wasted. Economic efficiency involves:

1) Allocative efficiency which involves allocating water with priority to uses with highest value to society as a whole;

2) Comparing costs of water management and water-related services with their value (i.e., do not misallocate economic resources); and

3) Regulation should ensure optimal risk allocation among stakeholders including users and taxpayers. 136

---

136 OECD, 24–25.

### 5.2.1 What Are Equitable or Fair Rates?

One of OECD's social concerns is access to water under fair and equitable conditions. Within the context of utility ratemaking, determining what is equitable or fair is a very subjective matter. Equity is a vague concept that can change meanings depending on the circumstances or environment being discussed. A survey of industry and academic publications on water rate design reveals at least five concepts held up under the banner of "equity." These include:

1) Affordability;
2) Cost of service;
3) Provision of a basic human right;
4) Social justice; and
5) Resource efficiency.

These concepts will be described in more detail below.

**Affordability** is a function of a utility's water rates and charges, a customer's income, and the prices of other goods and services that customers purchase. Affordability is most often associated with residential water utility customers. Economic development rates (discussed later in the chapter), which are usually applicable for commercial and industrial customers, are also based on some measure of affordability. Rate affordability is meaningful at the level of a customer's ability to pay whereas equity connotes fairness across many customers. The price of a good or service can be affordable but not equitable, or vise-versa. This chapter discusses various benchmarks for assessing affordable water rates.

**Cost of Service.** Of all the standards for equitable water rates, cost of service is perhaps the most highly regarded. Cost-of-service based rates rests on the principle that each customer should pay the costs a utility incurs to serve him. Cost of service equity is a distinct normative goal in itself. The mechanics of cost-of-service ratemaking is discussed in more detail later in the chapter.

**Basic Human Life.** Water is among a short list of goods essential for human life and therefore a precondition to any other normative or utilitarian good. (The other essential goods are food, shelter, and clothing.) Many policymakers include water service among the fundamental human rights that *governments* must ensure. Under this principle, normative considerations on rate structures are secondary to universal provision of water. Taken to its logical conclusion, the statement that "water is a human right" implies that utilities should provide at least a minimum quantity of potable water to its customers. However, what is reasonably debatable is how accessible water should be for the public. For instance, is it the utility's obligation to supply water to the customer's *premises* or at a reasonable accessible delivery point (e.g., the town's square).

**Social Justice.** Under the heading of social justice is a society's income distribution. The cost of water may be a significant portion of a household's budget or a trivial amount for society's more affluent members. Evidence suggests, however, that water rates alone can have little overall impact on income distribution. In the United States, policymakers rarely cite this factor as a consideration in ratemaking.

**Resource Efficiency.** The concept of resource efficiency as an attribute of fairness or equity is at the heart of resource economics. Chapter three makes a case that efficient water rates increase society's welfare. This chapter identifies resource efficiency as a primary goal of a sound rate structure.

### 5.2.2 Price Discrimination

As mentioned above, one of Dr. Phillips's policy goals of utility economic regulation relates to price discrimination. Three forms of price discrimination exist. They include:

1) Third-degree price discrimination. In this case, various prices are charged for different markets such as water for low-income customers. Normally, third-degree price discrimination breaks the market up into a few submarkets;

2) Second-degree price discrimination. As more of a good is purchased, the per-unit price falls. This is the case with declining block rate structures and discussed later in this chapter; and

3) First-degree price discrimination. In this case, a monopolist is able to obtain the full value that any single buyer places on each unit of his good (e.g., a lost person in the desert on a hot summer day will usually pay a high price for the first bottle of water and lower prices for each subsequent bottle).

According to Dr. Phillips, for a utility to practice price discrimination, four conditions must exist. 137 These conditions are summarized in Table 5.2.

**Table 5.2**
**Necessary Conditions for Price Discrimination**

| No. | Condition |
|---|---|
| 1 | Customers who are charged the higher rate cannot buy in the lower-rate sector (i.e., class). |
| 2 | Customers buying at the lower rate cannot resell in the higher-rate sector. Customers cannot shift from one rate class to another rate class. |
| 3 | Price elasticity of demand must be quite different among the sectors (classes). |
| 4 | The costs of separating the market into sectors cannot be too large. |

Source: Author's construct.

---

The ratemaking practice of grouping customers into classes entails a variety of assumptions such as all customers having identical preferences and incomes. 138 However, this is not true for all customers in the same rate class. For instance, a residential customer may be a single individual living in an apartment who travels considerably and is rarely home, or a four-person household in

137 Phillips, 440.

138 For a discussion of consumer preferences, see Hayward, 88–91.

the suburbs with a large lawn. However, Dr. Phillips claims that price discrimination cannot be justified unless four conditions exist. 139 These conditions are reflected in Table 5.3

**Table 5.3**
**Justification for Price Discrimination**

| No. | Condition |
|---|---|
| 1 | A utility has high fixed costs and chronic excess capacity exists. |
| 2 | Lower rates are needed to attract new business. |
| 3 | All rates cover at least variable (marginal costs), and they make some contribution to the utility's fixed costs. |
| 4 | Regulation is undertaken to keep a utility's total earnings reasonable and to keep price and service discrimination within bounds. |

Source: Author's construct.

## 5.3 Factors Influencing Tariffs

A myriad of economic, political, and social factors exist that influence a water utility's tariffs. These factors are summarized in Table 5.4. Figure 5.1 illustrates the constraints in supplying water.

**Table 5.4**
**Factors Influencing Tariffs**

| No. | Factor | Description/Example |
|---|---|---|
| 1 | Politics | Lifeline rates for low-income residential customers |
| 2 | Social attitudes | Water and water delivery is a free good, an entitlement, and not an economic good |
| 3 | Priority | "Must do" (e.g., environmental compliance) versus discretionary projects |
| 4 | Lack of funds | Insufficient cash flow from operations and/or funds from capital markets may not be available for projects at reasonable interest rates |
| 5 | Legal | Water quality that meets EPA's maximum containment levels (MCL) |
| 6 | Special Interests | Economic development rates; low water rates for farmers |
| 7 | Economic | Projects based on cost–benefit analysis, allocative efficiency |
| 8 | Local governments | Economic development rates |
| 9 | Technology | Use of desalination plants; cost–benefit analysis of supply-side and demand-side management (DSM) projects |
| 10 | Environmental | Pollution of rivers and streams |

Source: Author construct.

139 Phillips, 440.

**Figure 5.1**
**The Constraints in Supplying Water**

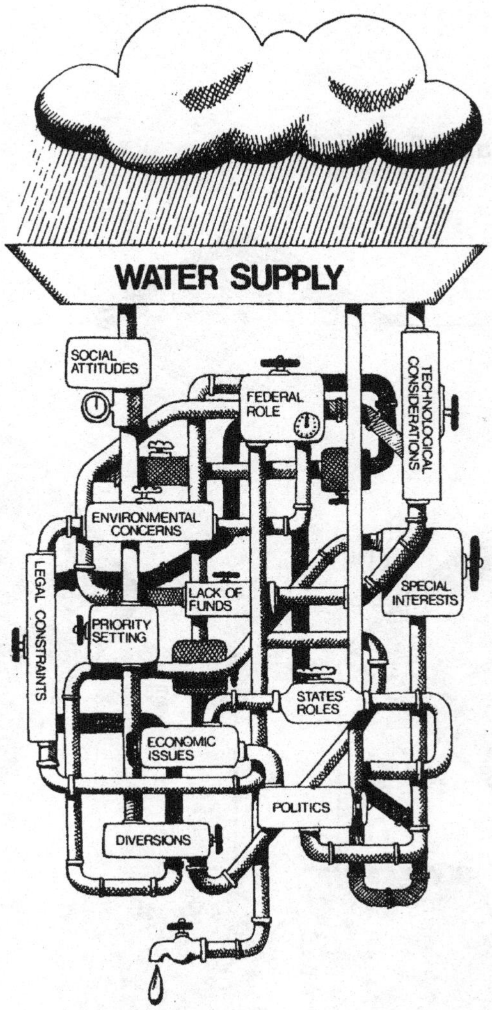


Source: Andrew A. Dzurik, *Water Resource Planning* (Lanham, MD: Rowman & Littlefield Publishers, Inc., 2003), 341.

---

## 5.4 Pricing Policies

When developing pricing policies, regulators often determine if uniform prices are desired. Figure 5.2 provides a flowchart for regulators to identify pricing options. Average pricing is relatively easy to implement as compared to two-part or multi-part pricing. The tradeoff, however, is a loss in economic efficiency. Ramsey pricing is a method developed by Frank Ramsey in 1927 that adjusts prices away from marginal costs in inverse proportion to the price elasticity of demand.

A major problem with average-cost pricing reflected in Figure 5.2 is that usually economically efficient rates are not the outcome. Recall from chapter three that average-cost pricing results in lost economic welfare even though this loss is less than under monopoly pricing. For example, if a water utility has significantly different summer and winter demands, a uniform rate throughout the year will likely result in efficiencies. That is because rates are too low in the summer when demand is highest and capacity is constrained; and rates are too high in the winter when excess capacity exists.

**Figure 5.2**
**Decision Rule in Adopting a Pricing Policy**

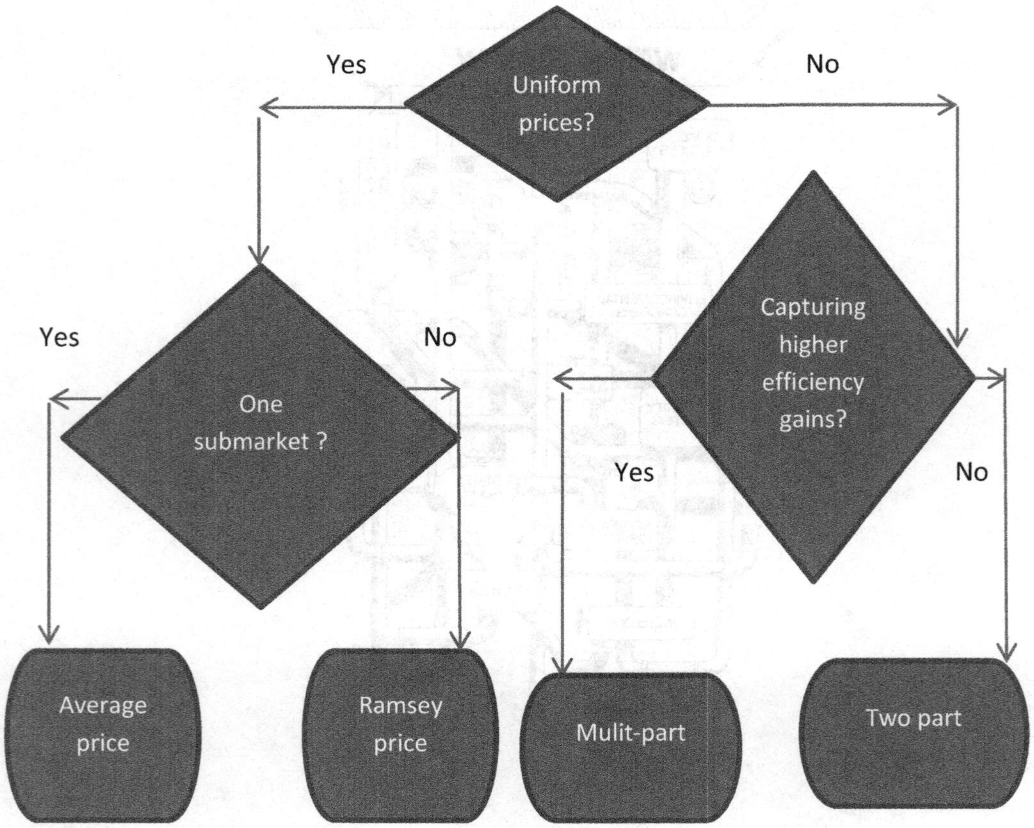


Source: Adopted from Nadira, Barkatullah, *Pricing, Demand Analysis and Simulation: An Application for a Water Utility* (Dissertation.com, 1999), 43.

---

Figure 5.3 provides an overview of pricing approaches for public utilities. Section 5.8 discusses second-best pricing and Section 5.11 summarizes pricing based on average incremental cost (AIC), peak-load pricing, and scarcity pricing. (Present worth incremental system costs—PWISC—is also known as Turvey marginal costs and was discussed in chapter two.) Other methods of calculating marginal costs (MC) were also discussed in significant detail in chapter two.

**Figure 5.3**
**Pricing Approaches**

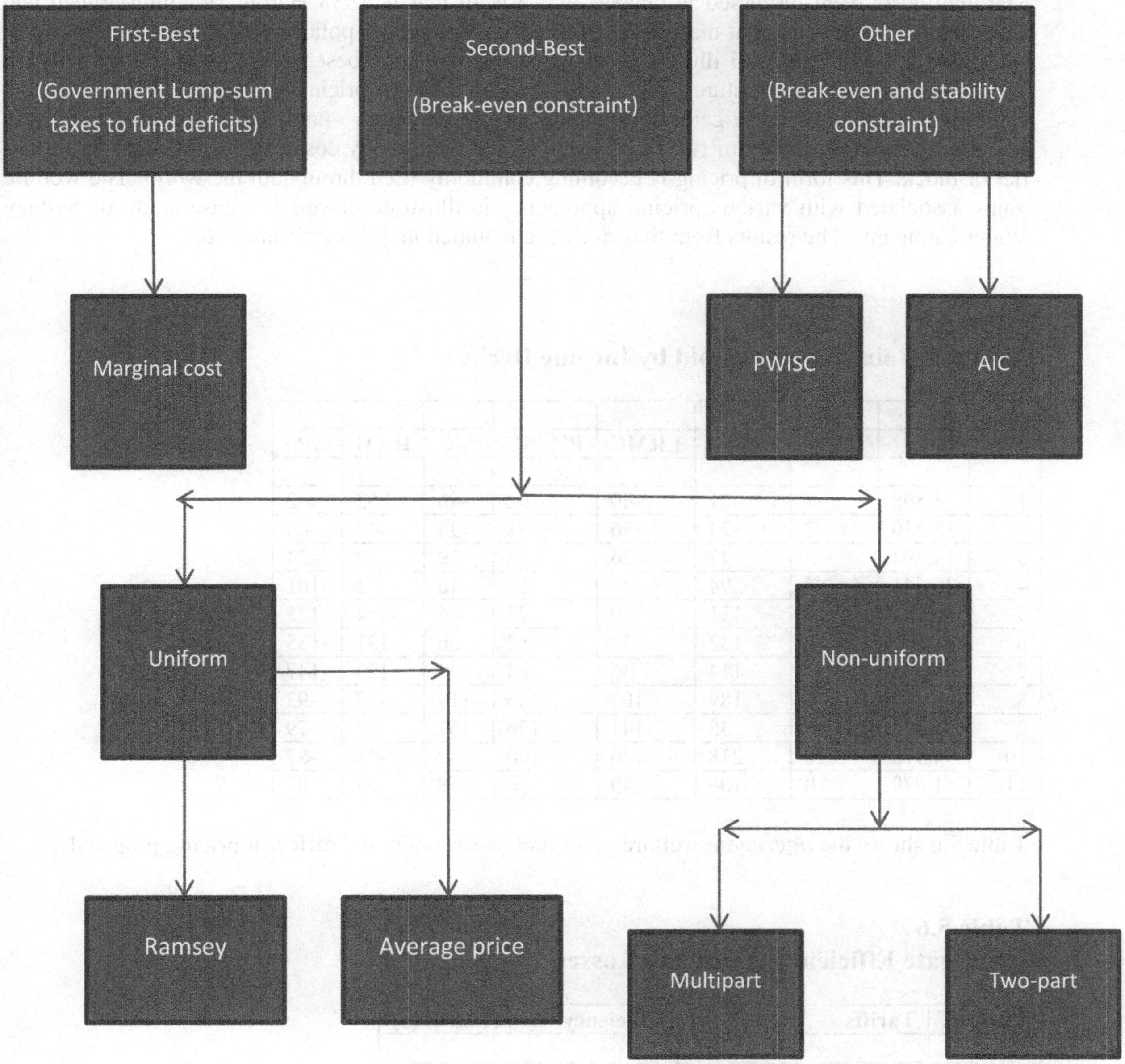


Source: Adopted from Nadira, Barkatullah, *Pricing, Demand Analysis and Simulation: An Application for a Water Utility* (Dissertation.com, 1999), 80.

---

In terms of economic efficiency, economists would rank the pricing approaches identified in Figure 5.3 in the following order:

1) First-best (marginal cost);

2) Second-best with a break-even (i.e., revenue requirements) constraint; and

3) Other pricing policies such as present worth incremental system costs (PWISC), average incremental costs (AIC), and fully distributed costs (FDC), (i.e., embedded costs).

Marginal costs were discussed in chapter two. Recall that in 1938 Harold Hotelling argued and defended his proposition that marginal-cost pricing is the proper policy in establishing utility rates. As Figure 5.3 and Table 5.5 illustrates, included in the second-best pricing approach are uniform and non-uniform tariff structures. By adopting a non-uniform pricing approach, utility regulators can capture higher efficiency gains through either multi-part or two-part tariffs. A multi-part tariff is best since with a minimum of two tiers, the marginal commodity costs can be reflected in the last tier or block. This form of pricing is becoming commonly used throughout the world. The welfare gains associated with various pricing approaches is illustrated through a case study of Sydney Water Company. The results from that study are included in Tables 5.5 and 5.6.

**Table 5.5**
**Average Gains by Household by Income Decile**

| Line No. | Ave Inc. | Decile | SRMC | LRMC | PWISC | AIC | RAM | AP |
|---|---|---|---|---|---|---|---|---|
| | | | | | | | | |
| 1 | 5,508 | 1 | -71 | -40 | -52 | -46 | 52 | 32 |
| 2 | 13,210 | 2 | -24 | -36 | -31 | -34 | -47 | -63 |
| 3 | 19,694 | 3 | 47 | 26 | 33 | 29 | -7 | -24 |
| 4 | 26,541 | 4 | 94 | 36 | 57 | 46 | -71 | -101 |
| 5 | 34,176 | 5 | 131 | 40 | 74 | 56 | -154 | -175 |
| 6 | 41,577 | 6 | 132 | 52 | 82 | 66 | -131 | -135 |
| 7 | 48,695 | 7 | 114 | 36 | 64 | 49 | -123 | -147 |
| 8 | 58,414 | 8 | 189 | 105 | 136 | 119 | -77 | -93 |
| 9 | 74,594 | 9 | 235 | 141 | 176 | 157 | -67 | -79 |
| 10 | 94,378 | 10 | 218 | 126 | 160 | 142 | -48 | -87 |
| 11 | 41,679 | All | 106 | 49 | 70 | 58 | -67 | -87 |

Table 5.6 shows the *aggregate* welfare gains and losses under the different pricing proposals.

**Table 5.6**
**Aggregate Efficiency Gains and Losses**

| Line No. | Tariffs | Efficiency Gains/Losses ($) |
|---|---|---|
| | | |
| | **Non-uniform two part** | |
| 1 | SRMC | 87,188 |
| 2 | LRMC | 39,733 |
| 3 | PWISC | 57,180 |
| 4 | AIC | 47,868 |
| | | |
| | **Uniform** | |
| 5 | RAM | -55,196 |
| 6 | AP | -71,544 |

Notes: In 1992/1993 dollars.. Adopted from Barkatullah, 168, 183.

Table 5.7 illustrates a hypothetical two-part tariff with all consumption priced at short-run marginal costs. This type of tariff incorporates concepts from embedded cost and marginal-cost pricing approaches. The commodity charge, based on short-run marginal costs, captures economic efficiency and provides proper price signals to consumers. The customer and/or access charge is derived residually such that the utility's revenue requirements are met. Appendix E provides an example of a multi-part tariff with two rate blocks or tiers.

**Table 5.7**
**Sample Two-Part Tariff**
**All Consumption Priced at Marginal Cost**

| Domestic (Metered) | Block | Description | Charge ($) | Volume (Units) | Monthly Bill ($) |
|---|---|---|---|---|---|
| | | Customer charge | 14.00 | | 14.00 |
| | 1 | Commodity charge | 3.00 | 19 | 57.00 |
| | | | | | 71.00 |

1 Unit = 100 cubic feet.

Source: Author's construct.

### 5.4.1 Welfare Gains Related to Water Utility Pricing Reforms (Sydney Water, Australia)

In January 1994 Sydney, Australia, faced severe water restrictions related to a drought. Therefore, a review of alternative water utility pricing strategies became useful. In a 1997 study [140] of Sydney Water (Australia), Nadira Barkatullah evaluated alternative pricing strategies for water against the criteria of *efficiency* and *equity* while maintaining the financial viability of the utility.

Her first step examined Sydney Water's cost structure by developing cost functions to estimate the utility's short and long-run marginal costs using quarterly time-series data from 1970/1971 to 1995/1996. The second step was to develop a residential water demand model using data comprising 822 cross-sectional units and 23 quarterly time periods from 1990/1991 to 1995/1996. The purpose of the demand model was to test the sensitivity of water demand to changes in the tariff structure and to use it to simulate the impact of alternative pricing strategies. (The cost functions and demand model will be described in more detail below.)

**Cost Functions.** Utility pricing based on short-run marginal costs is considered the theoretically correct approach and any deviations from these costs results in efficiency losses. The marginal cost of supplying an extra quantity of water depends on output, pumping and distribution costs relating to machinery and equipment needed to serve each customer class. Each utility is assumed to purchase inputs from the market at competitive prices to minimize the costs of producing output. For a water utility, generally the main inputs required are capital, labor, chemicals, and energy. Once a water utility's technology and costs are specified, it is necessary to determine the cost function's mathematical form. Often a linear functional form is assumed. In her study, the general cost function was expressed in equation 5.1 as:

140 Barkatullah, 164–84.

$$C = c(p,q) \tag{5.1}$$

Where:

p = the vector of input prices; and

q = the vector of output.

In the short-run, when some factors are fixed and others are variable, the fixed and variable input prices can be separately defined as reflected in equation 5.2:

$$C = c(pv, pf, q) \tag{5.2}$$

Where:

Pv = the vector of variable costs; and

Pf = the vector of fixed input prices.

The cost function specified above assumed certain properties. She used a linear short-run cost function given by the equation in 5.3:

$$C_t = a + bPL_t + cPE_t + eQR_t + fQNR_t \tag{5.3}$$

Where:

C = cost;

t = time;

$P_E$ = price of energy;

$P_L$ = price of labor;

$Q_R$ = residential output;

$Q_{NR}$ = non-residential output;

"a" is a constant (intercept term); and

b, c, e and f are coefficients.

Whereas in the short-run capital costs are ignored, in the long-run they are included. Thus, the linear short-run cost function was modified to the following long-run cost function shown in equation 5.4.

$$C_t = a + bPL_t + cPE_t + dPK_t + eQR_t + fQNR_t \tag{5.4}$$

Where:

$dPK_t$ = the cost of capital.

Given the linear functional forms for both the short-run and long-run cost functions, the coefficients of the output variables are the marginal costs. For instance, the short-run marginal cost for the nonresidential sector is the coefficient (f) of the nonresidential output variable $Q_{NRt}$.

The short and long-run cost functions were first estimated using the ordinary least squares (OLS) technique. The results indicated that autocorrelation and heteroscedasticity were problems. To address these problems, she used the Generalized Autoregressive Conditional Heteroscedasticity (GARCH) model. The GARCH model as compared to the OLS model produced superior results in terms of goodness of fit. The estimated short-run and long-run marginal costs were comparable to other studies.

**Demand Model**. Barkatullah developed a demand model under a non-uniform pricing structure consisting of an increasing or two-part tariff structure depending on the quarterly data used. The purpose of developing the model was to test the significance of marginal costs. An additional purpose was to provide an estimated behavioral model for simulation analysis.

The estimated parameters of the model had the expected signs and were nearly all significant at the one-percent level. Both peak and off-peak price elasticities were less than one, and the magnitude of the elasticities fell within the range of previous studies. In summary, Barkatullah concluded:

> *"The results suggest that consumers do respond to price when faced with a non-linear [multiple blocks] price schedule. Although price is an important determinant of water consumption and can be used in demand management strategies, the results show that due to the highly inelastic demand elasticity, substantial change in price would be required to motivate the consumers to any large changes in consumption."*[141] (emphasis added)

**Simulation Model**. Barkatullah used a simulation model to analyze various pricing reforms (discussed below) using both the cost and demand model results, where the individual welfare and aggregate efficiency gains were determined under each pricing policy. This process is illustrated in Figure 5.4. Figure 5.4 is a flowchart showing the process in simulating a multi-part tariff. In step No. 1, the marginal cost is estimated using one of the methods discussed in chapter three. Also in this step, the estimated demand coefficients are fed into a computer model. Step No. 2 simulates demand by incorporating either a uniform or non-uniform tariff structure. Step No. 3 predicts consumption quantities, which then determine the water utility's revenue. This step is an iterative process that generates predicted quantities and revenue by modifying the access charge until the model generates the revenue required to meet the target. Finally, in step No. 4 (once the predicted quantities and prices that meet the given revenue constraint are determined), welfare gains can be calculated using a variety of approaches (e.g., Marshallian consumer's surplus).

---

141 Barkatullah, 152.

**Figure 5.4**
**Multipart Tariff Simulation Process**

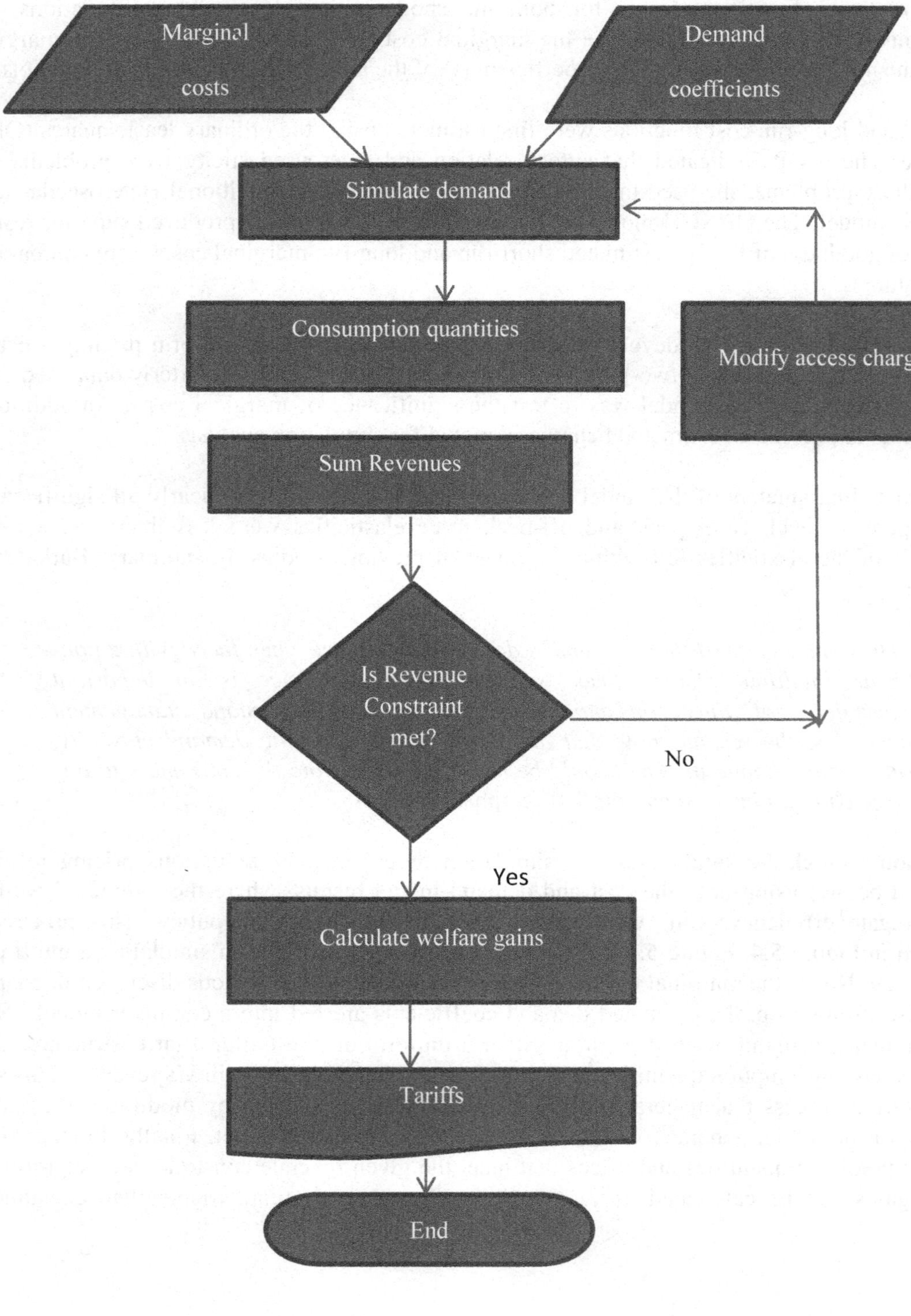


Source: Adopted from Nadira, Barkatullah, *Pricing, Demand Analysis and Simulation: An Application for a Water Utility* (Dissertation.com, 1999), 161.

**Pricing Approaches.** The distributional effects of various tariff structures were examined. (See Table 5.5.) Six pricing policies were studied and included the following:

1) Multipart tariff. This tariff had an increasing block structure. This was the actual 1992/1993 tariff structure in place at the time of the survey, and formed the base case.

2) Two-part tariff. This was a simple version of a non-uniform price consisting of two components—an access charge and a usage charge. The access charge was fixed and was set to meet the revenue requirements constraint. Four versions of the two-part tariff were used. They included:

    a. Two-part short-run marginal cost (SRMC). This tariff consisted of a constant flat rate which was fixed and a single per-unit price equal to the estimated short-run marginal cost;

    b. Two-part long-run marginal cost (LRMC). This tariff consisted of a constant flat rate which was fixed and a single per unit price equal to the estimated long-run marginal cost;

    c. Two-part present worth incremental system cost (PWISC). This tariff consisted of a constant flat rate, which was fixed and a single per unit price based on Ralph Turvey's methodology of PWISC. (This policy would be included in the "Other" category in Figure 5.3.);

    d. Two-part average incremental cost (AIC). This version of the two-part tariff consists of a constant flat rate which was fixed and a single per unit price based on the calculated average incremental cost. (This policy would be included in the "Other" category in Figure 5.3.)

3) Uniform pricing. This type of pricing consists of a single price where the consumer's total outlay increases proportionately to the amount of water consumed. Two types of uniform pricing tariffs were used and included:

    a. Ramsey (RAM). This method was based on Ramsey pricing principles. Two demand submarkets were identified—off-peak and peak. Peak periods contain the summer months where the price elasticity was higher than the off-peak months. The calculated prices were based on the Ramsey inverse elasticity rule. This method used the peak and off-peak demand elasticities and the estimated short-run marginal cost to calculate the prices for peak and off-peak periods.

    b. Average price (AP). The average price was calculated by dividing the total bill by the total consumption.

**Study Results**. Table 5.5 shows the *average* gains by household by income decile. The results show the largest gains where tariffs are set at short-run marginal costs (SRMC). Low-income customers (e.g., \$5,508 to \$13,210) experience losses under short-run marginal cost pricing practices.

Similar to the average efficiency gains, Table 5.6 shows the aggregate efficiency gains are the highest with the non-uniform, two-part, short-run marginal cost tariff.

Barkatullah found that the empirical results of the cost structure estimates were comparable with previous studies. As economic theory suggests, the demand estimates indicated that consumers respond to price. Thus, changing prices (rates) can be considered a tool in implementing demand-management strategies. In conclusion, she found:

> *"The empirical evidence shows that the two-part tariff with usage equal to short-run marginal cost is the most efficient pricing policy and leads to the highest welfare gains as compared to other uniform pricing policies. The results are consistent with second-best theory, which implies that when the usage charge is equal to the short-run marginal cost and the other costs are recovered as an access charge [similar to a demand charge] which is like a lump-sum tax, it leads to minimum efficiency losses. It is recommended [Coase (1946); Margolis (1957); Sherman (1967); Meyer (1979); Acton et al (1980); Albon (1988); Train (1989)], for the natural monopolies who want to adopt a pricing policy which dominates others on efficiency criteria alone."* (emphasis added) 142

## 5.4.2 Rate Block Quantities

When a water utility has two or more rate blocks (also called tiers) as is illustrated in Appendix E (sample residential water bill, charges, and rates—City of Oceanside, California), an important issue for ratemaking is the quantity of water in each block. 143 If a lifeline rate structure for the residential class is used, the quantity of water in the first rate block or tier can represent the minimum amount of water socially desirable (e.g., water needed for survival). As mentioned previously in this book, The World Health Organization estimates this amount at 25 liters per capita per day. Figure 5.5 illustrates potential rate block break points for residential water customers. For illustration purposes, the first tier would include the first 100 cubic meters. This amount would represent an individual's basic water necessity. The second tier for basic discretionary use would include quantities 101 to 200 cubic meters per month; and the last tier (also called the tail block) would include quantities in excess of 200 cubic meters per month.

A tabulation showing the number of bills and corresponding sales is a bill-frequency distribution. A simplified bill-frequency distribution is provided in Table 5.8. Table 5.9 shows the present and proposed revenues given current and projected rates using the data in Table 5.8.

---

142 Barkatullah, 184.

143 The techniques for establishing the quantities in the rate blocks are explained in more detail in American Water Works Association, *Principles of Water Rates, Fees, and Charges*, M1, 5th ed. (Denver, CO: American Water Works Association, 2000), Appendix C.

**Table 5.8**
**Simplified Bill Frequency Distribution**

| Line No. | | Number | Of Bills | Units | Units | Consolidation | Factor |
|---|---|---|---|---|---|---|---|
| | Interval (1) | Total In Interval (2) | No. in Excess of Interval (3) | Use In Interval (4) | Cumulative Use in Interval 1/ (5) | Units (6) | % of Total (7) |
| 1 | 0 | 72,264 | 3,495,879 | 0 | 0 | 0 | 0 |
| 2 | 1-5 | 126,626 | 3,369,253 | 439,732 | 439,732 | 17,285,997 | 10.48 |
| 3 | 6-10 | 299,919 | 3,069,334 | 2,510,510 | 2,950,242 | 33,643,582 | 20.39 |
| 4 | 11-15 | 373,176 | 2,696,158 | 4,962,320 | 7,912,562 | 48,354,932 | 29.30 |

1/ 1 unit = 1,000 gallons

Source: Adopted from American Gas Association, *Gas Rates Fundamentals* (Arlington, VA: American Gas Association, 1987), 247–48.

**Table 5.9**
**Computation of Revenue Using a Bill Frequency Distribution**

| Line No. | Present Rates $ (1) | Proposed Rates $ (2) | Rate Block Interval (3) | Billing Units 1/ (4) | Present Revenues $ (5) | Proposed Revenues $ (6) |
|---|---|---|---|---|---|---|
| 1 | 6.00 | 7.00 | Customer charge | 3,568,143 bills | 23,408,858 | 24,977,001 |
| 2 | .65 | .70 | 0-50 | 111,605,809 units | 72,543,776 | 78,124,066 |
| 3 | .55 | .58 | 51-200 | 50,181,583 units | 27,599,871 | 29,105,318 |
| 4 | .50 | .52 | Over 200 | 3,231,501 units | 1,615751 | 1,680,381 |
| 5 | | | | | **123,168,256** | **133,886,766** |

Notes: 1/ 1 unit = 1,000 gallons.

Source: Adopted from American Gas Association, *Gas Rates Fundamentals* (Arlington, VA: American Gas Association, 1987), 250.

Clearly, the quantities in each rate block will affect the utility's revenues. To determine the quantities in each block requires the preparation of a bill frequency distribution (i.e., compiling the size and number of bills by type of service such as residential). Figure 5.5 illustrates a sample water utility's cumulative monthly water sales. Note that if the utility has a three-tiered rate structure; possible break points could occur: (a) up to 400 cubic feet, which constitutes 50 percent of billed usage; (b) from 400 to 1,000 cubic feet, which constitutes another 35 percent of use; and (c) consumption in excess of 1,000 cubic feet, which constitutes 15 percent of use.

Present and proposed revenues from a hypothetical bill-frequency distribution are provided in Table 5.9, which shows only a portion of the total distribution. The total number of bills is 3,568,143 (column 4, line 1) and the total units sold is 165,018,893 (column 4, lines 2–4).

To estimate the impact of a rate change and to predict the resulting revenues, one must know the distribution of customers and their associated usage (e.g., how many customers use one unit, two units, etc., per billing period). Usage is grouped into intervals with wider intervals used at higher consumption levels. As usage increases, a smaller percentage of total sales occur in equal intervals of consumption. Intervals are selected so that the upper limit corresponds to each cumulative consumption block of the present rate and anticipated cumulative consumption blocks of any proposed rate. Thus, present and proposed rates can be analyzed. This is the minimum number of intervals. Additional intervals may be used.

In Table 5.8, note that column 7, line 4 reflects approximately 30 percent of the total units. The basic data appears in columns 2 and 4. Column 2 reflects the total number of bills in the interval. The data in the other columns are derived from the basic data. For example, column 5 is the sum of use in the interval and the cumulative use from the prior intervals (e.g., 439,732 + 2,510,510 = 2,950,242). The number of bills whose usage exceeds the upper limit of the given interval is shown in column 3. The cumulative usage in the given interval and in all preceding intervals is provided in column 5. In Table 5.8, the consolidated factor for a given interval is the upper limit usage for those bills that exceed the interval plus the accumulated usage through the interval. It is calculated by first multiplying the number of bills exceeding the considered interval by the interval upper limit and then adding the product to the cumulative use in the interval.

**Figure 5.5**
**Cumulative Monthly Water Sales (Ccf)**

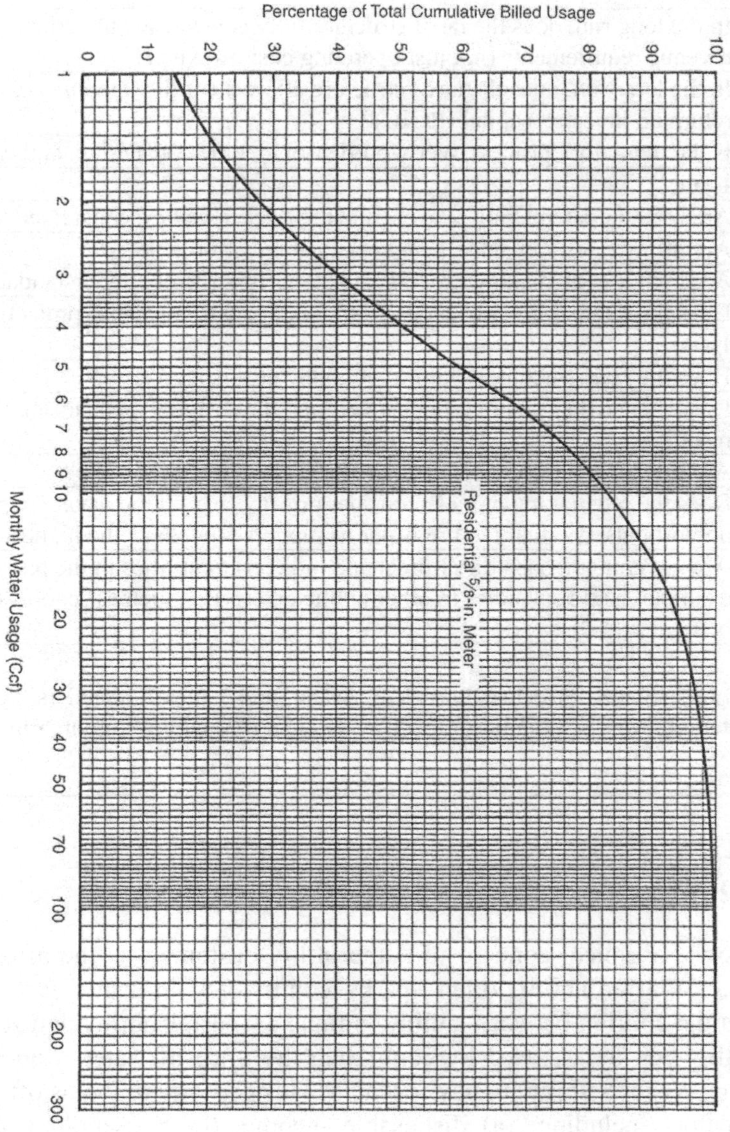


Source: American Water Works Association, *Principles of Water Rates, Fees, and Charges*, M1, 5th ed., (Denver, CO: American Water Works Association, 2000), 316.

---

## 5.5 Utility, Consumer, and Society Ratemaking Perspectives

In setting rates, many utility regulators view their job as balancing the interests of the utility, its customers, and society. Not all utility analysts agree on the perspectives and concerns of these three stakeholders. Table 5.10 represents the author's view of these perspectives and the key questions and issues raised by the stakeholders.

**Table 5.10**
**Ratemaking Perspectives of Stakeholders**

| Utility | No. | Issue |
|---|---|---|
| | 1 | In the long run, does the tariff structure fully compensate the utility such that its full revenue requirements (not just operating costs) are met? |
| | 2 | In the long-run, does the tariff structure allow the utility an *opportunity* to earn a fair return on invested capital (ROIC)? |
| | 3 | Is the regulatory process overly burdensome, time consuming, and expensive? |
| **Customer** | **No.** | **Issue** |
| | 1 | Are both the ratemaking *process* and the *tariff structure* considered fair? |
| | 2 | Are utility rates viewed as being reasonably "affordable?" |
| | 3 | Are both the ratemaking process and the tariff structure understandable? |
| | 4 | Does the ratemaking process provide for adequate consumer protection? |
| **Society** | **No.** | **Issue** |
| | 1 | Does the rate structure promote economic efficiency? |
| | 2 | Does the tariff structure reflect water (and the delivery mechanisms) as economic resources? |
| | 3 | Are the ratemaking process and the tariff structure reasonable? |
| | 4 | Does the ratemaking process consider priority (e.g., if the water supply is limited, do domestic users—that require water to support life—have the highest priority)? |
| | 5 | Are government subsidies (direct and indirect) to utilities in the public's interests? For example, could subsidies to other public enterprises such as schools or hospitals be better used? |

Adopted, in part, from Janice A. Beecher, Patrick C. Mann, and James R. Landers, "Cost Allocation and Rate Design for Water Utilities" (Columbus, OH: The National Regulatory Research Institute, 1990), 10.

---

### 5.5.1 Affordability

As Table 5.10 shows, a typical concern of some utility customers is the affordability of water service. The issue of affordability often sparks controversy in water utility rate hikes and illustrates the potential conflict between a utility's financial sustainability and access to affordable service. Affordability can be assessed by comparing the price of water services (i.e., the water bill) with a utility customer's ability to pay for them. This capacity to pay is often measured using a variety of indicators including: (a) disposable income, (b) household expenditures, or (c) expenditures on other essential services such as food, electricity, and housing. The measure of affordability can be assessed at a macro level (e.g., all households in an area or country), or at a micro level (specific groups, such as lower income or other vulnerable people). While a precise level of affordability usually does not exist, donors, international financial institutions, and other international organizations often quote the range of 3 to 5 percent of disposable income or household expenditure. 144

Related to the affordability issue, the effectiveness of any tariff structure (e.g., lifeline) is reduced if poor households do not have access (e.g., hookup) to the service whose consumption is subsidized. If access is systematically skewed against the poor, any tariff structure that provides negative incentives (or insufficient funds) for the extension of services will be regressive. In these

144 OECD, 28.

cases, subsidizing access has been demonstrated to be more effective than subsidizing consumption. 145

## 5.6 Criteria of a Sound Rate Structure

A discussion of a water utility's costs, prices (rates), values, and subsidies is not productive without reference to the criteria of a sound rate structure. As discussed in chapter eight, in the *Hope* decision, the U.S. Supreme Court found that the rates, and not the method employed to set them, is the key issue in determining "just and reasonable rates."

So what are the criteria for a sound rate structure? In 1961, James C. Bonbright, Albert L. Danielsen, and David R. Kamerschen (hereinafter referred to as "Bonbright") first published their book, *Principles of Public Utility Rates*. In March 1988, their second edition was released. In his book, Bonbright compiled a list of ten criteria of a sound rate structure and noted that they have emphasized normative economics (i.e., what should be done) as compared to positive economics (i.e., the study of what is and how the economy works). 146 Currently these criteria are used in water utility training courses and rate cases. 147 Rate experts testifying in natural gas, electric, and water utility rate cases often refer to Dr. Bonbright's attributes of a sound rate structure. These criteria are listed in Table 5.11.

**Table 5.11**
**Dr. Bonbright's Criteria of a Sound Rate Structure**

| No. | Criteria |
|---|---|
| 1 | Effectiveness in yielding total revenue requirements |
| 2 | Revenue stability and predictability |
| 3 | Stability and predictability of the rates themselves |
| 4 | Efficiency of the rate classes and the rate blocks in *discouraging wasteful use* (emphasis added) |
| 5 | Reflection of all of the present and future private and social costs and benefits occasioned by a service provider (i.e., *all internalities and externalities*) (emphasis added) |
| 6 | Fairness of the specific rates in apportionment of total cost of service (i.e., revenue requirements) among rate classes |
| 7 | Avoidance of undue discrimination in rate relationships (i.e., subsidy free without inter-customer burdens) |
| 8 | Responsive to changing demand and supply patterns |
| 9 | Practical attributes (e.g., simplicity, certainty, understandability, public acceptability, and feasibility of application) |
| 10 | Freedom from controversies as to proper interpretation |

Source: Author's construct.

145 Ibid,

146 [Intentionally left blank]

147 Keith Switzer, Vice President, Golden State Water Company, "Comparison of Water and Energy Utility Ratemaking," presentation at the 27th Annual Western NARUC Utility Rate School, May 14–19, 2006, San Diego, California, 13.

Dr. Bonbright then regrouped and emphasized five of the ten attributes into three criteria:

1) Capital attraction (No. 1);

2) Consumer rationing (Nos. 4 and 5); and

3) Fairness to ratepayers (Nos. 6 and 7). 148

This book focuses on the theory and tools economists can bring to water utility ratemaking and policy formation. Thus the book focuses on Bonbright's consumer rationing criteria—Nos. 4 and 5—(positive economics) as compared to social issues (e.g., fairness) included in normative economics.

It should be noted that not all utility regulatory agencies throughout the world subscribe to Bonbright's principles. For instance, the Queensland Competition Authority in Canada follows a different set of principles. These principles are listed in Table 5.12.

**Table 5.12**
**Water Utility Pricing Principles—Queensland, Australia**

| No. | Description |
|---|---|
| 1 | Reflect the costs of providing the service and, usually where the demand for water exceeds its supply, *potentially incorporate a value for the resource.* |
| 2 | Be *forward-looking* in that they represent the *least cost* that would now be incurred in providing the requisite level of service over the relevant period. |
| 3 | Ensure revenue adequacy—the revenue needs of the utility must be addressed where necessary. |
| 4 | Promote sustainable investment—where the services are to be maintained into the future, the investor must be given the opportunity to enjoy an appropriate return on invested capital (ROIC). |
| 5 | Ensure regulatory efficiency—the pricing method that minimizes regulatory intrusion and compliance costs relevant to a particular circumstance should be adopted. |
| 6 | Take into account matters relevant to the public interest. Many such matters are identified in the Queensland Competition Authority Act of 1997. |

Source: Marsden Jacob Associates, "Estimation of Long Run Marginal Cost (LRMC)," report prepared for the Queensland Competition Authority, Camberwell, Victoria, November 3, 2004, 1–2.

## 5.7 Water Utility Rate Structures

A utility's rate structure relates to the design and organization of billing charges by customer class. Once rate classes are established, the utility's revenue requirements are distributed among customer classes and rating periods. The structure should be consistent with the ratemaking perspectives and criteria of a sound rate structure previously discussed. Table 5.13 provides a brief definition of the rate structures commonly used in the U.S. water utility industry. For years, the most common structures were uniform rates and decreasing block rates. In the past decade or so, given water supply shortages in many areas, utility regulators have been switching to increasing block rate structures.

148 Bonbright, Danielson, and Kamerschen, 383–84.

**Table 5.13**
**Rate Structure Forms and Definitions**

| No. | Description | Definition |
|---|---|---|
| 1 | Flat Fee | A periodic fixed charge for water service that is unrelated to the amount of water consumed. |
| 2 | Fixture Rate | A periodic fixed charge for water service related to water-using fixtures on the customer's premises. |
| 3 | Uniform Rate | Price per unit is constant as consumption increases. |
| 4 | Decreasing Block | Price per unit decreases as consumption increases. |
| 5 | Increasing Block | Price per block increases as consumption increases. |
| 6 | Seasonal | Price level during season of peak use (e.g., summer) is higher than the level during the off-peak season. |
| 7 | Excess Use | Price level is significantly higher for all water used above average, usually determined by winter use. |
| 8 | Indoor/Outdoor | Price level for indoor use is lower than for outdoor use. |
| 9 | Lifeline Rate | Price for "necessary" water use is kept low. |
| 10 | Sliding Scale | Price level per unit for all water used increases based on average daily consumption. |
| 11 | Scarcity Pricing | Cost of developing new supply is attached to existing use. |
| 12 | Spatial Pricing | User pays for actual cost of supplying water to its establishment. |
| 13 | Interruptible | Special rates for consumers who are willing to have their delivery service interrupted by the utility when necessary. |

Adopted, in part, from Janice A. Beecher, Patrick C. Mann, and James R. Landers, "Cost Allocation and Rate Design for Water Utilities" (Columbus, OH: The National Regulatory Research Institute, 1990), 107–9.

---

### 5.7.1 Sample Rate Structure

Appendix E illustrates the rates, charges, consumption, and bill for a residential water utility customer in Oceanside, California. There, water utility service is provided by the City of Oceanside. The City receives its water from the San Diego County Water Authority (SDCWA), which provides wholesale service to various entities. The Metropolitan Water District of Southern California (MWD) provides bulk water supplies to various customers including SDCWA. It too provides wholesale service. The City of Oceanside uses an increasing block rate structure with the first tier—13 units (9,724 gallons) priced at $1.99/unit, and the second tier priced at $2.28/unit. The service charge is based on meter size; in this case a 5/8 inch meter. This rate structure is an example of a multi-part tariff. Note that the total monthly bill is $77.79. It consists of approximately 49 percent fixed charges and 51 percent variable charges. These amounts are in line with the cost structure of the average large IOU in the United States and reflected in Figure 2.1.

### 5.7.2 Rates Based on Cost of Service

Recall from chapter two that in the United States, utility rates based on cost-of-service pricing using embedded costs is by far the most common method of ratemaking. In chapter two, the concept of embedded (full supply costs) was introduced. The general process of determining rates based on cost of service is as follows. First, a utility's revenue requirements are determined. The revenue requirements are estimated for an upcoming year (called the test year) and usually consist of: (a) taxes, (b) depreciation expense, (c) operating and maintenance (O&M) expenses, and (d) a rate of return applied to rate base. Second, once the revenue requirements for a test year (usually a twelve-month historical period) is determined, a cost-of-service study is completed. Where possible, and a reasonable link is established, the cost-of-service study attempts to assign costs to specific customers and/or classes (e.g., residential, commercial).

Third, expenses and investment are often separated into functional accounts such as: supply production/procurement, pumping, transmission, treatment, storage, distribution, customer accounting, and administrative/general categories. Fourth, costs are often classified into three categories: customer, capacity (demand), and commodity. Fifth, various methods such as peak responsibility [149] are used to distribute common costs to the utility's customer classes. Sixth, various rate structures such as increasing block, declining block, or uniform rates are selected. One of the primary goals of the resulting rates is to provide proper price signals to customers. The process of moving from revenue requirements to tariffs (rates) is illustrated in Figure 5.6.

149 This method considers both the magnitude of peak demand and its timing, but does not incorporate average demand or volume of usage in the allocation of capacity costs.

**Figure 5.6**
**A Cost-of-Service Study**
**Process of Revenue Requirements to Tariffs**

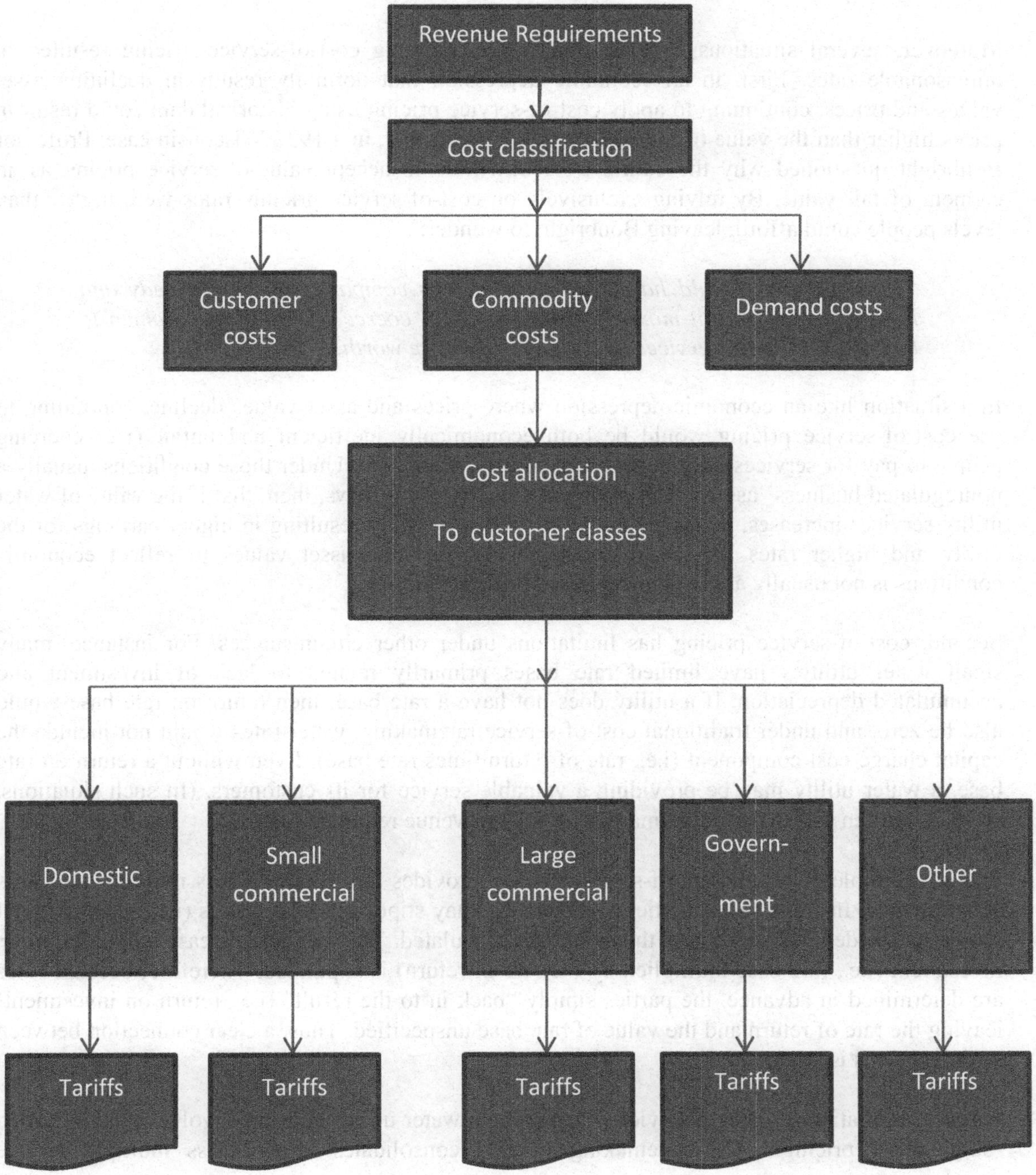


Source: Author's construct.

### 5.7.3 The Limitations of Cost-of-Service Pricing

Some regulators at PSCs are usually aware that cost-of-service studies are inherently subjective and judgmental, and for this reason, among others, cannot serve as the *exclusive* measure of just and reasonable rates. Other appropriate considerations necessarily include value of service to the customer, competitive conditions, and the historic rate design. [150]

Moreover, several situations have existed where applying cost-of-service pricing resulted in unreasonable rates. First, in an economic depression that normally results in declining asset values and prices, continuing to apply cost-of-service pricing using historical data could result in prices higher than the value of the service provided. In fact, in a 1939 Wisconsin case, Professor Bonbright questioned why the courts were unwilling to accept value-of-service pricing as an element of fair value. By relying exclusively on cost-of-service pricing, rates were higher than levels people could afford, leaving Bonbright to wonder:

> *"How the court could have assumed that any company, however greedy and however possessed of monopoly powers, could coerce free men and women to buy its products or services at more than they are worth?"* [151]

In a situation like an economic depression where prices and asset values decline, continuing to use cost-of-service pricing would be both economically inefficient and unfair (i.e., coercing people to pay for services at prices more than they are worth). Under those conditions, usually a nonregulated business' asset values and prices decline. It follows, then, that if the value of water utility services increases, assets should be revalued, possibly resulting in higher earnings for the utility and higher rates for customers. However, inflating asset values to reflect economic conditions is not usually allowed under cost-of-service pricing.

Second, cost-of-service pricing has limitations under other circumstances. For instance, many small water utilities have limited rate bases primarily related to lack of investment and accumulated depreciation. If a utility does not have a rate base, then return on rate base would also be zero, and under traditional cost-of-service ratemaking, water rates would not include the capital charge cost component (i.e., rate of return times rate base). Even without a return on rate base, a water utility may be providing a valuable service for its customers. (In such situations, regulators often use an operating margin [152] to set revenue requirements.)

A third example of where cost-of-service pricing provides limited usefulness is when rate cases are stipulated. In some cases, parties to a rate case may stipulate to the results (i.e., rates) without providing the details behind how the rates were calculated. This is often the case where return on investment (i.e., rate base multiplied by the rate of return) is stipulated. Therefore, because rates are determined in advance, the parties simply "back in to the result" (i.e., return on investment) leaving the rate of return and the value of rate base unspecified. Thus, a clear connection between rates and costs is not made.

A fourth limitation of cost-of-service pricing in the water utility industry involves what is called "single-tariff pricing." This ratemaking method consolidates rates across multiple service

---

150 Bonbright, Danielsen, and Kamerschen, 157.

151 Ibid, 127.

152 The operating margin method of ratemaking is where, in an attempt to derive revenue requirements, the economic regulator specifies a specific percentage above the utility's operating expenses as a proxy for return on rate base.

territories owned and operated by a multisystem utility that may or may not be contiguous or physically interconnected. Several states currently use single-tariff pricing to faciliate other social objectives (e.g., consolidating water systems). In some regions of the country such as California, a water utility may have various districts such as a desert region and a mountain region. In many cases, supplying water service to diverse geographic areas can have very different costs. Thus, a detailed cost allocation process typically used in a cost-of-service study appears to be undermined when the end result is where costs for a given class (e.g., residential) are aggregated to derive a uniform price.

Finally, traditional cost-of-service studies which are often used in establishing rates also have their limitations, including:

1) Considerable judgment is used in allocating common expenses and investment to customer classes;

2) Subsidies (particularly interclass) continue to be widespread; and

3) Embedded (historical) costs, in most cases, do not represent a water utility's future opportunity costs.

Thus, cost-of-service pricing can provide consumers with distorted price signals leading, in most cases, to wasteful consumption. As to the usefulness of embedded cost-of-service studies, Dr. Bonbright wrote:

> *"Many economists would like to see the fully distributed cost [FDS] concept dispatched to the museum of antiquated and irrelevant ideas."* [153]

### 5.7.4 Cost, Equity, and Efficiency in African Water Tariffs

The lessons learned by water utility economic regulators in Africa can be valuable to other water utilities and their regulators throughout the world. This case study was chosen for analysis because it was recently completed and it involved a large number of utilities. Now that the fundamentals of rates and tariffs including—(a) rate structure forms and definitions; (b) rate structure criteria; (c) cost of service; and (d) policy goals of economic regulation—have been discussed, their application for water utilities in Africa will be considered.

Many multilateral organizations such as the World Bank, United States Agency for International Development (USAID), the European Union (EU) and others have long been involved in assisting developing countries with public utility issues. This assistance has been in the form of institutional reforms (e.g., establishing an independent economic regulator and establishing tariffs), and engineering projects.

A July 2010 policy research working paper from the World Bank [154] discussed cost, equity, and efficiency issues for water utilities in Africa. Forty-five utilities were included in the study. In Africa, the World Bank uses a scorecard to grade water utilities against the criteria of cost

153 Bonbright, Danielsen, and Kamerschen, 481.

154 Sudeshna Banerjee, Vivien Foster, Yvonne Ying, Heather Skilling, and Quentin Wodon, "Cost Recovery, Equity, and Efficiency in Water Tariffs: Evidence from African Utilities" (Washington, DC: The World Bank, 2010), 1.

recovery, efficiency, and equity. 155 These are issues similar to those considered by U.S. utility regulators. Common questions they attempted to answer include:

1) Are customers metered?

2) Do tariffs recover costs?

3) Are water usage charges equitable?

4) Do cross-subsidies exist between large and small consumers, public standposts and private residential consumers, and water and wastewater customers? (The topic of subsidies is discussed in chapter six.) Often a water utility will provide standposts (a source of water available to the entire population at a reduced rate) as an alternative to piped water.

5) Are water connection charges fair?

The following is a discussion of these issues.

**Water metering** in Africa is widespread. Of the forty-four utilities surveyed, for thirty-five utilities for which detailed information was available, the average metering ratio is 75 percent. Water utilities in Nigeria and Sudan have almost negligible or no metering. In Africa, for utilities that use meters, the increasing block tariff structure with a fixed charge (i.e., customer charge) is the most common, and flat fees and uniform volumetric rates are rarely used. In theory, increasing block tariff structures allow utilities to meet the goals of efficiency and equity. The last block in the tariff structure is expected to be closer to the utility's long-run marginal cost. As would be expected, the initial rate block is a form of lifeline rate and is an attempt to make water affordable to low-income water utility customers. The size of the first block can vary; however, in most countries it is usually below ten cubic meters per month, where six cubic meters per month is considered subsistence consumption. (In comparison to these amounts, the World Health Organization has set a per capita consumption of 25 liters per day as the minimum consumption level for survival.) Most of the policy debates over the impact of tariffs on equity revolve around the quantity and price of the first block and whether it is actually serving the poor. 156

**Cost recovery.** As to the question of cost recovery, a large percentage of African water utilities do not recover all of their O&M costs from tariff revenues. Only 36 percent of the utilities surveyed were recovering their full O&M costs (assuming $0.40 per cubic meter for O&M cost recovery). Moreover, only nine percent were recovering their O&M costs and a portion of their capital costs. Obviously, externalities and opportunity costs (if any) were not recovered in tariffs.

What is particularly striking about African water utilities' cost recovery is the apparent notion that some costs are more important than others. In theoretical economics, a producer that cannot recover its variable O&M costs would shut down the business. This practice, however, is not realistic for a public utility that has a continuing obligation to serve and has a very high ratio of fixed to total costs. The majority of African countries report that their stated objective of water utilities is to recover all of their O&M costs. Only Chad reports that tariffs are set without a specified cost-recovery mandate. Two countries—Sudan and Ghana—indicated that there was no

155 For details regarding the scoring criteria, see Banerjee, 24.

156 Ibid, 14.

requirement to recover investment, only *O&M* expenses. For water utilities in developing countries, reaching the goal of recovering full O&M costs is important from the perspective of receiving funds from outside donors (e.g., the World Bank). As discussed in chapter three, an efficient tariff structure involves setting prices that signal the marginal benefits of water use to consumers. Prices should not only encompass financial costs (e.g., O&M, and capital), but also the externalities that the use of water imposes on the economy and environment.

**Equitable Tariffs and Subsidies.** Concerning the issue of equitable tariffs one measure is the extent of cross-subsidies. Many African utilities are responsible for providing wastewater services in addition to water supply. Wastewater charges are either included in the water bill or imposed separately in the form of a fixed or block structure. For the utilities that enforce a block tariff structure, it is possible to compare water and wastewater prices at similar levels of consumption. The study found that for three levels of monthly consumption—four cubic meters, ten cubic meters, and forty cubic meters—the consumers of wastewater services are subsidized by water users.

In terms of interclass subsidies (e.g., residential, commercial, industrial, and government) the effective tariffs of nonresidential consumers can be compared with high-end residential consumption at a hundred cubic meters. Of the forty-five utilities in the study, thirty-seven utilities had the nonresidential consumers pay more on a unit cost basis than the residential consumers. Not only were the absolute unit-cost levels higher for nonresidential consumers, the rate of increase in the tariffs of nonresidential customers were higher as compared to residential consumers.

**Fairness.** The final issue of the study concerned the fairness of connection charges. The costs of connecting to a water utility's distribution network can prove to be a significant barrier to consumers in Africa. Often the metric for evaluating the affordability of water-connection charges is cost as a percentage of per capita gross national income (GNI). On average, the connection charge is 28 percent of per capita GNI. [157]

In the context of this book, the main points regarding the African water utility study are:

1) A widespread belief exists that all costs are not equally important. That is, the bar for cost recovery has been lowered. Often these water utilities attempt to only recover their O&M expenses and not the return of and on capital. In effect, they are saying that the owners of some of the factors of production (e.g., labor) are more important than providers of other factors (e.g., capital).

2) The difference between full cost recovery and O&M costs are made up in the form of subsidies provided by the central government, regional governments, local governments, donors, and others. Little incentive exists to reduce or eliminate the subsidies.

3) Widespread subsidies exist between water and wastewater services, and classes (e.g., residential and commercial).

4) With a fixed charge and inclining block rate structure, poor consumers (the very consumers where financial assistance was intended) often pay higher effective water bills as compared to other consumers.

157 Ibid., 16.

## 5.8 Second-Best Pricing

Another utility pricing approach is the second-best or as it is also called, "theory of the second-best." This approach is reflected in Figure 5.3. Recall from chapter two, in the United States, water utility rates based on cost-of-service pricing using embedded costs are by far the most common method of ratemaking. In chapter two, the concept of embedded (full supply costs) was introduced. The general process of determining rates (tariffs) based on full supply costs was discussed previously.

This theory is concerned with a situation in which certain economic conditions are not met. [158] The principal conclusion of the theory of second-best is: since some of the conditions for efficiency remain unfulfilled, there is no assurance that the reduction in the number of unfulfilled conditions will result in increased welfare. [159] However, several studies have been more positive about implementing marginal-cost pricing. Bonbright cites several studies that downplay the significance of the unfulfilled conditions. For instance, one study concludes that the second-best option is probably close to the first-best option (i.e., marginal costs). Another study points out that the individual regulated sectors, such as water, are very small relative to the whole economy, and therefore the impact is minimal. Finally, a study suggests that since general rules for optimality in the second-best world do not exist and because the direction of distortions are unclear, the price equals marginal cost rule should still apply (i.e., first-best pricing). [160]

## 5.9 Rates Based on Value of Service

Value-of-service (VOS) pricing assumes that a utility's customers have both the ability and willingness to pay higher rates. The mechanics of implementing a system of prices based on value of service is called "differential pricing." Value-of-service pricing, without constraints, maximizes a regulated water utility's operating revenues. The legal precedents for value-of-service pricing are discussed in chapter eight.

### 5.9.1 The Perspectives of Three Well-Respected Regulatory Economists Related to Value-of-Service Pricing

During the last century, arguably some of the most prominent economists involved in public utility issues have been James C. Bonbright, Charles F. Phillips, Jr., and Alfred E. Kahn. These economists are well-respected authorities and have authored utility ratemaking books that have been widely used for decades. The following are summaries on their positions regarding value-of-service pricing.

---

158 The marginal rate of substitution between any two commodities must be the same for any two consumers; the marginal rate of technical substitution between any two inputs must be the same for any pair of producers; and the marginal rate of substitution between any two commodities must be the same as the marginal rate of transformation between these two commodities for any producer.

159 Ibid., 437.

160 Bonbright, Danielsen, and Kamerschen, 433.

### 5.9.1.1 James C. Bonbright

Dr. Bonbright devotes one full chapter in his text *Principles of Public Utility Rates* titled, "Value of Service as an Ancillary Standard." Note the words *ancillary standard.* In particular, *ancillary* suggests something supplemental and not something that should be totally dismissed.

Value-of-service pricing can serve as a ceiling for rates. On this topic, Dr. Bonbright wrote:

> *"Perhaps the most frequent position [taken by writers on public utility rates] is that a reasonable rate is one intermediate between cost of production [referring to marginal costs] as the lower limit and value of service as the upper limit, the precise point being set by practical considerations rather than by any scientific rule of ratemaking."* 161

As noted by Dr. Bonbright in the above quote, utility rates should range between a water utility's short-run marginal costs—SRMC—(i.e., its out-of-pocket or variable costs) at the low end and the value-of-service (i.e., willingness to pay) at the high end. 162 In utility ratemaking, this range is often referred to as the "zone of reasonableness." If a water utility's rates to a customer are above the customer's willingness to pay, the utility will likely lose the customer, have to absorb its contribution to fixed costs, and/or reallocate some of the fixed costs to other customer classes. Basic microeconomics tells us that if a company (in this case a water utility) cannot recover its variable operating costs, the rational choice would be for it to shut down and stop providing service. However, this solution is not an option for a regulated utility. By continuing to provide service, the utility would incur more financial losses. In most cases estimates of marginal costs (both short-run and long-run) and value of service are not included in typical water utility rate cases. However, for business planning purposes and possibly communicating with their customers, a utility should know the amounts of their marginal costs.

A high value of service is sometimes used to justify increasing rates above levels resulting from a fully allocated cost-of-service study. Similarly, when the value of service is low, rates are sometimes set below these levels. On this issue Dr. Bonbright wrote:

> *"Modifying rates in the light of service value to customers need not be considered improper. Rather, this practice may help a utility retain customers whose usage contributes to the recovery of its fixed costs and correspondingly lower rates for all customers."* (emphasis added) 163

Dr. Bonbright also notes that examples of value-of-service pricing exist in all regulated industries. In the telephone industry, companies have adopted a statewide system of rates designed to yield adequate total revenues through the levy of higher charges on subscribers in large cities than on subscribers for comparable service in smaller cities or towns. While both cost and value considerations have been used to support rate levels, the major emphasis has been on value considerations. Dr. Bonbright added:

> *"While telephone ratemaking evolved under the general principle of value-of-service pricing, residential versus industrial pricing practices for telephone (and*

161 Ibid., 125.

162 Colander, 272.

163 Bonbright, Danielsen, and Kamerschen, 127

> *electric) services have incorporated both cost-of-service and value-of-service concepts."* [164]

In the U.S. natural gas industry during the 1970s and 1980s, a common practice was to charge high-volume industrial users higher rates in order to subsidize low-volume residential customers. This form of interclass subsidy is discussed in chapter six. Later, PSCs used the principle of "opportunity cost" to charge large industrial customers a price just below the Btu-equivalent price of the next best alternative fuel, which was generally No. 6 residual fuel oil.

With respect to the natural gas industry, Dr. Bonbright concluded by stating:

> *"Clearly, rate differentials in the natural gas industry have not been completely supported by cost differentials."* [165]

With respect to rate differentials in the U.S. electric utility industry, Dr. Bonbright stated:

> *"Historically, rate differentials in the electric industry have by no means been justified on a cost basis...In some instances in the past, the long-run marginal cost of electricity has been shown to be 5 to 10 times the price being charged. Nor are specific rates, as opposed to rates as a whole, in this industry today entirely based on costs."* [166] (emphasis added)

### 5.9.1.2 Charles F. Phillips, Jr.

In addition to Dr. Bonbright, Dr. Charles F. Phillips, Jr., another well-known economist, has weighed-in on the topic of value-of-service pricing. According to Dr. Phillips, price discrimination (the result of value-of-service pricing) results when a firm sells the same service at rates that are not proportional to costs. Price discrimination can be both avoidable and unavoidable. It is unavoidable in that the cost of providing a particular service (e.g., delivered water to a residential customer) is difficult, if not impossible, to determine accurately. This difficulty occurs because of the numerous ways joint investment and expenses can be allocated to customer classes in a class cost-of-service study. Thus, Dr. Phillips stated:

> *"When the same plant or equipment is used to provide several types of service, there is no one correct way to allocate these costs among the different units of service. Any method of apportionment is subject to dispute. Even if firms tried to base their rates upon costs, a substantial element of judgment is involved."* [167] (emphasis added)

Dr. Phillips claims that price discrimination may be advantageous for two reasons. First, it may result in a fuller utilization of a utility's plant and equipment, and wider consumption of its service. Second, price discrimination may lead to lower prices for all customers.

---

164 Ibid.

165 Ibid., 128.

166 Ibid., 129.

167 Phillips, 438.

### 5.9.1.3 Alfred E. Kahn

Professor Alfred E. Kahn, at one time the chairman of the New York Public Service Commission and chairman of the Civil Aeronautics Board, was a strong believer in economic-based rates, particularly marginal-cost rates. One of his most famous illustrations was from the airline industry. Dr. Kahn argued that when an airplane was fueled and ready for takeoff, the rational pricing behavior was that anyone willing to pay at least the short-run marginal cost—SRMC—(e.g., extra fuel for the airplane, can of soda, pretzels) should not be turned away. This was particularly true of students who were then afforded "student standby rates." Students who typically had limited income and at the same time had significant free time were willing to "camp out" at an airline's gate waiting for an opportunity to get on the next flight. In short, they were willing to sacrifice time for money (with time being abundant but money limited). Thus, the opportunity cost of their time was low. This behavior is a good example of value-of-service pricing using a floor level. Again, using the airline example, people who have an urgent need for the service (e.g., a family emergency) are willing to pay significant sums in order to get on the earliest flight. This exchange between time and money is frequently seen where airlines overbook a flight and then ask volunteers to give up their seats in exchange for various sums of money or services (e.g., $400, paid overnight lodging, service upgrade, and a reservation on another flight).

## 5.9.2 The Implications of Different Value-of-Service Definitions

Critics of value-of-service pricing point to an imprecise definition of value as a major obstacle to its implementation. The term "value" often does not lend itself to quantitative expression as a measure of reasonable rates. (The terms "cost" and "full cost" can also be confusing in that it could represent: (a) long-run or short-run; (b) marginal or embedded; or (c) economic or accounting.) Three alternative definitions of rates have been used to describe the value-of- service standard. These are:

1) The most profitable rate;
2) Rate discrimination in the public interest; and
3) A market-clearing price.

These definitions are discussed below.

### 5.9.2.1 The Most Profitable Rate

In economics the "monopoly price" is used by monopolists to maximize profits by searching for the optimum price and quantity relationship. The monopoly price is higher and the quantities lower as compared to the competitive price and output level. This situation was illustrated in chapter three.

Dr. Phillips claimed that:

> *"The very fact that public utility rates are subject to regulation clearly disqualifies this version of the value-of-service standard as a general criterion of reasonable rates."* [168]

As mentioned previously, regulation is undertaken to keep total earnings reasonable and to keep price discrimination within bounds (i.e., rates should have ceilings and floors).

### 5.9.2.2 Rate Discrimination in the Public Interest

According to Dr. Phillips, public interest theory—regulation is viewed as a substitute for competition and, as such, has the objective of protecting a utility's customers from the potential abuses of a monopoly—is based on the premise that regulators set utility rates to maximize a perceived social welfare function subject to various constraints. One constraint is that a utility has an opportunity to earn a specified profit. This amounts to marginal-cost pricing when social welfare is defined as the sum of consumer's and producer's surplus. [169] [170] As previously discussed, Ramsey pricing is often used to adjust prices such that the utility's revenue requirements is met. In cases where marginal-cost pricing leads to excessive profits, "Ramsey pricing" or the inverse elasticity rule is often used.

As noted previously in this book, most water utilities and their regulators rarely know, or even attempt to know, consumer's and producer's surplus. Furthermore, for a water utility, this method assumes decreasing average costs and pricing at short-run marginal costs would result in a revenue deficiency. Because, in general, the water utility industry faces *increasing* average costs, this definition should also be disqualified.

### 5.9.2.3 Market-Clearing Price

What about using a market-clearing price as a value-of-service standard? Dr. Phillips defines a market-clearing price as "a price just sufficient to secure full but un-rationed use of service in whatever amounts are temporarily available in view of limited plant capacity."[171] The practical definition would result in raising rates for service up to the point at which no demand at these rates would long go unsatisfied. On this topic Dr. Phillips wrote:

> *"For as long as there is an absolute limit to the number of customers who can be supplied, the granting of service to any one customer involves a social cost in the resulting necessity of denying the service to some other customer. What this other customer would pay for the service may be said to reflect the cost of denial."* [172] (emphasis added)

The above definition is similar to the price-determining forces of a perfectly competitive market. Since rate regulation is generally viewed as a substitute for a competitive market, the market-

---

168 Ibid., 132.

169 Hayward, 60–65.

170 The argument that charging rates based on customers' willingness to pay "extracts consumer surplus" may be overstated. This is because the rates consumers pay could be significantly below "full costs."

171 Bonbright, Danielsen, and Kamerschen, 136.

172 Ibid.

clearing standard is the preferred definition. Also, note that this is the principle used in Queensland, Australia (see Table 5.11).

### 5.9.3 The Limitations of Value-of-Service Pricing

Opponents of value-of-service pricing for utilities claim that the concept is too theoretical to be useful. However, for decades, economists have used valuation concepts and methods in the context of pricing environmental goods and services. In addition, the U.S. Water Resources Council has determined that the contingent valuation method (CVM)—defined in Appendix B—is an acceptable method of establishing benefits. Thus, this method can be useful in estimating water utility customers' value of service.

A second limitation of implementing value-of-service pricing is the time and expense a utility would incur conducting a thorough WTP study. Third, as noted previously, critics of value-of-service pricing point to an imprecise definition of value as a major obstacle to its implementation. However, it is puzzling that decisionmakers are reluctant to accept value-of-service concepts because they are considered "speculative." Yet in traditional utility ratemaking, inferring a water utility's cost of equity capital requires judgment since it cannot be directly observed. Similarly, customers' WTP may not be directly observable yet is nevertheless important for utility decision-making.

## 5.10 Reconciling Economic-Based Pricing and Embedded Costs

As mentioned previously, full supply costs used in traditional utility ratemaking are often measured by accounting costs. A practical limitation of applying value-of-service (VOS) pricing (as well as marginal-cost pricing) is reconciling a utility's operating revenues with its revenue requirements. Only by coincidence would the operating revenues generated by economic-based pricing equal a utility's revenue requirements.

In contrast with accounting-based pricing, marginal costs (MC) and marginal benefits (MB) [173] used in economic-based pricing are *not* based on the premise that operating revenues equal costs. Using marginal cost pricing usually requires a method of adjusting rates to meet a utility's revenue requirements. [174]

Welfare economics is a branch of economics, which deals with the principles and criteria of evaluating alternative economic states and policies from the viewpoint of efficiency or social well-being. Welfare economics involves an assessment of the condition of society as a whole and not individuals or groups, (e.g., residential and commercial customers.) [175] As pointed out in chapter three, the use of consumer's surplus (CS) and producer's surplus (PS) is broadly accepted as appropriate for welfare analysis in public utility economics. [176] (See Figure 3.2, producer's and

---

173 A marginal benefit is the added satisfaction above what one has already derived.

174 A common reconciliation method is "Ramsey pricing." For a discussion, *see* Bonbright, 533–42. Another method is equal percentage of marginal cost. This method increases marginal costs in proportion to the revenue differential. For a discussion, see Lesser and Giacchino, 171.

175 For an elementary discussion of welfare economics and water utility pricing, see Hayward, chapter seven.

176 Michael A. Crew and Paul R. Kleindorfer, *The Economics of Public Utility Regulation* (Cambridge, MA: The MIT Press, 1986), 10.

consumer's surplus.) Thus, an identity exists between full costs reflected in Figure 1.3 and full value of service (V) reflected in Figure 4.5. This identity is reflected in equation 5.5.

$$\text{Full costs (FC)} = \text{Value of the market (V)}; \qquad (5.5)$$

The value of the market (established in chapter three) is the sum of consumer's and producer's surplus. This formula is presented in equation 5.6.

$$V = PS + CS \qquad (5.6)$$

Full costs are represented by a water utility's long-run marginal costs (LRMC). Full value is reflected as the market demand curve ($D_m$). The economic efficient price is where the supply and demand curves meet. Another way of saying this is economic efficiency results when the marginal costs (MC) to the utility equal the marginal benefits (MB) to their customers.

Finally, the aggregate subsidy (S) discussed in chapter six can be defined as the difference between full supply costs (FSC) underlying the calculations of the water price (under cost-of-service ratemaking) and full costs (FC). This relationship is summarized in equation 5.7 as:

$$FC - FSC = S \qquad (5.7)$$

If FC equals V in equation 5.5, and V equals PS and CS in equation 5.6, then FC equals the sum of PS and CS in equation 5.8.

$$FC = PS + CS \qquad (5.8)$$

## 5.11 Other Pricing Methods

Because of limited data, budget constraints, or other reasons, water utilities are often constrained in their pricing approaches. Other pricing methods include:

1) Peak-load pricing;

2) Average incremental cost (AIC); and

3) Scarcity pricing.

These approaches are approximations to long-run marginal costs. These methods, instead of estimating marginal costs and demand elasticities, rely on forecasted demand, cost projections, and the utility's capital expansion program. [177] The scarcity pricing approach used in Australia is summarized later in this chapter.

### 5.11.1 Peak-Load Pricing

Usually, moving water through a system requires pumps, which can require a significant amount of energy. Often, the longer the distance water needs to be moved, the more expensive

177 Barkatullah, 102–6.

transporting it becomes. During peak demand periods, more pumping and energy are required. Flattening a water utility's peak demand periods could lower its water supply costs and possibly future capacity additions. A general agreement exists among economists and various other industry experts that designing a water system should be done to enable a water utility to be able to meet its peak demand. Usually, a significant percentage (e.g., 20) is added to the historical peak demand as a reserve margin. Many water utilities, however, do not charge their customers appropriate rates to reflect this reserve margin.

Various studies of water use have consistently shown that residential demand is largely for outdoor uses, which are normally higher in the summer than the winter. Water demand also peaks at various times during the week and a typical day. For instance, for the city of Palo Alto, California, during a typical winter day, water demand peaks between approximately 8:00 and 10:00 AM. [178] Because of this usage pattern during peak hours, economists have developed a rule for pricing capacity. That is, capacity costs should be levied only on utilization at the peak, and none of the costs should be levied on off-peak users. For a water utility with significant variations in seasonal demand, seasonal rates might be appropriate.

### 5.11.2 Average Incremental Cost (AIC)

In 1976 R. J. Saunders and J. J. Warford developed the average incremental cost approach, which reduces price volatility and takes a longer view of costs as compared to PWISC. It considers a water utility's entire planning horizon and averages out any capital investment spikes. Unlike the PWISC approach, the AIC approach takes into account a water utility's entire planning horizon by including all the projected investment costs specified in the utility's long-run capital plan. The AIC approach emphasizes price stability and attempts to balance allocative efficiency with long-term investment signals in a practical manner. The AIC approach averages the price fluctuations and is based on a long-term view, which goes beyond the next planned investment. Analysts using the AIC method criticize the PWISC method because it only looks at the next *major* investment. The PWISC approach also overlooks the changes associated with the increase in output. Stated another way, AIC is the present worth (present value) of the future supply costs divided by the present worth of the incremental usage. The basic methodology for estimating the AIC is summarized as follows:

1) Forecast the relevant expected demand characteristics into the foreseeable future;
2) Estimate the system requirements and augmentations that would be required over time to meet expected demand levels;
3) Estimate the likely cost of these requirements; and
4) Calculate the MCC as the average cost per unit of anticipated demand of the total increment to capacity required during the forecast period. [179]

Appendix D, "Estimates of Long-Run Average and Marginal Costs for Alexandria Water Company (Alexandria, Egypt)" provides a numerical example of long-run average incremental

178 Hyman et al., 230.

179 Marsden, 13.

costs (LRAIC) and long-run average costs (LRAC). The major assumptions in the analysis include the following:

1) A twenty-year period from 2010 through 2030;

2) Total supply augmentation of 800 million cubic meters (i.e., capacity expansion);

3) Total investment over the period of eight million Egyptian pounds (LE8 million); and

4) A discount rate of 10 percent (that was intended to represent the cost of capital to the Government of Egypt);

The conclusion of the study was that Alexandria Water Company's LRAIC was approximately three times higher than its LRAC.

### 5.11.3 Scarcity Pricing in Australia

In August 2008 the Australian Bureau of Agricultural and Resource Economics prepared a report—"Urban Water Management: Optimal Price and Investment Policy Under Climate Variability." [180] The context for the report was an ongoing drought across the country. Australian urban water prices are set by utility regulators on the basis of long-run marginal costs (LRMC). The report noted that a fixed LRMC price does not respond to changes in scarcity levels and will be lower than optimal when storage levels are low, necessitating a rationing of demand through alternative measures such as water restrictions. Scarcity pricing was proposed as an alternative to water restrictions that involve complex rules that govern the use of outdoor water by urban households. The study found that water restrictions are a relatively inefficient method of demand management, as they impose inconvenience costs, generate allocative efficiency losses and require substantial enforcement effort. [181]

A scarcity pricing system would involve adopting a variable price that responds to changes in water scarcity where, for instance, the price varies inversely with storage levels. One of the primary conclusions from the study was:

> *"Scarcity pricing could also assist in supply augmentation decisions. Historically, urban water utilities have made relatively arbitrary judgments on the timing of supply augmentation, often involving the targeting of an 'acceptable level' of reliability as measured by the expected duration of water restrictions. Scarcity pricing would provide a more accurate measure of society's willingness to pay for urban water, which could be directly compared with the costs of supply augmentation."* [182] (emphasis added)

The main focus of the report considered how a scarcity pricing system could potentially operate. The implementation steps involve economic modeling to demonstrate how an urban water scarcity price would typically vary, given a specific set of assumptions over time and in response

---

180 As of May 2011, it is unclear if the scarcity pricing proposal was implemented.

181 Neal Hughes, Ahmed Hafi, Tim Goesch, and Nathan Brownlowe, "Urban Water Management: Optimal Price and Investment Policy under Climate Variability" (Canberra, Australia: Australian Bureau of Agricultural and Resource Economics, 2008), 1–2.

182 Ibid., 2.

to changes in storage levels. The report also involved considering a range of practical implementation issues, including the possibility that scarcity pricing could be implemented using a system of stages similar to that used for water restrictions.

# CHAPTER SIX

# SUBSIDIES IN THE WATER UTILITY INDUSTRY

## 6.1 Overview

Chapter five introduced the concept that subsidies often result when differences exist between full costs and supply costs. Government authorized water tariffs may (and often do) include prices below full costs. If this is the case, an implicit subsidy from producers to consumers exists. Price theory discussed in chapter three holds that a price below the equilibrium level will eventually result in a lower quantity of output and losses in producer's surplus. As was discussed in chapter three, a lower amount of producer's surplus results in a reduction in value of the market. A price ceiling below full costs is a combination implicit tax on suppliers and implicit subsidy to consumers of the same amount.

This chapter begins by analyzing the sources of revenues available to water utilities. Next, subsidies and social policy goals are discussed. Third, types of subsidies found in the water utility industry are identified and discussed. Fourth, four case studies related to subsidies in the water utility industry are presented. These are:

1) Current prices compared to full-cost pricing in college dormitories;

2) A study related to cross-subsidies in the Scottish water industry;

3) Subsidies in Chile's public utilities; and

4) The World Bank's analysis of water utility subsidies.

Chapter seven discusses a topic related to subsidies—economic analyses related to water projects and the differences in practices between financial and economic analysis. Finally, the pros and cons of subsidies in the water utility industry are discussed.

## 6.2 Sources of Revenue for Water Utilities

Subsidies can take the form of transfers among and between customers in different rate classes, within rate classes, between services (e.g., water and wastewater) and generations, or externally from various levels of government. One source of revenue for a water utility is from fees other than water tariffs and water-related charges. For example, a combination utility supplying water and wastewater services may transfer revenues from one service to the other. In the United States, government utilities are notorious for using revenues from utilities as a temporary source of funds for other uses. On the other hand, funds from other government sources may be available to pay for exceptional expenses such as an increase in purchased water costs from the utility's supplier.

General taxation and transfers account for revenues from government sources. These could be in the form of grants for: (a) new investment; (b) coverage of operational deficits; or (c) the transfer of buildings and equipment produced by an outside entity (usually the government). Indirect subsidies include: (a) low-interest loans; and (b) underpricing commodities and services by the public sector. For example, in developing countries it is common for the central government to supplement employee salaries through direct gifts of housing, food, and other commodities. A final source of revenue is non-operating revenue. This revenue could result from buying and/or selling securities.

Related to the topic of revenue sources is the idea of decoupling water utility sales and profits. This concept has been applied with certain energy utilities. When policymakers encourage (and in some cases mandate) water conservation measures, a lower level of sales can result in lower profits (and in some cases financial losses) for a water utility. In effect, a water utility could be penalized for reaching goals (e.g., conserving water) established by the policymakers. In chapter one, the concept was put forward that a water utility actually provides at least two distinct services. First, it acquires and treats water that meets specific water quality specifications. Second, it delivers the water to its customers—also known as "service on demand." An analogy to delivery services provided by water utilities is overnight shipping services such as FedEx and UPS. These companies are in the business of providing delivery services to their customers.

One option to the above problem (i.e., lower profits as the result of conservation) is to revise water tariffs such that most (if not all) of a water utility's fixed costs are obtained through fixed charges such as customer charges or demand charges (also known as readiness-to-serve charges). Appendix E provides examples of these charges. Such a shift in pricing coupled with performance criteria could reward or penalize a utility based on its delivery services to its customers (e.g., reliability of service, frequency and duration of outages, and customer service response time to customer inquiries). In some developing countries, regulators use a performance scorecard to grade a water utility's performance. The scorecard uses a variety of financial and operating criteria.

## 6.3 Subsidies and Social Policy Goals

Utility ratemaking is often described as part art and science. Tariffs where the rates and charges meet economic efficiency standards are a major theme of this book. However, in the United States, the courts have upheld utility regulators' decisions (e.g., rate levels) where social policy goals are also important. Social objectives were briefly discussed in chapter five, and chapter seven provides several examples. In the United States, utility regulators have often created special tariffs for low-income and elderly customers. Often, they are called "lifeline rates" and are a form of intraclass (and possibly interclass) subsidy. The rationale for these rates is that a certain quantity of water is necessary for life. (The World Health Organization estimates that twenty-five liters per day are necessary for a person to sustain life.) Because of this, regulators often believe that a certain quantity should be provided at rates that are "affordable" even if the rate is below the utility's average or marginal costs. From a purely economic perspective, and setting aside social policy concerns, lifeline rates do not make sense. By their very definition, these rates subsidize one or more groups of customers while other customers (or the utility) make up the difference. Most important, subsidies are inefficient because they distort consumption decisions. In addition, providing subsidies to some customers violates an important principle of ratemaking—having the customers that cause a utility to incur costs pay for them. An alternative to lifeline rates is a "water stamp" program similar to the federal government's food stamp program. Some economists have recommended this as a policy proposal. [183]

### 6.3.1 Tariff Subsidies in Chongquig, China

In some cases, the results of lifeline rates are inconsistent with the initial policy goals. For example, in Chongquig, China, the original intention of the government was to maintain the water tariff at a low level (through financial subsidy) to decrease living costs for low-income groups. However, an investigation of the subsidy disclosed an embarrassing finding—low income groups who consumed the most water were the primary beneficiaries.[184]

## 6.4 Types of Subsidies in the Water Utility Industry

As previously stated, utility economic regulation is intended to be a substitute for competition. Nevertheless, subsidies (intended and unintended) are often embedded in water utility rates. Table 6.1 reflects subsidies [185] in the water utility industry.

---

183 See Carriker and Dillman, 34.

184 Zhou Linjun, "Reform of Water Tariffs in Chongqing: A Case Study Review," World Bank Analytical and Advisory Assistance Program (Washington, DC: The World Bank, n.d.), 1.

185 The subsidies were based, in part, on a Water Policy Regulatory Reform (WPRR) project in Egypt and funded by the United States Agency for International Development (USAID). Task Order No. EPP-I-00-04-00020-00, January 2011.

**Table 6.1**
**Subsidies in the Water Utility Industry**

| No. | Description |
|---|---|
| 1 | Interclass (e.g., residential and commercial) |
| 2 | Intraclass (e.g., first and third blocks of a multiblock rate structure; e.g., lifeline rates) |
| 3 | Intergenerational |
| 4 | Multiservice (e.g., water and wastewater) |
| 5 | Intercompany (if part of a holding company structure) |
| 6 | Direct government—cash or grants to utilities. (This is usually limited to municipal utilities or utilities in developing countries.) |
| 7 | Indirect government (e.g., low-interest rate loans, deferred income taxes) |
| 8 | Regions and states within a utility's service territory |
| 9 | Seasonal pricing (e.g., winter and summer rates) |
| 10 | Time of day (if measurable or can be estimated) |
| 11 | Direct government—cash to specific customers (e.g., low income) |
| 12 | Utility/nonutility operations (i.e., cross-subsidization) |
| 13 | Lost income tax revenue to the government |
| 14 | Surcharge for funding various programs (e.g., low-income assistance) 186 |
| 15 | Utility-customer (i.e., profits above or below normal levels) |
| 16 | Certain conservation programs (e.g., costs and benefits) |
| 17 | Uncollectable revenues (bills) |
| 18 | Employment objectives (e.g., customers pay higher rates as the result of the government's objective to employ people) |

Source: Author's construct.

Policymakers are often aware that subsidies may exist. Typically, regulators are primarily concerned with Nos. 1, 2, 4, 5, 8, 9, 12, 14, and 15. However, in their rate orders, regulators rarely quantify the amounts of the subsidies. In addition, when they do address subsidies, they rarely mention their long-run policies related to them (e.g., continuation of the subsidy). Finally, once a subsidy is allowed by policymakers, they tend to remain in effect indefinitely. The federal government's treatment of water subsidies for agriculture is a prime example.

Given the potential subsidies in the water utility industry, how do regulators protect the public interest with respect to the following issues?

1) Ensuring a water utility's infrastructure enables a city, state, or region, to have long-term economic growth. This issue is generally described as an inter-generational subsidy (No. 3). (Recall the example from the City of Escondido, California.);

2) Providing fairness to all members of society—utility customers, utility, and other third parties. (Does fairness result when subsidies exist?); and

186 An example of this is San Jose Water Company's Water Rate Assistance Program for residential, low-income households. See www.sjc.com.

3) Identifying, justifying, quantifying, and possibly eliminating subsidies. (It is not reasonable for regulators to authorize a subsidy without knowing the amount.)

If policymakers are determined to remove subsidies in water rates, creating a "plain vanilla" water utility is one option. A plain vanilla water utility does not sell other products or services, operates in one jurisdiction, and is not part of a holding company structure. In such a case, subsidy Nos. 4, 5, 6, 11, 12, 13 would no longer be applicable. In addition, if a utility provides service with little if any variation in seasonal use, geographical terrain, or time of day use, subsidy Nos. 8, 9, and 10 would not be applicable. Next, if utility regulators are not constrained by other forces (e.g., state legislation that mandates various conservation programs, surcharges, and low-interest rate loans) subsidy Nos. 7, 11, 14, and 16 would no longer be applicable. Finally, if regulation has allowed managers of the utility to maintain or increase the value of the company or enterprise, intergenerational subsidies would not be an issue. Common subsidies in the water sector are discussed in more detail below.

### 6.4.1 Intergenerational Subsidies

Water utilities are capital-intensive companies with long-lived assets such as pipelines and treatment plants. It would not be fair to recover from today's customers all of the costs of construction (for instance, a new water treatment plant with a forty-year expected life), since that plant is expected to provide benefits to future customers as well. At the same time, the utility's current customers should contribute some amount toward recovering construction costs, as well as toward variable operating costs associated with the water treatment plant. A unique method does not exist for allocating common costs over time to ensure either efficient or equitable treatment of current and future customers. Therefore, utility regulators use their judgment to allocate these costs. The primary ratemaking approach is to recover the costs over the accounting life of the asset. What is clear is that currently the quality of the infrastructure for the average U.S. water utility is poor (i.e., given a grade of D− by the American Society of Civil Engineers). In addition, the cost of replacing a water utility's assets is generally much more expensive than their historical costs reflected on their balance sheet. Thus, for many utilities it is almost certain that an intergenerational subsidy exists in the water utility industry (i.e., current and new customers will pay much higher rates for a level of service as compared to previous customers).

### 6.4.2 Current Prices Compared to Full-Cost Pricing in College Dormitories

Failing to incorporate full costs in water prices can have long-term economic consequences. In a 2006 study, 187 Angela Arpke and Kelly Strong compared the lifecycle cost for a typical college dormitory using subsidized versus full-cost water pricing. The specific topics in the study having public policy implications were:

1) Operating subsidies for municipal water production and treatment;

2) Capital subsidies in the form of infrastructure grants to municipal water districts from states and the federal government;

3) Deferred recapitalization and maintenance; and

187 Angela Arpke and Kelly Strong, "A Comparison of life-cycle cost analysis for a typical college dormitory using subsidized versus full-cost pricing of water," *Ecological Economics*, 58, 1 (June 2006): 66–78.

4) Technology improvements required by more stringent water quality standards.

The study analyzed four cities in the United States and factored market imperfections into the consumer prices (as of 2002) of water to determine the full-cost price. Their analysis evaluated three design options, which included various technologies. The results are reflected in Table 6.2. Note that their definition of full costs only includes capital and O&M expenses. That is, opportunity costs and externalities were excluded from their analysis of full costs. In the case of Houghton, Michigan, the current consumer price was approximately one-half of the price based on full costs. The authors concluded that the four topics mentioned above created market imperfections that artificially altered the price of water.

**Table 6.2**
**Full-Cost Price of Water in College Dormitories**

| Municipality | Current Consumer Price | Current Capital Subsidy | Current Operating Subsidy | Infrastructure Recapitalization and Maintenance | Treatment Technology Costs | Prices Based on Full Costs |
|---|---|---|---|---|---|---|
| | Cents/gal. | Cents/gal. | Cents/gal. | Cents/gal. | Cents/gal. | Cents/gal |
| Houghton, MI | .860 | .56 | .000 | .222 | .004 | 1.646 |
| Ames, IA | .360 | .75 | .010 | .222 | .004 | .671 |
| Boulder, CO | .210 | .03 | .055 | .222 | .004 | .521 |
| Newark, NJ | .425 | .03 | .000 | .222 | .004 | .681 |

Source: Angela Arpke and Kelly Strong, "A Comparison of Life-Cycle Cost Analyses for a Typical College Dormitory Using Subsidized Versus Full-Cost Pricing of Water," *Ecological Economics*, 58, 1 (June 2006), 71.

By far the largest components in the analysis were the capital subsidy and the deferred infrastructure recapitalization and maintenance. 188 By failing to include the cost of maintaining and replacing the infrastructure required to produce, distribute, collect, and treat water, the municipalities shifted the cost from present customers to future customers. This action is a form of intergenerational subsidy and discussed previously. The authors of the study found that water users who were "consuming" the infrastructure will not be required to pay for it; thus, deferring those costs to unspecified future users. Therefore, this policy decision introduces a market imperfection into the current price of water. The authors also concluded that market imperfections created by public policy tend to change the results of lifecycle cost analyses for design solutions.

### 6.4.3 Multiservice, Intercompany, and Utility/Nonutility Subsidies

A common characteristic of a multi-service utility (e.g., water and wastewater), multi-business structure (e.g., operating utilities owned by a holding company), and utility/nonutility operations (e.g., water and real estate) is that common or joint costs need to be allocated between or among

188 This amount was estimated by adding the total U.S. EPA estimated Clean Water and Drinking Water Infrastructure Cost Analysis for 2002 ($26 billion) and dividing by the total volume of water treated annually in the United States (44 billion cubic meters).

the operations. For example, an office building is used for both water utility and nonutility operations. A second example is allocating labor costs among these entities. Frequently the allocation factors used to distribute costs among entities are, at best, approximations of the causation for the costs. A common principle in ratemaking is customers, subsidiaries, or other entities that cause the utility to make an investment or incur an expense should pay for them.

A common approach used to prevent cross-subsidies between regulated and nonregulated subsidiaries is called "ring-fencing." The intent of ring-fencing is designed to allocate costs fairly between regulated and non-regulated operations. A number of ring-fencing approaches exist. Most approaches establish clear guidelines for firm behavior, coupled with strict accounting overview. However, the effectiveness of ring-fencing remains questionable.

### 6.4.4 Interclass Subsidies

In practice, for a "plain vanilla" water utility, regulators generally focus on possible inter-class subsidies. Unless evidence exists that supports one customer class is more risky than other classes, customer classes should provide an equal rate of return on rate base. In a water utility rate filing, an exhibit often exists showing a class's rate of return before the tariff adjustment and a class's rates of return after the rate adjustment. Frequently, the residential class provides a rate of return lower than the utility's average. If this exists, one or more rate classes are subsidizing the residential class. Often interclass subsidies come about either intentionally or as the result of unjustifiable allocation methodologies associated with common plant and expenses.

Using the design basis, common costs are allocated to customer classes on the basis of engineering design criteria. The focus of the design basis is on engineering and economics in contrast with the functional basis where the focus is primarily accounting. The justification for this approach is that utilities predominately incur capital costs, operating expenses, and provide services to customers generally on the same basis as they were designed. Two general cost allocation methods exist—peak responsibility (also called coincident peak) and nonpeak responsibility. From cost causation and economic theory perspectives, the peak responsibility method is preferred. If certain common plant and expenses are allocated using the nonpeak method, class subsidies may result.

### 6.4.5 Subsidies for Conservation Programs

In some states, regulators require utilities to develop conservation programs with little or no economic analysis. (The optimum analysis would be comparing the net present value of programs' costs and benefits.) In some cases, all conservation measures are authorized until the average cost of the program equals the forecasted avoided costs. As was discussed in chapter three, this policy violates basic economic principles.

### 6.4.6 Subsidies in the Scottish Water Industry

With the widespread belief that subsidies existed in the water industry, in 2005 the Scottish government initiated a reform of economic regulation. One of the questions related to reform was: "If it is established that there are significant cross subsidies between consumer groups, should these be retained, or withdrawn gradually over time?" [189] Given this question, the Scottish government commissioned an empirical analysis of cross-subsidies between different customer groups served by Scottish Water. (Scottish Water operates as a multiproduct business; that is, it provides water and processes wastewater). The study was labeled "Analysis of Whether there are Significant Cross-Subsidies Between the Different Customer Groups Served by Scottish Water." The data used in the analysis came from Scottish Water's 2003–2004 Annual Return to the Water Industry Commissioner. The results of the study were published in February 2005.

Common costs were allocated to two groups (i.e., customer classes): households and non-households. The operating costs of wholesale water supply functions were allocated to customer groups on the basis of relative output shares (e.g., water quantity), and capital costs were allocated where possible on the basis of relative capacity shares.

The Scottish study determined that to measure the amount of subsidies three cost-allocation approaches could be used. These approaches are:

1) Stand-alone cost (SAC);
2) Incremental cost (IC); and
3) Fully distributed cost (FDC).

The stand-alone cost of any service or group of services of an enterprise is the cost of providing that service or group of services by themselves, without any other service provided by the enterprise. The IC method is the additional cost of providing that service or group of services over and above the cost of providing all remaining services. Fully distributed costs (FDC) and their limitations are discussed throughout this book. In the study, the FDC method was selected, and the SAC and IC approaches were rejected primarily as the result of poor or inadequate information. If the necessary information were available the IC approach would be preferred.

The results of the study showed a 6.8 percent subsidy from sewerage customers to water customers; and a 13.6 percent subsidy from non-households to households. [190] While the results (i.e., the direction, and amount of the subsidies) were not particularly surprising, what was noteworthy is the Scottish government's concern for the issue and its commitment to unwind part of the nondomestic to domestic cross-subsidy.

### 6.4.7 Subsidies in Chile's Public Utilities [191]

In the 1980s, the Chilean national government began a process of privatizing publicly-owned utilities including water and wastewater. In 1988, a new regulatory framework was set up for the water sector closely matching the electric sector. The government's long-run goal was to comply with the World Health Organization's (WHO) recommendation that families should not spend more than five percent of their income on water and sanitation services. As of 2000, the national average of the after-subsidy bill for a consumption of 15 cubic meters amounted to 5.5 percent of the average income earned by a family in the tenth decile; however, this figure varies widely

189 John W. Sawkins and Scott Reid, "The Measurement and Regulation of Cross Subsidy: The Case of the Scottish Water Industry," Utility Policy, 15, 1 (2007): 2.

190 Sawkins and Reid, 11.

191 The following case study was based on Pablo Serra, "Subsidies in Chilean Public Utilities," Policy Research Working Paper No. 2445, (Washington, DC: The World Bank, 2000).

across regions. To be eligible for the direct subsidy, potential beneficiaries had to apply for it by filling out a socioeconomic evaluation form. Filling out the form was necessary unless they had already done this for other purposes. In some cases, it was necessary for the water utility to make applications on behalf of their customers.

Part of the country's utility reform effort was to introduce cost-reflecting pricing rules. Pricing zones with relatively homogeneous costs were created. The new rate-setting schemes had two objectives: (a) allow firms to self-finance (i.e., be a going concern); and (b) encourage them to be efficient with rates based on the long-run marginal costs of a *simulated (hypothetical)* firm. The new regulatory framework meant raising charges when they did not cover the costs (i.e., implementing cost-reflective rates) of providing the service; or rebalancing them when cross subsidies existed. In Chile, utility charges consist of a monthly standing charge (primarily reflecting meter reading and billing) and a variable rate. (The variable rate changes depending on peak or off-peak periods.) Water utility rates are reviewed every five years and are adjusted in the interim period with an inflation index relevant to the sector.

The main reason for introducing cost-reflective rates was to eliminate economic inefficiencies. Chapter three argued that from a theoretical point of view, the price should reflect the marginal cost of providing service. As is common in developing countries, water rates were too low and in many cases did not allow the water utilities to recover their operation and maintenance expenses. For the period 1990 to 1994, real prices increased by 90 percent; in some rural areas they increased 500 percent. Regulatory reform made it possible to introduce an explicit consumption subsidy which targets the poorest 20 percent of the population and subsidizes the first 15 cubic meters of monthly consumption by between 40 percent and 85 percent.

As of 2000, cross-subsidies have been virtually eliminated and existing subsidies are funded from the national budget. The Chilean experience shows that it is possible to design direct subsidies, such as for drinking water, at a relatively low cost to the national government. One of the main conclusions of the study was:

> *"Chile's experience also shows that it is possible to use subsidies that do not distort people's behavior—by making sure that they perceive the marginal cost of providing the service."* 192

A second lesson from the Chilean experience shows that it is possible to design direct subsidies for water utility service at a relatively small cost to the state. A third lesson is that it is possible to design subsidies that do not cause deadweight losses (described in chapter three) by making sure beneficiaries perceive the marginal cost of providing the service. 193

### 6.4.8 The World Bank's Analysis of Water Utility Subsidies

Subsidies for water utility customers are popular among policymakers and the general public, yet despite persistent belief that subsidies favor the poor, a World Bank study: "Who Benefits from Water Utility Subsidies?" shows that they actually tend to benefit the middle class and the more affluent classes. 194 This conclusion was based on a sample of 32 programs from 13 water

192 Serra, p. i.

193 Ibid., p. 43.

194 World Bank press release No. 2006/317/ESSD, "World Bank Report: Water Utility Subsidies Benefit the 'Haves' , Not 'The Have Nots,' March 18, 2006.

utilities. Most of the programs involve quantity-based subsidies. The World Bank report identified two broad categories of explicit subsidies: (a) consumption or quantity-based subsidies reduce the charge for consuming water service; and (b) connection subsidies are a one-time reduction in connection charges.

The study used a survey of tariff structures in Latin America, Africa, and Asia. It found that roughly three-quarters of utilities include some form of quantity-based consumption subsidy. Consumption subsidies are available only to those households connected to the network which means that many poor households are often excluded from subsidy programs.

The study found that quantity-targeted utility subsidies perform poorly for the following reasons:

1) Poor households are less likely than other households to be connected to the water network. Households that lack access to utility service are unable to benefit from any consumption subsidy.

2) Differences in consumption between the poor and better off households are less than they are often assumed to be.

3) Even in the cases when the poor do consume less than more affluent households, various common features of tariff structures often fall heaviest on those who consume the least. Fixed charges mean that households that consume very small quantities may face a much higher unit price than larger consumers. Moreover, failure to apply full cost recovery tariffs to households consuming at higher levels means that even large consumers benefit from subsidization to a substantial degree.

The study concluded by identifying other measures that may be more promising than the current measures of subsidies. These measures include:

1) Reducing a utility's cost of service through efficiencies.

2) Elimination of minimum consumption requirements and fixed charges.

3) Removing legal barriers (e.g., restrictions that use inappropriate high-cost technologies) can work against the expansion of services to the poor.

4) To the extent they can be more accurately targeted to the poor, other measures of social protection may achieve redistributive goals better than utility subsidies.

A separate cross-country study of water utility subsidies by the World Bank found that consumption-based subsidies—prevalent in 80 percent of the sample—were starkly regressive in poor households, and they captured only half as much value of the subsidy as they would if the subsidies were distributed randomly. [195]

In the U.S. and other developed countries connection to the water network is generally not a significant issue. Therefore, if water utility regulators want to implement welfare redistribution through rates they should generally focus on consumption subsidies; and in particular, the amount of the fixed charge, minimum quantity requirements, and rate structure.

---

195 Joyce Meng, 2008, p. 1.

## 6.5 Pros and Cons of Subsidies in the Water Utility Industry

The following is a list of arguments for and against subsidies in the water utility industry. Some of the arguments are more applicable to water utilities in developing countries as compared to water utilities in the U.S. and other developed countries.

### 6.5.1 Arguments Against Subsidies

The following are the primary *economic* arguments (not necessarily listed in order of importance) against subsidies in the water utility industry and in favor of implementing full-cost pricing.

1) As discussed above, consumption-based subsidies have not benefited the intended recipients.

2) Low-priced water incentivizes excessive consumption. Since the supply of water is random, subsidized water prevents flexibility in adjusting prices upwards to temper demand during dry periods and droughts. This is particularly important in arid or desert regions. When natural sources of water supplies require non-price rationing, overall efficiency is reduced.

3) Full-cost pricing of water increases the supply of water and allows for the market to clear. As a corollary to the above argument, higher water prices incentivize the reduction of water losses and more efficient operations. With widespread subsidies, supply and demand may not necessarily clear leading to shortages in the short and/or long run.

4) Economic pricing of water facilitates the re-allocation of water from sectors of lower value-added (e.g., agriculture) to sectors of higher value-added, such as urban or industrial use. Often subsidies prop up irrigation uses that create net economic losses—in other words, the value of crops produced is substantially below the cost of the inputs when calculated with the full cost of water. Since the economic value of water differs across sectors in which urban water use has a substantially larger return than agricultural use, full-cost pricing optimizes the patterns of water consumption to support activities of higher productivity.

5) In some cases, subsidies are regressive against the poor.

6) Full-cost pricing of water promotes investment in infrastructure and expands network access, thus benefitting the poor and increasing equity. Even if the government owns and operates the water utility, limited fiscal resources and inability to break-even reduces long-term investment in water infrastructure. By allowing the price of water to reflect its full cost, the water utility would generate enough profit to invest in assets. Likewise, a water utility could re-invest its profits in more efficient production and distribution of water that not only decreases the marginal cost of water, but promotes better water quality.

7) As mentioned previously in this chapter, a water utility could have a tangled web of subsidies which could be interrelated and difficult to quantity.

8) Once a subsidy is in place it is seldom reviewed by decisionmakers; thus, a subsidy could (and often does) remain indefinitely.

### 6.5.2 Arguments in Favor of Subsidies

The following are the primary *economic* arguments in favor of subsidies in the water utility industry and *not* implementing full-cost pricing.

1) By increasing access to clean water, subsidies reduce the incidence of disease, thus improving public health and potentially generating net government savings. Subsidies could be a less expensive alternative to widespread medical expenses. From a total societal perspective, universal access to clean water moderates the risk of epidemics, which often propagate through contaminated water. This argument is clearly more applicable to water utilities in developing countries.

2) In certain areas where consumers have individual water wells, cheap and available water reduces the likelihood of depleting groundwater as a substitute good, potentially reducing environmental externalities. Excessive overdraft may permanently damage the water table, causing problems such as saltwater intrusion, subsidence, and land degradation, while harming river, lake, and wetland ecosystems that depend on groundwater. Similar to the argument presented above, this argument is more applicable in developing countries.

3) In affluent industrial countries such as the U.S., the public may demand that all of its citizens should have access to a minimum quantity of clean water regardless of ability and/or willingness to pay for it. (Note that this argument has nothing to do with economic efficiency; it is primarily a normative economic argument—i.e., what should be.)

4) To the extent that subsidies exist in other network industries, focusing exclusively on the water utility might appear to be unfair and illogical.

5) By allowing subsidies (primarily for low-income domestic customers) people could spend less time fetching water and spend that time in more productive ways. This is an argument primarily applicable to utilities in developing countries.

6) Universal access to water supplied by a water utility is necessary for economic growth. If a water utility imposes a fixed charge, access fee, or minimum bill, low-income customers could spend a significantly higher percentage of household income for water service as compared to more affluent domestic customers.

As noted above, at least three of the arguments in favor of subsidies are primarily applicable in developing countries.

# *CHAPTER SEVEN*

# ECONOMIC ANALYSIS IN THE WATER UTILITY INDUSTRY

## 7.1 Overview

Economic analysis is a term used to refer to the evaluation of social (as contrasted with private) profitability of alternative investments or programs. The terms *social* and *economic* may be used interchangeably. However, some analysts limit *economic profitability* to economic efficiency or net national income gains, while social profitability is used to refer to analysis that incorporates social considerations other than economic efficiency, such as income distribution. *In economic analysis, benefits and costs are valued in terms of real WTP or opportunity costs.* Subsidies, certain taxes, and other income transfer policies are not counted in economic analysis.

In the water utility industry, business planners, investors, and government entities generally use several complementary metrics to evaluate an investment or to choose among a set of investment options. 196 These metrics include:

1) Net present value (NPV);

2) Cost–benefit analysis (CBA);

3) Cost-effectiveness analysis (CEA);

4) Internal rate of return (IRR);

196 Other economic measures include total life-cycle cost, levelized cost, modified internal rate of return, discounted payback period, and savings-to-investment ratio.

5) Simple payback period (SPB); and

6) Consumer's surplus.

In terms of investment features in the utility industry, NPV, CBA, and SPB are recommended and commonly used. [197] The consumer's surplus method is a powerful tool; however, it is not used frequently. (Chapter three discusses the consumer's surplus method.)

**Cost–benefit analysis** involves the comparison of benefits and costs in decision making. Dollar values are assigned to benefits and costs in most cost–benefit analyses. Economic analysis answers questions such as:

1) Is the value of all the benefits of a project (or service) greater than the value of all the costs?

2) How does the cost of (or values generated by) one option (e.g., to supply a given amount of water) compare to the cost (or value) of other options?

Within the context of economic analysis is the economic decision rule for both individuals, businesses, and public entities. This rule states that if the marginal benefits of doing something exceed the marginal costs, do it. Alternatively, if the marginal costs of doing something exceed the marginal benefits, do not do it. To economists, investments that have already occurred are considered "sunk costs" and not relevent in making future decisions. In economic analysis, decisions are said to be made "at the margin."

In the context of water, two methods exist to estimate benefits. These are:

1) Estimate the market value of a product that results from using water (e.g., an agricultural crop); and

2) Estimate the value as the cost of the next least expensive alternative to providing the water or water service (e.g., the cost to a utility of purchased water in comparison to the cost of pumping water from a well).

Economic analysis can also be used to determine the allocation of costs and funding responsibility on an equitable basis, by identifying the proportion of total project benefits and costs a stakeholder is expected to receive (i.e., it can help identify who receives the benefits and who should bear the costs).

The use of economic analysis is embedded in Dr. Bonbright's criteria for a sound rate structure and was discussed in chapter five. For instance, the phrase "discouraging wasteful use" (criterion No. 4) as it pertains to rates suggests that a customer's marginal benefit of using the water is compared to the marginal costs. A second example is criterion No. 5 and the phrase "reflection of all of the present and future private and social costs and benefits." This phrase is clear on its face that water rates involve a form of cost–benefit analysis given a time dimension (e.g., present and future).

---

197 Walter Short, Daniel J. Packey, and Thoma Holt, *A Manual for the Economic Evaluation of Energy Efficiency and Renewable Energy Technologies*, for the National Renewable Energy Laboratory, U.S. Department of Energy (Honolulu, HI: University Press of the Pacific, 2005), 36.

Another related phrase used in economic analysis is cost-effective analysis. This is generally defined as "among alternatives, the one whose benefit, or payoff divided by its cost is the highest." [198]

**World Bank Study.** In 1992, the World Bank critiqued the methods of economic analysis for twenty-one Bank-approved water projects. [199] The study found four different approaches used in the economic analysis of projects. The methods were chosen, in part, based on the availability and accuracy of the data available for the analysis. These approaches and the number of studies were:

1) Only the least-cost solution was identified (i.e., cost-effectiveness analysis)—one study;
2) A financial internal rate of return (IRR) was calculated and briefly mentioned other non-quantifiable benefits—fourteen studies;
3) A financial IRR and an estimate of the consumer's surplus—three studies; and
4) An independent economic analysis without relying on the projected financial revenue stream—one study.

In conclusion, the World Bank's most rigorous analysis involves economic concepts of water projects.

### 7.1.1 Risk and Uncertainty in Economic Analysis

Economic analysis should incorporate measures of risk and uncertainty. A general definition of risk is the uncertainty associated with a key value criterion. Uncertainty is often, but not always, associated with variables that will be revealed at a later time, such as the outcome of an experiment of next year's oil price. An illustration of risk is the uncertainty in the net present value (NPV) of a project. Uncertainty refers to the analyst's state of information about a variable or parameter of interest, specifically when the quantity cannot be known perfectly. The state of the art in measurement is not sufficiently advanced to produce exact measures of value for many kinds and environmental and resource changes. The simplest approach is to base the calculations of benefits and costs on the expected values of the uncertain parameters and to base decisions on these expected values. A more formal approach is based on viewing probabilities as statements about the degree of confidence held about the occurrence of a possible event. The approach involves assigning probabilities to all of the values produced by the available estimates, where a higher probability reflects a greater degree of confidence in that estimate. Once the probabilities have been assigned, various statistical calculations can be performed. For example, the expected value of the parameter in question (the mean of its probability distribution) can be calculated and used for cost–benefit calculations. The variance of the distribution can be used to determine confidence intervals on the value to be used, thus preserving for policymakers information on the uncertainties about values. When multiple uncertainties exist, Monte Carlo methods can be used to draw from the assumed distributions to generate probability distributions of outcomes.

198 Hayward, 190.

199 Laszio Lovei, "An Approach to the Economic Analysis of Water Supply Projects" (Washington, DC: The World Bank, 1992), 1.

Later in this chapter, the value of a water utility concession is estimated. For both the social NPV and the financial NPV, an expected value is estimated along with probability distributions related to those estimates. Thus, the study incorporates risk and uncertainty.

## 7.2 The Importance of Economic Analysis in Utility Ratemaking

With various areas in the United States facing droughts and water "shortages" as well as vast future costs for water utility infrastructure replacement (and possibly growth) required, policymakers can no longer afford to get the prices wrong. If they do, a significant loss in economic welfare may result. (The definition of shortages may be different from the layperson's definition. A shortage is a situation in which more of a commodity is demanded in the market than is being supplied *at the going price*.) One key measure of economic efficiency is the concept of economic welfare. Economists argue that policymakers should strive to maximize total consumer's and producer's surplus. Failure to get the prices right results in lost welfare for society.

### 7.2.1 Economic Versus Financial Analysis

Valuing water and delivery services using economic analysis can be very different from business valuation (sometimes called "appraisal"), which is used in financial analysis. Various organizations such as the National Association of Certified Valuation Analysts (NACVA) teach techniques, methods, and approaches for valuing businesses. Both business valuation and utility ratemaking account for the interests of two parties—the buyers (consumers) and the sellers (utilities). Valuing water and water utility services can be trickier when the general public (a third party) is affected (e.g., incorporating externalities). This is because utility economic regulation also represents the interests of society at large and may not be a direct (or current) water user. Recall that water is both a public and private good. For instance, under California law, ownership of water is separate from the use of water. Water is the public property of the people of California and is considered a public resource. Therefore, policymakers in California have a continuing duty to protect the public under the Public Trust Doctrine. 200

The objective of economic analysis is to determine if a project represents the best use of resources over the analysis period. Economic analysis should answer questions such as:

1) Should the project be built?
2) Should the project be built now?
3) Should it be built to a different configuration or size?
4) Will the project have a net positive social value for society irrespective of to whom the costs and benefits accrue?

In contrast to economic analysis, financial analysis is from the perspective of the private individual or firm affected by a project (which can be producers, consumers, or both). The purpose of financial analysis is to ascertain the appeal of a project to its intended beneficiaries.

---

200 *Layperson's Guide to Water Marketing* (Sacramento, CA: Water Education Foundation, 2005), 6.

Profitability is calculated in terms of actual prices received or paid, and therefore reflects *income transfer program (taxes or subsidies). Thus, utility rates are usually based on financial analysis and not economic analysis.*

The objective of financial analysis is to determine financial feasibility (i.e., whether someone is willing to pay for a project and has the capability to raise the necessary capital). Financial analysis answers questions such as:

1) Who benefits from a project?

2) Who will repay the project costs, and are they able to meet repayment obligations?

3) Will the beneficiaries be financially better off compared to what they will be obligated to pay?

Financial costs are actual expenditures, "out-of-pocket" expenses that are required to construct and operate a project. Financial costs can be grouped into two primary categories: (a) capital costs, and (b) operating costs.

Another distinction between economic analysis and financial analysis is that using the income method of valuation, the discount or capitalization rate may be different between a private and a public entity. For instance, U.S. federal law requires the use of long-term bonds (e.g., 10-year Treasury notes) in evaluating federal water projects. 201 In utility regulation, an IOU's after-tax weighted average cost of capital (WACC) is often used as the discount rate. The difference in these rates can be substantial.

In some ways, it is puzzling to realize that economic analysis (as contrasted with financial analysis) of water services is conducted in third-world countries but not in the United States. For example, Alexandria Water Company (Alexandria, Egypt) prepares both embedded and marginal cost studies. 202 Appendix D shows the results of their marginal (incremental) cost study. These analyses are often required as conditions for loans and grants from the World Bank and other multilateral institutions. Yet in the United States, water utility pricing decisions are not normally based on economic analyses and in particular a customer's willingness-to-pay (WTP).

In conclusion, in the modern era, the ongoing reduction of federal subsidies and the general public desire for financial responsibility is causing economic analysis to be more closely related to financial analysis.

Table 7.1 provides a summary of the differences between economic and financial analyses.

---

201 Griffin, 75.

202 This was the goal as of July 1, 2010.

**Table 7.1**
**Comparison of Economic and Financial Analysis**

| No. | Issue | Economic Analysis | Financial Analysis |
|---|---|---|---|
| | | | |
| 1 | Analysis perspective | Can vary from individuals, communities, state, and/or national | Project beneficiaries |
| 2 | Evaluation period | Economic life of the project (usually fifty to a hundred years) | Usually bond repayment |
| 3 | Adjustment for inflation | Excludes inflationary effects, price changes different from inflation can be included (escalation) | Includes inflationary effects |
| 4 | Project input valuation | Project inputs valued using their economic opportunity costs | Project inputs valued using their purchase costs |
| 5 | Adjustment for benefits and costs over time | Determine present values using an economic discount rate | Determine present values using a financial discount rate |
| 6 | Discount rate | Economic discount rate, real rate of return (excluding inflation) that could be expected if money were invested in another project with similar risk | Financial discount rate; financial rate of return (including inflation) that could be expected if money we invested in another project |
| 7 | Interest paid on borrowed funds used during construction | Included; real rate of return that could be expected if construction funds were invested in another project (opportunity cost) | Included if CWIP is not allowed in rate base |
| 8 | Financial costs | Not included | Included |

Source: California Resources Agency, Department of Water Resources, "Economic Analysis Guidebook" (Sacramento, CA: Department of Water Resources, January 2008).

## 7.3 Cost–Benefit and Cost-Effectiveness Analysis

Cost–benefit analysis (CBA)—also called benefit–cost analysis—is the commonly used procedure for economic evaluation of public and private projects. It was discussed in chapter four in the context of IRP. A market mechanism does not exist for making decisions in most water resource projects so a procedure must be used to determine whether projects are justified on economic grounds. Cost-effectiveness analysis is also used in evaluating water projects. However, differences exist between the two analyses. These differences are explained below.

Cost-effectiveness analysis seeks to identify the *least-cost* alternative to achieving a given objective. It involves the following distinct processes:

1) Identification, quantification, and analysis of the costs of each alternative project proposal;

2) Estimation and analysis of each alternative's effectiveness; and

3) Analysis of the relationship between the costs and effectiveness of each alternative, usually expressed as a ratio.

Cost-effectiveness analysis (CEA) does *not* require the valuation of benefits. The major limitations of CEA are that it cannot be used to compare alternatives with different goals nor can it help determine whether a project is worthwhile. CEA would be appropriate in situations where the following four requirements are met:

1) The costs and effects of each alternative are measured;

2) The alternatives identified must be comparable;

3) A well-defined objective must exist; and

4) An alternative means of achieving that objective must be identified and formulated as project proposals.

Water projects are typically evaluated using a variety of criteria, however, the primary method is cost–benefit analysis. Specifically, the present value of net benefits (i.e., the present value of all benefits minus the present value of all costs) is used. Critical issues in this type of analysis are measuring and accounting for all costs and benefits, and the appropriate discount rate used. Benefits are either primary versus secondary, tangible versus intangible, and private versus public. Cost–benefit analysis should be evaluated given the appropriate geographical region. For instance, a project may have negative net benefits for the nation as a whole while an individual region may have positive net benefits.

Economic analyses (whether recognized or not) have been common in the water industry for quite some time. Applications of economic analysis have been made by state utility regulators and the federal government. Examples of these applications are discussed below.

### 7.3.1 Utility Regulation

For years, conservation and demand-side management (DSM) programs have been persued by natural gas, electric, and water utilities. Economic analyses have been a major part of determining if specific programs are cost-effective, and if so, their cost-effectiveness. One common method of evaluating costs and benefits is from *society's* perspective. [203] Of particular importance, this method recognizes externalities. Again, recall the criterion used by Dr. Bonbright—reflection of *all* of the *present and future private and social costs and benefits* occasioned by a service's provider (i.e., all internalities and *externalities*). When society's perspective is used, analysts attempt to capture all benefits and costs including externalities.

A second example of economic analysis used in utility regulation involves economic development (negotiated) rates. These rates are offered to select customers that are not available to an existing customer class (e.g., commercial). For instance, the Pennsylvania Public Utility Commission has approved economic development rates subject to the customer meeting various criteria including:

203 Other perspectives commonly evaluated include: program participants only, nonparticipant rate-level impacts, utility, and all ratepayers.

> *"long-term economic gain…The potential long-term economic gain to the community should be greater than any short-term subsidies provided."* (emphasis added) [204]

As a second example, in Missouri, rate discounts are available to water utility customers that demonstrate that net benefits (i.e., present value of benefits minus the present value of all costs) will accrue to the State. [205] In both of the above examples, the wider society perspective is used thus supporting the societal perspective in performing economic analyses of water utility projects. The societal perspective is discussed later in this chapter.

A third illustration of economic analysis in water utility ratemaking is the National Association of Regulatory Utility Commissioners' (NARUC) resolution [206] supporting consideration of regulatory policies deemed as best practices. The language in the resolution is unmistakable—"to help ensure sustainable practices in promoting needed capital investment and *cost-effective rates*" (emphasis added). A fourth example of economic analysis used in utility regulation was a consumer's surplus study related to installing water meters in New York City. This study was discussed in chapter three.

### 7.3.2 The Government

For more than a *century*, the federal government has required the use of cost–benefit analysis (CBA) in terms of water projects. For instance, the Water Reclamation Act of 1902 requires the systematic comparison of the estimated benefits with the estimated costs. In addition to the Water Reclamation Act of 1902, The National Environmental Policy Act (NEPA) was adopted in 1970. The primary purpose of NEPA was to require full disclosure of potential environmental consequences of a proposed action. NEPA mandated a balancing process in which environmental costs must be weighed against economic and technical benefits on a case-by-case basis. [207] Presumably, as mentioned previously in this book, withholding water from the Sacramento delta to southern California is an example of the use of CBA related to public water projects.

Sometime after 1950, resource economists began using rigorous microeconomics and welfare economic concepts in evaluating public investment of water projects. In the analysis of water projects, economists use concepts such as opportunity cost, demand as WTP, marginal analysis, non-market costs and benefits, and the distinctions between private and social benefits and costs.

Federal, state, and/or city governments may also mandate certain types of water efficiency for commercial and industrial water customers. For instance, the Energy Policy Act of 1992 mandated that certain types of water-using devices newly installed after January 1, 1994—including urinals, toilets, faucets, and showerheads—must not exceed a maximum level of water use. In addition, the Energy Policy Act of 2005 place further standards on other devices including dishwashing equipment, certain clothes washers, and automatic icemakers.

---

204 Scott Rubin, "What Does Water Really Cost? Rate Design Principles for an Era of Supply Shortages, Infrastructure Upgrades, and Enhanced Water Conservation" (Silver Springs, MD: NRRI, 2010), 19.

205 Ibid.

206 *2010 NAWC Water Policy Forum Summary Report* (Washington, DC: NAWC, April 2010), 58–59.

207 Dzurik, 122.

## 7.4 Key Issues in Cost–Benefit Analysis

Cost–benefit analysis uses economic efficiency as the choice criterion. In general, the aim of this analysis is to maximize the present value of all benefits less the present value of all costs subject to specified constraints.

Cost–benefit analysis requires answering the following questions:

1) Which costs and benefits should be included?
2) Which perspective should be used in analyzing proposals?
3) How should benefits be calculated?
4) What is the appropriate time period?
5) What is the appropriate discount rate?
6) What are the relevant constraints?

These questions will now be explored.

### 7.4.1 Which Costs and Benefits Should Be Included?

The first question relates to the benefits and costs included in the analysis. Total benefits equal direct (primary) benefits (both tangible and intangible) plus indirect (secondary) benefits (both tangible and intangible). Total costs equal direct (primary) costs (both tangible and intangible) plus indirect (secondary) costs (both tangible and intangible). Admittedly, identification and quantification of intangible costs and benefits can be challenging. The benefits and costs are usually expressed in terms of money. When market prices are not available, shadow prices should be used. (See Appendix F for a definition of shadow prices.)

### 7.4.2 Which Perspective Should Be Used in Analyzing Projects?

Some state public service commissions have wrestled with the issue of the appropriate discount rate in assessing demand-side management (DSM) programs. A given perspective can have a significant impact on the discount rate as well as the components of costs and benefits. Supply-side and demand-side water utility projects can be evaluated from numerous perspectives, which include:

1) Participant test: participant's perspective;
2) Total resource cost test: utility and ratepayer perspective;
3) Ratepayer impact measure test: nonparticipant perspective;
4) Utility cost test: utility perspective; and

5) Societal test; societal perspective.[208]

The societal test is a measure of the net benefits of projects from the point of view of society as a whole. This test attempts to capture all benefits and costs including externalities. Benefits associated with this perspective include direct and indirect benefits. Since water is both a public and private good, this perspective is most appropriate. The formula for the societal test is included in equation 7.1

$$B/C\ (societal) = Bs \div Cs \quad (7.1)$$

$$Bs = \sum [(\Delta W * MC_t) + B_{ext})] \div (1+r)^t \quad (7.2)$$

$$Cs = \sum [(DC_t) + UC_t\ \ C_{ext})] \div (1+r)^t \quad (7.3)$$

Where:

Bs = societal benefits;

Cs = societal costs;

$\Delta Wi$ = change in water use in year t;

MCi = marginal cost of water in year t;

DCi = consumers' direct costs in year t;

UCi = utility's direct costs in year t;

$B_{ext}$ = external or indirect benefits in year t;

$C_{ext}$ = external or indirect costs in year t;

r = discount rate; and

n = number of years in the analysis.

### 7.4.3 How Should Benefits Be Calculated?

Various federal agencies calculate benefits using a variety of methods. Table 7.2 identifies the methods used by various federal agencies in calculating benefits. Note that the Federal Energy Regulatory Commission (FERC), which has a similar regulatory function as state PSCs, uses willingness-to-pay (WTP) as the method for calculating benefits.

208 For details regarding these tests, see: Short, Packey, and Holt, 65–69.

**Table 7.2**
**Methods of Calculating Benefits Used by Federal Agencies**

| Line No. | Type of Benefit | Agency Responsible | Method |
|---|---|---|---|
| 1 | Flood control | Army Corps of Engineers | Estimated damage avoidance |
| 2 | Navigation | Army Corps of Engineers | Estimated savings of shippers |
| | Recreation | | |
| 3 | | Bureau of Outdoor Recreation | Visitor-days times dollar value per visitor-day (travel cost) |
| 4 | | Bureau of Sport Fisheries and Wildlife | Visitor-days times dollar value per visitor-day (travel cost) |
| 5 | | National Marine Fisheries Service | Visitor-days times dollar value per visitor-day (travel cost) |
| | Fish and Wildlife Enhancement | | |
| 6 | | Fish and Wildlife Service | Various methods |
| | | National Park Service | Various methods |
| 7 | Power | FERC | Willingness-to-pay |
| 8 | Regional development | Army Corps of Engineers | Estimating increased income accruing to a region |

Source: Nancy Y. Moore, Morlie H. Graubard, and Robert Shishko, "Efficient Water Use Planning in California: Water Supply Planning" (Santa Monica, CA: RAND Corporation, 1978), 26.

---

### 7.4.4 What Is the Appropriate Time Period?

Investment analysis requires comparisons of time and value. With respect to the issue of time, water projects can have a very long time dimension. For example, depleting an aquifer could have implications for society for hundreds of years or longer. Conventional cost–benefit analysis approaches would regard one dollar of future damage as being less important than one dollar of damage now because of the phenomenon of discounting. The problem that arises with discounting is that it discriminates against future generations—and is referred to as the "intergenerational equity problem." Such discrimination assumes that satisfying today's generation is more important than meeting future generations' wants.

### 7.4.5 What Is the Appropriate Discount Rate?

The issue of the appropriate discount rate has resulted in significant debate. Many planners of federal water resource projects (e.g., U.S. Army Corp of Engineers and the Bureau of Reclamation) have been criticized for using low discount rates. The actual discount rate is set by federal legislation such that all U.S. agencies are consistent in their selection of the rate. [209] That rate is the 10-year Treasury note. One well-respected environmental economist, David W. Pearce, claims the appropriate range is between 2 and 5 percent. [210] This is a "real" interest rate (i.e., it excludes inflation). (At the time of this writing, the rate on 10-year Treasury notes was approximately 2 percent.)

---

209 Ibid, 132–33.

210 Pearce, 61.

Economists Jack Hirshleifer, James C. Dehaven, and Jerome W. Milliman have been very critical of analysts using low discount rates in cost–benefit analysis. They contend that conventional project analysis for government investments discount future benefits and costs at the rate that does not necessarily represent the risk of failure of the project in question. The risks of failure in the most closely comparable private class of investments—privately owned regulated water utilities—require companies to finance new projects at their marginal cost of capital of approximately 10 percent (at the time their book was published). 211 Another recommended after-tax *real* discount rate for utilities is 4.9 percent. 212 Discount rates should be adjusted to reflect risk.

Table 7.3 provides discount rate recommendations provided by various experts. Although the information is somewhat dated, the real rates (i.e., adjusted for inflation) are still useful.

**Table 7.3**
**Discount Rate Recommendations**

| Line No. | Author | Year | Recommended Nominal Rate (%) | Adjusted for Expected Inflation (%) |
|---|---|---|---|---|
| 1 | Krutilla and Eckstein | 1958 | 6.00 | 4.58 |
| 2 | Hirshleifer et al. | 1960 | 10.00 | 8.39 |
| 3 | Bain, Caves, and Margolis | 1966 | 6.00 | 4.65 |
| 4 | Haveman | 1966 | 7.30 | 5.95 |
| 5 | DoD Directive | 1966 | - | 10.00 |
| 6 | Stockfisch | 1949–1965 | 12.00 | 10.67 |
| 7 | Harberger | 1968 | 10.68 | 8.33 |
| 8 | Baumol | 1968 | 10.00 | 7.65 |
| 9 | OMB Directive | 1972 | - | 10.00 |
| 10 | Dorfman | 1975 | - | 7.50 |

Source: Nancy Y. Moore, Morlie H. Graubard, and Robert Shishko, "Efficient Water Use Planning in California: Water Supply Planning" (Santa Monica, CA: RAND Corporation, 1978), 81.

---

With respect to accounting for future generations, two distinct options exist. The first requires that some intergenerational criterion of sustainability be imposed, leaving the conventional discount rate unmodified as a means of allocating resources within a generation. The problem with this option is that few specific rules for practical operation have emerged. A second option is to adjust the discount rate. Four discount rate options include:

1) Setting the discount rate equal to zero;

2) Computing a consumer discount rate;

3) Computing a producer discount rate; and

---

211 Hirshleifer, DeHaven, and Milliman, 360.

212 Short, Packey, and Holt, 9.

4) Computing a weighted average of consumer and producer rates (i.e., a synthetic discount rate).

### 7.4.6 What Are the Relevant Constraints?

The constraints in cost–benefit analysis may include: (a) a socially desirable pattern of income distribution; (b) level of employment; and (c) improvement/preservation of the quality of the environment. Other constraints may be physical (e.g., choice of design, size), or legal (e.g., price controls, budgetary, environmental).

### 7.4.7 What Are the Steps in Cost–Benefit Analysis?

The economic analysis of investment projects and public policies must be flexible enough to capture the specific characteristics of each case study. However, the following are the primary steps that have to be followed independently of the particular aspects of the project under evaluation. These steps are summarized below.

1) Determine the objective of the project and examine the relevant alternatives;
2) Identify costs and benefits;
3) Measure costs and benefits;
4) Aggregate costs and benefits;
5) Interpret the results and decision criteria;
6) Compare the project with a base case; and
7) Estimate the economic return and financial feasibility of the project.

The application of cost–benefit analysis in the water utility industry will now be illustrated with summaries of various case studies.

## 7.5 Cost–Benefit Analysis Case Studies

### 7.5.1 Cost–Benefit Analysis of a Water Concession 213

This case study evaluates a policy of privatizing (through a concession contract) the water supply in a medium-sized city. In the past decade, such privatization contracts have been relatively common worldwide. The purpose of this case study is to show how the theoretical framework of cost–benefit analysis can be applied to data on costs and prices in a market. To calculate the increase in social surplus (SS) (i.e., the sum of all surplus), the formula in 7.4 is used:

213 Gines de Rus, *Introduction to Cost-Benefit Analysis, Looking for Reasonable Shortcuts* (Cheltenham, UK: Edward Elgar, 2010), 192–98.

$$\Delta SS = \sum 1/(1 + i)^t [\Delta S(t) + \gamma_g \Delta\pi(t)] \qquad (7.4)$$

Assume that the value of money in private hands is equal to the value of money in public hands.

Where:

t = time; ΔSS = change in social surplus;

π = profit;

i = interest rate, ΔS = change in surplus;

$Y_p$ = income under private ownership (discussed below);

$Y_{pp}$ = income under public ownership (discussed below); and

$\gamma_g$ = shadow price of money.

**Assumptions Used in the Analysis.** This calculation requires information about the values $\gamma_g$ ,$Y_p$, $Y_{pp}$ and also about water demand. To proceed with the analysis, the following assumptions are made. First, the shadow price of money in public and private hands is equal to one: $\gamma_g = \gamma_p = 1$. This assumption is included in the above simplified formula. Second, water demand is linear and therefore the "rule of a half" 214 is applied to calculate the consumer's surplus. Using this assumption, the changes in consumer's surplus and profits are reflected in equations 7.5 and 7.6, respectively.

$$\Delta S(t) = ½(P_g(t) - P_p(t)) (X_g(t) + X_p(t)) \qquad (7.5)$$

$$\Delta\pi(t) = (P_p(t) - C_p(t))X_p(t) \qquad (7.6)$$

Where:

$C_p$ = private cost of ownership,

$P_p$ = private ownership price,

$P_g$ = government ownership price,

$X_g$ = government-owned production level, and

$X_p$ = privately-owned production level.

Third, the average cost is lower when the firm is under private ownership ($C_p < C_g$), where $C_p$ is the cost of a private firm and $C_g$ is the cost under government ownership. Fourth, subsidies do not exist. The public company covers costs ($P_g = C_g$), while regulated private companies are allowed to set $P_p = KC_p$, where $K \geq 1$ is determined by the economic regulator. This assumption is imposed to abstract the problem discussed here—the evaluation of the increase in welfare through a change in ownership—from considerations of optimal pricing and optimal subsidies, plus the

214 The phrase "rule of a half" is often used in practical cost-benefit analysis. The change in consumer surplus is determined by multiplying three elements: (1) .5, (2) change in price, and (3) change in quantity.

problem of asymmetric information. The fourth assumption allows a determination of the price levels $P_g$ and $P_p$ required to evaluate the change in social surplus (SS). Relaxing this assumption would imply making additional assumptions about the level of subsidy.

The above assumptions allow the equation in 7.7 to be simplified as follows:

$$\Delta SS = \sum 1 \div (1 + i)^t \,[1/2(P_g - KC_p)(X_g + X_p) + (K - 1)C_pX_p] \quad (7.7)$$

Where $(K-1) \geq 0$ is the mark-up (the margin of the price over the cost) that the regulated private firm is allowed to set.

Figure 7.1, the value of privatizing a water utility, shows that D is a linear function of water demand. (Production per year on the horizontal axis is reflected as "X per year.") The terms in brackets in the above formula represent the value of the area $P_gabdc_p$. The area $p_gabp_p$ is the change obtained in consumer's surplus, while $p_pbdc_p$ represents the profits of the company in the case $K > 1$.

**Figure 7.1**
**The Value of Privatizing a Water Utility**

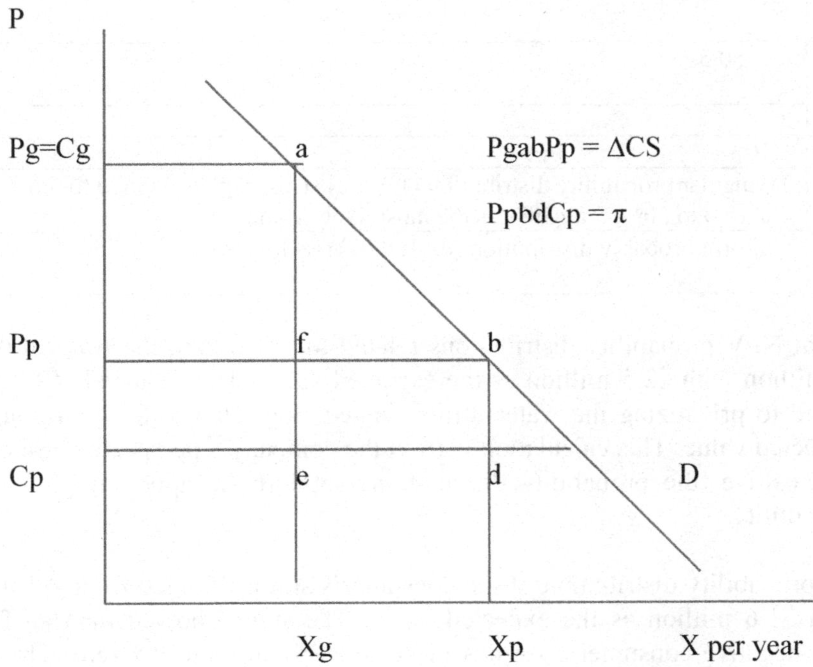


Source: Adopted from Gines de Rus, *Introduction to Cost–Benefit Analysis: Looking for Reasonable Shortcuts* (Cheltenham, UK: Edward Elgar, 2010), 195.

---

To evaluate the change in welfare obtained through privatization using the formula in equation 7.7, the only new values that are needed are: $P_g$, $C_p$, $X_p$, i, and k. It is known that $P_g$ and $X_g$ are the observed values of the price (equal to the marginal cost in this case) and the production level of the public enterprise.

Table 7.4 shows the basic data of the project, which is privatizing the publicly-owned water utility. The additional facts include: (a) the concession will last thirty years; (b) the benefits are produced at the end of each year, and the terminal value is zero; (c) the discount rate and rate of interest are equal and 5 percent; and (d) the water utility sells three hundred thousand cubic meters of water per year at a price equal to the marginal cost of $2.00 per cubic meter. The private company will be allowed a mark-up of 10 percent per year over its private marginal cost ($C_p$). This mark-up is the return on invested capital (ROIC) for the company. The reduction in the post-privatization cost (i.e., the operational efficiencies) is unknown; however, a range is assumed between a maximum of 50 percent and a minimum of zero. The most likely value is 20 percent. Next, the demand after privatization needs to be estimated. The range of the price elasticity of demand is -0.7 to -0.2 with -0.4 as the most likely value.

## Table 7.4
## Basic Data for Water Utility Concession Analysis

| | |
|---|---|
| I | 0 |
| T | 30 |
| I | 5% |
| Xg | 300,000 cubic meters |
| Demand price elasticity | -0.7;-0.4,-0.2 |
| Demand income elasticity | 0.25; 0.5 |
| Pg = Cg | 2 |
| Pp | 1.1Cp |
| Cp | Triangular probability distribution (1;1.6;2). This implies a range for cost reduction (%) of 0 to 50%, with 20% as the most likely value. |
| Income growth rate | Uniform probably distribution (0.01; 0.03) (each year). |

**Results.** The social NPV probability distributions related to privatizing the water utility ranged from $0 to $5.9 million with $2.5 million as the expected value. The financial NPV probability distributions related to privatizing the water utility ranged from $0.5 to $1.0 million with $0.8 million as the expected value. This calculation is from the company's perspective. Since the NPV in both cases is positive, the probability distributions support the approval of the policy to privatize the water utility.

Nevertheless, the probability distribution of the consumer's surplus ranged from -$1.0 million to $5.1 million, with $1.6 million as the expected value. The study showed than an 8.3 percent chance exists of a negative consumer's surplus of between $1 million and zero. The reason for this segment of negative values for the consumer's surplus rests on the possibility of a 10 percent mark-up combined with a cost reduction that ranges between 0 and 50 percent. A 10 percent increase in price with insufficient cost reduction can produce an increase in price for the consumer, which in terms of the social NPV is partially compensated for by an increase in producer's surplus. The deadweight loss in efficiency is generally compensated for, in this particular case, by the gain in efficiency as the result of the cost reduction.

Note that the analysis in this case involves both social and financial NPV. This is because an analysis must be conducted from the perspectives of the utility (requiring a financial NPV) and society (requiring a social NPV).

### 7.5.2 Cost–Benefit Analysis of a Water Recycling Project

For each project evaluated, a clear baseline should be established as the basis for comparison before costs and benefits are estimated. A baseline could be a "do nothing" scenario or the most likely projects that would be built in the absence of the option evaluated. Take the case of a water recycling project where the most likely alternatives could include a new water supply contract, desalination plant, or a new dam. The first step in the analysis is to separate costs and benefits that can be quantified. Direct costs to the water utility are usually established through engineering estimates. Usually a range of costs is established to reflect uncertainty in the estimates. Other costs and benefits can be monetized using the methods listed in Appendix B. The second step in the process is to make annual estimates of the costs and benefits, and to project the years that they apply to in the future. The present value of the benefit stream should be calculated to ensure a consistent analysis across projects. The issue of the appropriate discount rate was discussed previously in this chapter.

Table 7.5 provides a template for recording the key inputs used for monetizing the benefits of a project option. In this example, two benefit categories are estimated—improved water supply reliability, and nonuse values for sustaining habitat for threatened or endangered species. Comparable templates should be used for key cost elements of each option. A key value of this template is recording the assumptions and inputs used in the calculations of costs and benefits.

**Table 7.5**
**Benefit Detail for Water Recycling Project**

| No. | Benefit Category | Annual Quantity | Unit Value Used | Comments |
|---|---|---|---|---|
| 1 | Improved water supply reliability | 20,000 AF of use by a large customer | \$140-\$200/AF of added value to the customer | Use based on interview with the company. Based on avoiding production cutbacks due to periodic use restrictions |
| 2 | Nonuse values for sustaining habitat for threatened or endangered species | 200,000 households in impacted counties assumed to hold nonuse values related to the species and habitat impacted | A low of \$6.88 per household per year, to a high of \$10.24 per year per taxpayer | The low-end and high-end values are based on previous studies |

The next step in the analysis is to record all costs and benefits for a project. In the analysis, to the extent that variability or uncertainty of the costs and benefits exist a range should be included. Benefits requiring qualitative assessment should also be recorded. Finally, the various stakeholders affected by the project should be noted.

Table 7.6 provides a description of costs and benefits of the project, their amounts in 2002 dollars, and the stakeholder(s) affected.

**Table 7.6**
**Cost–Benefit Analysis of Water Recycling Project**

| Line No. | Cost or Benefit Description | Dollars (000) (2002) | Stakeholder |
|---|---|---|---|
| | **Costs** | | |
| 1 | Capital construction costs | 5,000 | Water utility |
| 2 | Treatment O&M | 900 | Water utility |
| 3 | Distribution capacity costs | 9,000 | Water utility |
| 4 | Distribution system O&M | 1,100 | Water utility |
| 5 | **Total Costs** | **16,000** | |
| | | | |
| | **Benefits (monetized)** | | |
| 6 | Avoided supply acquisition costs | 4,000-6,000 | Water utility |
| 7 | Avoided wastewater treatment capacity expansion | 8,000-10,000 | Wastewater district |
| 8 | Avoided wastewater treatment variable costs | 300 | Wastewater district |
| 9 | Improved water supply reliability | 3,000-4,000 | Company |
| 10 | Improved in-stream recreation | 500-800 | General public |
| 11 | Improved nonuse value for threatened or | | |
| | endangered species | 150-200 | General public |
| | | | Sierra Club |
| 12 | **Total monetized benefits** | **15,950-21,300** | |
| | | | |
| | **Benefits requiring qualitative assessment** | | |
| | | | |
| 13 | Impact on source-water ecosystem (fisheries' impact) | + | General public |
| 14 | Differential access to recycled water according to geographic impact | - | General public |
| 15 | Community economic development | + | Irrigation district |
| | | | |
| 16 | **Total monetized net benefits (benefits minus costs)** | **> (50) – 5,300** | |

Notes:

1/ + indicates positive benefits anticipated, but not monetized with readily available data.

2/ - indicates costs anticipated, but not monetized with readily available data.

3/ Present value using a 10 percent discount rate.

---

All estimates have a certain amount of deviation from their "true" value. The reasons for imprecise estimates are generally related to omissions, biases, and uncertainties. Omissions are information gaps that affect a project's valuation. It is important to identify them and assess if they are likely to have positive or negative impacts on the analysis. Biases refer to any factor causing cost or benefit estimates to be smaller or larger than their actual value. Uncertainties result because quantification involves estimating or predicting changes in the physical world or in socioeconomic relationships that may not be completely understood. This knowledge gap can cause estimated values to be different from their true value. These uncertainties should be acknowledged and addressed through sensitivity analyses. Sensitivity analysis involves changing a key input variable and determining how it affects the outcome of the analysis.

The final step in a cost–benefit analysis is to estimate the impact of uncertainties or key assumptions, such as discount rates, through the use of sensitivity analysis. Sensitivity analysis is often performed by varying a particular input by equal amounts greater to and less than the current value. In Table 7.7, a discount rate of 9 percent was chosen as the most likely amount. Alternative discount rates in 3 percent increments are used to determine the impact on the monetized net benefits.

**Table 7.7**
**Water Recycling Project**
**Sensitivity Analysis Applied to the Discount Rate**

| Discount Rate (%) | Monetized Benefit ($) (000) | Cost ($) (000) | Monetized Net Benefit ($) (000) |
|---|---|---|---|
| | | | |
| 0 | 49,000–51,500 | 30,000 | 19,000–21,500 |
| 3 | 39,500–41,700 | 26,000 | 13,500–15,700 |
| 6 | 29,500–34,000 | 22,000 | 7,500–12,000 |
| 9 | 15,950–21,300 | 16,000 | (50) – 5,300 |
| 12 | 8,500–14,000 | 11,000 | (3,500) – 3,000 |
| 15 | 2,500–8,000 | 8,000 | (5,500) – 0 |

Sources for Tables 7.5–7.7: Adopted from R. D. Raucher et al., *The Value of Water: Concepts, Estimates, and Applications for Water Managers* (Denver, CO: American Water Works Research Foundation, 2005), 120–26.

---

### 7.5.3 Estimating the Benefits of Water-Use Efficiency Programs for Denver Water
215

Many water utilities evaluate the effectiveness of water-efficiency programs relative to supply-side resources. This task is often difficult to accomplish because the benefits of improved efficiency are not easily quantified. To accomplish this task, two tools developed by the California Urban Water Conservation Council have been used. These are: (a) the avoided-cost model (AC model) and (b) the environmental-benefit model (EB model). RAND economists used these tools to evaluate efficiency programs to help Denver Water meet its ten-year conservation goals. Their findings were:

> *"When long-run avoided costs and efficiency and recreational benefits are estimated and added to the marginal benefit calculation, an additional five programs were cost-effective."* 216

---

215 David G. Groves, James Griffen, and Sara Hajiamiri, "Estimating the Value of Water-Use Efficiency in the Intermountain West" (Santa Monica, CA: RAND Corporation, 2008), xi-xiii.

216 Ibid, 39.

By including both short-run and long-run avoided costs as well as short-run and long-run environmental benefits, the combination yields results that are significantly higher than just analyzing avoided costs. For example, when just short-run avoided costs are included, total savings amounted to $8,000–$13,000 per million gallons. When total environmental benefits were added, the savings increased to between $41,000 and $100,000 per million gallons.

### 7.5.4 Commercial Building Retrofit

Water is a critical input to commercial buildings, yet the amount of water required to meet the uses in these structures is highly variable. Water use depends on:

1) The technology used in water-using devices;

2) System maintenance;

3) Water rates and charges; and

4) The intensity of building use.

Depending on the location and the expected change in water and energy utility rates, commercial building retrofits can provide substantial savings to the owner. Building retrofits are one of several types of demand-side management (DSM) programs water utilities include in their integrated resource plans (IRP). To illustrate the potential for saving water, The RAND Corporation prepared an analysis of various retrofits for its commercial building headquarters in Santa Monica, California. 217 The analysis could also be used for retail and wholesale businesses, hotels and motels, laundry facilities, restaurants, car washes, and many other organizations. In short, the analysis is applicable to all nonresidential applications.

To conduct the analysis, RAND's analysts developed a spreadsheet-based model, "Building Water Efficiency Analysis Model" (BEAM). Specifically, BEAM considers the avoided water, wastewater, and energy costs realized through increased water efficiency.

The standard financial framework for evaluating investment decisions weighs the present value (PV) of all costs against the PV of all benefits associated with an investment. Owners of commercial buildings realize direct monetary benefits from efficiency in the form of avoided future resource costs. In this case, the avoided costs (i.e., benefits) fall into three categories:

1) Water costs: The amount of money spent on water for all end uses at the building;

2) Wastewater costs: The amount of money charged by the utility that disposes of any wastewater leaving the building; these costs are often tied to the amount of water leaving the building; and

3) Energy costs: The costs associated with heating water (typically by electricity, natural gas, or both).

---

217 David G. Graves, Jordan Fischbach, and Scot Hickey, "Evaluating the Benefits and Costs of Increased Water-Use Efficiency in Commercial Buildings" (Santa Monica, CA: RAND Corporation, 2007), 27.

The costs of the projects include operating and maintenance expenses over the life of the fixtures, and the initial investment costs of efficiency improvements in building cooling systems as well as restrooms including toilets, urinals, sinks, and showers. Other DSM projects such as replacing landscaping with low-water-using designs were not considered. If included in the analysis, these improvements would likely provide even more benefits. Seven combinations of efficiency devices were compared in the analysis. Finally, the analysis considered two baseline efficiency conditions—a hypothetical older building constructed prior to 1992, and a building similar to RAND's headquarters, which was constructed in 2004.

A water utility's rate structure discussed in chapter five can affect the amount of water cost savings due to efficiency. Three common rate structures—uniform, declining block, and increasing block—can affect total costs as follows:

1) Uniform rate structure. In this case the average and marginal costs are the same. A reduction in use will lead to a direct reduction in water costs. For instance, a 10 percent reduction in water use will reduce water bills by 10 percent.

2) Declining block rate structure. In this case, the marginal cost of water is less than the average cost. For example, a 10 percent reduction in water use will reduce water cost savings by less than 10 percent.

3) Increasing block rate structure. In this case the marginal cost of water is higher than the average cost. A reduction in use will lead to a higher percentage reduction in water costs. For instance, a 10 percent reduction in water use will reduce water bills by more than 10 percent.

Thus, the rate structure in place after the retrofit will affect the efficiency savings. The BEAM model allows the user to specify the prices and amounts for each tier in a block rate structure. The RAND Corporation purchases water from its supplier that uses a three-tier increasing block rate structure, and natural gas based on a three-tier declining block rate structure. For wastewater, the rate charged is uniform for each 100 cubic feet. The BEAM model uses scenario analyses that offer an approach for situations in which analysts cannot uniquely characterize all the important uncertain parameters with probability distributions. In scenario analysis, the model user develops a set of scenarios, each corresponding to a single value for the parameters. Decisions based on a set of independent scenarios, rather than a single probabilistic result, require subjective reasoning on the part of the decisionmaker.

The commercial building retrofit analysis included various assumptions, such as:

1) Toilet and urinal use per day;

2) Number of people using faucets and faucet use of water per flush;

3) Showers (average shower duration) and number of employees using showers;

4) Average temperature for water heating (hand washing and shower);

5) Gas and electric heater efficiency;

6) Cost of capital of 8 percent;

7) A service life of twenty-five years for toilets and urinals; and ten years for faucets;

8) Rated capacity for technology (e.g., toilet—gallons per flush); and

9) Annual O&M expenses for each technology.

The analysis looked at seven packages (options) ranging from no new efficiency to replacing fixtures with maximum efficiency. Six scenarios were evaluated, with weighted price trends ranging from zero price growth to a worst-case scenario of high price growth. After calculating water and energy use, the model produces financial metrics that include net present value (NPV), internal rate of return (IRR), payback period, and equivalent annual net benefits (EANB). Equivalent annual net benefits represents the equivalent amount of income required annually to achieve the overall NPV of the project throughout its service life. As the metric is annualized, EANB can be compared across projects without concern for differing horizon values. 218

Package No. 6 was the most promising and included installing non-water-using urinals, and bringing all technologies up to at least the minimum federal standards for devices manufactured after 1992. The package included ultra-low-flow toilets, ultra-low-flow urinals, 1.0 gpm faucets, and 1.7 gpm showers.

The results of the study showed a $41,000 investment pays for itself in about 3.6 years and provides an NPV ranging from $91,000 to $122,000, depending on the scenario of future utility prices.

This case study illustrates several key points stressed in this book. These include:

1) The rate structure that regulators approve can make a big difference in water consumption and the economic analysis of a project;

2) In some cases, subsidies for water saving equipment are not necessary, since for many users, investment in the equipment is financially rewarding. Thus, in this case water utility customers' money is not necessary to achieve the social goal of saving water; and

3) Commercial customers value water by the amount and price used for various applications, and can make future investment choices consistent with their marginal cost of capital.

### 7.5.5 Cost of Water Utility Infrastructure Failure

Failure of a water system's infrastructure can result in numerous adverse economic consequences, which include direct and indirect costs. The direct costs related to a failure are obvious and include labor and materials to fix the problem. Other costs are indirect and may include: (a) inconvenience to customers; (b) disruption of traffic; (c) damage to property and goods; (d) disruption of business activity; (e) disruption of parallel utilities; (f) human injury; and (g) diminished firefighting capability. Various methods of estimating indirect costs are included in Appendix B.

---

218 Ibid, 9.

One example of economic analysis is estimating the cost of infrastructure failure (or the avoided cost of infrastructure failure) in network industries such as the water utility industry. Examples of this are from the U.S. electric utility industry that experiences occasional power outages. The American Water Works Research Foundation (AwwaRF) has done some work in estimating the costs of infrastructure failures related *only* to water transmission and distribution systems. They have found that from the electric utility industry, market-based methodologies exist for estimating customer outages costs could easily be applied to estimating costs of customer service interruptions (a type of externality) resulting from water infrastructure failure. [219] In the context of this discussion, these are the water delivery mechanisms.

The various methods of valuing outage costs are grouped into three categories, which are: (a) aggregated data; (b) customer behavior; and (c) market survey. The aggregated data approach uses statistical data such as: (a) gross domestic product (GDP) per cubic feet of water consumed; (b) the wage rate; or (c) the average water price per hundred cubic feet as proxies for customers' willingness to pay for reliable service.

Included in the customer behavior approach is the consumer's surplus method. Recall that consumer's surplus was discussed in chapter three. This method involves estimating customers' willingness to pay for a specific level of water delivered to a customer's premises.

The market survey approach asks customers to identify their probable responses to different hypothetical scenarios. Examples of this approach include the contingent valuation method (CVM) and cost decomposition analysis. Market survey approaches are the most prevalent of the reliable outage cost estimation methodologies. [220]

As an example of the cost of infrastructure failure in the water utility industry, AwwaRF reports that two-thirds of the twenty-eight corporations surveyed by the Silicon Valley Manufacturing Group reported that a thirty-day water service interruption would shut them down entirely, while over half reported that they would expect multi-million dollar economic losses. The report also estimated total losses in the San Francisco Bay Area (including residential, business, and fire damage) from water service interruptions resulting from earthquakes at between \$17.2 and \$28.7 billion. This range is based on earthquake magnitudes of 7.1 and 7.9, respectively. [221]

In the water utility industry, the repair-replace-refurbish (RRR) decisionmaking process often does not reflect the entire array of social costs that result from infrastructure failures. [222] When considering RRR decisions, water utilities typically consider the cost of a hypothetical failure as one criterion in prioritizing projects. The cost of a main break is often estimated using actual cost data from previous breaks in similar mains within the utility's system. However, utilities usually do not quantitatively estimate nor include less tangible social costs (i.e., indirect costs) that usually result from a failure (e.g., property loss, water damage, service outage, traffic delays). If this is the case, true full costs and ultimately water rates will be understated. The AwwaRF claims that quantifying and including these costs will provide a more accurate and effective tool for prioritizing main rehabilitation and replacement choices than exists with current practices. [223]

---

219 John E Cromwell, III, Hayden Reynolds, Norman Pearson, Jr., and Michael Grant, *The Cost of Infrastructure Failure* (Denver, CO: Awwa Research Foundation and American Water Works Association, 2002), xiii.

220 Cromwell, 9.

221 Raucher et al., 182–83.

222 Cromwell, 1.

223 Ibid, 3.

### 7.5.6 Analysis of a Residential Low-Flow Showerhead

Table 7.8 reflects the assumptions, calculations, results, and conclusion of the costs and benefits of a low-flow showerhead. This analysis is common in evaluating various demand-side management (DSM) programs.

**Table 7.8**
**Cost–Benefit Analysis of a Residential Low-Flow Showerhead**

| Line No. | Assumptions | Description |
|---|---|---|
| 1 | | The cost of a new low-flow showerhead is \$8.00 |
| 2 | | The showerhead uses 1.9 gallons per minute |
| 3 | | A non-conserving showerhead uses 3.4 gallons per minute |
| 4 | | The life expectancy of the showerhead is 15 years |
| 5 | | The average household has 2.5 people |
| 6 | | There are 1.7 showerheads per household |
| 7 | | The average shower is five minutes per person, per day |
| 8 | | The marginal cost of an alternative water supply is \$700/acre-foot |
| 9 | | The discount rate is 8% |
| 10 | | The escalation rate is 10% |
| | **Calculations** | |
| 11 | | Water savings = 11 gallons per day = 0.012 acre-foot/year |
| 12 | | The present value of the avoided cost of supply is \$104 |
| 13 | **Results** | The benefit/cost ratio = \$104/\$8 = 13>1 |
| 14 | **Conclusion** | The low-flow showerhead passes the economic screen |

Source: American Water Works Association, *Integrated Resource Planning: A Balanced Approach to Water Resources Decision Making,* VI–5.

# CHAPTER EIGHT

# THE LEGAL FRAMEWORK IN RATEMAKING

## 8.1 Overview

The legal authority for approving tariffs is based primarily on the type of ownership of a specific utility. Two general ownership types exist: private and public. Ratemaking authority for private utilities (also called investor-owned utilities—IOU is determined by state law. Usually it is regulated by a state regulatory commission (often called public service commission—PSC—or public utility commission—PUC). The ratemaking methodology is usually cost of service using embedded costs. In the case of government-owned utilities—GOU—the ratemaking authority is also determined by state law. The regulatory body may be a city council, district commission, or similar government entity.

For IOUs, the ratemaking process is considered quasi-judicial and requires a set of rules of practice and procedures in order to present, process, and rule on utility regulatory matters. Various safeguards to protect the public are implemented and include, among others:

1) Rules of evidence;

2) Burden of proof;

3) No ex-parte communications;

4) Due process; and

5) The right to cross-examine witnesses.

In the context of ratemaking, the rules of practice and procedures are important because even though a general agreement on a specific issue (e.g., rate structure) may exist among rate case participants in a rate proceeding, the utility regulator needs sufficient facts included in the record to justify changing rates or other regulatory matters.

The courts have held that discriminatory rates among customers are not necessarily unlawful. Discrimination among customers may refer to discrimination among different customer classes or among customers in the same customer class. Only unjust or unreasonable rate discrimination is not permitted. For example, different rates for two residential customers with the same customer service characteristics, often described as "similarly situated," constitute unreasonable or unjust discrimination. Furthermore, legal experts claim that these standards do not require that a rate design chosen and implemented by a particular utility must be the best rate design, nor have mathematical exactitude, but merely be reasonable.

Common legal issues involved in appeals of utility regulatory commission decisions include:

1) Is the rate order supported by competent and substantial evidence?

2) Is the rate order based on a mistake of fact or law?

3) Does the rate order contain adequate findings of fact?

4) Did the PSC act beyond its statutory authority?

5) Is the decision arbitrary, unreasonable, or contrary to the overwhelming weight of the evidence? [224]

## 8.2 Key U.S. Supreme Court Decisions Regarding Utility Pricing [225]

### 8.2.1 *Munn v. Illinois*, 94 U.S. 113,74 L.Ed. 77 (1877)

In this case, the state of Illinois required Munn to secure a business license to operate warehouses used to store grain. The U.S. Supreme Court upheld the state statute and found that it did not violate the commerce clause or due process amendments of the U.S. Constitution. Furthermore, the Court held that a state can determine the level and kind of service; and it can fix rates as long as those rates are fair, "just and reasonable," and "affected with a public interest." The Court also concluded that the licensing of price and service (i.e., regulation) is a legislative matter and not one that should be left to the judicial branch. The significance of the Munn case in the context of utility ratemaking is that virtually any good or service (including water and sewer) sold to the public is potentially affected with the public interest. [226]

---

224 Wendell F. Holland, Chairman, Pennsylvania Public Utility Commission, "Legal Framework of Water Utility Regulation," presentation at the 27th Annual Western NARUC Utility Rate School, May 14–19, 2006, San Diego, California, 6.

225 For a summary of other key U.S. Supreme Court decisions affecting utility ratemaking and pricing, see Hayward, 223–29.

226 John R. Marks III, Adorno & Yoss, LLP, "The Legal Aspect of Utility Regulation," presentation at the 27th Annual Western NARUC Utility Rate School, May 14–19, 2006, San Diego, California, 16.

### 8.2.2 *Nebbia v. New York,* 291 U.S. 502, 54 S. CT. 505, 78 L.Ed. 940 (1934)

In another U.S. Supreme Court case, *Nebbia v. New York*, the state of New York sued Nebbia for setting the price of milk in excess of the level established by the Milk Control Board. The essential question in the case was: does a state statute fixing the minimum and maximum price for milk violate the due process clause of the 14th amendment to the U.S. Constitution? The Court held that fixing prices by state legislative mandate does not violate the due process clause. The Court's rationale was that the due process clause does not prohibit government regulation, but there are conditions imposed when government decides to regulate. The conditions included:

1) Just compensation must be given if the government confiscates property;

2) Regulation must be reasonable, not arbitrary, not capricious or "unduly discriminatory;" and

3) Regulation must be reasonably related to the objective.

The key point for the purposes of this book is that regulation must be reasonable, not arbitrary, not capricious or unduly discriminatory.

### 8.2.3 *Hope Natural Gas Company v. FPC,* 320 U.S. 519 (1944)

In the context of utility pricing, another key U.S. Supreme Court case affecting regulated utilities was *Federal Power Commission (FPC) v. Hope Natural Gas Company*. This case was significant in that the majority opinion held:

> *"It is the result reached, not the method employed which is controlling. If the total effect of the rate order is just and reasonable, the court will not overturn the Commission."*

In other words, the Court did not care how a utility commission sets rates as long as the result was "just and reasonable," enabling the utility to operate successfully, remain financially viable, attract capital, and compensate investors. If the investment community (e.g., *Value Line Investment Survey*) repeatedly finds that a utility or industry's rates provides inadequate cash from operations, then their financial viability remains questionable.

The second key finding in the case was the need for the commission to balance the interests of businesses and consumers. In conclusion, the U.S. Supreme Court gave wide latitude to state regulators and considerably broadened the "affected with the public interest" concept.

### 8.2.4 *Smyth v. Ames*, 169 U.S. 466 (1898)

The issue of value or worth came up in this famous utility case. In its decision, the U.S. Supreme Court issued a dictum stating, in effect, that a company supplying a public service might not be denied an opportunity to charge rates that would yield a "reasonable return on fair value" of its property devoted to public service. But the Supreme Court qualified this statement by declaring that the consuming public has an overriding right to enjoy service at rates *not higher* than "what the service is reasonably worth" [227]—(i.e., the ceiling price of a customer's value of service).

## 8.3 Legal Precedents for Value-of-Service Pricing

The early application of value-of-service pricing in the United States occurred in the railroad industry. In the mid-nineteenth century, railroads often used "first class" and "second class" pricing without any distinction in the services offered. In some cases, the first-class fare was more than double the second-class fare. [228] Economists have usually supported the railroad companies' efforts to employ differential pricing. (The mechanics of implementing a system of prices based on value of service is called differential pricing.) In a 1962 article, ten well-known economists strongly supported the railroads' system of differential pricing and stated:

> *"Differential pricing is consistent with the public interest in the economical utilization of resources. It can yield significant benefits to the users of rail services by encouraging the retention of traffic and the development of greater traffic volumes and improved profits, thus fostering the adoption of improved technology and service, as well as lower rates."* [229]

The rationale behind value-of-service (VOS) pricing is not only economic efficiency, but social policy. In 1990, the Oregon Public Utility Commission explained that "the impetus behind value-of-service pricing was the social policy goal of providing affordable, quality telephone service to the greatest number of local network subscribers, a concept now generally referred to as universal service." [230]

In the natural gas industry, the California Public Utilities Commission (CPUC) incorporated value-of-service pricing for gas pipeline transportation service. It believed that market-based pricing is the most efficient way of allocating a scarce resource. [231] Also in the natural gas industry, the North Carolina PSC with regard to the emergence of transportation-only rates has caused a new awareness of value-of-service considerations by holding:

> *"as transportation and negotiations increase, as they have since 1985...cost-of-service studies became less important and value of service becomes more important."* [232] (emphasis added)

When a utility regulatory agency has conservation, social, or other noncost recovery goals, it may favor value-of-service pricing. In a telephone case, the Tennessee PSC held that in its regulation of local exchange carriers, regulatory policies that promote economic development, convenience, and other goals was appropriate. The courts have also supported regulatory promotion of noncost legislative goals even if a regulated company supplied service at less than compensatory rates.

227 Bonbright, Danielsen, and Kamerschen, 126.

228 Goodman, 887.

229 Ibid, 898.

230 Ibid.

231 Ibid, 889.

232 Ibid, 893.

Finally, in some cases, the quality and quantity of a utility's service may override cost considerations. In the water utility industry, service quality is often measured, in part, by service interruptions. For instance, in a water utility case, the Washington Utilities and Transport Commission found that the company's requested 13 percent return on equity (ROE) was unreasonable. It found that given the utility's failure to provide safe and adequate water service and to meet its public service obligations, a normal ROE was neither fair nor reasonable. [233]

233 Ibid, 893.

# *CHAPTER NINE*

# IMPORTANT POINTS TO REMEMBER

The recommendations in chapter ten are based on the following facts and arguments.

## 9.1 The Problems

1. Currently in America, the water utility industry has serious problems, such as: (a) an infrastructure graded by the American Society of Civil Engineers (ASCE) as D–; (b) irrational pricing and use; and (c) deteriorating financial viability reflected by:

   A. Insufficient operating cash flow to fund infrastructure replacement and growth, and;

   B. Low return on invested capital (ROIC).

   In particular, ASCE's grade has changed very little over the past decade. The causes of these problems may vary from utility to utility.

2. Underpricing water (the commodity) and services (e.g., delivery) is seen by many economists as a key element contributing to the industry's problems.

3. Water utilities often have poorly defined (and in many cases ignored) sustainability metrics.

4. For many water utilities, annual sales are flat, per capita consumption is declining, and costs are increasing.

## 9.2 Value

1. When the value of water or water services is being estimated, what is being measured is the welfare change associated with some policy-induced change in the attributes of the commodity or service (e.g., reliability).

2. The full value of water includes: (a) intrinsic value; (b) value to society; (c) value to water users (the most common); and (d) externalities (positive or negative).

3. A working definition of value of service is: assigning monetary measures of individuals' preferences for outcomes of policy proposals or events (e.g., water delivered with a specified reliability).

4. Experts in the fields of natural resource and environmental economics have long known the methods [234] of valuing water supply, but other analysts in the field of public utility economics have generally failed to incorporate this knowledge in the context of pricing water utility services.

5. Key water industry organizations (e.g., AWWA, NAWC) claim that the price of water is a great value, but very few facts and supporting information are included in utility rate decisions or communicated to the public.

6. Various nonmarket valuation methods have been used throughout the world to estimate water customers' willingness to pay for goods and services (e.g., water delivered to a customer's tap). Perhaps the most widely used approach is the contingent valuation method (CVM).

7. Nonmarket valuation cases studies related to water have included: (a) waste disposal; (b) recreation and fish/wildlife habitat; (c) navigation; (d) hydropower; (e) irrigation; (f) industrial processing; (g) thermoelectric power; and (h) domestic uses.

8. Willingness-to-pay studies for water service are rarely undertaken in the United States, while such studies are common in developing (third-world) countries.

9. The most commonly used method of valuing the benefits of power used by the Federal Energy Regulatory Commission (FERC) is willingness-to-pay.

10. Various willingness-to-pay studies have found that some water utility customers were willing to pay 3 to 5 percent of their disposable income or household expenditures to receive reliable water service.

11. A recent paper by the National Regulatory Research Institute (NRRI) calls upon state public service commissions (PSC) to establish reliability standards for water utilities before billions of dollars are spent replacing aging infrastructure.

12. Often a water utility's value of service for a customer class serves as the ceiling for rates in what is called the "zone of reasonableness." The floor of the zone is usually the water utility's short-run marginal costs.

---

234 The general methods of valuing a natural resource such as water are summarized in Appendix B.

13. Even if a value-of-service study is not directly used to set rates, it can provide useful information to water utilities and their regulators regarding the magnitude of potential rate increases.

14. Often it is useful to value and price water as a commodity separately from water delivery services (e.g., reliability). This is often referred to as unbundling services.

15. In the U.S., a huge range exists related to the value of water by sector (e.g., domestic, agricultural, industrial). The value of water is site-, time-, and use-specific, and these parameters account for this range.

16. Water has value as a private and public good.

## 9.3 Pricing/Costs

1. In the United States, the most common practice of pricing utility services is based on cost-of-service using primarily historical costs (i.e. full supply costs).

2. Both cost-of-service pricing and value-of-service pricing approaches have limitations.

3. Most businesses attempt to satisfy their customers' needs, outcomes, or events. In the water utility industry, customers normally focus on three issues—quality, quantity, and reliability of service at specific times, locations, and conditions. Current water utility pricing practices normally do not efficiently capture these value-related issues. Water quality issues are normally addressed by health officials and are generally outside the scope of utility economic regulation.

5. Full-cost pricing has been recommended by numerous water utility experts. Full costs include: O&M expenses, capital charges, opportunity costs, and costs resulting from externalities (economic and environmental). Denmark is an example of a country that has adopted the full-cost pricing concept.

6. In a study of the full-cost of water in college dormitories, in some cases the current prices were approximately one-half the price based on full costs. The primary areas of underpricing were related to: (a) infrastructure recapitalization and maintenance, and (b) capital subsidies.

7. For most U.S. water utilities, implementing full-cost pricing would likely result in excessive revenues and profits. Utility economic regulators have several options for dealing with this issue including phasing in full-cost rates and using the surplus to fund infrastructure programs, and possibly assistance for low-income customers.

8. Full-cost pricing is not the same as cost-of-service pricing. In the traditional revenue requirements formula externalities and opportunity costs are assumed to be zero. Furthermore, the formula ignores nonuse value of water (e.g., option value and existence value).

9. An accounting identity exists between full-cost pricing and the full value of water. The full value of water is reflected in value-of-service pricing.

10. Using the concepts from welfare economics in terms of valuing water and water services could improve utility pricing practices—specifically incorporating marginal-cost and peak-load pricing principles. Central to welfare economics is the notion of maximizing aggregate economic welfare. To maximize economic welfare, efficient prices are necessary. Economic efficient rates are one of Dr. Bonbright's (an established expert in the field of public utility economics) primary criteria of a sound rate structure. Given the industry's current problems, it should be regulators' primary goal in the context of pricing (rate) decisions.

11. Pricing based on value of service (as contrasted with pricing based on cost of service) is endorsed by well-respected economists, assuming necessary conditions are met and justification exists for price discrimination.

12. Water utilities rarely have price elasticity of demand information regarding their customer classes. This is one of four conditions most economists view as necessary for price discrimination and implementing value-of-service pricing.

13. A tariff study for Sydney Water Company (Australia) found the tariffs that produced the maximum efficiency gains were non-uniform, two-part tariffs based on short-run marginal costs. The least-effective tariffs were uniform rates based on average cost pricing often used in the United States.

14. In many countries throughout the world, economic regulators do not believe that all costs are equal. This is particularly true of externalities. In extreme cases, a measure of cost recovery is limited to O&M costs. Thus, recovery of capital and other costs are not considered as significant.

15. Marginal costs as the basis for pricing are common in the United Kingdom, Canada, and Australia. A deviation of marginal costs—average incremental costs (AIC)—is often used for practical reasons. The World Bank endorses AIC-pricing and it is used in World Bank–funded projects.

16. The most common forms of marginal cost pricing are: (a) simple, (b) traditional (textbook), (c) Turvey (also called the present worth incremental system cost—PWISC), and (d) average (also called long-run average incremental costs).

17. In the water utility industry in the United States, only two states—Massachusetts and New York—have implemented marginal cost pricing for regulated investor-owned water utilities.

18. As the appropriate basis for cost-reflective pricing and for practical reasons, several prominent economists believe that long-run marginal costs (LRMC) are preferable to short-run marginal costs (SRMC).

19. In the United States, in most instances estimates of marginal costs and value of service are not included in water utility rate cases. However, for business planning purposes and possibly communicating with their customers, a utility should know the amounts of their marginal costs.

20. The costs and benefits (i.e., cost–benefit analysis) for a society are often used as a basis for setting water rates. For example, incentive rates in Missouri and Pennsylvania were approved if the long-run benefits to society were greater than the long-run costs.

## 9.4 Subsidies

1. Current pricing practices incorporate up to eighteen subsidies depending on the characteristics and ownership of a water utility. Rate decisions issued by utility regulators rarely identify these subsidies and amounts. Also, regulators usually do not provide explicit policies regarding future subsidies. For example, should the subsidy be kept, eliminated, or the amount modified?

2. In a study of commercial building retrofits, in some cases customer subsidies for water saving equipment are not necessary, since for many users the investment in the equipment is financially rewarding.

3. In 2005 the Scottish government initiated a reform of economic regulation in the water utility industry. One question related to the reform was: If it is established that there are significant cross-subsidies between customer groups, should these be retained, or withdrawn gradually over time? The results of the study found, among other things, a 13.6 percent subsidy from non-households to households. The Scottish government is committed to unwinding part of the nondomestic to domestic cross-subsidy.

## 9.5 Legal

1. The U.S. Supreme Court has given utility regulators wide discretion in setting rates.

2. Economic regulation must be reasonable, not arbitrary, not capricious, or unduly discriminatory.

3. Utility regulators must balance the interests of stakeholders.

4. Numerous legal precedents exist for value-of-service pricing. The courts have held that a rate design (i.e., pricing) chosen and implemented by a particular utility need not be the best, nor have mathematical exactitude, but merely be reasonable.

## 9.6 Policy

1. The thirty member countries of the Organization for Economic Co-operation and Development (OECD) have organized their water utility policy objectives around four sustainable dimensions which include: (a) environmental sustainability, (b) financial sustainability, (c) economic efficiency, and (d) social concerns.

2. In Africa, the World Bank uses a scorecard to grade water utilities against the criteria of cost recovery, efficiency, and equity. These are issues similar to those considered by U.S. utility regulators. However, scorecards are rarely used.

3. In some areas of the world, a widespread belief exists that all costs are not equally important. That is, the bar of cost recovery has been lowered. Some water utilities attempt to only recover their O&M expenses and not the return of and on capital. In effect, they are saying that the owners of some of the factors of production (e.g., labor) are more important than providers of capital. However, in the long run for a utility to remain a going concern all factor inputs must be paid full market prices (assuming subsidies do not exist).

4. While a precise level of affordability for water utility service usually does not exist, donors, international financial institutions, and other international organizations often quote the figures of 3 to 5 percent of disposable income or household expenditure.

5. The scarcity pricing study in Australia found that water restrictions are a relatively inefficient method of demand-side management (DSM); they impose inconvenience costs, generate allocative efficiency losses, and require substantial enforcement effort.

6. The use of consumer's and producer's surplus is broadly accepted as appropriate for analysis in public utility economics. Consumer's surplus has been used by the World Bank in evaluating water projects.

7. Utility economic regulators should make a reasonable attempt to incorporate full costs in water utility rates.

8. Since water is both a public and private good, the most appropriate method of evaluating water projects (e.g., DSM) is from a societal perspective.

9. To capture the impact of negative externalities, some countries (e.g., France) have imposed a 15 percent tax on water rates.

# CHAPTER TEN

# RECOMMENDATIONS FOR UTILITY REGULATORS

## 10.1 Overview

Nearly two decades ago, Dr. Patrick C. Mann, economics professor at West Virginia University and Institute Associate at NRRI, proposed various policy measures related to water utility rates and cost recovery. The context of his recommendations included many of the issues currently facing the water utility industry such as:

1) Financial pressures related to a deteriorating infrastructure and meeting more stringent drinking water regulations;

2) Pricing (rate) practices that have generated several forms of inefficiencies; and

3) Potentially numerous subsidies that may not be equitable or meeting their initial goals.

He identified five cost, finance, and rate initiatives. According to Dr. Mann, if the initiatives were implemented, they could reduce the inefficiencies inherent in traditional rate regulation.[235] Table 10.1 provides the status of his rate and cost recovery mechanism recommendations and the typical governmental authority responsible for implementing changes.

235 Mann, 1–2.

**Table 10.1**
**Status of Dr. Mann's Rate and Cost Recovery Recommendations**

| No. | Recommendation | Status | Authority |
|---|---|---|---|
| 1 | Integrating marginal costing into rate design | Rarely done | PSC or City Council |
| 2 | Where feasible, implement: seasonal, zonal, conservation surcharges, availability charges, system development charges | Some states use seasonal rates and surcharges (e.g., DISC) | PSC or City Council |
| 3 | Install incentive regulation mechanisms (e.g., PBR) | Rarely done | PSC or City Council |
| 4 | Selective state deregulation of IOUs | Limited | State legislature |
| 5 | Selective regulation of GOUs | Limited | State legislature |

Source: Author's construct.

## 10.2 Policy Recommendations

By most accounts very little progress has been made over the past twenty years in accomplishing Dr. Mann's recommendations. Furthermore, many of the problems in the water utility industry (particularly financial) have gotten worse. Water utility economic regulators have a variety of tools and options at their disposal that may solve some of the industry's challenges. Based on the facts and arguments set forth in this book, the options mentioned below should be implemented by the appropriate authority. In addition, Appendix D provides a proposed resolution on water utility costing and pricing reform for the National Association of Regulatory Utility Commissioners (NARUC) for consideration by its Water Committee. NARUC should pass this or a similar resolution.

1) Adopt the above-mentioned rate and cost recovery mechanisms identified by Dr. Mann.

2) As a policy, require that full costs included in Figure 1.3 and full value reflected in Figure 4.5 is an accounting identity for ratemaking purposes. This would fulfill one of Dr. Bonbright's ratemaking criteria—reflecting of *all* the present and future private and *social costs* and benefits occasioned by a service provider (i.e. all *externalities*).

3) Recognize that a water utility's customers may prefer, and are willing to pay for, different service reliability levels and/or other services. For instance, the value customers receive as the result of increased reliability may be higher or lower than prices based on embedded costs.

4) Provide water utilities with financial incentives for meeting various targets (i.e., performance-based regulation—PBR). For example, the CPUC will consider providing utility managers with financial incentives to encourage conservation, 236 and investment

236 CPUC "Water Action Plan," 19.

in infrastructure needed to improve water quality. [237] However, these two incentives may be too limited in that other measures of importance such as reliable service are excluded.

5) Require water utilities to identify their customers' willingness-to-pay as part of base rate cases. If companies complete these studies, they should be allowed to recover the associated prudent costs incurred in producing the study.

6) Use cost–benefit analysis (CBA) as the primary decisionmaking criterion in evaluating projects.

7) Similar to the Scottish water utility regulator, U.S. regulators should commit to unwinding subsidies. A good way to start is to reorganize a water utility into a "plain vanilla" company; however, certain economies of scope may not be achieved by the reorganized water utility.

8) In the context of setting water utility rates, establish maximizing economic welfare as the primary goal.

9) Similar to utility regulators in OECD countries, water utility regulators in the United States should establish ratemaking objectives around four dimensions: (a) economic efficiency, (b) financial sustainability, (c) environmental sustainability, and (d) social goals. Economic efficiency, however, should have the highest priority.

10) To the extent that regulators want to subsidize low-income water utility customers, consider implementing a "water stamp" program in lieu of altering rate structures. [238]

11) Require a utility to regularly assess the condition of its infrastructure; and disclose the results and potential rate increases (related to all causes such as increasing costs of water supplies) to the public (investors and customers). Thus, in an effort to promote the availability of information, the public will be in a position to make reasonable investment decisions (e.g., customer-paid conservation mechanisms).

12) Define sustainability metrics, and measure and report the financial health of the water utility to the public.

### 10.2.1 Pricing Reform

When marginal-cost pricing (particularly short-run) was first proposed for utilities, the proponents recommended funding any revenue *deficiency* with a tax. (Short-run marginal cost below average cost would not provide sufficient funds to pay for a utility's capital investments.) Today, instead of a revenue deficiency, a revenue surplus is more likely (assuming a water utility's LRMC is used). In Egypt, water utilities as part of their tariff applications are required to file embedded cost and marginal cost studies. As reflected in Appendix D, in the case of Alexandria Water Company, their LRMC is three times higher than their LRAC.

---

237 Ibid, 3.

238 Other economists have suggested this. For example, see Carriker and Dillman, 33–34.

As a result of implementing pricing reform based on marginal costs, a utility's surplus revenue (if any) could be used to:

1) Fund infrastructure projects. To implement this practice, new balance sheet and income statement accounts would need to be created. However, great care should be taken in choosing the projects with the highest cost-benefit ratios. A NRRI research paper calls upon regulatory commissions to establish reliability standards for water utilities before billions of dollars are spent replacing aging infrastructure; 239

2) Fund a PBR program to reward water utilities that exceed operational and financial performance standards established by utility regulators;

3) Invest in water conservation programs using the methodology used for Denver Water; and

4) Potentially rebate surplus revenues (if any) to water utility customers.

Finally, such a dramatic shift from cost-of-service pricing to full-cost pricing could be implemented over a couple of years. Regarding the potential issue of a utility's surplus revenue, it may be useful for U.S. policymakers to recall that residential customers from around the world have been willing to pay 5 to 8 percent of their household income for reliable water-utility service. (A commonly used rule of thumb used by the World Bank and multilateral institutions is a maximum of 5 percent of household income.) In comparison to other areas of the world, in the United States, the average portion of total household income used for water and wastewater services is less than 1 percent. Furthermore, in Germany, water rates are 3.7 times higher than in the United States 240 Thus, relative to other nations, water utility rates and charges in the United States still have plenty of room to increase. However, water rate increases should be predicated on the utility's reasonable estimate of its full costs and the achievement of meeting service standards and performance metrics.

## 10.3 Steps to Implementing Water Utility Costing and Pricing Reform

Table 10.2 identifies the recommended steps necessary for policymakers and utilities to implement water utility costing and pricing reform.

239 Rubin, iii.

240 Kathy L. Pape, Esq. Vice President, Treasurer and Rate Counsel, Aqua America, Inc. "Rate Setting & Full Cost Pricing," 3rd National Drinking Water Symposium, Broadmoor Hotel, Colorado Springs, Colorado, November 1, 2005.

**Table 10.2**
**Steps to Implementing Water Utility Costing and Pricing Reform**

| No. | Description | Regulator | Utility |
|---|---|---|---|
| 1 | Adopt a policy of recovering full costs in rates and maximizing economic welfare | X | |
| 2 | Complete a long-run marginal cost (or LRAIC) study | | X |
| 3 | Require full integrated resource plans (IRP) 241 | X | |
| 4 | If appropriate, analyze the necessary conditions and justifications for price discrimination | | X |
| 5 | Undertake and complete willingness-to-pay studies including estimating price elasticity of demand for each customer class | | X |
| 6 | Identify and disclose the amounts of all subsidies; routinely review and justify the need and appropriateness of the subsidies | | X |
| 7 | Regularly assess the condition of a utility's infrastructure 242 | | X |
| 8 | Disclose to the public (investors and customers) the condition of a utility's physical assets (i.e., plant in service) 243 | | X |
| 9 | Set a schedule for infrastructure improvements based on cost–benefit analysis | | X |
| 10 | Use cost–benefit analysis as the primary criteria in evaluating water projects | X | X |
| 11 | Define sustainability metrics | X | |
| 12 | Measure and report the financial health of the water utility to ensure sustainability 244 | | X |

Source: Author's construct.

241 Even if regulators do not require water utilities to complete full integrated resource plans, prudent business planning would suggest that utility managers complete them.

242 For example, in Dade County, Florida, the entire water and wastewater system is evaluated over a three-year cycle.

243 It is very unlikely that a utility's customers and investors understand the quality of a company's infrastructure and thus the likelihood of system failure. For instance, American Water Company's 2010 10-K Report states, "We believe that our properties are generally maintained in good operating condition and in accordance with current standards of good water and wastewater works industry practice, and units of property are replaced as and when necessary" (36). This information does not address the percentage of infrastructure that has passed its useful life, nor does it address a specific operating company.

244 For instance, see NRRI's Distress Classification Model. NRRI's model attempted to allow regulators to consistently identify water utilities that were distressed and in need of regulatory attention. David W. Wirick, John D. Borrows, and Steven Goldberg, "Evaluating Water Utility Capacity with Ratio Analysis and Discounted Cash Flows" (Columbus, OH: National Regulatory Research Institute, July 1997), 14–18.

# APPENDIX A

## Challenges Facing the U.S. Water Utility Industry

For many years, the U.S. water utility industry has incurred a number of challenges including, but not limited to:

1) Irrational water pricing and use (e.g., using subsidized water to grow low-value crops);

2) The need to replace large portions of the country's water infrastructure;

3) Declining sales related to conservation and other issues;

4) Many water utilities (particularly small) are not viable (i.e., sustainable) in terms of financial, managerial, and operational criteria; and

5) Unique characteristics of the water utility industry that is different from the natural gas and electric utility industries.

The following is a brief discussion of these challenges.

### Irrational Water Pricing and Use

In many countries including the United States, regardless of the scarcity of water, government entities subsidize water for irrigation and domestic uses. In the United States, a classic example is how the federal government made water cheap for farmers and miners in developing the West. The U.S. Department of Interior's Bureau of Reclamation is the largest supplier of irrigation water. The Bureau diverts 40–85 percent of major Western river systems and of that quantity, 85 percent is allocated to agriculture. The allocated amount is through long-term contracts with water or irrigation districts, and the districts provide water to individual farmers. The contracts between the agency and the districts specify below-cost (subsidized) prices and fixed water allotments to ensure that water is available to farmers. 245

Many people believe that water is a free good, an unlimited resource, and an entitlement. Other areas of the world have recognized the need to use water more efficiently. For example, the Water Framework Directive of the European Union requires countries to ensure that water pricing policies provide incentives to use water efficiently, and for all sectors to contribute to *full cost recovery*, including environmental costs.

Many studies in the United States argue that water is underpriced. 246 For example, a U.S. General Accounting Office (GAO) study collected data from approximately 75 percent of U.S. drinking water and wastewater utilities serving populations of more than ten thousand. In the

245 Raucher et al., 49.

246 Robert Renner, Executive Director, Water Research Foundation, "Current Water Infrastructure Research," presentation at the NARUC Winter Committee Meetings, February 16, 2010.

study, more than half of the utilities whose revenues from user charges and local sources did not provide sufficient funds to cover their cost of providing service raised their rates only two times for fewer between 1992 and 2001. 247 In addition, not a single reputable study has been found supporting the conclusion that water is overpriced. Furthermore, another study pertaining to water pricing is a 1994 national rate survey conducted by the accounting firm, Ernst and Young. They found:

> *"a crazy-quilt pattern of charges that bears almost no relationship to water scarcity or surplus."* 248

An examination of water rates within the United States (as well as in other nations) shows unusual relationships. For example, for residential customers who consume 3,750 gallons of water per month, on a scale of 1 (lowest) and 50 (highest), Phoenix, Arizona, is ranked 34th while Tucson, Arizona, (approximately 60 miles south) has a score of 18. Similarly, Colorado Springs, Colorado, is ranked 42 while Denver is ranked 13. Again, these cities are approximately 60 miles apart. 249

The United States is not alone regarding inappropriate water pricing practices. In establishing a proper policy, legal, and institutional framework in India, economists Katar Singh and Anil Shishodia made various recommendations to policymakers, including setting water prices to account for their real resource cost and ability of water users to pay for the commodity.

## Infrastructure Replacement

In addition to irrational water pricing and use, a September 2003 study by the American Society of Civil Engineers (ASCE) gave the water and wastewater infrastructure a mark of "D." 250 As of 2008, their grade dropped to a "D–." 251 Unfortunately, as of 2010 the grade has remained the same. 252 Water main breaks, sinkholes, and sewer overflow incidents are on the rise. Approximately three hundred thousand water main breaks occur each year. 253 254 For example, in the fourth quarter 2010, cities in Missouri suffered hundreds of broken water mains due to the drought. Aging infrastructures, especially water mains made of cast iron, are particularly vulnerable to weather-related conditions that cause the earth to shift and pipes to break. 255

---

247 Melissa J. Stanford, "Replacing and Securing Water Utility Infrastructure" (Columbus, OH: National Regulatory Research Institute, 2004), 5.

248 Simon, 130–31.

249 Black & Veatch, "2009/2010 50 Largest Cities Water/Wastewater Rate Survey" (Overland Park, KS: Black & Veatch), 4. www.bv.com/consult.

250 Stanford, 6.

251 Tim Winter, Jesup & Lamont Securities, "Which Came First…The CHICKEN or the EGG The Importance of Allowed ROE's in the Water Utility Sector," presentation at the 111th NAWC Annual Conference, October 21, 2008, Santa Fe, New Mexico.

252 Debra G. Coy, Svanda & Coy Consulting, "Attracting Capital to Water Utilities and Water Projects," presentation at the 113th NAWC Annual Conference, October 11, 2010, Tucson, Arizona, 2.

253 Robert Renner, Executive Director, Water Research Foundation, "Current Water Infrastructure Research," presentation at the NARUC Winter Committee Meetings, February 16, 2010.

254 Ibid, 2.

255 First Research, "Water & Sewer Utilities," 4.

The challenge of replacing the country's water infrastructure is not limited to small water utilities. For instance, in 2008 *Value Line Investment Survey* was concerned about the industry's ability to fund its growing infrastructure needs. 256 Unfortunately, this problem has not significantly improved. In a October 2010 report, the *Value Line Investment Survey* stated:

> "*None of the companies in this industry have the cash coffers to meet the upcoming maintenance costs associated with decaying water systems and pipelines. These pressures are not likely to abate anytime soon and ought to continue climbing higher, based on the current shape of America's water systems.*" (emphasis added) 257

Even some AWWA members refer to the problem as "the infrastructure crisis." Members of AWWA's Water Utility Council and Public Affairs Council are not optimistic regarding the likelihood that the nation's water infrastructure problems will be solved. The following are views from some AWWA members related to fixing the water infrastructure:

> "*Unfortunately, it seems to require a disaster or catastrophe.*"

> "*The tyranny of the immediate has taken over public decision-making.*"

> "*For most communities, it will probably take a significant critical event where it is perceived that the public's health or safety has been put in jeopardy. Then elected officials can champion the solution and position themselves as protecting the public from imminent disaster.*" 258

The AwwaRF estimates the costs associated with maintenance and replacement of water infrastructure over the next twenty years are projected to be approximately $335 billion and distributed in the following manner:

1) Transmission and distribution mains, 60 percent;

2) Water treatment, 22 percent;

3) Water storage, 11 percent;

4) Source, 6 percent; and

5) Miscellaneous/other, 1 percent. 259

Furthermore, the projected "gap" in infrastructure spending amounts to between $500 billion to $1.2 trillion over twenty years, and that federal assistance will likely fund only 10–15 percent of the estimated investment. 260 The gap reflects the projected infrastructure investment needs and current levels of spending. One industry expert estimates that as of 2008 infrastructure

---

256 *Value Line Investment Survey*, July 25, 2008, 1416.

257 *Value Line Investment Survey*, October 22, 2010, 1791.

258 Steve Maxwell, ed., *The Business of Water A Concise Overview of Challenges and Opportunities in the Water Market* (Denver, CO: American Water Works Association, 2008), 119.

259 Renner presentation, 25.

260 Maxwell, 37.

replacement is 20 percent below the needed levels. [261] Finally, one-third of government-owned water/wastewater utilities report that 20 percent or more of their pipes are reaching the point where they can no longer provide reliable service. [262] Finally, AwwaRF reports that many water utilities are replacing less than one percent of their pipes annually. [263]

With respect to U.S. IOUs, the financial statements filed with the United States Securities and Exchange Commission (SEC) often do not identify the age of their assets. One investor-owned water utility reported (in confidence) that more than 90 percent of their wells were beyond the point where they can no longer provide reliable service.

Finally, for years the so-called "infrastructure funding gap" has been discussed at almost every major water utility conference. Other capital-intensive industries such as airline, steel, and auto also have vast future capital investment requirements. In those cases, however, market forces are presumed to result in attracting the needed capital. This is not the case in the water utility industry where the sources of additional capital necessary to solve the infrastructure replacement problem are not clear.

## Declining Sales

The water utility business is considered a "mature" industry where total sales are correlated with the growth of the local population. Total annual water withdrawals peaked around 1980 and have remained relatively flat since that time. [264] With various conservation measures, total demand is expected to remain flat through the year 2030. [265] In addition, per capita consumption has been declining for several years. Finally, in many cases, regulators have required water utilities to implement water conservation programs even if they are not economically viable. These trends coupled with increasing costs related to water treatment, water supply, and replacing an aging infrastructure have placed financial strains on many water utilities.

## The Water Industry as Compared to the Natural Gas and Electric Utility Industries

The water utility industry is unlike the natural gas and electric utility industry in numerous areas. First, water is injected in the human body and necessary for survival. Second, water quality standards are set by the EPA and/or state health authorities. Third, water is very heavy and difficult/expensive to transport over long distances. Fourth, a national water policy does not exist. Fifth, water is found in basins that overlap state boundaries (e.g., Delaware River Basin Commission). Sixth, state and regional water laws (e.g., riparian doctrine, prior appropriation) are not uniform. Seventh, water has historically been considered a local issue and city, county, and state authorities are extremely sensitive to controlling supply. As a result, various water management districts have been formed. Eighth, water transfers and exchanges have historically been difficult to complete. Ninth, water is often considered an entitlement, and social and political forces tend to require a water utility to provide a minimum amount of water at affordable

---

261 Tom Curtis, "Models for National Infrastructure Investment Programs," presentation at the 111th National Association of Water Companies Annual Conference, October 19–22, 2008, Santa Fe, New Mexico.

262 Maxwell, 37.

263 Ibid, 37.

264 Janice A. Beecher, "The conservation conundrum: How declining demand affects water utilities," *Journal AWWA* (Denver, CO: American Water Works Association Journal, February 2010), 79.

265 Ibid., 80.

rates. Tenth, water is often both a private and public good. Eleventh, economic regulation in the United States has been difficult due to the extremely large number of water utilities. Recently, more than 50,000 water utilities (mostly public) have operated in the United States.

Table A.1 illustrates how water quality, quantity, and price issues overlap federal, interstate, state, substate, and local jurisdictions.

**Table A.1**
**Regulatory Jurisdiction for Water Utilities**

| Issue | Federal | Interstate | State | Substate | Local |
|---|---|---|---|---|---|
| Quality | EPA | | Drinking water primary agencies | | Public health departments |
| Quantity | | River basin commissions | Water resource agencies | Water management districts | |
| Prices | | | PSC or PUC (mostly investor-owned systems) | | Public ownership, other local controls |

Source: Janice A. Beecher, "Economic Regulation of Water Utilities: A Primer" (Washington, DC: National Association of Water Companies, 2001), 2.

---

A good example of conflicting water laws and policies relates to how projects are evaluated. Cost–benefit analysis of federal water projects can be quite different from how a state regulatory commission or other government water authorities may evaluate the same project. Key differences include:

1) The discount rate used (i.e., social discount rate for public projects as compared to a private discount rate for investor-owned utilities);

2) The time horizon used in the analysis; and

3) Which costs and benefits are to be included in the analysis.

## Summary

The U.S. water utility industry creates enormous challenges for policymakers. This is one reason why policymakers might consider revising their long-established approaches to pricing water and utility services based on supply costs and place more emphasis on full costs.

Consider the situation facing many U.S. water utilities:

1) A combination of institutional (particularly political) issues have limited rate increases;

2) A public perception that water should be provided either free or at a nominal cost;

3) An unwillingness of policymakers to apply economic methods (e.g., value-of-service pricing); and

4) Supplying water (the good and the service) is an *increasing*-cost industry resulting primarily from, among various factors:

   - More stringent environmental standards;
   - Decreased per capita consumption;
   - Increasing costs of supply (e.g., water from desalination plants);
   - Diseconomies of scale involving transporting water; and
   - Replacing basic water infrastructure.

# APPENDIX B

## Primary Types of Nonmarket Water Valuation Methods

### Inductive Valuation Techniques

Inductive valuation techniques are nonmarket valuation techniques, including *expressed preferences* and *revealed preferences*, which use inductive reasoning (i.e., reasoning from specific empirical observations to broader generalizations, usually statistical methods) to infer *willingness-to-pay* from empirical observations of behavior, including market transactions or responses to questionnaires.

**Benefit Function Transfer/Meta-Analysis:** Statistical synthesis of the results of previously reported studies of the same phenomenon or relationship to distill generalizations.

**Choice Modeling:** An express preference method that infers *willingness-to-pay* in the absence of markets by directly asking a sample of respondents to make choices among alternative policies; the technique assumes preferences are based on several attributes of a product or situation, and values proposals by assessing tradeoffs among attributes.

**Contingent Valuation Method (CVM):** An *expressed preference method* that asks individuals the value (in monetary terms) of specified changes in quantities or qualities of environmental goods and services. The method is especially useful where nonuse values are important.

**Damage Cost Methods:** Maximum willingness-to-pay given as monetary value of damages avoided.

**Defensive Behavior Method:** A revealed preference method using reductions in the costs of actions taken to mitigate or avoid incurring an external cost as a partial measure of the benefits of policies from reducing the externality.

**Econometric Estimation of Production and Cost Functions:** Primary or secondary data on industrial and agricultural inputs and outputs analyzed with statistical (usually regression) techniques.

**Econometric Estimation of Water Utility Demand Functions:** Primary or secondary water utility data analyzed with statistical methods.

**Expressed Preference Method:** The class of methods, including contingent valuation and choice modeling, which determine, by questionnaire, how much a respondent would be willing to pay for a change in quantity or quality of an environmental good. It is useful where no complementary or substitute private goods are available from which to derive behavior-based willingness-to-pay.

**Hedonic Property Value Method:** A *revealed preference* method of isolating the value of one attribute of a complicated multiattribute good or service (usually farm land or residences) by statistically seperating the contributions of the various attributes using data from market transactions on a selected good or service.

**Observations of Water Market Transactions:** Observed prices from transactions for short-term leases or permanent sale of water rights.

**Property Damage Avoided (PDA):** The estimated present value of real (inflation-free), expected property damages avoided by a project or policy. It is the principal technique for estimating urban flood risk reduction benefits. This method is criticized for ignoring nonproperty effects such as individual and community disruption, medical expenses, productivity losses, and preflood anxiety.

**Revealed Preferences Method:** Nonmarket valuation methods, including *travel cost* and *hedonic pricing*, which infer economic value from analysis of actual consumer decisions or market transactions.

**Travel Cost Method (TCM):** A revealed preference approach to valuing recreational sites that derives a demand schedule from statistical analysis of the costs of travel.

## Deductive Valuation Techniques

Deductive valuation techniques are models (including residual, alternative cost, and benefit transfer methods) that primarily use *deductive reasoning* (i.e., reasoning from general principles and assumptions to specific conclusions using logical or mathematical rules. Conclusions are only as valid as the initial assumptions.)

**Alternative (Avoided) Cost:** Value attributable to cost savings from next-best alternative source of service.

**Benefit Transfer:** Benefits estimated for one or more sites or policy proposals employed to assign benefits or value to other sites or policy proposals.

**Change in Net Rents:** Constructed residual models for deriving an interval estimate of net producers' income or rents attributable to an increment of water via budget or spreadsheet.

**Computable General Equilibrium Models:** Constructed models for deriving net producers' income or rents attributable to water via price-endogenous optimization models.

**Mathetical Programming:** Constructed residual models for deriving net producers' rents or marginal costs attributable to water via (usually) fixed-price optimization models.

**Residual Methods:** A class of methods used primarily for valuing nonmarketed producers' or intermediate goods. They approximate the net rent or value of the marginal product of a nonpriced productive input by subtracting all other estimated costs of production from forecasted total value of output. The remaining (residual) value is assigned to the nonpriced input (water).

**Value Added:** Constructed models of net producers' income or rents attributable to water via value-added measures from input-output models.

Source: Young, *Determining the Economic Value of Water, Concepts and Methods*, 47–49.

**Table B.1**
**Selected Nonmarket Valuation Case Studies in the Water Industry**

| No. | Topic | Method |
|---|---|---|
| 1 | Residential customer water supply reliability | CVM |
| 2 | Groundwater values | Avoided cost method |
| 3 | Agricultural water rights | Hedonic property method; change in net rents |
| 4 | Agriculture—Drought water banks | Change in net rents |
| 5 | New York City, water demand study | Lost consumer's surplus |
| 6 | At-source residential water value | Benefit transfer method |

Source: David L. Hayward, *The Economic Value of Water Utility Services: A Survey of Theory, Methods, and Applications* (West Conshohocken, PA: Infinity Publishing Company, 2009), 147–57.

# APPENDIX C

## Proposed NARUC Resolution Supporting Consideration of Water Utility Costing and Pricing Methods

**WHEREAS,** key water industry organizations (e.g., NAWC, Clean Water America Alliance) claim that the price of water is a great value, but very few facts and supporting information are included in utility base rate cases or communicated to the public.

**WHEREAS**, currently in America the water utility industry has serious problems such as: (a) an infrastructure graded by the American Society of Civil Engineers (ASCE) as D–; (b) inefficient pricing and use; (c) deteriorating financial viability reflected, in part, by insufficient operating cash flow to fund infrastructure replacement and growth; and low returns on equity (ROE) and returns on assets (ROA).

**WHEREAS,** various studies have found that some water utility customers were willing to pay hundreds of dollars more per year to receive reliable service. However, this desire is rarely incorporated in prices (i.e., water utility rates).

**WHEREAS**, various studies show a high correlation between the quality of water infrastructure and economic growth.

**WHEREAS,** in the United States, the most common practice of pricing utility services is based on historical costs, and a cost-of-service study is used to allocate costs among a utility's customer classes.

**WHEREAS,** in the United States, current pricing practices often incorporate numerous subsidies depending on the characteristics of a water utility. Rate orders issued by utility regulators rarely identify these subsidies and amounts. Moreover, utility regulators rarely provide explicit policies regarding future subsidies. Once subsidies are established, they tend to last indefinitely.

**WHEREAS**, In the U.S. water utility industry, customers normally focus on three issues—quality, quantity, and reliability of water delivered at specific times, locations, and conditions. Current water utility pricing practices normally do not efficiently capture these costs and customer desires.

**WHEREAS,** full-cost pricing has been recommended by numerous water utility experts and institutions (e.g., World Bank, EU). Full costs include: O&M expenses, capital charges, opportunity costs, and costs resulting from externalities.

**WHEREAS,** full-cost pricing is not the same as cost-of-service pricing based on accounting figures.

**WHEREAS,** the full value of water often includes: intrinsic value, value to society, value to water users, and externalities.

**WHEREAS**, well-recognized and accepted methods exist to estimate value of service.

**WHEREAS,** water as a commodity and reflected in terms of quality, taste, color, and smell is different from the delivery service (e.g., degree of reliability). However, water utility prices (rates) usually do not capture the true value of the commodity and delivery service.

**WHEREAS,** a working definition of value of service is: assigning monetary measures of individuals' preferences for outcomes of policy proposals or events (e.g., water of a minimum quality delivered with a specified level of reliability).

**WHEREAS,** value-of-service pricing has been used in various regulated industries (e.g., railroad, telephone, natural gas, and electric).

**WHEREAS,** the market-clearing price is the most appropriate definition for value-of-service pricing.

**WHEREAS,** limitations exist to both cost-of-service pricing and value-of-service pricing.

**WHEREAS**, an accounting identity exists between full-cost pricing and the full value of water.

**WHEREAS,** using the concepts from welfare economics in terms of valuing water and water services could improve utility pricing practices. Economic efficient rates are an important criteria of a sound rate structure, and (given the challenges in the water utility industry—particularly a decaying infrastructure) should be regulators' primary goal in the context of pricing (rate) decisions.

**WHEREAS,** a water utility's value of service for a customer class serves as the ceiling for rates in what is called the "zone of reasonableness." The floor of the zone is usually the water utility's short-run marginal costs.

**WHEREAS,** pricing based on value of service (as contrasted with pricing based on cost of service) is endorsed by well-respected economists, assuming necessary conditions are met and justification for price discrimination exists.

**WHEREAS,** price discrimination (the result of value-of-service pricing) results when a firm sells the same service at rates that are not proportional to costs.

**WHEREAS,** numerous legal precedents exist for value-of-service pricing. When a utility regulatory agency has conservation, social, or other non-cost recovery goals, it may favor value-of-service pricing.

**WHEREAS**, the courts have held that a rate design (i.e., pricing) chosen and implemented by a particular utility need not be the best, nor have mathematical exactitude, but merely be reasonable.

**WHEREAS,** the AwwaRF has determined that market-based methodologies exist for estimating customer outages costs (COC) could easily be applied to estimating costs of customer service interruption (a type of externality) resulting from water infrastructure failure. Infrastructure failure relates to reliability of service.

**WHEREAS,** water utility willingness-to-pay studies (necessary for value-of-service pricing) are rarely undertaken in the United States while such studies are common in developing (third-world) countries.

**WHEREAS,** water utilities rarely have price elasticity of demand information regarding their customer classes. This is one of four conditions most economists view as necessary for price discrimination and implementing value-of-service pricing.

**WHEREAS,** for most U.S. water utilities, implementing value-of-service pricing would likely result in excessive revenues and possibly (but not necessarily) profits. Utility economic regulators have several options for dealing with this issue including phasing in value-based rates.

**WHEREAS,** the argument that charging rates based on customers' willingness-to-pay "extracts consumer surplus" may be overstated. This is because the rates consumers pay are often significantly below "full costs."

**RESOLVED, water utility economic regulators should make a reasonable attempt to incorporate full costs in water rates.**

# APPENDIX D

## Estimates of Long-Run Average and Marginal Costs for Alexandria Water Company (Alexandria, Egypt)

**EWRA Tariff Review Submission - Long-Term Projections of Development Strategy (2010-2039)**

**Operating Company** ~Alexandria water company

Discount rate 10%

Total supply augmentation investment over 2010-2039: 800 $M\ m^3$ capacity expansion; 8000 M EGP capital cost (excluding inflation)

| | | LRAIC | LRAC |
|---|---|---|---|
| NPV Incremental/Total Costs | *M EGP* | 4,727 | 10,705 |
| NPV Incremental/Total Water Supply | *$M\ m^3$* | 1,578 | 10,672 |
| **Long-run costs** | *$EGP/m^3$* | 3.00 | 1.00 |

Data

Control variables - note that investment phasing has to be redone if reduction in per capita demand is changed or loss reduction is significant.

| | | *Units* | **2010** | **2011** | **2012** | **2013** | **2014** | **2015** | **2016** | **2017** | **2018** | **2019** | **2020** | **2021** | **2022** | **2023** | **2024** | **2025** | **2026** | **2027** | **2028** | **2029** | **2030** |
|---|---|---|---|---|---|---|---|---|---|---|---|---|---|---|---|---|---|---|---|---|---|---|---|
| **Demand** | Population | *million* | 4.100 | 4.186 | 4.274 | 4.364 | 4.455 | 4.549 | 4.644 | 4.742 | 4.842 | 4.943 | 5.047 | 5.153 | 5.261 | 5.372 | 5.485 | 5.600 | 5.717 | 5.837 | 5.960 | 6.085 | 6.213 |
| | change p.a. | % | - | 2.1% | 2.1% | 2.1% | 2.1% | 2.1% | 2.1% | 2.1% | 2.1% | 2.1% | 2.1% | 2.1% | 2.1% | 2.1% | 2.1% | 2.1% | 2.1% | 2.1% | 2.1% | 2.1% | 2.1% |
| | Per Capita Demand | *m3/capita* | 200 | 200 | 200 | 200 | 200 | 200 | 200 | 200 | 200 | 200 | 200 | 200 | 200 | 200 | 200 | 200 | 200 | 200 | 200 | 200 | 200 |
| | change p.a. | % | | 0.0% | 0.0% | 0.0% | 0.0% | 0.0% | 0.0% | 0.0% | 0.0% | 0.0% | 0.0% | 0.0% | 0.0% | 0.0% | 0.0% | 0.0% | 0.0% | 0.0% | 0.0% | 0.0% | 0.0% |
| | Total demand | *$M\ m^3$ p.a.* | 820 | 837 | 855 | 873 | 891 | 910 | 929 | 948 | 968 | 989 | 1,009 | 1,031 | 1,052 | 1,074 | 1,097 | 1,120 | 1,143 | 1,167 | 1,192 | 1,217 | 1,243 |
| **Losses** | Losses | % | 15% | 15% | 15% | 14% | 14% | 14% | 14% | 13% | 13% | 13% | 13% | 13% | 13% | 12% | 12% | 12% | 12% | 12% | 11% | 11% | 11% |
| | Improvement p.a. | % | - | 1.5% | 1.5% | 1.5% | 1.5% | 1.5% | 1.5% | 1.5% | 1.5% | 1.5% | 1.5% | 1.5% | 1.5% | 1.5% | 1.5% | 1.5% | 1.5% | 1.5% | 1.5% | 1.5% | 1.5% |
| | Total losses | *$M\ m^3$ p.a.* | 145 | 145 | 146 | 146 | 147 | 147 | 147 | 148 | 148 | 149 | 149 | 150 | 150 | 151 | 152 | 152 | 153 | 153 | 154 | 154 | 155 |
| **Supply** | Total supply | *M m3 p.a.* | 965 | 982 | 1,000 | 1,019 | 1,038 | 1,057 | 1,076 | 1,096 | 1,117 | 1,138 | 1,159 | 1,181 | 1,203 | 1,225 | 1,248 | 1,272 | 1,296 | 1,321 | 1,346 | 1,371 | 1,398 |
| | Incremental supply | *$M\ m^3$ p.a.* | 0 | 18 | 36 | 54 | 73 | 92 | 112 | 132 | 152 | 173 | 194 | 216 | 238 | 261 | 284 | 307 | 331 | 356 | 381 | 407 | 433 |
| **Shortfall** | Before investment | *$M\ m^3$ p.a.* | 0 | 0 | 16 | 35 | 54 | 73 | 92 | 112 | 133 | 154 | 175 | 197 | 219 | 241 | 264 | 288 | 312 | 337 | 362 | 387 | 414 |
| | After Investment | | 0 | 0 | 0 | 0 | 0 | 0 | 0 | 0 | 0 | 0 | 0 | 0 | 0 | 0 | 0 | 0 | 0 | 0 | 0 | 0 | 0 |
| **Capacity** | Current Capacity | *$M\ m^3$ p.a.* | 984 | 984 | 984 | 984 | 984 | 984 | 984 | 984 | 984 | 984 | 984 | 984 | 984 | 984 | 984 | 984 | 984 | 984 | 984 | 984 | 984 |
| | Additional Capacity | *$M\ m^3$ p.a.* | 0 | 0 | 200 | 200 | 200 | 200 | 200 | 200 | 200 | 200 | 200 | 200 | 400 | 400 | 400 | 400 | 400 | 400 | 400 | 400 | 600 |
| | Total Capacity | *$M\ m^3$ p.a.* | 984 | 984 | 1,184 | 1,184 | 1,184 | 1,184 | 1,184 | 1,184 | 1,184 | 1,184 | 1,184 | 1,184 | 1,384 | 1,384 | 1,384 | 1,384 | 1,384 | 1,384 | 1,384 | 1,384 | 1,584 |
| **Existing costs** | Volume related O&M | *$EGP/m^3$* | 0.45 | 0.45 | 0.44 | 0.44 | 0.43 | 0.43 | 0.42 | 0.42 | 0.42 | 0.41 | 0.41 | 0.40 | 0.40 | 0.39 | 0.39 | 0.39 | 0.38 | 0.38 | 0.38 | 0.37 | 0.37 |
| | Improvement p.a. | % | - | 1.0% | 1.0% | 1.0% | 1.0% | 1.0% | 1.0% | 1.0% | 1.0% | 1.0% | 1.0% | 1.0% | 1.0% | 1.0% | 1.0% | 1.0% | 1.0% | 1.0% | 1.0% | 1.0% | 1.0% |
| | Fixed costs | *M EGP p.a.* | 150.0 | 149.3 | 148.5 | 147.8 | 147.0 | 146.3 | 145.6 | 144.8 | 144.1 | 143.4 | 142.7 | 142.0 | 141.2 | 140.5 | 139.8 | 139.1 | 138.4 | 137.7 | 137.1 | 136.4 | 135.7 |
| | Improvement p.a. | % | - | 0.5% | 0.5% | 0.5% | 0.5% | 0.5% | 0.5% | 0.5% | 0.5% | 0.5% | 0.5% | 0.5% | 0.5% | 0.5% | 0.5% | 0.5% | 0.5% | 0.5% | 0.5% | 0.5% | 0.5% |
| | Annual costs - opex | *M EGP p.a.* | 584 | 587 | 590 | 593 | 596 | 599 | 602 | 605 | 608 | 611 | 614 | 618 | 621 | 624 | 628 | 631 | 635 | 639 | 642 | 646 | 650 |
| **Capacity expansion or** | Additional capacity | *$M\ m^3$ p.a.* | | | 200 | | | | | | | | | | 200 | | | | | | | | 200 |
| **enhancement** | Year of new capacity | | | | **2012** | | | | | | | | | | **2022** | | | | | | | | **2030** |
| **projects** | New capex | *M EGP* | | | 2,000 | | | | | | | | | | 2,000 | | | | | | | | 2,000 |
| **Replacements** | Replacement capex | *M EGP* | 50 | 500 | 500 | 500 | 500 | 500 | 125 | 100 | 100 | 100 | 100 | 100 | 150 | 150 | 150 | 150 | 150 | 150 | 150 | 150 | 200 |
| | Annual costs - capex | *M EGP p.a.* | 50 | 500 | 2,500 | 500 | 500 | 500 | 125 | 100 | 100 | 100 | 100 | 100 | 2,150 | 150 | 150 | 150 | 150 | 150 | 150 | 150 | 2,200 |
| **Total costs** | Total Annual costs | *M EGP* | 634 | 1,087 | 3,090 | 1,093 | 1,096 | 1,099 | 727 | 705 | 708 | 711 | 714 | 718 | 2,771 | 774 | 778 | 781 | 785 | 789 | 792 | 796 | 2,850 |
| | Incremental costs | *M EGP* | 0 | 453 | 2,456 | 458 | 461 | 464 | 92 | 71 | 74 | 77 | 80 | 83 | 2,137 | 140 | 144 | 147 | 151 | 155 | 158 | 162 | 2,216 |

# Social Tariff and Economic Costs Assumptions and Methodology

The purpose of this figure is to show the potential range of Alexandria Water Company's unit costs given the definition of "costs" in the Draft Water Law. In addition, we have attempted to quantify various subsidies (e.g., subsidies resulting from lost income taxes). To the extent that subsidies exist, policymakers are frequently interested in knowing the form of subsidy and the amount.

Possible subsidies in the Egyptian water sector include: (a) interclass, (b) intraclass, (c) cash subsidies from the Government of Egypt (GOE), (d) plant built by NOPWASD—an agency of the Egyptian Government, (e) intergenerational, (f) lost tax revenues, (g) below-market cost of capital, (h) subsidies from the Holding Company to the operating utilities (e.g., Alexandria Water), (i) interoperating company, (j) loan guarantees from the GOE related to public–private partnership (PPP) projects, and (k) inflated labor costs resulting from an excessive number of utility employees.

| Bar Title | Description | Analysis |
|---|---|---|
| 1 | Social tariff | The social tariff is presently LE .23/cubic meter for domestic customers for the first 10 cubic meters per month. This rate does not have any clear connection to the utility's costs (i.e., it is a political decision)<br><br>**LE0.23 per cubic meter** |
| 2 | O&M (historical) | O&M costs of LE99,764,000 and sales of 211,005 million cubic meters<br><br>**LE0.47 per cubic meter** |
| 3 | Ave. cost | Average costs include book value O&M, depreciation, indirect taxes, interest expenses, and equity return. Note that we have not made any normalization adjustments. That is, book values are identical to the amounts used for ratemaking.<br><br>O&M 99,746<br>Depreciation 31,000<br>Indirect taxes 1,962<br>Equity return 3,665<br>Interest expense 0<br>Total 136,373<br>Sales 211,005<br>**LE0.646 per cubic meter** |
| 4 | Ave. cost + return (gov.) | This scenario reflects the above costs with the following exceptions: (a) the capital structure is 100% equity, (b) the cost of capital is assumed to be 10%, (c) operating income is rate base multiplied by 10%, (d) income taxes are paid on profits (operating income) at the current tax rate of 20%.<br><br>O&M 99,746<br>Depreciation 31,000<br>Indirect taxes 1,962<br>Operating inc. 3,665<br>Income taxes 0<br>Total 206,676<br>Sales 211,005<br>**LE0.98 per cubic meter** |

<table>
<tr>
<td>5</td>
<td>Ave. cost + market return</td>
<td>
The historical O&M expenses, plus depreciation plus return to government (debt and equity) plus indirect taxes consistent with the GOE's long-run goal of allowing up to 49% private equity ownership interest in the operating companies, the following capital structure and cost of capital are assumed. The cost of debt and equity represent marginal costs.
The mix of long-term debt and equity is similar to large well-managed water utilities in the United States having an S&P bond of "A." The cost of equity capital of 25 percent is conservative for a variety of reasons: (a) minority interest owner, (b) marketability discount; (c) economic regulatory structure not operational; and (d) historical track record of losing money (i.e., little if any profitability—the return on invested capital (ROIC) for the year was .6 percent) (The range of the utility's marginal cost of equity capital is likely to be 25–35 percent.) The assumption is the water utility is a "stand-alone" entity without any government guarantees or nonutility operations.
<table>
<tr><td>O&M</td><td>99,746</td></tr>
<tr><td>Depreciation</td><td>31,000</td></tr>
<tr><td>Indirect taxes</td><td>1,962</td></tr>
<tr><td>Interest expense</td><td>31,436</td></tr>
<tr><td>Income taxes</td><td>15,102</td></tr>
<tr><td>Net income</td><td>75,509</td></tr>
<tr><td>Total</td><td>254,755</td></tr>
<tr><td>Sales</td><td>211,005</td></tr>
<tr><td>Operating income</td><td>106,945</td></tr>
</table>
<table>
<tr><th>Type of Capital</th><th>%</th><th>Cost</th><th>WACC</th></tr>
<tr><td>Equity</td><td>49</td><td>0.25</td><td>12.25</td></tr>
<tr><td>Long-term debt</td><td>51</td><td>0.10</td><td>5.10</td></tr>
<tr><td>TOTAL</td><td>100</td><td></td><td>17.35</td></tr>
</table>
Cost of debt times percent in capital Structure times rate base net income multiplied by the tax rate of 20%
Note: sum of interest expense and net income equals operating income
RATE BASE
<table>
<tr><td>Net Plant in Service</td><td>603,929</td></tr>
<tr><td>Cash working capital</td><td>12,468</td></tr>
<tr><td>Total Rate Base</td><td>616,397</td></tr>
<tr><td>WACC</td><td>.1735</td></tr>
<tr><td>Operating income</td><td>106,945</td></tr>
</table>
LE1.21 per cubic meter
</td>
</tr>
</table>

| Bar Title | Description | Analysis |
|---|---|---|
| 6 | LRAIC | LRAIC is long-run average incremental cost. A rough analysis was completed by Mott MacDonald for Alexandria Water Company. The analysis includes a 10% "social discount rate." **LE3.00 per cubic meter.** |

## Subsidies

1. Low-Income Subsidies

Assuming full accounting costs of 1.21/LE per cubic meter and the social tariff of LE.23 per cubic meter the differential is as follows:

| | |
|---|---|
| Average accounting unit costs | 1.21 |
| Social tariff | .23 |
| Social tariff subsidy | .98 |
| Sales at the social rate | 85,560,757 cubic meters |
| Annual subsidy | LE83,621,881 |

2. Lost-Income Tax Revenues

LE15,102,000 per year based on average cost plus market return (No. 5 above).

Since the Company showed limited profits (given its financial statements), it did not pay income taxes. This represents a form of subsidy in that an equivalent amount of revenues must be derived from other sources and/or social services are foregone.

3. Opportunity Costs

Finally, the difference between the Company's average historical cost per unit determined from the cost of service study, and the long-run average incremental cost represents another form of subsidy. That is, water is underpriced in relation to its economic cost. The annual subsidy is as follows:

| | |
|---|---|
| LRAIC | 3.00 |
| Ave. accounting cost | .65 |
| Difference | LE2.35 per cubic meter |
| Annual sales | 211,005,000 cubic meter |
| Subsidy | LE495,861,750 per year. |

# APPENDIX E

## Table E.1

## Sample Residential Water Bill, Charges, and Rates
## City of Oceanside, California
## Service Period: 03/07/11 To 04/07/11

| Line No. | Description | Rate/Unit ($) | Consumption 5/ Units 2/ | Charge ($) | Total ($) |
|---|---|---|---|---|---|
| 1 | Service Charge 1/ | | | 13.71 | |
| 2 | Commodity Tier 1 | 1.99 | 13.0 | 25.87 | |
| 3 | Commodity Tier 2 | 2.28 | 6.0 | 13.68 | |
| 4 | MWD Readiness-to-Serve 3/ | | | 1.52 | |
| 5 | SDCWA Infrastructure 4/ | | | 2.49 | |
| 6 | SDCWA Surcharge | | | 19.19 | |
| 7 | Clean Water Program | | | 1.33 | 77.79 |

Notes:

1/ Meter size: 5/8 inch
2/ 1 unit = 100 cubic feet (748 gallons)
3/ MWD: Metropolitan Water District of Southern California
4/ SDCWA: San Diego County Water Authority
5/ Based on the consumption of three adults

Source: Author's construct. Data from the City of Oceanside, California.

# APPENDIX F

## Glossary of Terms

Note: Letters in parentheses correspond to a list of sources at the end of this glossary.

**Ability-to-pay principle** (S&S) A concept used in welfare and environmental economics. It implies that publicly provided goods and services should be priced on the basis of what potential consumers are able to pay. See *willingness-to-pay.*

**Acre-foot** (WEF) The amount of water that would cover an acre of land one foot deep (325,851 gallons). An acre-foot of water can support the annual indoor and outdoor needs of one to two urban households.

**Allowance for funds used during construction (AFUDC)** (B) A noncash item representing the estimated composite interest costs of debt and a return on equity funds used to finance construction.

**Annualization** (SPH) The conversion of a series of transactions to an equivalent annuity.

**Annuity** (SPH) A series of equal annual payments occurring over a period of time.

**Aquifer** (WEF) A geologic formation that stores, transmits, and yields significant quantities of water to wells and springs.

**Asset management** (M&B) A combination of management, financial, economic, engineering, and other practices applied to (physical) assets with the objective of maximizing the value derived from an asset stock over the whole life cycle, within the context of delivering appropriate levels of service to customers, communities, and the environment and at a acceptable level of risk.

**At-site value** (Y) The value of water calculated at the site of use (farm, home, factory). By convention (but not by necessity) this is the value used in investment evaluations, to be compared with costs of supply. See *at-source value.*

**At-source value** (Y) The value of water calculated at the source (stream, reservoir, aquifer). A derived demand less than at-site value by any costs of capture, transport, and treatment for use. Appropriate for use in comparing intersectoral allocations. See *at-site value.*

**Averting behavior** (Y) See *defensive behavior.*

**Avoided cost** (B) The cost of producing or providing one less unit.

**Base rate case** (H) A regulatory proceeding usually before a state PSC whereby the utility's cost of service is examined and rates for different customer classes are established. Contrast with changes in a utility's rates due to factors beyond a utility management's control, such as fuel, purchased power, or purchased water recovered through an adjustment clause. Also called general rate case.

**Benefit, economic** (Y) A monetary measure of preference, satisfaction, or welfare improvement from some change in quantity or quality of a good or service; the maximum amount that a person would be *willing to pay* to obtain the improvement.

**Bequest value** (S&S) The term is used to describe a value that individuals may place on the environment that represents their consideration for its use by future generations.

**Business valuation** (P) The act or process of determining the value of a business enterprise or ownership interest therein.

**Capacity costs** (BE) As used in the commodity-demand method, costs associated with providing facilities to meet the peak rates of use, or demands, placed on the system by the customers, including capital-related costs on plant designed to meet peak requirements plus the associated operation and maintenance expenses. This cost component may be broken down into costs associated with meeting specific demands, such as maximum-day, maximum-hour, or other periods of time that may be appropriate for the utility.

**Capital asset** (B) A term (imprecisely used) to describe plant and equipment.

**Capitalized value** (Y) The present discounted value of a stream of *per-period values* of indefinite length; the value of an asset (a property right to a stream of *per-period values*).

**Carrying charge factor (rate)** (SPH) The amount of revenue per dollar of investment that must be collected from customers in order to pay the carrying charges on that investment. The carrying charge factor (rate) is expressed as a decimal that is multiplied by the original investment to obtain a dollar amount. The carrying charge rate can be a present value or annualized quantity, over a specified period of time (up to the book life of the asset), or an annual quantity in a specific year of life.

**Cash from operations** (H) Net income plus noncash expenses.

**Commercial customer** (BE) A class of utility customers that includes commercial business other than industries.

**Commission** (P) An agency of government usually composed of three or more members charged with specified duties, functions, and responsibilities.

**Commodity (operating) costs** (BE) Costs that tend to vary with the quantity of water produced, including costs of chemicals, a large part of power costs, and other elements that increase or decrease almost directly with the amount of water supplied.

**Common costs** (A) Those that are common to all rate classes yet not directly caused by any single class. Common costs are associated with and indirectly caused by all rate classes. An example of a common cost is the chief executive officer's salary.

**Common pool resource (CPR)** (S&S) Natural resources that are used in common by a group of identifiable people who have property rights in the resource.

**Constant dollar analysis** (SPH) An analysis made without including the effect of inflation, although real escalation is included.

**Construction Work in Progress** (B) Plant not yet operational, which may or may not be included in a utility's rate base.

**Consumer's surplus** (Y) The excess in money value that an individual would pay for a good over and above the total expenditures that would be made at a given price for the good. Changes in consumer's surplus associated with changes in quantity or quality of *consumers' goods* are the primary basis for measuring economic benefits of consumers' goods.

**Contigent valuation method CVM** (Y) An express preference method that asks individuals the value (in monetary terms) of specified changes in quantities or qualities of environmental goods and services. Especially useful where nonuse values are important.

**Cost allocation** (A) The apportionment of joint costs among two or more rate classes in accordance with each class's relative share of a measurable cost-defining service characteristic.

**Cost–benefit analysis** (S) The comparison of benefits and costs in decisionmaking. Dollar values are assigned to benefits and costs in most cost–benefit analyses. Also called *benefit–cost analysis.*

**Cost classification** (A) The division of costs into groups bearing a relationship to a measurable cost-defining service characteristic. Typical groups include customer, commodity, and capacity (demand).

**Cost-effectiveness analysis** (B) Among alternatives, the one whose benefit, or payoff, divided by cost is highest. Sometimes said of an action whose expected benefits exceed expected costs whether or not there are other alternatives with larger benefit/cost ratios.

**Cost of capital** (B) The composite rate of cost for debt interest, preferred stock dividends, and common stockholder earnings requirements. It is the composite of the cost of the various capital sources used to provide the facilities utilized in supplying utility service.

**Cost of service** (B) Operation and maintenance expenses, depreciation and amortization expenses, and income and other taxes found just and reasonable by the regulatory agency for rate-making purposes plus, in the case of public utilities, an allowance for capital (usually computed by applying a rate of return to the rate base). See *revenue requirements.*

**Cost-of-service study** (BE) Detailed analysis of how a utility allocates the cost of serving different classes of customers.

**Costs** (Y) The value of goods or services sacrificed or used up in the allocation decision; measured by the opportunity costs (foregone benefits in the best alternative use) of the resources used.

**Cross-section analysis** (E) Statistical analysis of the members of a population at one point in time. It contrasts with time-series analysis, in which the population is drawn from a number of time periods (generally months, quarters, or years).

**Cross-subsidization** (P) Using the resources or profits from one line of business (or customer) to support another line of business (or customer).

**Constant dollar analysis** (SPH) An analysis that includes the effect of inflation and real escalation. Also called *nominal dollars.*

**Customer costs** (BE) Those costs associated with serving customers, irrespective of the amount or rate of water use, including meter reading, billing, and customer accounting and collecting expense, as well as maintenance and capital costs related to meters and services.

**Deadweight loss** (E) A loss in social welfare deriving from a policy or action that has no corresponding gain. Deadweight losses represent economic inefficiency and usually result when there is some flaw in the price-setting mechanism.

**Decision analysis** (SPH) The evaluation of decision options and the estimation of the value of additional information or testing, using the time and risk preferences of the decisionmaker.

**Deductive valuation technique** (Y) Valuation models (including residual, alternative cost, and benefit transfer methods) that primarily use *deductive reasoning* (i.e., reasoning from general principles and assumptions to specific conclusions using logical or mathematical rules. Conclusions are only as valid as the initial assumptions.)

**Demand function or schedule** (Y) Indicates the quantities of a good or service that individuals purchase a various prices. A single person has an individual demand schedule; all indivuduals in the market contribute to the market demand schedule. Also called *demand curve*.

**Demand-side management** (P) Activities or programs undertaken by a utility or its customers to influence the amount and timing of water usage.

**Depletion** (BE) The loss in service value incurred in connection with the exhaustion of a natural resource (e.g., water) during the course of providing service.

**Depreciation** (S) A periodic cost assigned for the reduction in value and usefulness of a long-term tangible asset.

**Desalination** (WRF) Specific treatment processes to demineralize sea water or brackish (saline) water for reuse.

**Differential pricing** (BO) The mechanics of implementing a system of prices based on value of service.

**Direct approaches** (NRC) Valuation approaches that use survey-based techniques to elicit preferences for nonmarket goods and services (e.g., the contingent valuation method.)

**Discount rate** (B) Interest rate used to convert future payments to present values (CO). The rate of interest the Federal Reserve charges for loans it makes to banks (SPH). Also the rate used for computing present values, which reflects the fact that the value of a cash flow depends on the time in which the flow occurs.

**Distribution system infrastructure charge (DSIC)** (B) A surcharge mechanism designed to pay for system improvements and enhance revenue recovery between rate cases.

**Distribution systems** (P) The system of pipes that connect the transmission network and customer load. That portion of a water utility system that delivers service directly to the end user. Most investor-owned water utilities own production, transmission, and distribution assets.

**Dollar year** (SPH) The year in which constant dollar results of an analysis are reported.

**Econometrics** (E) The setting up of mathematical models describing economic relationships, testing the validity of such hypotheses, and estimating the parameters in order to obtain a measure of the strengths of the influences of the different independent variables.

**Economic analysis** (Y) Term used in World Bank project evaluation literature to refer to evaluation of the social (contrasted with private) profitability of alternative investments or programs. In the project evaluation literature, "social" and "economic" may be used interchangeably. However, some writers limit "economic profitability" to economic efficiency or net national income gains, while social profitability is used to refer to analysis that incorporates social considerations other than economic efficiency, such as income distribution. In economic analysis, benefits and costs are valued in terms of real willingness-to-pay or opportunity costs. Subsidies, certain taxes, and other income transfer policies are not counted in economic analysis. See *financial analysis.*

**Economic cost** (F) The value of the alternative that is being given up in order to obtain some specified item. Economic cost is the same as *opportunity cost.*

**Economic development rate** (BE) Special discount rates offered to attract new business to the area or to entice existing business to expand.

**Economic efficiency** (CO) Achieving a goal at the lowest possible cost.

**Economic forces** (CO) The necessary reactions to scarcity.

**Economic regulation** (WB) The rules and organizations that set, enforce, and change the allowed tariffs and service standards for service providers.

**Economic welfare** See *welfare economics.*

**Economies of scale** (P) The principle that increased size of operations yields increased efficiency as well as greater output.

**Economies of scope** (BE) When the average cost of combined services (e.g., water service and fire protection service) is less than the cost of providing the services separately; when the unit cost of providing multiple services is less than if they were provided by separate utilities.

**Efficient prices** (CO) See *economic efficiency.*

**Elasticity** See *price elasticity of demand.*

**Embedded costs** (B) Those costs that are in existence at any point in time regardless of the date originally incurred and that affect current operations on a continuing basis.

**End-use forecast** (H) A method of demand forecasting that disaggregates demands into end uses for particular customer classes. For example, residential end uses include toilet flushing, lawn watering, and so on.

**Excess capacity** (P) Utility plant that is determined by regulators to be in excess of that necessarily used and useful to the provision of utility service.

**Existence value** (Y) See *nonuse value.*

**Expected unserved demand** (EUD) The average shortage that is expected.

**Expressed preference method** (Y) The class of methods, including contingent valuation and choice modeling, which determines by questionnaire how much a respondent would be willing to pay for a change in quantity or quality of an environmental good. Useful where no complementary or substitute private goods are available from which to derive behavior-based willingness-to-pay.

**Externality** (S&S) This term connotes an unintended side-effect of the actions of an individual, company, or community on others or the environment, and these effects are not taken into account in the decision making of the parties causing them. Can be either positive or negative.

**Financial analysis** (Y) In World Bank project evaluation terminology, evaluation from the perspective of the private individual or firm affected by a project (which can be producers, consumers, or both). The purpose of financial analysis is to ascertain the appeal of the project to its intended beneficiaries. Profitability is calculated in terms of actual prices received or paid, and therefore reflects any income transfer program (taxes or subsidies). See *economic analysis.*

**Fire-protection charge** (BE) A charge made to recover the cost of providing both public and private fire-protection service to the communities served by the water utility.

**Fixed charge rate** (SPH) The factor by which the present value of capital investment is multiplied to obtain the annual cost attributable to the capital investment.

**Fixed costs** (H&S) The annual costs that must be paid whether or not a facility or piece of equipment is used. Generally includes capital cost (see fixed charge rate) and some fixed operating and maintenance costs.

**Free goods** (S&S) Goods that are so abundant that they have no market price. Paradoxically, free goods can be the most essential, such as the air we breathe.

**Free rider** (S&S) An individual who benefits from the actions and efforts of others without contributing to the costs incurred in generating the benefits.

**Full costs** (RA) In the context of a regulated water utility components include: O&M expenses, capital charges, opportunity costs, economic externalities, and environmental externalities.

**Full supply costs** (RA) In the context of a regulated water utility costs include: O&M expenses, depreciation, taxes, and return on capital.

**Fully distributed costs** See *embedded costs.*

**Functional accounts** (BE) Groupings of plant and expense accounts prescribed by regulatory authorities according to the specified function or part they play in the rendition of utility service.

**Funds from operations** (W) Net income plus noncash expenses.

**Going concern assumption** (B) For accounting purposes, a business is assumed to remain in operation long enough for all its current plans to be carried out. This assumption is part of the justification for the acquisition cost basis, rather than a liquidation or exit value basis of accounting.

**Government-owned utility** (AWWA) A water utility created by legislative action of a state or other government agency. A government-owned water utility may be part of a municipal government operation, a county agency, or a regional authority, or it may take such other forms as are appropriate for its service area.

**Gross domestic product** (CO) The total market value of all final goods and services produced in an economy in a one-year period.

**Groundwater** (WRF) Water stored underground in pore spaces between rocks and other alluvial materials and in fractures of hard rock occurring in the saturated zone.

**Hedonic property valuation method** (Y) A revealed preference method of isolating the value of one attribute of a complicated multiattribute good or service (usually farmland or residences) by statistically separating the contributions of the various attributes using data from market transactions on a selected good or service.

**Incentive regulation** (BE) Methods of economic regulation, including but not limited to the use of price caps, designed to provide utilities with incentives for cost control, efficiency, and/or other desirable activities.

**Income elasticity of demand** (CO) The percentage change in demand divided by the percentage change in income.

**Increasing block rate structure** (BE) A rate structure also known as inverted block rate structure, in which the average and marginal price per block of use increases as consumption increases. It can be used for reducing average (and sometimes peak) use, and large volume users consider its use inequitable.

**Incremental costs** (BE) The change in total cost resulting from a change in capacity, output, or services provided. See *marginal costs.*

**Incremental value** See *marginal value.*

**Indifference curve** (CO) A curve that shows combinations of goods among which an individual is indifferent.

**Industrial customer** (BE) A class of utility customers that usually manufacture a product.

**Integrated resource planning** (PUR) A planning process that balances supply and demand-side investments by utilities to achieve the greatest efficiency. Also known as *least-cost planning.*

**Integrated water resource management** (D) A specific application of the more general notion of integrated environmental management, which seeks to deal holistically with the natural environment. Integrated environmental management can be considered as that set of proactive or preventive measures that maintain the environment in good condition for a variety of long-range sustainable uses.

**Intergenerational equity** (S&S) The notion that the present generation should consider the needs of future generations in current decisionmaking. Intergenerational equity is a fundamental feature of sustainable development.

**Internal rate of return** (SPH) The discount rate required to equate the net present value of a cash flow stream to zero.

**Intrinsic value** (Y) Value assigned to things, actions, or outcomes for their own sake, independent of means of providing or attaining other items or situations of value for humans. See *extrinsic value.*

**Interruptible rates** (P) Rates offered to customers who are willing, upon the utility's request, to have their service interrupted.

**Investment** (B) An expenditure to acquire property or other assets in order to produce revenue; the asset so acquired; hence a current expenditure made in anticipation of future income. Said of securities of other companies held for the long-term and shown in a separate section of the balance sheet; in the context, contrast with marketable securities.

**Investor-owned utility** (BE) A utility owned by and responsible to its shareholders.

**Joint costs** (A) Costs clearly caused by two or more rate classes or schedules. Also called joint investment.

**Joint use** (BE) More than one entity uses an entity's property or facilities, such as utility poles used for telephone lines, usually for compensation to the owner.

**Land** (B) An asset shown at acquisition cost plus the cost of any nondepreciable improvements. In accounting, implies use as a plant or office site rather than as a natural resource, such as timberland or farmland.

**Leakage (losses)** (BE) All water that is lost from the system through leaks and breaks and includes all unavoidable leaks, and all recoverable leaks and breaks.

**Least-cost planning** (PUR) See *Integrated resource planning.*

**Levelization** (SPH) Conversion of a series of transactions to an equivalent value per unit of output.

**Life-cycle cost** SPH) The present value over the analysis period of all system resultant costs.

**Life expectancy** (BE) The time period during which an article is expected to render efficient service.

**Lifeline rate** (BE) A pricing structure in which the price for "necessary" use is kept low. It can be used to reduce average use and is usually used to ensure that low-income users are not unduly burdened by high prices.

**Load** (BE) The amount of utility product delivered at any specified point or points on a system.

**Load factor** (PUR) A measure of the degree to which physical facilities such as a pipeline are being utilized; the ratio of average usage to peak usage.

**Load management** (BE) Techniques designed to reduce demand at peak times.

**Load profile curve** (SPH) A chart showing chronological demand plotted against time of occurance. It illustrates the varying magnitude of the load during the period covered.

**Long-run** (Y) In Alfred Marshall's simplified analytic price theory, the situation in which plant and equipment capacity is assumed to be variable, rather than fixed as it is in the short-run. Short-run and long-run are distinguished not by the actual time in days, weeks, or months but by the degree to which economic actors can adapt to changing conditions.

**Losses** (BE) See *leakage.*

**Marginal cost** (B) The cost of producing or providing an additional unit.

**Marginal rate of subsititution** (CO) The rate at which one good must be added when the other is taken away in order to keep the individual indifferent between two combinations.

**Marginal revenue** (CO) The change in total revenue associated with a change in quantity.

**Marginal social benefit** (CO) The marginal private benefit of consuming a good plus the benefits of the positive externalities resulting from consuming that good.

**Marginal social cost** (CO) The marginal private costs of production plus the cost of the negative externalities associated with that production.

**Marginal utility** (CO) The satisfaction one gets from consuming one additional unit of a product above and beyond what one has consumed up to that point.

**Marginal value** (NRC) The value of another (hypothetical or last) increment of water when used in the most efficient manner.

**Market-clearing price** (PH) A price just sufficient to secure full but unrationed use of service in whatever amounts are temporarily available in view of limited plant capacity.

**Market demand curve** (CO) The horizontal sum of all individual demand curves.

**Market power** (H) The ability of a buyer or seller to command a price or terms of service other than what would occur in a competitive market.

**Market supply curve** (CO) Horizontal sum of all individual supply curves. Also: horizontal sum of all the firm's marginal cost curves, taking account of any changes in input prices that might occur.

**Microeconomics** (CO) The study of individual choice and how that choice is influenced by economic forces.

**Monopoly** (CO) A market structure in which one firm makes up the entire market.

**Monopoly (natural)** (BE) A public utility that operates most efficiently when it is the only seller in the market. A natural monopoly is sanctioned to achieve efficient production and distribution. Utility monopolies are controlled through regulation instead of competition.

**Natural resource economics** (S&S) A subdiscipline of economics concerned with the allocation, use, and management of renewable and nonrenewable resources.

**Neoclassical economics** (S&S) The term is used to refer to the most popular mode of economic analysis at present. It is based on the premises of rational behavior by economic agents, that is, individuals and firms who try to optimize their utility/profit given their constraints.

**Net national income** (CO) The net total income earned by citizens and businesses of a country.

**Net present value** (SPH) The value in the base year (usually the present) of all cash flows associated with a project.

**Nondiscrimination** (BE) In general usage, reasonably equal treatment for all of a utility's customers.

**Nonmarket valuation** (Y) The study of economic behavior (especially consumption, demand, production, and supply relationships) for the purpose of assigning economic values in contexts where market prices are absent or distorted. See *accounting price.*

**Nonuse values** (Y) Benefits received from a *public good* by knowing that it exists, even though the individual may never directly experience the good. People are *willing to pay* for environmental services they will never use or experience. Sometimes called *passive or existence values*. See *total economic value* and *use value*.

**Normal goods** (CO) Goods whose consumption increases with an increase in income.

**Normative economics** (CO) The study of what the goals of the economy should be.

**Obligation to serve** (BE) The legal obligation of a utility to provide service on a nondiscriminatiory basis within its service territory.

**Off-peak** (BE) A period of relatively low system demands.

**Operating margin ratio** (WS) The ratio of operating income to sales.

**Operating revenues** (BE) The amounts billed by the utility for utility services rendered and for other services incidental thereto.

**Opportunity cost** (Y) The monetary value or foregone value of a good or service in its next best alternative use; the maximum amount it could receive elsewhere for use as a production input for final consumption.

**Option value** (S&S) A value, beyond an expected use value, derived from the willingness to pay for the option of using a resource at a future date.

**Ordinary least squares regression** (E) A statistical technique for estimating the relationship between a dependent variable and independent variables. The method derives estimates for the parameters and constants in the equation postulated as representing the nature of the relationship between the variables in the model.

**Overdraft** (WRF) A condition that occurs in a groundwater basin when pumping exceeds recharge over an extended period of time.

**Payback period** (SPH) The time required for net revenues associated with an investment to return the cost of the investment.

**Peak load** (PUR) The maximum load consumed or produced in a stated period of time.

**Peak load pricing** (BE) A pricing structure in which charges are based on both the quantity of water used and the maximum rate at which it is used.

**Perfectly competitive market** (CO) A market structure in which economic forces operate unimpeded.

**Performance-based regulation** (BE) An alternative to traditional rate of return regulation (RORR) that focuses on meeting performance objectives rather than covering the cost of service; includes price cap rates, yardstick regulation, and profit-sharing.

**Positive economics** (CO) The study of what is, and how the economy works.

**Possibility of shortage** (H) The likelihood that full-service demand will exceed available supply. That is, the probability of a shortage of any magnitude.

**Present value** (SPH) The value in the base year (usually the present) of a cash flow adjusted for the time-value differences in those cash flows between the time of the actual flow and the base year.

**Price elasticity of demand** (P) The degree to which demand for a product or service will vary with a change in the price of a product or service. Also called *elasticity.*

**Prior appropriation** (D) A doctrine of water law that allocates the right to use water on a first-come, first-served basis.

**Private cost** (F) All implicit and explicit costs encountered by a person or a firm.

**Private goods** (Y) Goods and services one person's consumption or use of which reduces the amount available to other consumers and from which nonpayers can be excluded. Contrast with *public goods.*

**Producer's surplus** (Y) The returns to a producer in excess of variable costs; also payments for fixed inputs.

**Production function** (CO) The relationship between the inputs (factors of production) and outputs.

**Property rights** (S&S) A bundle of rights that have legal recognition. The rights include the right to consume, sell, exchange, and bequeath.

**Prudence** (BE) A consideration of whether investments or expenses were wasteful or dishonest.

**PSC or PUC** A public service commission or a public utilities commission.

**Public good** (S&S) A pure public good is nonexclusive (anyone can use it) and nonrivalrous (the number of users does not affect the benefits derived from its consumption). Public goods may be publicly provided (such as national defense) or may be privately provided (such as a lighthouse).

**Public interest theory** (E) The area of welfare economics concerned with the ways in which society can and should make decisions. The concern of how different alternatives should be ranked. Also called *public choice theory.*

**Public trust doctrine** (WEF) A 1983 California Supreme Court decision in *National Audubon Society v. Superior Court of Alpine County*, which required the state to serve as trustee of the navigable waters and underlying beds within the state. In particular, the state has the affirmative duty to take the public trust into account in planning and allocating water resources.

**Public utility** (B) Enterprise providing essential public services, such as electric, gas, telephone, water, and sewer, under legally established monopoly conditions.

**Quantity demanded** (CO) A specific amount that will be demanded per unit of time at a specific price, other things constant.

**Quantity supplied** (CO) A specific amount that will be supplied at a specific price.

**Ramsey pricing** (SH) A method developed by Frank Ramsey in 1927 that adjusts prices away from marginal costs in inverse proportion to the elasticity of demand.

**Rate base** (B) The investor-supplied plant facilities and other assets used in supplying utility service to the consumer. This investment base is the amount to which the rate of return is applied (i.e., rate base x rate of return = net operating income).

**Rate-base method of ratemaking** (B) Also called *cost-of-service ratemaking.*

**Rate case** (PUR) A proceeding usually before a state PSC involving the rates to be charged for public utility service. Also called *base rate case.*

**Rate design** See *rate structure.*

**Rate equalization** (BE) See *single tariff pricing.*

**Ratemaking** (B) The process of setting rates.

**Rate order**: (B) Order establishing a regulated enterprise's revenue requirementss and rates.

**Rate proceeding** (B) The administrative proceeding to establish rates. Also called rate case.

**Rate of return** (B) The realized rate of return is the percentage factor obtained by dividing the net operating income from utility operations by the rate base. An adequate rate of return is the percentage factor that, when multiplied by the rate base, produces earnings that will meet the interest and equity requirements of the capital used to support the rate base. The measure of the adequacy of the rate-of-return factor is usually based upon cost-of-capital measurements.

**Rate-of-return regulation** See *rate-base method of ratemaking.*

**Rate shock** (PUR) The presumed psychological effect on a utility's customers of sudden, drastic rate increases.

**Rates** (B) Prices that enterprises in certain industries, usually regulated, charge for services or, occasionally, goods.

**Rate structure** (BE) The design and organization of billing charges by customer class to distribute the revenue requirements among customer classes and rating periods.

**Regulation** (B) The function of regulating enterprises in certain specified industries. Regulation may involve one or more activities, including rate making, accounting, financing, type and area of service, and construction and operating standards. *See economic regulation.*

**Regulatory agency** (B) A governmental body that regulates enterprises in certain industries (e.g., a state PSC, or the U.S. Environmental Protection Agency).

**Reliability** (H&S) The degree to which a utility delivers service to its customers within accepted standards and in the amount desired; reliability may be measured by the frequency, duration, and magnitude of adverse affects on service to the customer.

**Remaining life** (BE) The expected future service life of an asset at any given age.

**Reserve margin** (H) The excess of available capacity (i.e., capacity not on scheduled maintenance) over peak load; usually expressed as a percentage of peak load.

**Residential customer** (BE) A primary customer class of a water utility usually consisting of private housing dwellers.

**Return flow** (WRF) Water that is applied to a crop but not consumptively used, which makes its way back to a waterway and is available for use by downstream users.

**Return on assets** (C) Operating income expressed as a percentage of a utility's average assets.

**Return on equity** (BE) The return to shareholders, that is, the utility's net income expressed as a percentage of that portion of a utility's total investment provided by the common shareholders.

**Revealed preferences method** (Y) Nonmarket valuation methods, including *travel cost* and *hedonic pricing*, which infer economic value from analysis of actual consumer decisions or market transactions. See *expressed preference methods.*

**Revenue requirements** (B) The sum total of the revenues required to pay all operating and capital costs of providing service. See *cost of service.*

**Riparian rights (D)** A doctrine of water law under which the right to use lakes and streams rests with the owners of riparian land, or land that borders on the surface water.

**Risk analysis** (SPH) A method of quantifying and evaluating uncertainty.

**Scarcity** (S&S) A situation when demand for a good/service is greater than its supply at zero price.

**Scenario analysis** (H) The examination of the joint impact of changes in several assumptions as contrasted with sensitivity analysis that focuses on only a single assumption at a time.

**Seasonal pricing** (BE) A pricing structure in which the price level during the season of peak usage is higher than the level during the off-peak period.

**Sensitivity analysis** (H) Quantitative analysis of a particular problem where specific values of variables are changed to determine how significant the range of values are to the given analysis.

**Service area** (P) The territory in which a utility company has the right to supply or make available its utility service.

**Service obligation** (P) A term used to mean the obligations a public utility has to perform. They usually include the duty: (a) to serve all; (b) to provide adequate service; and (c) to render safe, efficient, and nondiscriminatory service.

**Shadow prices** (Y) The value used in social or public economic analysis when the market price is unknown or judged not to be an appropriate measure of economic value.

**Shortage** (HIR) A situation in which more of a commodity is demanded in the market than is being supplied at the going price.

**Short-run** (Y) In Alfred Marshall's simplified analytic price theory, the situation in which plant and equipment capacity is assumed to be fixed, rather than variable as it is in the *long run.* Short run and long run are distinguished not by the actual time in days, weeks, or months but by the degree to which economic actors can adapt to changing conditions.

**Single-tariff pricing** (BE) A method of setting utility rates that consolidates rates across multiple service territories owned and operated by a multisystem utility that may or may not be contiguous or physically interconnected.

**Social benefits** (S&S) The total value of an economic activity that accrues to society as a whole and thus leads to an increase in social welfare. In effect, it is the sum of two benefits: (a) the benefit to the agent performing the action (producer's surplus, profit made), and (b) the benefit accuring to society as a result of action, for example, increase in tax revenue.

**Social cost** (S&S) The total cost to society of an economic activity, that is, private costs plus value of externalities.

**Social discount rate** (Y) The shadow or accounting rate of interest used by public agencies to discount (calculate the present value of) future benefits and costs of public projects or policies. Determining the social rate of discount remains a controversial issue in evaluation of public water and environmental projects.

**Social welfare** (S&S) A measure of the collective well-being of a society.

**Strategic plan** (BU) A top-down approach to business planning, with an emphasis on long-term business-wide issues.

**Surcharge** (BE) An amount added to customers' bills for a special period of time, and the revenues from the surcharge are used to fund a specific project or purpose.

**Subsidies** (EU) The difference between actual costs underlying calculations of the water price and full economic costs.

**Sunk cost** (BE) Costs incurred in the past that are not affected by, and hence irrelevant for, current decisions, aside from income tax effects.

**Supply curve** (CO) Graphical representation of the relationship between price and quantity supplied.

**Supply main** (BE) Any pipe, main, aqueduct, or canal, the primary purpose of which is to convey water from one unit to another unit in the source of supply, water treatment or pumping plant and generally providing no service connections with customers.

**Tariff** (B) A schedule filed by a regulated enterprise with a regulatory agency describing the transactions between the enterprise and its customers in terms of type of service, conditions of service, rates (prices) to be charged, and payment.

**Test year or test period** (B) The twelve-month operating period selected to evaluate a utility's cost of service and the adequacy of the rates in effect or being sought. Frequently the term "test period" is used, and may refer simply to the test year or expressly to the adjusted test year.

**Third-party-impacts** (WRF) Direct and indirect economic, social, or environmental effects of a water transfer to a party other than the seller or buyer.

**Time-series analysis** (E) The application of statistical methods to find explanations for movements of variables over time. Contrast with *cross-section analysis*.

**Total economic value** (Y) The sum of *use values* plus *nonuse values.* (S&S) The total willingness-to-pay to preserve, maintain, or possess a natural resource or environmental good. The total economic value includes use and nonuse values.

**Transaction costs** (S&S) The costs incurred in exchanging and enforcing property rights. High transaction costs can be a major impediment to trade and exchange.

**Transmission and distribution main** (BE) A main with the primary purpose of conveying water (requiring no further processing except incidental chlorination or pressure boosting from a unit in the source of supply), water treatment of pumping plant, and generally providing no service connections with customers.

**Transmission system** (PUR) The system that transports water in bulk, usually from a source of supply to the distribution systems or major parts of the system.

**Travel-cost method** (Y) A revealed preference approach to valuing recreational sites that derives a demand schedule from statistical analysis of the costs of travel.

**Unbundled rate** (BE) Serveral services disaggregated from a tariff previously offered as a single charge.

**Uniform rate** (BE) A pricing structure in which the price per unit is constant as consumption increases.

**Unit cost** (BE) The cost of producing a unit of a product, or a service.

**Universal service** (BE) An effort by the utility to extend service to all inhabitants of a service territory who desire the service.

**Use value** (Y) Values assigned to goods and services that are actually used or experienced. See *nonuse value.*

**Value of service** (B) A concept in utility pricing practices whereby the usefulness or necessity of the service to a customer group replaces cost factors as a major influence on the rates charged to the group. Other names for value of service include: quasi-optimal, Ramsey, and inverse elasticity rule.

**Variable charge** (BE) Charges to a utility's customers that vary with water use.

**Variable costs** (B) Costs that change as activity levels change. Strictly speaking, variable costs are zero when the activity level is zero. In accounting, this term most often means the sum of direct costs and variable overhead.

**Weighted average cost of capital** (SPH) The weighted average of the component costs of debt, preferred stock, and common equity. This is sometimes used as a proxy for discount rates in the industrial and utility sectors.

**Welfare economics** (S&S) A branch of economics that deals with the principles and criteria of evaluating alternative economic states and policies from the viewpoint of "efficiency or social welfare."

**Wholesale service** (BE) A situation where water is sold to a customer at one or more major points of delivery for resale to retail customers within the wholesale customer's service area.

**Willingness-to-accept** (Y) A monetary measure of the minimum amount an individual would accept rather than experiencing a lesser amount or quality of a good or service.

**Willingness-to-pay** (Y) A monetary measure of the value an individual would pay for a specified change in quantity or quality of a good or service.

**Withdrawal** (Y) The amount of water delivered from a surface or removed from a groundwater source for human use. Withdrawal minus conveyance loss equals delivery to the point of use.

**Zone of reasonableness** (PUR) The range between the absolute maximum of value of service and the absolute minimum of cost of service in which a rate must fall to be deemed reasonable.

## SOURCES OF TERMS

(A) Alt, Lowell E. *Energy Utility Rate Setting*, lulu.com, 2006.

(AWA) American Water Works Association, *Water Utility Capital Financing*, 1998.

(B) Berk, Joel, "Glossary of Utility Finance and Accounting Terms," *Public Utility Finance and Accounting: A Reader,* 2nd ed., 1989.

(BE) Beecher, Janice A., *Sourcebook of Regulatory Techniques For Water Utilities*, 2nd ed., 1999.

(BO) Bonbright, James C., Albert L. Danielsen, and David R. Kamerschen, *Principles of Public Utility Rates*, 1988.

(BU) Bannock, Graham, Evan Davis, Paul Trott, and Mark Uncles, *The Economist Dictionary of Business*, 2003.

( CO) David Colander, *Microeconomics*, 2001.

(C) Copeland, Tom, Tim Koller, and Jack Murrin, *Valuation: Measuring and Managing the Value of Companies*, 2nd ed., 1996.

(D) Dzurik, Andrew A., *Water Resource Planning*, 3rd ed., 2003.

(E) Bannock, Grahm, R. E. Baxter, and Evan Davis, *The Economist Books Dictionary of Economics*, 1972.

(EU) Roth, Eva, "Water Pricing in the EU, A Review," Publication No. 2001/002 (Brussels: European Environmental Bureau [EEB], 2001).

(F) Fogiel, M., *The Essentials of Microeconomics*, 2001.

(H) Hayward, David, *Valuing A Water Utility*, 2006.

(H&S) Hayward, David, and Michael R. Schmidt, *Valuing an Electric Utility: Theory and Application*, 1999.

(HIR) Hirshleifer, Jack, James C. De Haven, and Jerome W. Milliman, *Water Supply Economics, Technology, and Policy*, 1960.

(M&B) David R. Marlow and Stewart Burn, "Effective Use of Condition Assessment within Asset Management" (Denver, CO: Journal AWWA, January 2008).

(NRC) National Research Council, *Valuing Ground Water, Economic Concepts and Approaches*, 1997.

(P) Pratt, Shannon P., *Business Valuation Body of Knowledge*, 2003.

(PH) Phillips, Charles F., Jr., *The Regulation of Public Utilities*, 3rd ed., 1993.

(PUR) "Glossary of Utility Terms," P.U.R. Guide, 1996.

(RA) Raucher, R., D. Chapman, J. Henderson, M. Hagenstad, J. Rice, J. Goldstein, A. Huber-Lee, W. DeOreo, P. Mayer, B. Hurd, R. Linsky, E. Means, and M. Renwick, *The Value of Water: Concepts, Estimates, and Applications for Water Managers* (Denver, CO: American Water Works Research Foundation, 2005).

(R) Ross, Stephen A., Randolph W. Westerfield, and Bradford D. Jordan, *Fundamentals of Corporate Finance*, 3rd ed., 1995.

(S) Scott, David L., *Wall Street Words: An Essential A to Z Guide for Today's Investor*, 2003.

(SH) Shaw, W. Douglass, *Water Resource Economics and Policy: An Introduction*, 2005.

(SPH) Short, Walter, Daniel J. Packey, and Thoma Holt, *A Manual for the Economic Evaluation of Energy Efficiency and Renewable Energy Technologies*, 2005.

(S&S) Singh, Katar, and Anil Shishodia, *Environmental Economics Theory and Applications*, 2007.

(WEF) Layperson's Guide to Water Marketing, 2005.

(WB) World Bank.

(WS) White, Gerald I., Ashwinpaul C. Sondhi, and Dov Fried, *The Analysis and Use of Financial Statements*, 1998.

(Y) Young, Robert A., *Determining the Economic Value of Water, Concepts and Methods*, 2005.

# APPENDIX G

## Suporting Tables for Massachusetts-American Marginal Cost Study

**Table G.1**
**Unit Marginal Cost by Customer Classification**

| | Annual Marginal Cost ($) | Effective Sales (TG's) | Unit Marginal Cost ($) |
|---|---|---|---|
| **Residential** | | | |
| A. Supply | 106,129 | 118,443 | 0.90 |
| B. Pumping | 50,134 | 118,443 | 0.42 |
| C. Treatment | 22,143 | 118,443 | 0.19 |
| D. Storage | 48,079 | 84,607 | 0.57 |
| Total | 226,486 | | 2.08 |
| **Commercial** | | | |
| A. Supply | 106,129 | 148,081 | 0.72 |
| B. Pumping | 50,134 | 148,081 | 0.34 |
| C. Treatment | 22,143 | 148.081 | 0.15 |
| D. Storage | 48,079 | 105,777 | 0.45 |
| Total | 226,486 | | 1.66 |
| **Other Industrial** | | | |
| A. Supply | 106,129 | 169,214 | 0.63 |
| B. Pumping | 50,134 | 169,214 | 0.30 |
| C. Treatment | 22,143 | 169,214 | 0.13 |
| D. Storage | 48,079 | 131,619 | 0.37 |
| Total | 226,486 | | 1.43 |
| **Large Industrial** | | | |
| A.Supply | 106,129 | 211,518 | 0.50 |
| B.Pumping | 50,134 | 211,518 | 0.24 |
| C.Treatment | 22,143 | 211,518 | 0.10 |
| D.Storage | 48,079 | 164,506 | 0.29 |
| Total | 226,486 | | 1.13 |
| | | | |
| **Public Authorities** | | | |
| A.Supply | 106,129 | 148,081 | 0.72 |
| B.Pumping | 50,134 | 148,081 | 0.34 |
| C Treatment | 22,143 | 148,081 | 0.15 |
| D.Storage | 48,079 | 105,777 | 0.45 |
| Total | 226,486 | | 1.66 |

## Table G.2
## Effective Sales and Production Cost Data

| **Effective Sales by Class** | **Demand Ratio** | **Sales Ratio** | **Annual Sales Per MGD of Capacity** |
|---|---|---|---|
| | | | |
| **Residential** | | | |
| Maximum Day | 2.50 | .3245 | 118,443 |
| Peak Hour | 3.50 | .2318 | 84,607 |
| | | | |
| **Commercial** | | | |
| Maximum Day | 2.00 | .4057 | 148,081 |
| Peak Hour | 2.80 | .2898 | 105,777 |
| | | | |
| **Other Industrial** | | | |
| Maximum Day | 1.75 | .4636 | 169,214 |
| Peak Hour | 2.25 | .3606 | 131,619 |
| | | | |
| **Large Industrial** | | | |
| Maximum Day | 1.40 | .5795 | 211,518 |
| Peak Hour | 1.80 | .4507 | 164,506 |
| | | | |
| **Public Authorities** | | | |
| Maximum Day | 2.00 | .4057 | 148,081 |
| Peak Hour | 2.80 | .2898 | 105,777 |
| | | | |
| TOTAL PRODUCTION | Average Day | 5.51 mgd | |
| | Annual Volume (TG) | 2,011,150 | |
| Company Use and Unaccounted For (TG) | | 379,483 | |
| Effective Total System Sales | | 1,631,667 | |
| Calculation of System Sales per 1.0 MGD | | | |
| Of Additional Capacity | | | |
| Ratio of Total System Sales to Total Production | | .8113 | |
| System Demand Ratio | 2.00 | | |

**Table G.3**
**Estimated Cost of Facilities**
**Required to Provide 1 MGD of New Capacity**

| No. | Facilities Required | Equipment Details | Capital Costs |
|---|---|---|---|
| | | | $ |
| | | | |
| 1 | Well | Exploration & Development | 150,000 |
| | | Mass. DEP Permitting | 25,000 |
| | | Structures & Appurtenances | 25,000 |
| | | | 200,000 |
| | | | |
| 2 | Pumping | Structure | 100,000 |
| | | Equipment | 50,000 |
| | | | 150,000 |
| | | | |
| 3 | Treatment | Equipment | 50,000 |
| | | | |
| 4 | Storage | 250,000 gallons 1/ | 250,000 |
| | | | |
| 5 | Transmission Mains Required | Well | 250,000 |
| | to Connect New Well and | Storage Tank 3/ | 60,000 |
| | Storage Facilities to Existing | | |
| | Distribution Network 2/ | | |
| | | | |
| 6 | Land for Well Site | | 250,000 |
| | | | |
| 7 | Land for Tank Site 4/ | | 12,500 |

Notes:

1/ Based on 1 MG structure costing $1,000,000. Volume required to equalize 1 MGD of maximum day demand is assumed to be 250,000 gallons or 25 percent of the total.

2/ Based on 2,500 feet of 12 inch main at $100 per foot.

3/ Based on 25 percent of $250,000 for transmission main.

4/ Based on 25 percent of $50,000 for land.

**Table G.4**
**Marginal Pumping Costs**

| **Pumping** | **Capital Cost ($)** | **Life Cycle** | **Present Value ($)** | **Equal Periodic Payment ($)** |
|---|---|---|---|---|
| | | | | |
| Structure | 100,000 | 50 | 133,939 | 14,827 |
| Equipment | 50,000 | 25 | 63,305 | 7,522 |
| **Total Investment** | 150,000 | | 197,244 | 22,349 |
| Variable Costs | | | | |
| Purchased Power | | | 282,249 | |
| Equipment Maintenance | | | 23,906 | |
| **Total System Expenses** | | | 306,155 | |
| Effective Total System Sales | | | 1,631,667 | |
| Unit Variable Costs | | | | 27,785 |
| **Annual Marginal Cost** | | | | 50,134 |

**Table G.5**
**Marginal Supply Costs**

| **Supply** | **Capital Cost ($)** | **Life Cycle** | **Present Value ($)** | **Equal Periodic Payment ($)** |
|---|---|---|---|---|
| | | | | |
| Well | 200,000 | 40 | 264,449 | 29,569 |
| Transmission main | 250,000 | 100 | 343,418 | 37,811 |
| Land | 250,000 | | 351,931 | 38,749 |
| **Total Fixed Costs** | 700,000 | | 959,799 | |
| | | | | |
| **Annual Marginal Cost—Supply** | | | | 106,129 |

## Table G.6
## Marginal Treatment Costs

| Treatment | Capital Cost ($) | Life Cycle | Present Value ($) | Equal Periodic Payment ($) |
|---|---|---|---|---|
| | | | | |
| Equipment | 50,000 | | | |
| **Total Fixed Costs** | 50,000 | 20 | 62,276 | 7,825 |
| | | | | |
| Variable Costs | | | 147,649 | |
| Chemicals | | | 10,116 | |
| **Total Variable Costs** | | | 157,765 | |
| | | | | |
| Effective Total System Sales (TG/YR) | | | 1,631,667 | |
| | | | | |
| Unit Variable Costs | | | $0.10 | |
| System Sales for IMGD Capacity | | | 148,081 | |
| | | | | |
| **Annual Variable Cost** | | | | 14,318 |
| | | | | |
| **Annual Marginal Costs—Treatment** | | | | 22,143 |

## Table G.7
## Marginal Storage Costs

| Storage | Capital Cost ($) | Life Cycle | Present Value ($) | Equal Periodic Payment ($) |
|---|---|---|---|---|
| | | | | |
| Storage Tank | 250,000 | 50 | 334,847 | 37,067 |
| Transmission Main | 60,000 | 100 | 82,420 | 9,075 |
| Land | 12,500 | | 17,597 | 1,937 |
| **Total Fixed Costs** | 322,500 | | 434,864 | |
| | | | | |
| **Annual Marginal Costs—Storage** | | | | 48,079 |

**Table G.8**
**Supporting Calculations**

| | $ |
|---|---|
| **Land Cost Required for Increased Well Capacity** | **250,000** |
| | |
| Return at 11.01% | 27,525 |
| Property Taxes at 1.147% | 2,868 |
| Income Taxes at 20.36% | 8,356 |
| | |
| **Total Annual Cost (Equal Periodic Payment)** | |
| | |
| **Land Cost Required for Increased Storage Capacity** | **12,500** |
| | |
| Return at 11.01% | 1,376 |
| Property Taxes at 1.147% | 143 |
| Income Taxes at 30.36% | 418 |
| | |
| **Total Annual Cost (Equal Periodic Payment)** | **1,937** |

Tables G.1 through G.8 adopted, in part, from Janice A. Beecher, Patrick C. Mann, and James R. Landers, "Cost Allocation and Rate Design for Water Utilities" (Columbus, OH, The National Regulatory Research Institute, 1990), 164–69.

# APPENDIX H

## Numerical Examples of Natural Monopolies and Pricing Policy [266]

The following discussion provides numerical examples and illustrations of average-cost (AC) and marginal-cost (MC) pricing. Assume that a price regulated water utility has the following demand and cost-related curves:

| | |
|---|---|
| Demand: | $P = 100 - Q$ |
| Marginal revenue: | $MR = 100 - 2Q$ |
| Average cost: | $AC = 15 + (400 \div Q)$ |
| Marginal cost: | $MC = 15$ |

As was discussed in chapter two, the relative position of the AC and MC curves gives the natural monopolist a cost advantage over its competition. Also, AC is always going to be greater than MC. These relationships are illustrated below.

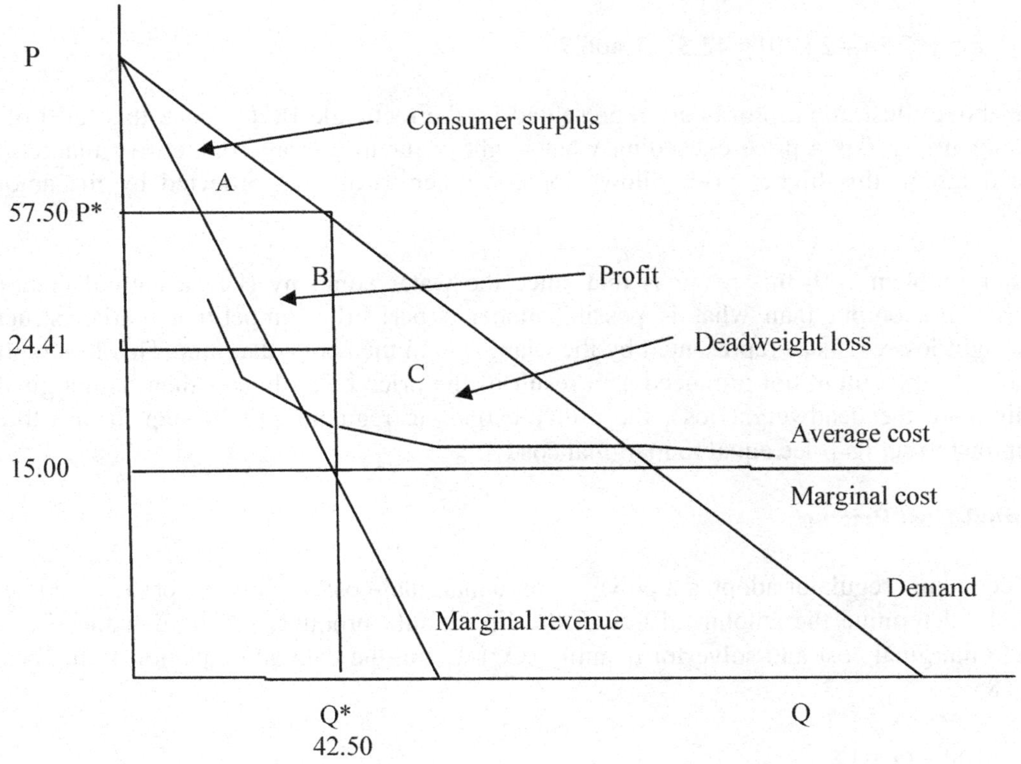


266 Adopted in part from Barry Haworth, University of Louisville, Department of Economics, Economics 201, http://econpage.com/201/handouts/natmonop.html.

If left to decide for itself, the monopolist would produce where MR = MC. This is the profit maximizing quantity (Q). The first step is to set MR = MC and solve for Q* as is shown below. Using the MR and MC formulas previously stated then:

MR = MC
100 – 2Q = 15
Q* = 42.5

To find the price (P*), plug the value of Q* (42.5) into the demand equation:

P* = 100 – (42.5) = 57.5

Therefore, the equilibrium price and quantity are: Q* = 42.5 and P* = 57.50

To find the water utility's profits, use the formula: (P – AC)Q. It is first necessary to calculate AC. The value for AC is found by plugging Q* into the AC equation to get AC = 24.41. That is, AC = 15 + (400 ÷ 42.5).

Profits (π) are price minus average cost multiplied by quantity as calculated as follows:

π = [57.50 – 24.40] * 42.5 = 1,406.75

In the above illustration, profits are represented by the rectangle B. To make this level of profit the water utility sets a price exceeding what might occur in a more competitive market. In the above diagram, this higher price allows for consumer surplus as reflected by the amount in triangle A.

A major problem with this result is that since the water company (i.e., a natural monopolist) produces less output than what is possible under a perfectly competitive market structure a deadweight loss exists as represented by the triangle C in the above diagram. This loss represents the value of the output not produced as a result of the price being higher than its marginal cost. To eliminate the deadweight loss, the utility economic regulator might step in and force the monopolist to set its price equal to marginal cost.

**Marginal-Cost Pricing**

If the economic regulator adopted a policy of pure marginal-cost pricing, the price would be equal to 15. To determine the amount of output the firm would produce, set the demand (i.e., price) equal to marginal cost and solve for quantity (Q*). Using the data and equation from above, Q* equals 85.

100 – Q = 15
Q* = 85

When the price is set at marginal cost, the firm's profits are -400.35 as calculated by the area in the rectangle abcd shown below:

If P* = MC = 15, Q* = 85, AC = 19.71 [AC = 15 + (400 ÷ 85) = 19.71] profits become

π = [15.00 – 19.71]85 = -400.35

On the graph below, these values and the areas for consumer surplus and profits are illustrated. Notice that the area of consumer surplus overlaps that corresponding with profit (loss), and that a deadweight loss does not exist since price equals marginal cost.

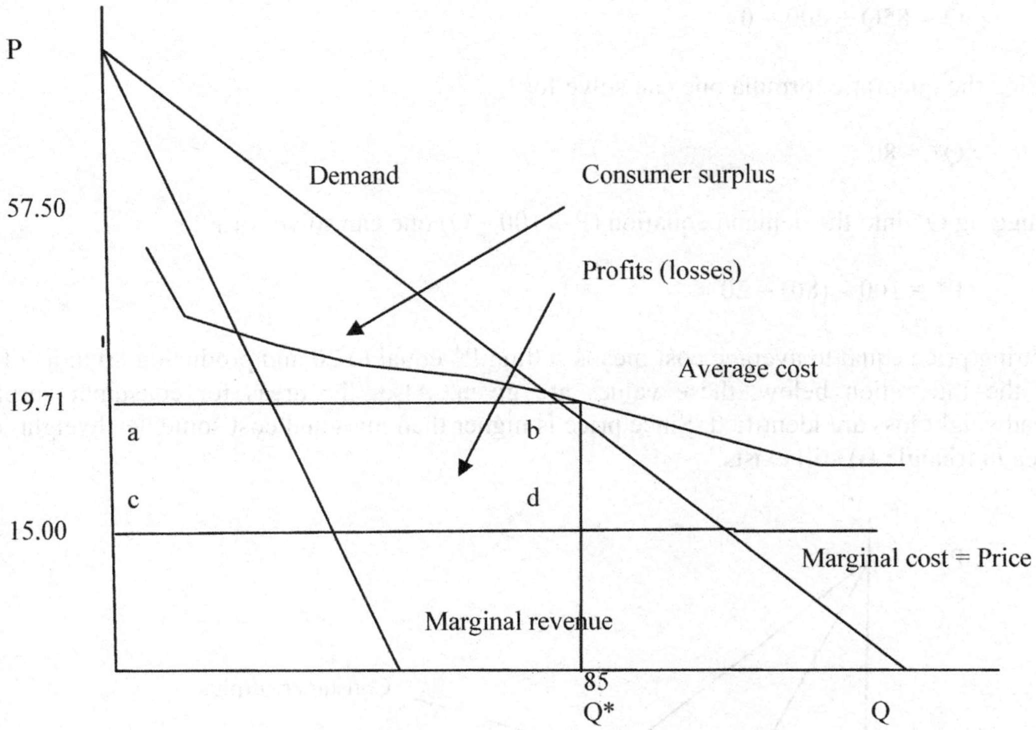


With a price and marginal cost equal to 15.00 the firm will experience a loss (-400.35) and if this continues it will exit the industry. The point of government involvement stems from the fact that utility economic regulators want to make the firm more efficient (in terms of allocative efficiency). With efficiency based on price equals marginal cost the firm will eventually become bankrupt and leave the industry. This would result in a solution that is unacceptable from a social perspective—without subsidies, consumers would not receive water at reasonable prices and under fair terms and conditions of service. To prevent the firm from leaving the industry, the government could subsidize the water utility in the amount of its loss (-400.35). A second option would be that regulators give up on the idea of pricing based on marginal cost. This second option usually results in the water company setting rates based on average-cost pricing.

**Average-Cost Pricing**

The usual solution to the above mentioned problem (i.e., P = MC resulting in financial losses) is for utility regulators to authorize rates based on average-cost pricing. This allows the utility to charge a price in excess of marginal cost and earn a normal (not an excessive) rate of return on investment (profit). In this case, price equals average price.

Determining the appropriate price is somewhat more complicated than that done above. To find the price that would equal average cost, demand (price) is equal to average cost (AC), then solve for Q* and finally plugging Q* into the demand equation to get P*. These steps are summarized as follows. First, set P = AC

$$100 - Q = 15 + (400 \div Q)$$

Rearranging terms, this equation yields the following:

$$Q^2 - 85Q + 400 = 0$$

Using the quadratic formula one can solve for Q:

$$Q^* = 80$$

Plugging Q* into the demand equation (P = 100 – Q) one can solve for P*

$$P^* = 100 - (80) = 20$$

Setting price equal to average cost means setting P* equal to 20 and producing 80 units of output. In the illustration below, these values are given. Also, the areas for consumer surplus and deadweight loss are identified. Since price is higher than marginal cost some deadweight loss (the area in triangle B) still exists.

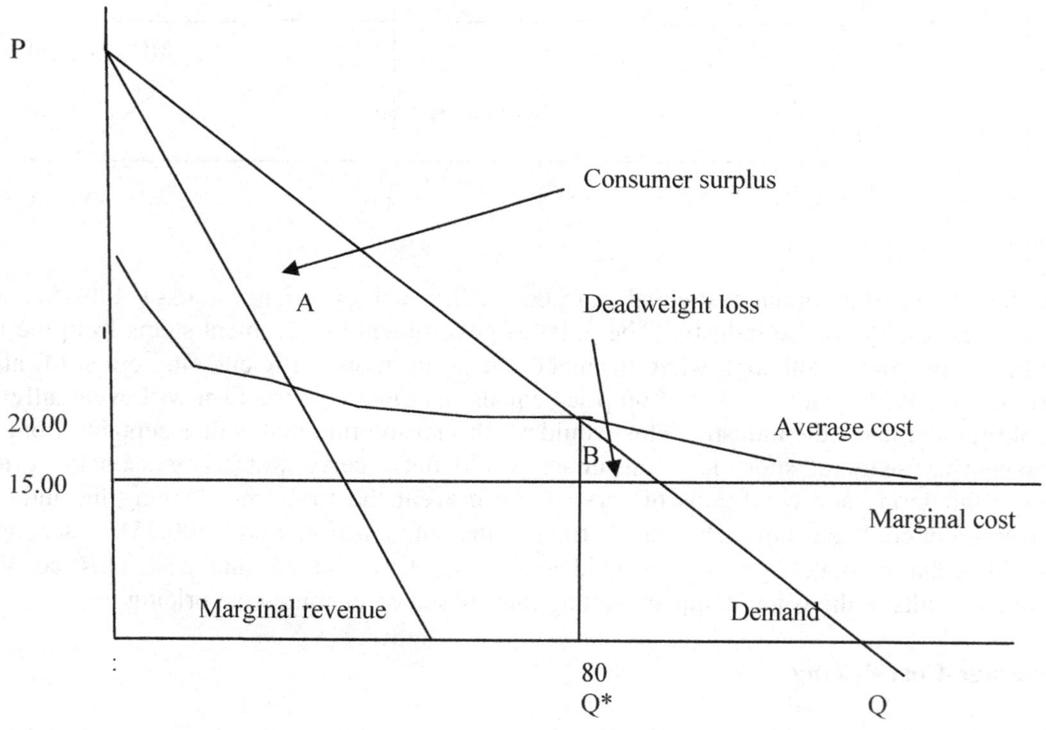


Another potential problem with regulators using average-cost pricing is that this practice may create an incentive for the utility to inflate its fixed costs—a practice called overcapitalization. This is because under traditional rate of return regulation a utility's profits are based on the amount of its investment in plant. Therefore, as the amount of investment in plant and equipment increases profits also increase.

Assuming that all of the water utility's customers are in the same rate class, when charging a single price for all consumers, a natural monopolist's costs force regulators to choose between allocative efficiency and allowing the utility a fair return on its investment. Another solution to this problem involves setting two prices in what is referred to as a two-part tariff.

**Two-Part Tariff**

Assume the utility economic regulator forces the water utility to sell every unit of output at 15 (i.e., P = MC), but also allows the utility to charge customers a fixed fee. This fee could be called a customer charge and/or a demand charge. Said another way, this fixed fee could be thought of as a "readiness-to-serve charge."

Before this extra fee, a price of 15 caused the monopolist to lose 400 in profits. But with the fixed fee the water utility is able to recoup the losses (by setting the fixed fee = 400 ÷ N, where N is the number of customers who want to purchase the firm's product). For example, if 50 customers want to purchase water from a utility then the firm should be allowed to charge a flat fee of 8. Doing so allows the firm to produce 85 units of output and make zero excessive profits. This means that the utility regulators get what they want—no deadweight loss—and the firm gets what it wants—a fair return on its investment.

# Commonly Used Symbols, Formulas, and Conversion Factors

## Table of Symbols

| No. | Name | Symbol |
|---|---|---|
| 1 | Annuity factor | A |
| 2 | Benefit | B |
| 2 | Capital investment | K |
| 3 | Capital recovery factor | R |
| 4 | Change | Δ |
| 5 | Cost | C |
| 6 | Consumer's surplus | CS |
| 7 | Depreciation | D |
| 8 | Elasticity | ε |
| 9 | Entrepreneurial ability | E |
| 10 | Externality (economic and environmental) | Ext |
| 11 | Income | Y |
| 12 | Interest or discount rate | i |
| 13 | Operation and maintenance | O&M |
| 14 | Opportunity costs | OC |
| 15 | Percentage change | %Δ |
| 16 | Price | P |
| 17 | Producer's surplus | PS |
| 18 | Profit | Π |
| 19 | Quantity | Q |
| 20 | Labor | N |
| 21 | Land | L |
| 22 | Rate Base | RB |
| 23 | Rate of return | RoR |
| 24 | Revenue | R |
| 25 | Social surplus | SS |
| 26 | Subsidy | S |
| 27 | Sum | ∑ |
| 28 | Taxes | Tax |
| 29 | Time | t |
| 30 | Total | T |
| 31 | Utilization factor | U |

Source: Author's construct.

## Table of Equations

| No. | Description | Formula |
|---|---|---|
| 1 | Arc elasticity | $(\Delta Q \div (Q_1 + Q_2)) \div (\Delta P \div (P_1 + P_2))$ |
| 2 | Annuity factor (A) | 1- (1+i) – N ÷ i |
| 3 | Average cost (AC) | TC ÷ Q |
| 4 | Average incremental cost (per million gallons) | TAIC ÷ (u * Wmg) |
| 5 | Average marginal costs | PV(K) + PV(Q) |
| 6 | Average revenue (AR) | TR ÷ Q |
| 7 | Average total cost (ATC) | AFC + AVC |
| 8 | Average variable cost (AVC) | VC ÷ Q |
| 9 | Capital recovery factor | $(i(1+i)^n) \div ((1 + i)^{n-1})$ |
| 10 | Cobb-Douglas production function | $\phi P^{\varepsilon}$ |
| 11 | Consumer's surplus (CS) | q(q, Q) – P(q) |
| 12 | Cost–benefit ratio | ∑C ÷ ∑B |
| 13 | Cost function | C = *f*(Q) |
| 14 | Equal Annual Net Benefit (EANB) | NPV ÷ A |
| 15 | Full costs (FC) | RR + Ext + OC |
| 16 | Full-supply costs (FSC) | same as revenue requirements |
| 17 | Future value (FV) | $(1 + i)^t$ |
| 18 | Income elasticity of demand | (%Δqd) ÷ (%ΔY) |
| 19 | Internal rate of return (IRR) | $0 = NP = \sum [Fn \div (1 + i)^n]$ |
| 20 | Levelized cost | $LCC \div \{\sum[Q \div (1 + i)^n]\}$ |
| 21 | Life-cycle cost | $\sum (Cn \div (1 + i)^n$ |
| 22 | Marginal benefit (MB) | ΔB ÷ ΔQ |
| 23 | Marginal capital cost (MCC) | rKt ÷ (Qt – Qt-1) |
| 24 | Marginal cost (MC) | ΔC ÷ ΔQ |
| 25 | Marginal revenue (MR) | ΔTR ÷ ΔQ |
| 26 | Marginal social cost (MSC) | MPC + Tax |
| 27 | Net present value (NPV) | $\sum(Bt - Ct) \div (1+i)^t$ |
| 28 | Present value (PV) | $Yt \div (1+i)^t$ |
| 29 | Present worth incremental system cost (PWISC) | SRMCt + MCCt |
| 30 | Price elasticity of demand | %ΔQ ÷ %ΔP or (dQw ÷ Qw) ÷ (dP/P) |
| 31 | Producer's surplus (PS) | (P(q) – MC) |
| 32 | Production function | Q = *f*(L, N, K, E) |
| 33 | Profit (Π) | TR – TC |
| 34 | Profit maximizing point | P = MC |
| 35 | Ramsey (inverse elasticity rule) | (P-MC) ÷ P |
| 36 | Revenue requirement (RR) | O&M + D +Tax + RoR(RB) |
| 37 | Short-run marginal cost | ΔO&M ÷ ΔQ |
| 38 | Simple marginal cost (SMC) | (Rt – Rt-1) + Kt(Qt – Qt-1) |
| 39 | Simple payback period | ∑n ΔIn ≤ ∑n ΔCF |
| 40 | Subsidy | FC – FSC |
| 41 | Traditional "textbook" marginal cost (TMC) | SRMCt + MCCt |
| 42 | Total cost (TC) | TFC + TVC |
| 43 | Total economic value (TEV) | UV + NUV |
| 44 | Total revenue (TR) | PxQ |
| 45 | Turvey marginal cost | (MCCt + SMCt) ÷ Q |
| 46 | Value of the market (V) | CS + PS |
| 47 | Welfare loss | PS + CS < V |

## Conversion Factors

| |
|---|
| 1 acre foot = 325,851 gallons = 1,233.4 cubic meters; enough to supply an average family of four for one year |
| 1 acre foot covers 1 acre of land with water 1 foot deep |
| 1,000,000 gallons = 3.07 acre feet |
| 1 cubic foot = 7.48 gallons = 62.4 pounds of water |
| 1 cubic foot per second (cfs) = 1.98 acre feet per day, or 448.8 gallons per minute |
| 1 ccf = 100 cubic feet |
| 1 liter = 1.06 quarts |
| 1,000 gallons per minute (gpm) = 4.42 acre-feet per day |
| 1 million gallons = 3.07 acre-feet |
| 1 cubic foot per second (cfs) = 646.272 gallons per day |

# ABBREVIATIONS

| | |
|---|---|
| **AC** | average cost |
| **AF** | acre-foot |
| **AFUDC** | allowance for funds used during construction |
| **AIC** | average incremental cost |
| **AMC** | average marginal cost |
| **ANTC** | annual net total cost |
| **AR** | average revenue |
| **ASCE** | American Society of Civil Engineers |
| **AWWA** | American Water Works Association |
| **AwwaRF** | Awwa Research Foundation |
| **BEAM** | Building Efficiency Analysis Model |
| **Btu** | British thermal unit |
| **CBA** | cost–benefit analysis |
| **Ccf** | hundred cubic feet |
| **CEA** | cost-effectiveness analysis |
| **CPUC** | California Public Utilities Commission |
| **COC** | customer outage costs |
| **COS** | cost of service |
| **CPR** | common pool resource |
| **CRRA** | Certified Rate of Return Analyst |
| **CS** | consumer's surplus |
| **CUWA** | California Urban Water Agencies |
| **CVM** | contingent valuation method |
| **CWIP** | construction work in progress |
| **CWWWA** | Canadian Water Waste Water Authority |
| **D** | depreciation |
| **DL** | deadweight loss |
| **DSIC** | distribution system investment charge |
| **DSM** | demand-side management |
| **EANB** | equivalent annual net benefit |
| **EPA** | Environmental Protection Agency (U.S.) |
| **EU** | European Union |
| **EWRA** | Egyptian Water Regulatory Authority |
| **FC** | full cost |
| **FCR** | full cost recovery |
| **FDC** | fully distributed costs |
| **FERC** | Federal Energy Regulatory Commission |
| **FPC** | Federal Power Commission |
| **FSC** | full supply cost |
| **GARCH** | generalized autoregressive conditional heteroscedastcity |
| **GAO** | General Accounting Office (U.S.) |
| **GDP** | gross domestic product |
| **GNI** | gross national income |
| **GOU** | government-owned utilities |
| **GPM** | gallons per minute |
| **IC** | incremental cost |
| **IOU** | investor-owned utility |

| | |
|---|---|
| **IRP** | integrated resource planning |
| **IRR** | internal rate of return |
| **ITC** | investment tax credit |
| **£** | British pounds |
| **LE** | Egyptian pounds |
| **LRAC** | long-run average cost |
| **LRAIC** | long-run average incremental cost |
| **LRMC** | long-run marginal cost |
| **MB** | marginal benefit |
| **MC** | marginal cost |
| **MCC** | marginal capacity cost |
| **MCL** | maximum containment level |
| **MGD** | million gallons per day |
| **MGY** | million gallons per year |
| **MPB** | marginal private benefit |
| **MPC** | marginal private cost |
| **MR** | marginal revenue |
| **MSB** | marginal social benefit |
| **MSC** | marginal social cost |
| **MTBE** | Methyl Tertiary Butyl Ether |
| **MWD** | Metropolitan Water District of Southern California |
| **NACVA** | National Association of Certified Valuation Analysts |
| **NARUC** | National Association of Regulatory Utility Commissioners |
| **NAWC** | National Association of Water Companies |
| **NED** | national economic development |
| **NEPA** | National Environmental Policy Act |
| **NIS** | New Israeli Shekel |
| **NRC** | National Resource Council |
| **NRRI** | National Regulatory Research Institute |
| **NPV** | net present value |
| **NUV** | nonuse value |
| **OECD** | Organization for Economic Co-operation and Development |
| **Ofwat** | Water utility economic regulator in the UK and Wales |
| **O&M** | operating and maintenance |
| **OLS** | ordinary least squares |
| **P** | price |
| **PDA** | property damage avoided |
| **Q** | quantity |
| **Qm** | quantity (monopolist) |
| **PBR** | performance-based ratemaking |
| **PS** | producer's surplus |
| **PSC** | public service commission |
| **PUC** | public utilities commission |
| **PUR** | Public Utility Reports |
| **PURPA** | Public Utilities Regulatory Policies Act |
| **PWISC** | present worth incremental system cost |
| **RB** | rate base |
| **ROA** | return on assets |
| **ROE** | return on equity |
| **ROIC** | return on invested capital |
| **RR** | revenue requirement |

| | |
|---|---|
| **RRR** | repair-replace-refurbish |
| **S** | subsidy |
| **SAC** | stand-alone cost |
| **SCR** | sustainable cost recovery |
| **SMC** | simple marginal cost |
| **SS** | social surplus |
| **SEC** | Securities and Exchange Commission (U.S.) |
| **SRMC** | short-run marginal cost |
| **T** | taxes |
| **TC** | total cost |
| **TG** | thousand gallons |
| **TCM** | travel cost method |
| **TEV** | total economic value |
| **TMC** | traditional (textbook) marginal cost |
| **TVMC** | Turvey marginal cost |
| **USAID** | U.S. Agency for International Development |
| **USD** | U.S. dollar |
| **UV** | use value |
| **V** | value of the market |
| **VOS** | value of service |
| **WHO** | World Health Organization |
| **WPRR** | Water Policy Regulatory Reform |
| **WTA** | willingness-to-accept |
| **WTP** | willingness-to-pay |

# SELECTED BIBLIOGRAPHY

Albouy, Yves. *Marginal Cost Analysis and Pricing of Water and Electric Power, Methodology Notes*. Washington, DC: Inter-American Development Bank, 1983.

Al-Ghuraiz, Yusuf and Adnan Enshassi. "Ability and Willingness to Pay for Water Supply Service in the Gaza Strip." *Building and Environment* 40, 8 (August 2005).

American Gas Association, *Gas Rate Fundamentals*, 4th ed. Arlington, VA: American Gas Association, 1987.

American Water Works Association. *Integrated Resource Planning: A Balanced Approach to Water Resouces Decision Making*. Denver, CO: American Water Works Association, n.d..

American Water Works Association. *Principles of Water Rates, Fees, and Charges*. M1, 5th ed. Denver, CO: American Water Works Association, 2000.

———. *Water Infrastructure at a Turning Point: The Road to Sustainable Asset Management*. Denver, CO: American Water Works Association, 2006.

———. *2010 Annual Report and 10-K*.

Aqua America, Inc. *2010 Annual Report and 10-K*.

Arpke, Angela and Kelly Strong. "A Comparison of Life-Cycle Cost Analyses for a Typical College Dormitory Using Subsidized Versus Full-Cost Pricing of Water." *Ecological Economics* 58, 1 (June 2006).

Aspen Institute, *Sustainable Water Systems. Report of the Dialogue on Sustainable Water Systems*. Aspen, CO: Aspen Institute, 2010.

Awwa Research Foundation. *A Strategic Assessment of the Future of Water Utilities*. Denver, CO: Awwa Research Foundation, American Water Works Association, IWA Publishing, 2006.

American Water Works Foundation, *Guidelines for Implementing an Effective Integrated Resource Planning Process*. Denver, CO: Awwa Research Foundation, American Water Works Association, IWA Publishing, 1997.

Bacon, Robert, "Measurement of Welfare Changes Caused by Large Price Shifts, An Issue in the Power Sector." *World Bank Discussion Paper No. 273*, Washington, DC: The World Bank, 1995.

Banerjee, Sudeshna, Vivien Foster, Yvonne Ying, Heather Skilling, and Quentin Wodon. "Cost Recovery, Equity, and Efficiency in Water Tariffs, Evidence from African Utilities," Policy Research Working Paper. Washington, DC: The World Bank, 2010.

Barakat & Chamberlin, Inc. *The Value of Water Supply Reliability: Results of a Contingent Valuation Survey of Residential Customers (Summary)*. Oakland, CA: Barakat & Chamberlin, Inc., 1994.

Barkatullah, Nadira. *Pricing, Demand Analysis and Simulation: An Application to a Water Utility*. Dissertation.com, 1999.

Beecher, Janice A. "The Conservation Conundrum: How Declining Demand Affects Water Utilities." Denver, CO: American Water Works Association Journal. February 2010.

Beecher, Janice A., "Economic Regulation of Water Utilities: A Primer." Washington, DC: National Association of Water Companies, September 2001.

Beecher, Janice A. "Full-Cost Pricing." La Jolla, California, 2007 National Drinking Water Symposium, October 1–2, 2007.

Beecher, Janice A. *Sourcebook of Regulatory Techniques For Water Utilities*. Washington, DC: National Association of Water Companies, 2006.

Beecher, Janice A. "Primer on Water Pricing," East Lansing, MI: Institute of Public Utilities, Michigan State University, November 1, 2011.

Beecher, Janice A., Patrick C. Mann, and James R. Landers. "Cost Allocation and Rate Design for Water Utilities." Columbus, OH: The National Regulatory Research Institute, 1990.

Black & Veatch. "2009/2010 50 Largest Cities Water/Wastewater Rate Survey." Overland Park, KS: Black & Veatch, 2011. www.bv.com/consult.

Bonbright, James C., Albert L. Danielsen, and David R. Kamerschen. *Principles of Public Utility Rates*, 2nd ed. Arlington, VA: Public Utilities Reports, Inc., 1988.

Brouwer, Roy and David Pearce, Eds., *Cost-Benefit Analysis and Water Resources Management*. Northhampton, MA: Edward Elgar Publishing, 2005.

California Public Utilities Commission. "2010 Water Action Plan." San Francisco, California, California Public Utilities Commission, October 2010. cpuc.ca.gov/puc/hottopics/3water/051109-wateractionplan.htm.

California Resources Agency, Department of Water Resources. "Economic Analysis Guidebook." Sacramento, CA: Department of Water Resources, January 2008.

Campbell, Harry and Richard Brown. *Benefit-Cost Analysis, Financial and Economic Appraisal Using Spreadsheets*. New York: Cambridge University Press, 2003.

Carle, David. *Introduction To Water In California*. Berkeley, CA: University of California Press. 2009.

Carriker, Gordon L. and Buddy L. Dillman. "A Full-Cost Water Pricing Strategy for South Carolina Rural Water Utilities." Clemson, SC: The Strom Thurmond Institute, 1988.

Casey, James F., James R. Kahn, and Alexandre Rivas. "Willingness to Pay for Improved Water Service in Manaus, Amazonas, Brazil." *Ecological Economics* 58, 2 (June 2006).

Champ, Patricia A., Kevin J. Boyle and Thomas C. Brown, eds. *A Primer on Nonmarket Valuation*. Boston, MA: Kluwer Academic Publishers, 2003.

Coase, Ronald H. "The Problem of Social Cost." *Journal of Law and Economics* (October 1960).

Colander, David. *Microeconomics*. 4th ed. Boston, MA: McGraw-Hill Irwin, 2001.

Coy, Debra G., Svanda & Coy Consulting. "Attracting Capital to Water Utilities and Water Projects." Presentation at the 113th NAWC Annual Conference, Tucson, Arizona, October 11, 2010.

Crew, Michael A. and Paul R. Kleindorfer. *The Economics of Public Utility Regulation*. Cambridge, MA: The MIT Press, 1986.

Cromwell, John E. III, Haydn Reynolds, Norman Pearson, Jr., and Michael Grant. *The Cost of Infrastructure Failure*. Denver, CO: Awwa Research Foundation and American Water Works Association, 2002.

Curtis, Tom. "Models for National Infrastructure Investment Programs." Presentation at the 111th National Association of Water Companies Annual Conference, Santa Fe, New Mexico, October 19–22, 2008.

DeHaven, James C. "Water Supply, Economics, Technology and Policy." Santa Monica, CA: RAND, 1963.

Denig-Chakroff, David. "The Water Industry at a Glance." Silver Springs, MD: National Regulatory Research Institute, April 2008.

De Rus, Gines. *Introduction to Cost-Benefit Analysis, Looking for Reasonable Shortcuts*. Cheltenham, UK: Edward Elgar, 2010.

Dixon, Lloyd S., Nancy Y. Moore and Ellen M. Pint, "Drought Management Policies and Economic Effects in Urban Areas of California, 1987–1992." Santa Monica, CA: RAND, 1996.

Dzurik, Andrew A. *Water Resource Planning*. 3rd ed. Lanham, MD: Rowman & Littlefield Publishers, Inc., 2003.

Financial Summary for Investor-Owned Water Utilities (2007). Economic Research Program. Washington, DC: National Association of Water Companies, 2008.

Financial Survey for Investor-Owned First Research. "Water & Sewer Utilities." February 28, 2011. www.hoovers.com.

Frederick, Kenneth D., Tim VandenBerg, and Jean Hanson. "Economic Values of Freshwater in the United States." Washington, DC: Resources for the Future, 1996.

Freeman, A. Myrick. *The Measurement of Environmental and Resource Values: Theory and Methods*. 2nd ed. Washington, DC: Resources for the Future, 2003.

Gascon, Sharon, Deputy Director, National Association of Water Companies. "Reflections on the Business of Water." Presentation at the 27th Annual Western NARUC Utility Rate School, San Diego, California, May 14–19, 2006.

Gibbons, Diana C. *The Economic Value of Water*. Washington, DC: Resources for the Future, 1986.

Goodman, Leonard Saul. *The Process of Ratemaking*. 2 vols. Vienna, VA: Public Utilities Reports, Inc., 1998.

Griffin, Ronald C., *Water Resource Economics, The Analysis of Scarcity, Policies, and Projects.* Cambridge, MA: The MIT Press, 2006.

Groves, David G., Jordan Fischbach, and Scot Hickey. "Evaluating the Benefits and Costs of Increased Water-Use Efficiency in Commercial Buildings." Santa Monica, CA: RAND Corporation, 2007.

Groves, David G., James Griffen, and Sara Hajiamiri. "Estimating the Value of Water-Use Efficiency in the Intermountain West." Santa Monica, CA: RAND Corporation, 2008.

Greene, Robert Lee. *Welfare Economics and Peak Load Pricing*. Gainesville, FL: University of Florida Press, 1970.

Grigg, Neil S. *Total Water Management Practices for a Sustainable Future*. Denver, CO: American Water Works Association, 2008.

Hanke, Steve H. and Robert K. Davis. "Potential for Marginal Cost Pricing in Water Resource Management." *Water Resources Research* 9, 4 (August 1973).

Hardin, Garrett. "The Tragedy of the Commons." *Science* 162 (1968).

Hausmann, J. "Exact Consumer Surplus and Deadweight Loss," *American Economic Review*. Vol. 71.

Hayward, David L. *The Economic Value of Water Utility Services: A Survey of Theory, Methods, and Applications*. West Conshohocken, PA: Infinity Publishing Company, 2009.

Hayward, David L. *Egypt Water Regulatory Authority Cost of Service Self-Study Course.* Vol. 1–4. Leucadia, CA: Hayward Consulting Group, 2010.

Hill, Walton, United Water. "MTBE Litigation and the Regulatory Treatment of Damage Awards." Presentation at the NARUC Winter Committee Meetings, Chicago, Illinois, NARUC Annual Meeting, 2009.

Hirshleifer, Jack, James C. DeHaven, and Jerome W. Milliman. *Water Supply Economics, Technology, and Policy*. Chicago, IL: University of Chicago Press, 1960.

Hirshleifer, J. and J. W. Milliman. "Urban Water Supply: A Second Look." *American Economic Association* (May 1967).

Hite, James C. and Holly H. Ulbrich. "Subsidizing Water Users or Water Systems," *Land Economics.* 1988.

Holland, Wendell F., Chairman, Pennsylvania Public Utility Commission. "Legal Framework of Water Utility Regulation." Presentation at the 27th Annual Western NARUC Utility Rate School, San Diego, California, May 14–19, 2006.

Hotelling, Harold. "The General Welfare in Relation to Problems of Taxation and Railway and Utility Rates." *Econometrica* (July 6, 1938).

Howe, C. W., and M. G. Smith. "The Value of Water Supply Reliability in Urban Water Systems." *Journal of Environmental Economics and Management* 26 (1994).

Hughes, Neal, Ahmed Hafi, Tim Goesch, and Nathan Brownlowe. "Urban Water Management: Optimal Price and Investment Policy under Climate Variability." Canberra, Australia. *Australian Bureau of Agricultural and Resource Economics* (2008).

Hyman, Leonard S., Andrew S. Hyman, Robert C. Hyman, Edward P. Meehan, James D. Hempstead, and Jose V. Kochen. *The Water Business: Understanding the Water Supply and Wastewater Industry*. Vienna, VA: Public Utilities Reports, Inc., 1998.

Iimi, Atshshi, "Effects of Improving Infrastructure Quality on Business Costs: Evidence from Firm-Level Data," *Policy Research Working Paper No. 4581*, Washington, DC: The World Bank, March 2008

Johansson, Per-Olov. *The Economic Theory and Measurement of Environmental Benefits*. Cambridge, Cambridge University Press, 1987.

Kahn, Alfred E. *The Economics of Regulation, Principles and Institutions*. 2 vol. Cambridge, MA: The MIT Press, 1995.

Klein, Michael. "Economic Regulation of Water Companies." Policy Research Working Paper No. 1649. Washington, DC: The World Bank, 1996.

Lesser, Jonathan A. and Leonardo R. Giacchino. *Fundamentals of Energy Regulation*. Vienna, VA: Public Utilities Reports, Inc., 2007.

Linjun, Zhou "Reform of Water Tariffs in Chongqing: A Case Study Review." World Bank Analytical and Advisory Assistance Program. Washington, DC: The World Bank, n.d.

Lovei, Laszio. "An Approach to the Economic Analysis of Water Supply Projects." Washington, DC: The World Bank, 1992.

Mann, Patrick C. "Water Utility Regulation: Rates and Cost Recovery." Policy Study No. 155. Los Angeles, CA: Reason Foundation, March 1993.

Mansfield, Edwin. *Microeconomics, Theory and Applications*. New York, NY: W. W. Norton & Company, Inc., 1970.

Mansfield, Edwin and Gary Yohe, *Microeconomics, Theory and Applications*, 11th ed., New York, NY: W.W. Norton & Company, Inc., 2004.

Marks, John R., III, Adorno & Yoss, LLP. "The Legal Aspect of Utility Regulation." Presentation at the 27th Annual Western NARUC Utility Rate School, San Diego, California, May 14–19, 2006.

Marlow, David R. and Stewart Burn. "Effective Use of Condition Assessment within Asset Management." *Journal AWWA*_100:1:54–63 (January 2008).

Marsden, Jacob Associates. "Estimation of Long Run Marginal Cost (LRMC): A Report Prepared by Marsden Jacob Associates for the Queensland Competition Authority." Camberwell, Victoria, November 2004.

Maxwell, Steve, ed. *The Business of Water: A Concise Overview of Challenges and Opportunities in the Water Market.* A Compiliation of Recent Articles from Journal AWWA. Denver, CO: American Water Works Association, 2008.

McConnell, Kenneh E. and Marcia A. Rosado. "Valuing Discrete Improvements in Drinking Water Quality Through Revealed Preferences." *Water Resource Research* 36, 6 (2000).

McKenzie, George W. *Measuring Economic Welfare.* London: England, Cambridge University Press, 1983.

Metropolitan Water District of Southern California. "Integrated Water Resource Plan, 2010 Update." Los Angeles, CA: MWD, 2010.

Milliman, Jerome W. "Policy Horizons for Future Urban Water Supply." *Land Economics* 39 (May 1963).

Mitchell, Robert Cameron, Richard T. Carson. *Using Surveys to Value Public Goods: The Contingent Valuation Method.* Washington, DC: Resources for the Future, 1989.

Monsma, David, Executive Director, The Aspen Institute. "Sustainable Water Systems: Step 1—Redefining the Nation's Infrastructure Challenge, Aspen Institute's Dialogue on Sustainable Water Infrastructure." NARUC's Winter Committee Meetings, February 16, 2010.

Moore, Nancy Y., Morlie H. Graubard, and Robert Shishko. "Efficient Water Use Planning in California: Water Supply Planning." Santa Monica, CA: RAND Corporation, 1978.

National Association of Regulatory Utility Commissioners. Western NARUC Utility Rate School, Course Materials and Mock Rate Case, San Diego, California, May 14–19, 2006.

National Association of Water Companies (NAWC). The Third National Drinking Water Symposium. Washington, DC: National Association of Water Companies, The Broadmoor Hotel, Colorado Springs, Colorado, October 30–November 3, 2005.

———. 109th Annual Conference, Washington, DC: National Association of Water Companies, La Quinta, California, October 8–11, 2006.

———. 111th Annual Conference, Washington, DC: National Association of Water Companies, Santa Fe, New Mexico, October 19–22, 2008.

National Association of Water Companies. *2010 NAWC Water Policy Forum Summary Report.* Washington, DC: National Association of Water Companies, April 2010.

OECD [Organization for Economic Co-Operation and Development]. *Pricing Water Resources and Water Sanitation Services.* London: IWA Publishing, 2010.

Ofwat (Office of Water Services). "The Role of Long-Run Marginal Cost in the Provision and Regulation of Water Services." 2001.

Ofwat (Office of Water Services). "Tariff Structure and Charges: 2002–2003 Report." Birmingham, England: Ofwat.

Pape, Kathy, Esq., Vice President, Treasurer and Rate Counsel, Aqua America, Inc. "Rate Setting & Full Cost Pricing." Presentation at the 3rd National Drinking Water Symposium, Broadmoor Hotel, Colorado Springs, Colorado, November 1, 2005.

Pearce, David W. *Economic Values and the Natural World.* Cambridge, MA: The MIT Press, 1993.

Phillips, Charles F. Jr. *The Regulation of Public Utilities Theory and Practice*. 3rd ed. Arlington, VA: Public Utilities Reports, Inc., 1993.

Pierce Jr., Richard J., *Economic Regulation, Cases and Materials*. Cincinnati, OH: Anderson Publishing Co., 1994.

*Public Utilities Reports, Guide*. Vienna, VA: Public Utilities Reports, Inc., 2004.

Raucher, R., D. Chapman, J. Henderson, M. Hagenstad, J. Rice, J. Goldstein, A. Huber-Lee, W. DeOreo, P. Mayer, B. Hurd, R. Linsky, E. Means, and M. Renwick. *The Value of Water: Concepts, Estimates, and Applications for Water Managers*. Denver, CO: American Water Works Research Foundation, 2005.

Raucher, R. "The Value of Water: What It Means, Why It's Important, and How Water Utility Managers Can Use It." *AWWA Journal*. Denver, CO: American Water Works Association, 2005.

Renner, R., Executive Director, Water Research Foundation. "Current Water Infrastructure Research." Presentation at the NARUC Winter Committee Meetings, February 16, 2010.

Roth, Eva. "Water Pricing in the EU, A Review," Publication No. 2001/002. Brussels: European Environmental Bureau (EEB), 2001.

Rubin, Scott J. "A Call for Water Utility Reliability Standards: Regulating Water Utilities' Infrastructure Programs to Achieve a Balance of Safety, Risk, and Cost." Silver Spring, MD: National Regulatory Research Institute, November 2010.

__________. "What Does Water Really Cost? Rate Design Principles for an Era of Supply Shortages, Infrastructure Upgrades, and Enhanced Water Conservation." Silver Spring, MD: National Regulatory Research Institute, July 2010.

San Jose Water Company. sjw.com.

Sawkins, John W. and Scott Reid. "The Measurement and Regulation of Cross Subsidy. The Case of the Scottish Water Industry." *Utilities Policy* 15, 1 (March 2007).

Segerfeldt, Fredrik. *Water For Sale: How Business and the Market Can Resolve the World's Water Crisis*. Washington, DC: Cato Institute, 2005.

Serra, Pablo, "Subsidies in Chilean Public Utilities," *Policy Research Working Paper No. 2445*, Washington, DC: The World Bank, September 2000.

Shaw, W. Douglass. *Water Resource Economics and Policy, An Introduction.* Northhampton, MA: Edward Elgar Publishing, 2005.

Short, Walter, Daniel J. Packey, and Thomas Holt. *A Manual for the Economic Evaluation of Energy Efficiency and Renewable Energy Technologies*, for the National Renewable Energy Laboratory, U.S. Department of Energy. Honolulu, HI: University Press of the Pacific, 2005.

Simon, Paul. *Tapped Out: The Coming World Crisis in Water and What We Can Do About It*. New York, NY: Welcome Rain Publishers, 1998.

Singh, Katar, and Anil Shishodia. *Environmental Economics Theory and Application*. Los Angeles, CA: Sage Publications, 2007.

Squire, Lyn, and German G. van der Tak. *Economic Analysis of Projects*. Baltimore, Maryland: The Johns Hopkins University Press, 1975.

Stanford, Melissa J. "Replacing and Securing Water Utility Infrastructure: Selected Regulatory Approaches in a Time of Heightened Threats and Burgeoning Costs." Columbus, Ohio: The National Regulatory Research Institute, 2004.

Strand, Jon, "The Full Economic Cost of Groundwater Extraction," *Policy Research Working Paper No. 5494*, Washington, DC: The World Bank, December 2010.

Switzer, Keith, Vice President, American States Water Company. "Comparison of Water and Energy Utility Ratemaking." Presentation at the 27th Annual Western NARUC Utility Rate School, San Diego, California, May 14–19, 2006.

Teodoro, Manuel P. "Measuring Fairness: Assessing the Equity of Municipal Water Rates." *AWWA Journal* (April 2005).

Texas A&M University, www.waterecon.tamu.edu.

Thornburg, Eric, President and CEO, Connecticut Water. "Sustainable Water Systems: Redefining the Nation's Infrastructure Challenge," Aspen Institute's Dialogue on Sustainable Water Infrastructure, NARUC's Winter Committee Meetings, February 16, 2010.

Turvey, R. "Analyzing the Marginal Cost of Water Supply." *Land Economics* (May 1976).

U.S. EPA. "Guidelines for Preparing Economic Analyses." EPA 240-R-00-003. Washington, DC: U.S. EPA, 2010.

*Value Line Investment Survey*. New York: The Value Line Investment Survey, July 25, 2008.

———.New York: The Value Line Investment Survey, October 22, 2010.

Wade, William W. and Brian Roach, "Economic Benefits of Municipal and Industrial Water Supply Reliability for Metropolitan Atlanta," Columbia, TN: Energy and Water Economics, draft paper, February 2003.

Warford, Jeremy J. "Marginal Opportunity Cost Pricing for Municipal Water Supply." Ottawa, Canada: International Development Research Centre, 1997.

Water Education Foundation. *Layperson's Guide To Water Marketing*. Sacramento, CA: Water Education Foundation, 2005.

Young, Robert A. *Determining the Economic Value of Water, Concepts and Methods*. Washington, DC: Resources for the Future, 2005.

Young, Robert A. "Measuring Economic Benefits of Water Investments and Policies." Technical Report No. 338. Washington, DC: World Bank, 1996.

Winter, Tim, Jesup & Lamont Securities. "Which Came First…The CHICKEN or the EGG: The Importance of Allowed ROE's in the Water Utility Sector." Presentation at the 111th NAWC Annual Conference, Santa Fe, New Mexico, October 21, 2008.

Wirick, David W., John D. Borrows, and Steven Goldberg. "Evaluating Water Utility Financial Capacity with Ratio Analysis and Discounted Cash Flows." Columbus, OH: National Regulatory Research Institute, 1997.

World Bank, "World Bank Report: Water Utility Subsidies Benefit The 'Haves', Not The 'Have Nots,'" World Bank Press Release No. 2006/317/ESSD, March 18, 2006.

# ABOUT THE AUTHOR

**David L. Hayward** is a principal at Hayward Consulting Group (www.haywardconsulting-group.com), a utility valuation and policy consulting firm in Leucadia, California. He has a B.S. degree in business and a M.S. degree in economics, both from the University of Utah, and is a Certified Rate of Return Analyst (CRRA)—an expert in utility cost of capital and utility finance.

Mr. Hayward has authored five books, a manuscript, and computer model, including:

- *The Economic Value of Water Utility Services: A Survey of Theory, Methods, and Applications* (Infinity Publishing Company);
- *Valuing a Water Utility* (National Association of Water Companies—NAWC);
- *Valuing an Electric Utility: Theory and Application* (primary author) (Public Utilities Reports, Inc.);
- *EWRA Cost of Service Training Self-Study Course* (Vol. 1–4) (Arab Republic of Egypt); and
- *FinMod: A Valuation Model for Water Utilities* (NAWC).

Mr. Hayward has more than twenty-five years of experience in the field of public utilities (water, natural gas, and electric) and has consulted throughout the world in eleven developing countries on World Bank and United States Agency for International Development (USAID)-funded projects. His most recent overseas project was serving as Senior Policy Advisor to the Egyptian government through the USAID-sponsored project, Water Policy Regulatory Reform (WPRR).

Mr. Hayward has prepared expert witness testimony and/or project work in thirty-five cases (fourteen jurisdictions in the United States) on a wide range of utility issues such as: cost allocation, rate design (marginal and embedded cost), cost of capital/capital structure, utility financing, policy issues, revenue requirements, and resource economics. He has been active in the California water industry, including preparing expert witness testimony regarding tariff issues, consolidation of water utilities, financial risk, and water industry best practices. He has also consulted on fourteen domestic and international utility valuation studies.

He has spoken at various utility-related seminars/conferences such as the Institute of Public Utilities at Michigan State University, the National Association of Regulatory Commissioners (NARUC) Rate School, the National Association of Water Companies (NAWC), and the National Association of Certified Valuation Analysts (NACVA). Mr. Hayward was also a part-time economics instructor at the University of Phoenix, San Diego.

Made in the USA
Monee, IL
08 November 2026

68020210R00162